Body Positive

What would it be like to feel *good* about your body? Does anyone really fully appreciate their body? If diverse body shapes and sizes were shown in the media, would this change your perception?

While this book addresses all of these questions and more, it is not simply a standard scientific exploration of poor body image. Instead, it examines a new movement focused on understanding what it is that leads people to love, appreciate, take care of, and embrace their bodies. Featuring chapters written by leading international experts in the science and practice of body image, *Body Positive* is a provocative and engaging look at how we feel about our physical selves in the twenty-first century – and how we can all come to feel better than we currently do.

ELIZABETH A. DANIELS, PhD, is Associate Professor of Psychology at the University of Colorado Colorado Springs. She is a feminist developmental psychologist and has been conducting research on body image, media, and gender for fifteen years. Her work has been featured in the national and international press, including *The New York Times*, *Los Angeles Times*, *Washington Post*, *Huffington Post*, *Time*, *New York Magazine*, *BBC News*, *The Telegraph*, and *International Business Times*.

MEGHAN M. GILLEN, PhD, is Associate Professor of Psychology at Penn State Abington. She has been conducting research on body image, gender, and physical appearance issues for fifteen years. She has won a college-wide teaching award and was a featured convocation speaker at her college. Her work has appeared in the *Washington Post*, *Self Magazine*, and *U.S. News and World Report*.

CHARLOTTE H. MARKEY, PhD, is Professor of Psychology and Director of the Health Sciences program at Rutgers University, Camden. She has been conducting research on eating, dieting, body image, and obesity risk for twenty years. Her book *Smart People Don't Diet* (2014) was described by *Scientific American* as "possibly the best book on weight loss ever written," and she regularly blogs for *U.S. News and World Report*, *Psychology Today*, and *Science of Relationships*. Her research has also been discussed in outlets including the *New York Times*, *The Today Show*, and *WHYY* radio.

Body Image in

Edited by

Elizabeth A. Daniels

University of Colorado Colorado Springs

Meghan M. Gillen

Pennsylvania State University

Charlotte H. Markey

Rutgers University

CAMBRIDGE
UNIVERSITY PRESS

CAMBRIDGE
UNIVERSITY PRESS

University Printing House, Cambridge CB2 8BS, United Kingdom

One Liberty Plaza, 20th Floor, New York, NY 10006, USA

477 Williamstown Road, Port Melbourne, VIC 3207, Australia

314-321, 3rd Floor, Plot 3, Splendor Forum, Jasola District Centre, New Delhi - 110025, India

79 Anson Road, #06-04/06, Singapore 079906

Cambridge University Press is part of the University of Cambridge.

It furthers the University's mission by disseminating knowledge in the pursuit of
education, learning and research at the highest international levels of excellence.

www.cambridge.org
Information on this title: www.cambridge.org/9781108410427
DOI: 10.1017/9781108297653

First published 2018
First paperback edition 2020

A catalogue record for this publication is available from the British Library

Library of Congress Cataloging in Publication data
Names: Daniels, Elizabeth A., 1976– editor. | Gillen, Meghan M.,
1979– editor. | Markey, Charlotte H., 1975– editor.
Title: Body positive : understanding and improving body image in science and
practice / edited by Elizabeth A. Daniels, University of Colorado, Colorado
Springs, Meghan M. Gillen, Pennsylvania State University, Charlotte
H. Markey, Rutgers University, New Jersey.
Description: 1 Edition. | New York : Cambridge University Press, [2018] |
Includes bibliographical references and index.
Identifiers: LCCN 2018003700 | ISBN 9781108419321 (hardback) |
ISBN 9781108410427 (pbk.)
Subjects: LCSH: Body image.
Classification: LCC BF697.5.B63 B636 2018 | DDC 306.4/613–dc23
LC record available at https://lccn.loc.gov/2018003700

ISBN 978-1-108-41932-1 Hardback
ISBN 978-1-108-41042-7 Paperback

To our families, students, friends, and colleagues who inspire us to promote positive body image and improve the culture we all reside in.

Contents

Figures

Tables

Notes on Contributors

CASEY L. AUGUSTUS-HORVATH, PhD, is employed as a staff psychologist at the Chalmers P. Wylie VA Ambulatory Care Center in Columbus, Ohio, where she uses evidence-based and strengths-based psychotherapy. She enjoys balancing a generalist practice with clinical and research interests centered on intuitive eating, body image, and the spectrum of eating and weight-related concerns.

MARIE L. CALTABIANO, PhD, is Associate Professor of Psychology at James Cook University, Cairns, Australia. As a health psychologist, she has researched numerous areas but has returned to the area of body image and disordered eating several times during the past twenty years.

DAWN CLIFFORD PhD, RD, is Associate Professor of Nutrition at Northern Arizona University. She is a registered dietitian and writes and conducts research in the areas of nondiet approaches and motivational interviewing. She coauthored *Motivational Interviewing in Nutrition and Fitness* (2016).

CATHERINE COOK-COTTONE, PhD, is Associate Professor at the University at Buffalo, State University of New York. A licensed psychologist and registered yoga teacher, she leads a research team that studies positive embodiment and self-regulation.

ELIZABETH A. DANIELS, PhD, is Associate Professor of Psychology at the University of Colorado Colorado Springs. She is a developmental psychologist and has been conducting research on body image, media, and gender for fifteen years.

LAURA D. D´ANTUONO is currently completing her Bachelor of Psychological Science at the University of Adelaide, Australia. She has been researching positive body image and other related behaviors over the past two years.

JAMIE L. DUNAEV, PhD, is Assistant Teaching Professor in Health Sciences and Psychology at Rutgers University, Camden. Jamie is a health psychologist with interests in body image, weight stigma, and health.

KRISTINA HOLMQVIST GATTARIO, PhD, is Senior Lecturer of Health Psychology in the Department of Psychology, University of Gothenburg, Sweden. She conducts research on youth development and health, in particular in relation to body image, bullying, gender norms, and cultural context.

MEGHAN M. GILLEN, PhD, is Associate Professor of Psychology at Penn State Abington. She has been conducting research on body image, gender, and physical appearance issues for fifteen years.

CAROLINA LUNDE, PhD is Senior Lecturer/Associate Professor in the Department of Psychology, University of Gothenburg, Sweden. Her research focuses on topics such as body image and peer relations, body image and physical activity, body image and cosmetic surgery attitudes, and sexuality on the internet.

CHARLOTTE H. MARKEY, PhD, is Professor of Psychology and Director of the Health Sciences Program at Rutgers University, Camden. She has been publishing research about body image and weight management for nearly twenty years, including her book *Smart People Don't Diet: How the Latest Science Can Help You Lose Weight Permanently* (2014).

LINA A. RICCIARDELLI, PhD, was Professor of Psychology at Deakin University, Melbourne, Australia (now deceased). She conducted research on body image and sociocultural factors across the lifespan with a health psychology focus for twenty-eight years.

TOMI-ANN ROBERTS, PhD, is Professor of Psychology at Colorado College and President of the Society for Menstrual Cycle Research. She is a feminist psychological scientist whose research on objectification theory seeks to uncover the cognitive, emotional, and behavioral costs to girls and women whose value in a sexually objectifying culture comes almost entirely from their physical appearance.

BRIAN SOUZA, PhD, is Assistant Professor in the Department of Food and Nutrition at Framingham State University. He earned his degree in Exercise and Sport Psychology from Oregon State University and integrates the Health at Every Size® principles into his teaching and research in health, wellness, and fitness.

VIREN SWAMI, PhD, is Professor of Social Psychology at Anglia Ruskin University. His main research focus is on the psychology of human appearance and body image, with a particular consideration of the impact of sociocultural influences. He is the author of *Attraction Explained* (2015) and *The Missing Arms of Vénus de Milo* (2007).

TRACY L. TYLKA, PhD, FAED, is Professor of Psychology at the Columbus and Marion campuses of The Ohio State University. She is a counseling psychologist and has been conducting research on negative body image for twenty years and positive body image since the inception of such research. She has been a part of the development teams for the Body Appreciation Scale (original and revised), the Functionality Appreciation Scale, and the Broad Conceptualization of Beauty Scale. She is Editor-in-Chief of *Body Image: An International Journal of Research*.

VIRGINIA RAMSEYER WINTER, PhD, MSW, is Assistant Professor in the School of Social Work at the University of Missouri. Her research explores relationships between body image and physical, mental, and sexual health.

PATTI LOU WATKINS, PhD, earned her degree in Clinical Psychology at Virginia Tech. She is currently Associate Professor at Oregon State University, where she teaches Fat Studies, with her research focusing on fat pedagogy and Health At Every Size® interventions. She recently coedited a special issue of *Fat Studies: An Interdisciplinary Journal of Body Weight and Society* on fat pedagogy.

NICHOLE L. WOOD-BARCALOW, PhD, is a psychologist at the Chalmers P. Wylie VA Ambulatory Care Center in Columbus, Ohio, who enjoys providing psychotherapy with a specialty focus on body image, eating disorders, and grief/loss issues. She is passionate about assisting clients in achieving their optimal potential and engaging in research projects focused on positive body image.

Acknowledgments

We thank Molly Hartig for her invaluable work on this project including her work creating the index for this volume. We also thank Amanda Hood and Samantha Buxton for their assistance.

In addition, we are grateful to have assembled an outstanding group of authors who worked so cooperatively on their chapters and helped us compile a volume we are all proud of.

Introduction

Becoming Positive – Our Growing Understanding of Positive Body Image

Meghan M. Gillen, Charlotte H. Markey, and Elizabeth A. Daniels

As body image researchers, we have recently witnessed the significant growth of research on positive body image. This change is exciting and revolutionary in the field, representing a shift in the way researchers – and hopefully the public – think about body image. As contributors to this volume have articulated in their chapters, body image is not simply what people do not like, or wish they could change, about their bodies. Instead, it is a much more holistic, multifaceted concept that consists of both positive and negative body image. Researchers disagree, however, about how to conceptualize these aspects of body image. Some view them as distinct constructs on separate poles that reflect thoughts, feelings, and attitudes toward the body, whereas others see them as overlapping, given that some components of both constructs are strongly correlated. What is clear is that both positive and negative body image are multifaceted and carry significant implications for health and well-being. In fact, working to develop a positive body image, rather than striving to reduce negative body image, may be a better approach to sustaining long-term health and well-being.

Research is only just beginning to unravel the meanings, antecedents, and consequences of positive body image. Historically, research has focused on the causes and consequences of negative body image, yielding much less knowledge about the positive aspects of body image. Thus, less is known about what it means to feel good about one's body, who feels good about their body, and how to encourage positive body image across different groups of people. This imbalance in the literature has been cited as problematic by leading body image scholars, both for the direction of the field and for clinicians' ability to foster well-being in their clients (Smolak & Cash, 2011; Tylka & Wood-Barcalow, 2015).

Researchers have responded to these concerns. A recent search on PsycInfo (August 2017) with "positive body image" as a key word yielded ninety results. In contrast, a similar search with the general term "body image" as a key word yielded 7,356 results. Thus, positive body image is a small but growing area within this larger field. The result of the positive body image search represents significant progress since the 2005 publication of the first version of the Body Appreciation Scale, a widely used and psychometrically sound measure of positive body image which has subsequently been revised and expanded. To that end, we saw this as an important time to create a volume that summarizes and reflects on the work that has gone before it. The aim of this book is to provide an overview of the existing research on positive body image. In the volume, we have included related topics such as positive health behaviors and body image interventions. Leading researchers in the field have synthesized existing evidence and offered future directions for the field. Below, we highlight some of the key points from each of their chapters.

Chapter 1, "Overview of the Field of Positive Body Image" by Tracy L. Tylka, provides an introduction to and review of the field of positive body image research. Tylka details the origins of the study of positive body image, including an operational definition of the construct, as well as the development of measures to assess the various components of positive body image. She also reviews existing research on positive body image, the majority of which has focused on outcomes for psychological well-being and physical health. Finally, Tylka concludes the chapter with a discussion of future directions for research on positive body image.

Chapter 2, "Positive Body Image by Gender and across the Lifespan" by Lina A. Ricciardelli, Marie L. Caltabiano, and Laura D. D'Antuono, synthesizes research on populations that have not received much research attention, such as pregnant and postpartum women, Canadian Aboriginal adults, adults with spinal cord injuries, and middle-aged and older women. The research included is both qualitative and quantitative and highlights themes related to positive body image (e.g., body pride, gratitude for the body's capabilities). The authors concluded that more research is needed among boys and men as well as middle-aged and older women and men, and that the field should move beyond measuring body appreciation to tap into additional components of positive body image.

Chapter 3, "Considering Positive Body Image through the Lens of Culture and Minority Social Identities" by Viren Swami, explores positive body image within different social and cultural contexts, and reminds us that positive body image – and, in fact, body image in general – is culturally constructed. From a small body of research, findings suggest that there are generally few between-group racial/ethnic differences (within the United States and across different countries) in positive body image. However, rural residents may be conducive to positive body image development. Further, sexual minority status may pose a risk factor for men's, but a buffering effect for women's, positive body image. Swami points out that there is work to be done, however, to determine more than group similarities and differences and to discover the explanatory mechanisms leading to the potential for positive body image to emerge in diverse contexts.

Chapter 4, "Moving beyond Body Dissatisfaction and Risky Sexual Behavior: A Critical Review of Positive Body Image and Sexual Health Scholarship" by Virginia Ramseyer Winter, includes research on positive body image and multiple components of sexual health. Winter reports that positive body image is generally associated with better sexual health and offers some compelling recommendations for research, practice, and policy. She argues that improving research is the foundation for enhancing practice and policy, and that this should include drawing on existing theories and creating new ones, developing new measures, and increasing diversity among participants. Throughout the chapter, she highlights the importance of diversity and theory in moving research on positive body image forward.

Chapter 5, "Appearance-Related Practices: Can They Be Part of a Positive Body Image" by Kristina Holmqvist Gattario and Carolina Lunde, reminds us of the complexities associated with living in one's body in a world where body modification of all sorts is accepted and even promoted. However, unlike many past conceptualizations of body modification as inherently "bad" or "antifeminist," Gattario and Lunde propose that appearance-related practices may be conducive to positive body image. They explain how enhancing one's appearance *may* be a statement about one's identity and/or an act of self-care, and can elicit positive social feedback, which in turn may enhance positive body image. Further, they describe the conundrum of whether or not to engage in appearance-related practices that is faced by women in particular. It is clear that refraining from engagement in such practices may have social costs. Although they frame their discussion in terms of theory and research, Gattario and Lunde also make it clear that some of the issues pertaining to appearance-related practices are cultural and philosophical. For example, they pose the question: To what extent is body modification a suitable part of body acceptance?

Chapter 6, "Mindful Self-Care and Positive Body Image: Mindfulness, Yoga, and Actionable Tools for Positive Embodiment" by Catherine Cook-Cottone, describes the constructs of positive embodiment and mindful self-care and their relationships with positive body image. Positive embodiment entails being present in the body and attuned to its needs and desires. Mindful self-care involves behaviors aimed at taking care of the body (e.g., planning for and preparing healthy meals). Cook-Cottone presents a theoretical model of positive embodiment as well as a new measure of mindful self-care. She also describes how individuals can implement self-care practices and yoga into their lives to enhance body image and cultivate positive embodiment.

Chapter 7, "The Health at Every Size® Paradigm: Promoting Body Positivity for All Bodies" by Patti Lou Watkins, Dawn Clifford, and Brian Souza, introduces the Health at Every Size® (HAES) paradigm, which rejects the traditional weight-centric approach to health in favor of a wellness-focused approach. In the HAES approach, weight loss is decentered as a target for interventions intended to improve health. In contrast, enhancing physical, emotional, and spiritual health without focusing on weight loss is the aim of the HAES approach to health. The authors review existing intervention research using the HAES approach. They also describe how the HAES paradigm can be applied in clinical, fitness, and educational settings and provide resources for accessing HAES curricula and other materials.

Chapter 8, "Better than Before: Individual Strategies for Body Image Improvement" by Jamie L. Dunaev and Charlotte H. Markey, highlights evidence-based practices that individuals can engage in on their own to enhance positive body image, such as therapeutic writing, physical activity, and mindfulness training. However, most studies are qualitative or have used small samples, so more research is needed to support use of these programs. Considering the challenges involved in changing the current sociocultural context (e.g., media) and, for some, in gaining access to interventions or treatments to improve body image (e.g., individual therapy), their strategies are practical and have wide implications for use.

Chapter 9, "Programmatic Approaches to Cultivating Positive Body Image in Youth" by Elizabeth A. Daniels and Tomi-Ann Roberts, describes body image programs for youth in three critical settings – school, sport, and dance – that have the potential to impact positive body image. Many of these existing programs focus on reducing negative body image, yet the authors argue, importantly, for a shift toward the inclusion of curricula that also foster positive body image. This approach may be better for maintaining well-being and may also "undo" the negative emotions generated by body image disturbance. The authors also include an important point about bridging research and practice, to incorporate theory into the design of body image programs.

Chapter 10, "Clinical Applications of Positive Body Image" by Nichole L. Wood-Barcalow and Casey L. Augustus-Horvath, discusses positive body image work in clinical contexts. As both clinicians and researchers, the authors offer insight into facets of positive body image that can be addressed through specific clinical interventions. They stress the importance of both clinicians and clients being committed to body acceptance, as opposed to behaviors aimed to alter the body to meet a particular ideal. Some of the possible avenues for intervention described include nurturing gratitude and self-compassion, educating about beauty ideals, and promoting self-care (e.g., healthy nutrition, sleep, and physical activity). Further, the authors discuss how clients can be taught to filter information that is not conducive to the development and maintenance of positive body image.

In conclusion, there clearly seems to be some cultural movement in popular media toward an aim to promote positive body image. Celebrities post pictures of their curvy physiques on Twitter, athletes proudly promote muscular bodies, and YouTube users post how-to videos about loving your body. As researchers, we may have fallen behind the cultural milieu when it comes to how we think about body image. However, the research discussed in this volume brings us closer to thinking about body image in a more holistic way; studying our view of our bodies as dynamic and full of potential instead of objects in need of fixing. We hope you find these chapters as novel, informative, and practical as we did. We encourage body image scholars and clinicians to continue their important work in unraveling what positive body image means and how to cultivate it. Similar to the movement toward promoting positive body image in the wider culture, we hope that researchers begin to adopt a "body positive" outlook in their research as well.

References

Smolak, L., & Cash, T. F. (2011). Future challenges for body image science, practice, and prevention. In T. F. Cash & L. Smolak (Eds.), *Body image: A handbook of science, practice, and prevention*, 2nd ed. (pp. 471–478). New York: Guilford Press.

Tylka, T. L., & Wood-Barcalow, N. L. (2015). What is and what is not positive body image? Conceptual foundations and construct definition. *Body Image, 14*, 118–129. doi: 10.1016/j.bodyim.2015.04.001

1   Overview of the Field of Positive Body Image

Tracy L. Tylka

Spanning nearly a century, the scientific study of body image has revealed many insights into its correlates, predictors, and consequences (Cash & Smolak, 2011). Yet, this research has been heavily slanted toward understanding its pathological side – body image disturbance – and consequently has neglected its adaptive side – positive body image (Tylka, 2011). Body image disturbance, or negative body image, encompasses many forms, such as body/appearance dissatisfaction, body surveillance, body shame, and internalization of media appearance ideals. Prominent researchers have argued that focusing on alleviating symptoms of negative body image without considering how to promote positive body image has precluded a comprehensive understanding of body image and have considered research on positive body image to be "essential to the future of the field" (Smolak & Cash, 2011, p. 472).

There are several reasons why scholars have predominantly focused on the pathological side of body image. First, body image disturbance is intertwined with eating disorder diagnoses. To prevent and treat eating disorders, researchers need to understand body image disturbance. Second, a focus on pathology has been the trend of psychological research in general (Seligman & Csikszentmihalyi, 2000). Third, there is an assumption that negative and positive body image are opposite poles of the same construct – in other words, information on body image disturbance can be reversed, leading to a full understanding of positive body image. However, positive body image is a more complex, nuanced construct than simply low levels of negative body image and therefore is worthy of study in its own right (Tylka & Wood-Barcalow, 2015c).

Regardless, ignoring positive body image in research may translate into clinicians being poorly equipped to promote health and well-being as they relate to embodiment (i.e., connection to how the body is feeling and functioning), and, ironically, prevent and treat body image disturbance. If body image therapies reduce symptoms of negative body image but do not enhance aspects of positive body image, clients may settle at a "neutral" body image (i.e., where the body is simply tolerated)

6

at best, which could limit self-care practices and allow disembodiment, or disconnection from how the body is feeling and functioning (Tylka & Wood-Barcalow, 2015c). In contrast, guiding clients toward positive body image may help them appreciate, respect, celebrate, and honor their body, which may make treatment gains more effective and enduring.

This chapter presents an overview of the current standing of the field of positive body image. What do we currently know about positive body image? What disciplines and actions contributed to its rise as a distinct field of study? What are its components and expressions? What scales measure it? How do we know that it is distinct from low negative body image? What has research revealed about its links to psychological well-being and physical health? Where does research go from here? This chapter will address these questions.

The Rise of Positive Body Image as a Distinct Field of Study

Two broad disciplines – psychology and Buddhism – situated positive body image as ripe for discovery. First, strength-based specialties within psychology emphasize that hygiology, or the preservation of health, is just as important as pathology for consideration within theory, research, and practice (Tylka & Wood-Barcalow, 2015c). Second, the practice of Buddhism facilitates the resilience and self-compassion needed to process and adaptively handle threats to body image and maintain positive actionable body practices (i.e., self-care) in the face of these threats (Webb, Butler-Ajibade, & Robinson, 2014).

Since the early to mid-twentieth century, counseling psychology and humanistic psychology have emphasized the need to consider strengths alongside psychopathology, appreciate cultural and body-related diversity, prevent illness by promoting health, accept others and the self unconditionally, and transcend beyond the physical (e.g., body appearance) to the meaningful (e.g., the joys that the body can offer; Tylka & Wood-Barcalow, 2015c). Since the early 2000s, positive psychology has reinvigorated and expanded the study of human strengths. A central tenet of positive psychology is that removing maladaptive characteristics in the absence of fostering adaptive characteristics does not promote human flourishing; it teaches us what not to be, but does not teach us what we should become (Seligman & Csikszentmihalyi, 2000). Soon after, scholars started to recognize the importance of promoting positive body image (Avalos, Tylka, & Wood-Barcalow, 2005) and began to champion a culture that appreciates body diversity, values body functionality, resists engaging in body shaming (of self and others), promotes self-compassion, and challenges unrealistic media appearance ideals (Tylka & Wood-Barcalow, 2015c).

In addition to cultural reform, the practice of attending to internal experiences, such as emotions and thoughts, is valuable for promoting positive body image. Buddhism conceptualizes psychopathology as the rigid and inflexible avoidance or control of internal experiences, and conceptualizes well-being as the mindfulness and acceptance of internal experiences while pursuing meaningful and valued goals (Webb et al., 2014). When negative internal experiences are brought on by body-related threats, the practice of being mindful and accepting of the distress, while proceeding to engage in self-care, elicits self- and body-related compassion (Neff, 2003; Webb et al., 2014). Thus, Buddhism contributes to positive body image theory, research, and practice by identifying mindfulness, self-compassion, and self-care as ways to process body-related threats, and by advising people to remain attuned to the internal self while engaging with the external world.

The interaction of these disciplines creates an understanding of how positive body image emerged as an independent area of investigation. Within the newly developed area of positive psychology, Seligman and Csikszentmihalyi (2000) called for researchers to investigate human strengths and resilience – this call provided the impetus for body image researchers to conceptualize positive body image as a distinct field of scholarship. Counseling psychology, humanistic psychology, and Buddhism provided a rich reservoir of ideas about human strengths and resilience for these researchers to consult to shape the study of positive body image.

Two years after Seligman and Csikszentmihalyi (2000) published a call to research human strengths, Cash and Pruzinsky (2002) highlighted the need to study the development and experience of positive body image and move beyond the study of appearance to instead focus on embodiment, in *Body Image: A Handbook of Theory, Research, and Clinical Practice*. In 2004, Cash provided an outlet for this research with the advent of *Body Image: An International Journal of Research*. This journal (*Body Image* for short) has encouraged submissions on positive body image development, adaptive body image processes and their clinically relevant consequences, and interventions to promote positive body image. Scholars were now assured that a journal would appreciate their rigorous and seminal contributions to the study of positive body image, which likely helped them invest resources in conducting such research. In 2011, Cash and Smolak devoted a chapter within the second edition of *Body Image: A Handbook of Science, Practice, and Prevention* that synthesized the "handful of published studies on positive body image" (Tylka, 2011, p. 56). Subsequently, positive body image research blossomed between 2011 and 2015, and this research was reviewed in the 2015 Special Series, *Positive Body Image: Avenues for Assessment, Application, and Advancement*, published in *Body Image*. Positive body image scholarship has since progressed even more rapidly, as it is understood as a unique domain in need of a great deal of research. As a personal reflection, positive body image is a rewarding area to investigate. Indeed, studying strengths often fuels researchers' enthusiasm for their research and clinical practice (Tylka & Wood-Barcalow, 2015b).

What Is Positive Body Image?

Until 2010, no definition of positive body image had been proposed. For her dissertation, Nichole Wood-Barcalow set out to understand the nuances of this construct and conducted a mixed methods study to achieve this goal. She first utilized the Multidimensional Body-Self Relations Questionnaire (Brown, Cash, & Mikulka, 1990; Cash, 2000) and a general question, "I feel that I have a positive body image," to identify college women who espouse a positive body image. She then conducted in-depth individual interviews with these women to explore fully what it means to endorse a positive body image. To further substantiate information, she interviewed body image researchers and clinical experts to discern their definition and description of this construct which was then interwoven with the women's reports. Together, Nichole, Casey Augustus-Horvath, and I identified themes that emerged from these interviews. As we looked across the themes, we generated the following definition of positive body image:

An overarching love and respect for the body that allows individuals to (a) appreciate the unique beauty of their body and the functions that it performs for them; (b) accept and even admire their body, including those aspects that are inconsistent with idealized images; (c) feel beautiful, comfortable, confident, and happy with their body, which is often reflected as an outer radiance, or a "glow;" (d) emphasize their body's assets rather than dwell on their imperfections; and (f) interpret incoming information in a body-protective manner whereby most positive information is internalized and most negative information is rejected or reframed. (Wood-Barcalow, Tylka, & Augustus-Horvath, 2010, p. 112)

This definition provided a base from which body image scholars and clinicians could understand the construct of positive body image. Notably, most aspects of this definition emerged in additional interviews with diverse participants who have positive body image, including samples of adolescent girls and boys from Sweden (Frisén & Holmqvist, 2010; Holmqvist & Frisén, 2012), African American girls from the United

States (Pope, Corona, & Belgrave, 2014), Aboriginal girls from Canada (McHugh, Coppola, & Sabiston, 2014), and Canadian residents with spinal cord injuries (Bailey, Gammage, van Ingen, & Ditor, 2015). Results of these studies are reported throughout the remainder of this section. Additional work is needed to ensure that the definition of positive body image represents a range of social identities and their intersections (Tiggemann, 2015; see also Chapter 3 in this book).

From this definition, it is evident that positive body image transcends appearance satisfaction and instead represents love and acceptance of the body regardless of its appearance. Also, it is evident that positive body image is multifaceted – consisting of distinct yet interrelated components that together form a cohesive and holistic view of the construct.

Components of Positive Body Image

Body appreciation. Body appreciation involves respecting, honoring, loving, and displaying gratitude toward the features, functionality, and health of the body. It includes praising the body for what it is able to do, what it represents, and its unique features. College women in the United States stated that they appreciate features of their body that they disliked or ignored during adolescence and are grateful for the ways their body can function (Wood-Barcalow et al., 2010). Swedish and African American adolescents reported appreciating the functionality and "average" appearances of their body (Holmqvist & Frisén, 2012; Pope et al., 2014). Aboriginal Canadian girls indicated that they appreciate their Native features and their body's ability to partake in the customs of their culture, such as powwow dance (McHugh et al., 2014). Canadian adults with spinal cord injuries revealed that they are grateful for improvements in the health, function, independence, and strength of their body (Bailey et al., 2015).

Body acceptance and love. Those with positive body image love their body, are comfortable with their body, and accept their unique physical features. This component of positive body image does not reflect vanity or preoccupation with appearance, nor is it contingent on the body's alignment with sociocultural appearance ideals. College women in the United States reported focusing on body assets (rather than perceived body flaws) and admiring (or at least accepting) how their body is unique rather than attempting to conform to unrealistic societal appearance ideals (Wood-Barcalow et al., 2010). Swedish adolescents revealed that they accept unique features of their body and are not troubled by them (Frisén & Holmqvist, 2010). African American adolescent girls stated that they emphasize their body assets, with roughly a third indicating that they like everything about their body (Pope et al., 2014). Aboriginal Canadian girls indicated that they are comfortable in their body and do not want to change their appearance, even if others want them to make changes (McHugh et al., 2014). Finally, Canadian adults with spinal cord injuries revealed that they had to learn to accept their body after their disability and now focus on loving their body despite its limited mobility (Bailey et al., 2015).

Broadly conceptualizing beauty. This component of positive body image reflects the perception that a diversity of appearances (e.g., body sizes and shapes) and looks (e.g., personal style) are beautiful, and the belief that inner features, such as confidence and generosity, can shape beauty. Swedish adolescents and Canadian adults with spinal cord injuries emphasized that being beautiful does not imply having an appearance that is consistent with societal definitions of beauty and that beauty encompasses many different appearances and inner qualities (Bailey et al., 2015; Holmqvist & Frisén, 2012). College women in the United States revealed that they appreciate different appearances and emphasized that beauty cannot be compared and is embodied in an indefinite number of ways (Wood-Barcalow et al., 2010). African American adolescent girls emphasized creating a style that makes a personal statement and projects a unique presence, suggesting that they have a flexible definition of beauty and beauty ideals (Parker et al., 1995). Aboriginal Canadian girls conceptualized beauty as experienced on the "inside" yet expressed outwardly in their choice of style and grooming (McHugh et al., 2014).

Adaptive body investment. Those with positive body image are invested in taking care of their body. This investment involves regularly engaging in self-care, such as grooming behaviors, adequate sleep, joyful physical activity, eating foods that give one's body energy, and enhancing one's natural features via benign methods (e.g., a new hairstyle). College women in the United States revealed that they invest in behaviors such as nutritious eating, physical exercise, and regular rest, and view these behaviors as acts of kindness toward and acceptance of their body (Wood-Barcalow et al., 2010). African American girls emphasized that they value being "well-kept" and "making what they had work for them," which they described as being well-groomed and having their body project their sense of style, personality, and confidence (Parker et al., 1995, p. 108). Canadian adults with spinal cord injuries reported increased self-care (e.g., physical activity appropriate for their body, nutritious eating) after their injury to assist their body in performing the best it possibly can. This self-care promotes body attunement, or the integration of awareness of their needs with engagement in practices that serve and support those needs, which helps them manage secondary complications and minimize pain with greater success (Bailey et al., 2015).

Inner positivity influencing outer demeanor. This component involves the interplay between positive feelings about the body, positive feelings in general (e.g., confidence, optimism, happiness), and the manifestation of these feelings in behavior (e.g., helping others, self-care, smiling, asserting oneself, holding one's "head up high," and emanating a "special glow or "outer radiance"; Tylka, 2011, p. 59). College women in the United States revealed that their inner happiness is expressed as a confident glow and fuels their engagement in pleasurable exercise, yoga, and joyful eating that honors their body (Wood-Barcalow et al., 2010). Swedish adolescents indicated that their inner positivity is tied to physical activity, as many are involved in sports and exercise for enjoyment and challenge rather than to control the size and shape of their body (Frisén & Holmqvist, 2010). Aboriginal Canadian girls reported that their positive body image is experienced internally (e.g., being comfortable in and loving their body) and expressed externally (e.g., via confidence, self-respect); they believed that joyful movement (e.g., powwow dance) and nutritious eating both stem from and maintain their positive body image (McHugh et al., 2014).

Protective filtering. Filtering information in a body-protective manner involves accepting information that is consistent with positive body image while rejecting messages that could endanger it, termed by Wood-Barcalow et al. (2010, p. 109) a "protective filter." College women in the United States, Swedish adolescents, and Canadian adults with spinal cord injuries reported being aware of the unrealistic and fabricated nature of media images, rejecting and challenging these images, and internalizing messages that are compassionate toward their body (Wood-Barcalow et al., 2010). Swedish adolescents noted that they are not particularly bothered by negative appearance-related comments (Frisén & Holmqvist, 2010) and are aware of and actively criticize unnatural and unrealistic appearance ideals and the media's use of these ideals for profit (Holmqvist & Frisén, 2012). Aboriginal Canadian girls spoke about the need to develop a "mind frame" that does not "listen to" negative appearance comments and body-related pressures from influential others or the media in order to build and maintain positive body image (McHugh et al., 2014, p. 321). Importantly, the protective filter is not foolproof, as some participants reported not being able to ward off the distress prompted by body image-related threats at particularly vulnerable times (e.g., when tired, when stressed, when the threat comes from someone particularly meaningful; Holmqvist & Frisén, 2012; Wood-Barcalow et al., 2010).

Interactions among Components: The Role of Attunement

The components of positive body image are interdependent and need to be interpreted together. Cook-Cottone (2015; see Chapter 6 in this book) refers to this process as *attunement*, reflecting the reciprocity between the internal self (i.e., thoughts, affect, physiology) and environment (i.e., family, community, culture). Indeed, those with positive body image indicated that they change, shape, and alter their environments in growth-enhancing ways, which then benefit their internal experiences (Tylka & Wood-Barcalow, 2015c). As an illustration, college women in the United States indicated that they avoid participating in negative body-related talk, engage in regular self-care (e.g., yoga), befriend those who accept their body, and reduce their consumption of appearance-related media in order to protect their physical health and psychological well-being (Wood-Barcalow et al., 2010). Aboriginal Canadian girls revealed that they engage in powwow dance to show their body and cultural pride, which then further reinforces this pride (McHugh et al., 2014). Swedish adolescents reported that participating in athletics helps them appreciate the functionality of their body, which then facilitates their engagement in sports for self-care, enjoyment, and challenge (Frisén & Holmqvist, 2010). Canadian adults with spinal cord injuries spoke about choosing friends who accept their body, which then facilitates self-care and their appreciation of their own body (Bailey et al., 2015).

Summary

Although qualitative research provides a great deal of insight into the nuances of the positive body image construct, quantitative studies test the veracity of the claims that positive body image is distinct from low body image disturbance, multifaceted, and tied to indices of physical health and psychological well-being. Quantitative studies further refine what is known about the positive body image construct and examine whether it can be nurtured and protective against psychological distress. To facilitate this research, scales were developed to assess one or more components of positive body image.

Assessment of Positive Body Image

Several positive body image scales have been developed and refined; this section identifies, discusses, and presents psychometric evidence for these scales. To be included, the scale has to assess one or more of the identified components of positive body image; predominantly contain items that are positively worded (rather than worded in the direction of body image disturbance and reverse scored); and have accrued considerable psychometric evidence, including examinations of factor structure, internal consistency and test–retest reliability, and construct, convergent, discriminant, and incremental validity.

Body Appreciation Scale-2

The original thirteen-item Body Appreciation Scale (BAS; Avalos et al., 2005) was designed to measure the extent to which individuals accept, hold favorable opinions toward, and respect their body, as well as the extent to which they reject media-promoted appearance ideals as the only form of human beauty. Although this unidimensional scale has a great deal of evidence supporting its psychometric properties (Avalos et al., 2005), it was recently revised because (a) it was written before comprehensive qualitative examinations of the positive body image construct were conducted; (b) three items produce lower factor loadings which result in a two-factor structure in some cultural groups; (c) women and men have different forms due to gender-specific language within one item; (d) two items were written as though it is normative to see the body as flawed; and (e) two items conceptualize positive body image as the absence of body shape/weight concern. Thus, eight BAS items were revised, reworded, discarded, or replaced to rectify these issues and better reflect current knowledge of the positive body image construct.

This revised scale, the BAS-2, contains five original BAS items and five new items (Tylka & Wood-Barcalow, 2015a). Its items reflect the body appreciation, body acceptance and love, broadly conceptualizing beauty, and inner positivity components of positive body image. Some items include: "I respect my body," "I appreciate the different and unique characteristics of my body," "I feel love for my body," "I feel like I am beautiful even if I am different from media images of attractive people (e.g., models, actresses/actors)," and "My behavior reveals my positive attitude toward my body; for example, I hold my head high and smile." Thus, while brief, the BAS-2 represents the positive body image construct. Its items are each rated along a five-point scale ranging from *never* (scored as 1) to *always* (5) and averaged, with higher scores reflecting greater body appreciation.

The psychometric properties of the BAS-2 have been upheld among college and community samples of women and men in the United States (Tylka & Wood-Barcalow, 2015a). Within these samples, the BAS-2 conformed to a unidimensional factor structure, and demonstrated strong internal consistency (αs = .93 to .96) and stability over a three-week period

($r = .90$). It was positively related to self-esteem and proactive coping and inversely associated with body dissatisfaction, internalization of societal appearance ideals, and body surveillance, upholding its convergent validity. It accounted for unique variance in intuitive eating (i.e., a flexible pattern of eating largely based on internal hunger and satiety cues rather than emotional and situational cues) and disordered eating above and beyond appearance evaluation and body dissatisfaction, supporting its incremental validity. It was negligibly related to impression management, demonstrating its discriminant validity. Measurement invariance analyses revealed that its structure is similar between men and women, as well as between college and community samples.

Recently, the BAS-2 was modified for children as young as age nine, and the psychometric properties of this version (BAS-2C) have been established in a sample of girls and boys aged nine to eleven (Halliwell, Jarman, Tylka, & Slater, 2017). A state version of the BAS-2 that is sensitive to fluctuations in body appreciation also exists (SBAS-2; Homan, 2016). The BAS-2 has also been translated into many languages, with its unidimensional factor structure and psychometrics supported (see Chapter 3 in this book), aiding in cross-cultural research on positive body image.

Functionality Appreciation Scale

Body functionality includes everything that the body can do or is capable of doing, and encompasses functions related to physical capacities (e.g., walking, carrying groceries), internal processes (e.g., healing from an illness), bodily senses and perceptions (e.g., seeing, feeling physically relaxed), creative endeavors (e.g., drawing, singing), communication (e.g., speaking, hugging), and self-care (Alleva, Martijn, Van Breukelen, Jansen, & Karos, 2015). Because body functionality may be limited by various factors (e.g., diseases, acquired injuries, lack of flexibility), the specific construct upon which researchers need to focus is individuals' appreciation of, respect for, and honoring of their body for what it can do or is capable of doing (Alleva et al., 2015; Bailey et al., 2015; Webb, Wood-Barcalow, & Tylka, 2015). Although the BAS-2 assesses body appreciation more generally, none of its items assesses the appreciation of body functionality.

The Functionality Appreciation Scale (FAS; Alleva, Tylka, & Kroon Van Diest, 2017) has been developed for this purpose. The FAS includes seven items, such as "I appreciate my body for what it is capable of doing," "I am grateful for the health of my body, even if it isn't always as healthy as I would like it to be," "I am grateful that my body enables me to engage in activities that I enjoy or find important," and "I feel that my body does so much for me." Items in the FAS are rated along a scale ranging from *strongly disagree* (scored as 1) to *strongly agree* (5) and averaged, with higher scores indicating greater functionality appreciation. In three studies of community women and men in the United States, Alleva et al. (2017) found that the scale had a unidimensional factor structure and demonstrated measurement invariance across sex. Its internal consistency (αs = .86 to .91) and three-week test–retest reliability (rs = .74 to .81) were also established. It was positively related to body appreciation, broadly conceptualizing beauty, intuitive eating, gratitude, self-esteem, life satisfaction, self-compassion, and proactive coping and inversely related to body surveillance, self-objectification, symptoms of anxiety and depression, and cosmetic surgery acceptance, upholding its convergent validity. It was unrelated to impression management, supporting its discriminant validity. Functionality appreciation also was found to be a novel construct different from body appreciation, self-compassion, and low appearance-focused attitudes and behavior, upholding its incremental validity.

Broad Conceptualization of Beauty Scale

The nine-item Broad Conceptualization of Beauty Scale (BCBS; Tylka & Iannantuono, 2016) assesses the degree to which women perceive that a wide range of physical appearances are beautiful and internal personality characteristics shape beauty. Its items are tailored to women, and it is administered only to women because beauty, and its evaluation, is gendered. Some items include: "I think that a wide variety of body shapes are beautiful for women"; "I define a woman's beauty differently than how it is portrayed in the media"; "Even if a physical feature is not considered attractive by others or by society, I think it can be beautiful"; "A woman's confidence level can change my perception of her physical beauty"; and "A woman's acceptance of herself can change my perception of her physical beauty." Items are rated along a seven-point scale ranging from *strongly disagree* (scored as 1) to *strongly agree* (7) and averaged, with higher scores indicating a broader conceptualization of beauty.

Among samples of community women in the United States, Tylka and Iannantuono (2016) found that the BCBS conforms to a unidimensional factor structure, and it demonstrates internal consistency (αs = .84 to .91) and stability over a three-week period (r = .88). The BCBS was positively related to body appreciation, self-compassion, and body image quality of life and inversely related to anti-fat attitudes, body surveillance, thin-ideal internalization, acceptance of cosmetic surgery, and body comparison, supporting its convergent validity. It was unrelated to impression management and narcissism, upholding its discriminant validity. The BCBS was also found to be a novel measure different from body appreciation, low thin-ideal internalization, and anti-fat attitudes, upholding its incremental validity.

Because the BCBS only assesses women's tendency to broadly conceptualize other women's beauty, Tylka and Iannantuono (2016) suggested that a variable representing beauty that extends to others *and* the self can be generated by multiplying the total BCBS score with the last BAS-2 item that assesses perceptions of self-beauty ("I feel like I am beautiful, even if I am different from media images of attractive people"). Thus, perceptions of self-beauty and other-beauty are weighed equally. Tylka and Iannantuono (2016) found that this variable, BCB (others and self), is positively related to body appreciation, self-compassion, and body image quality of life and inversely related to anti-fat attitudes, body surveillance, thin-ideal internalization, endorsement of cosmetic surgery, and body comparison. It contributed to indices of psychological well-being above and beyond body appreciation. These findings suggest that BCB (others and self) is a holistic conceptualization of broad conceptualization of beauty – extending beyond others to the self – that is not redundant with body appreciation.

Summary

Most research on positive body image has been conducted with the BAS (original and BAS-2), given its relative longevity in the positive body image literature. Other strengths of the BAS-2 include its comprehensiveness in assessing the positive body image components, its excellent psychometric properties, and its translations into various languages that allow researchers to explore positive body image cross-culturally. The more recently developed FAS and BCBS have demonstrated excellent psychometric properties. Evidence supports each measure as novel and incremental to the study of positive body image. However, is the positive body image construct itself novel and incremental to the study of body image?

Novelty of Positive Body Image as a Construct

Is positive body image best conceptualized as one endpoint along a body image continuum, anchored at the opposite end by negative body image? Several research teams have demonstrated that this conceptualization is inaccurate. Four arguments for the construct distinction between positive and negative body image are provided.

First, positive body image is uniquely associated with well-being after excluding its shared variance with negative body image. Body appreciation contributed to well-being (self-esteem, optimism, and proactive coping), intuitive eating, and eating disorder symptomatology after extracting its shared variance with negative body image among samples of college women and men in the United States (Avalos et al., 2005; Tylka & Wood-Barcalow, 2015a). Body appreciation was associated with Australian women's higher use of sun protection (e.g., SPF products) and skin cancer screenings and lower engagement in weight-loss behaviors after removing its shared variance with body dissatisfaction (Andrew, Tiggemann, & Clark, 2016a). Body appreciation was also positively related to sexual functioning in women when controlling for appearance dissatisfaction (Robbins & Reissing, 2017). Furthermore, functionality appreciation contributed to higher body appreciation and intuitive eating after excluding its shared variance with body image disturbance in women and men in the United States (Alleva et al., 2017). Broad conceptualization of beauty was inversely associated with anti-fat attitudes after excluding its shared variance with thin-ideal internalization in women in the United States (Tylka & Iannantuono, 2016). Therefore, positive body image is uniquely associated with well-being, self-care, eating behaviors, and (lower) weight stigma above and beyond negative body image.

Second, individuals may endorse high body appreciation yet still remain somewhat dissatisfied with their body. Tiggemann and McCourt (2013) examined relationships between body appreciation, body dissatisfaction, and age among Australian women. The strength of the inverse correlation between body appreciation and body dissatisfaction decreased as women's age increased. Also, body appreciation was positively related to age, whereas body dissatisfaction was unrelated to age. Tiggemann and McCourt concluded that body appreciation and body dissatisfaction are not mirror images of one another – it becomes increasingly possible for women to simultaneously experience some level of body dissatisfaction but also to appreciate and respect their body, especially with age. Moreover, in their qualitative study of women over age fifty-five at an exercise facility, Bailey, Cline, and Gammage (2016) found that participants experience negative and positive body image simultaneously – they are invested in and somewhat dissatisfied with their appearance, but appreciate the functionality of their body. Pope et al. (2014) found that African American adolescent girls identify features they would like to change about their body, but concurrently hold positive feelings about their body.

Third, the conceptual overlap (as determined by r^2) between measures of positive body image and measures of negative body image is not large, illustrating that these constructs are sufficiently distinct and should not be considered as opposite ends on the same continuum. For example, there was only a 19 percent conceptual overlap between body appreciation and body dissatisfaction among a sample of African American adolescent girls (Webb et al., 2014). While the conceptual overlap between body appreciation and body dissatisfaction appears to be larger in predominantly White samples of college women (i.e., 53 percent) and men (41 percent) in the United States and Australian women (44 percent), there is still evidence of construct differentiation within these estimates (Tiggemann & McCourt, 2013; Tylka & Wood-Barcalow, 2015a). Functionality appreciation overlapped by only 5 percent and <1 percent with body surveillance and 10 percent and <1 percent with self-objectification among women and men in the United States, respectively (body surveillance and self-objectification were tested because they position appearance against body functionality; Alleva et al., 2017). Broadly conceptualizing beauty resulted in a conceptual overlap of only 27 percent with anti-fat attitudes and 18 percent with thin-ideal internalization among women in the United States (anti-fat attitudes and thin-ideal internalization were chosen based on their narrow [thin] conceptualization of female beauty; Tylka & Iannantuono, 2016).

Fourth, some activities increase participants' body appreciation but have little to no impact on their negative body image. For instance, Swami (2017) found that women and men in the United Kingdom who attended a six-week life drawing course with nude models increased their body appreciation and had greater feelings of embodiment compared to baseline (i.e., pre-course) levels, whereas the course did not have a significant impact on their negative body image (however, findings should be taken with caution since no control group was included). Thus, interventions may have differential effects on positive and negative body image.

Summary

Substantial evidence demonstrates that positive body image is its own construct – it is not simply low negative body image (Tylka & Wood-Barcalow, 2015c). This evidence lends support to the research on positive body image that has been occurring, with increasing momentum, pace, and rigor, since the publication of the original BAS.

Research on Positive Body Image

In 2011, few published quantitative studies on positive body image existed. Now, research on positive body image is burgeoning. Although most of this research has been correlational and cross-sectional, these designs are needed to set the foundation and rationale for expensive, time-consuming, and long-term prospective and experimental designs. For instance, it is important to know that positive body image and intuitive eating are related before investing resources in exploring whether positive body image predicts higher levels of intuitive eating across time. The bulk of research on positive body image has focused on how positive body image relates to psychological well-being and physical health – an area with great clinical, empirical, and theoretical relevance – and therefore is reviewed below. Unless otherwise noted, study designs are cross-sectional and findings are based on samples from the United States, Canada, the United Kingdom, Australia, or the Netherlands.

Psychological Well-Being

Positive body image is related to multiple indicators of positive psychological well-being such as optimism, self-esteem, proactive coping, positive affect, life satisfaction, subjective happiness, emotional intelligence, and feeling/being connected to nature (Alleva et al., 2017; Avalos et al., 2005; Dalley & Vidal, 2013; Gillen, 2015; Swami, Barron, Weis, & Furnham, 2016; Swami, Begum, & Petrides, 2010; Swami, Tran, Stieger, Voracek & the YouBeauty.com Team, 2015; Tylka, Calogero, & Daníelsdóttir, 2015; Tylka & Iannantuono, 2016; Tylka & Kroon Van Diest, 2013). Body appreciation and functionality appreciation are also inversely related to negative affect and depressive symptomatology (Alleva et al., 2017; Gillen, 2015; Iannantuono & Tylka, 2012; Tylka et al., 2015; Tylka & Kroon Van Diest, 2013).

Body appreciation was first explored in Avalos and Tylka's (2006) acceptance model of intuitive eating. According to this model, body acceptance by others encourages individuals to appreciate their body and focus less on their appearance, which then facilitates intuitive eating. In two studies, Avalos and Tylka (2006) found that body appreciation mediates the relationship between body acceptance by others and intuitive eating – that is, women who perceive that important others accept their body have higher body appreciation, which is, in turn, associated with higher intuitive eating. These associations are also upheld in samples of men (Kroon Van Diest & Tylka, 2010); adolescent girls (Andrew, Tiggemann, & Clark, 2015a); women in emerging, early, and middle adulthood (Augustus-Horvath & Tylka, 2011); and female college athletes (Hahn Oh, Wiseman, Hendrickson, Phillips, & Hayden,

2012). Expanding the model, Tylka and Homan (2015) found that, among physically active college students, the connection between body appreciation and intuitive eating is disrupted when participants exercise for appearance reasons (e.g., to lose weight).

Andrew, Tiggemann, and Clark (2016c) prospectively examined the acceptance model of intuitive eating, as well as body appreciation's connection to disordered eating, substance use, and physical activity, among adolescent girls assessed at two time points separated by one year. They found that body acceptance by others predicted increased body appreciation, and body appreciation predicted increased intuitive eating and physical activity as well as decreased dieting, alcohol, and cigarette use over the year. These findings highlight body appreciation as an important variable to target for interventions addressing eating behavior, physical activity, and substance use.

Much research also has upheld the strong connection between body appreciation and self-compassion, even after controlling for self-esteem (Wasylkiw, MacKinnon, & MacLellan, 2012). Self-compassion refers to being mindful, kind, and nurturing toward the self during situations that threaten self-adequacy (Neff, 2003). Andrew, Tiggemann, and Clark (2016b) revealed that the strong positive relationship between self-compassion and body appreciation was mediated by lower appearance-related processing or focusing less on appearance such as lower thin-ideal internalization and appearance comparison. Thus, being kind and compassionate toward the self is linked to decentering appearance, which is then connected to appreciating the body regardless of appearance. Self-compassion also buffered the relationship between body comparison and body appreciation such that when self-compassion was very high, body comparison was not related to body appreciation, and when self-compassion was low, body comparison was associated with lower body appreciation (Homan & Tylka, 2015). Furthermore, increases in self-compassion facilitate increases in body appreciation. For example, Albertson, Neff, and Dill-Shackleford (2015) delivered a three-week self-compassion meditation training to adult women with existing body image concerns. Women who received this training reported significantly greater gains in body appreciation at post-intervention compared to a waitlist control group, and maintained these gains at a three-month follow-up. Kelly and Stephen (2016) found that, over a seven-day period, college women's day-to-day fluctuations in self-compassion were connected to their day-to-day fluctuations in body appreciation. That is, on days when women treat themselves more compassionately than usual, they are more appreciative of their body.

Physical Health

Some scholars have asserted that individuals who have a holistically favorable body image may not be motivated to engage in healthy behaviors (Heinberg, Thompson, & Matzon, 2001). To date, no empirical research substantiates this claim. Instead, research supports the opposite – positive body image is linked to health in an adaptive direction.

Yoga is an embodying physical activity that provides the opportunity to cultivate positive body image (Cook-Cottone, 2015). Women who practice Iyengar and Bikram yoga reported higher body appreciation than women who do not practice yoga, with lower self-objectification and higher embodiment among the yogis accounting for this difference (Mahlo & Tiggemann, 2016). Whereas positive body image was linked to higher engagement in physical activity (Wasylkiw & Butler, 2014), this relationship may only exist when appearance-related motives for exercise are low. Indeed, engaging in exercise to alter appearance weakened the positive link between body appreciation and physical activity among college women (Homan & Tylka, 2014). Conversations about exercise orient women to consider what their body can do, which was connected to higher body appreciation, whereas conversations about weight loss and dieting prompt women to evaluate their appearance, which was linked to lower body appreciation (Wasylkiw & Butler, 2014).

This appearance-versus-functionality focus is also relevant to body appreciation in dance. Some forms of dance are appearance-oriented and may thus lower body appreciation, whereas other forms encourage dancers to experience their body in a functional, strong, empowered, and embodied way and thus may strengthen body appreciation. Indeed, beginner ballet dancers reported higher body appreciation compared with advanced ballet dancers, whereas advanced contemporary dancers reported higher body appreciation compared with beginners (Swami & Harris, 2012). In other studies, female modern, street, belly, and recreational pole dancers reported higher body appreciation compared to nondancers (Langdon & Petracca, 2010; Pellizzer, Tiggemann, & Clark, 2016; Swami & Tovée, 2009; Tiggemann, Coutts, & Clark, 2014), with higher embodiment and lower self-objectification among the dancers likely accounting for these differences (Tiggemann et al., 2014).

In terms of sexual health, body appreciation is connected to higher sexual functioning among women. Among a diverse sample of women, body appreciation was found to be connected to higher sexual arousal, orgasm, and satisfaction, even when controlling for their sexual orientation, partner status, and age (Satinsky, Reece, Dennis, Sanders, & Bardzell, 2012). Similarly, in a separate study, body appreciation uniquely contributed to women's higher sexual functioning and satisfaction and lower sexual distress when controlling for their age and appearance dissatisfaction (Robbins & Reissing, 2017). In addition, body appreciation buffered age-related changes in sexual satisfaction, suggesting that body appreciation may be a promising clinical intervention in the treatment of sexual problems that may emerge with age. In other research, body appreciation was linked to greater sexual liberalism and more positive attitudes toward unconventional sexual practices in women and men when controlling for sexual orientation, relationship status, age, and BMI (Swami, Weis, Barron, & Furnham, 2017). Further, body appreciation was related to lower pornography use among men (Tylka, 2015) and lower perceived partner use of pornography among women (Tylka & Kroon Van Diest, 2015), suggesting that people higher in body appreciation value actual bodies rather than the idealized bodies often depicted in pornography, and therefore may choose to not view pornography or partner with men who do.

Similar adaptive links have been found between body appreciation and reproductive health. In one study, body appreciation was associated with women's greater feelings of menstrual well-being and pride and fewer beliefs that their menstrual cycle is annoying and embarrassing (Chrisler, Marván, Gorman, & Rossini, 2015). In another study, awareness and appreciation of body functionality were linked to fewer depressive symptoms and less engagement in unhealthy prenatal behaviors in pregnant women, with the appreciation of body functionality buffering the relationship between body surveillance and unhealthy prenatal behaviors (Rubin & Steinberg, 2011).

Body appreciation is also associated with a range of positive routine self-care behaviors and the avoidance of harmful behaviors. Adolescent girls and college women and men who report higher body appreciation also endorse greater intentions to protect their skin from UV exposure and damage and conduct skin cancer screenings (Andrew et al., 2016a; Gillen, 2015). Higher body appreciation among first-year medical students was connected to their oral health (Dumitrescu, Zetu, Teslaru, Dogaru, & Dogaru, 2008). Furthermore, college students with higher body appreciation reported lower abuse of prescription stimulants for weight loss compared to those with lower body appreciation (Jeffers & Benotsch, 2014). Several researchers have found that body appreciation is inversely linked to disordered eating and the endorsement of cosmetic surgery for women and men (Andrew et al., 2016a; Avalos et al., 2005; Gillen, 2015; Swami, 2009; Tylka & Iannantuono, 2016; Tylka & Kroon Van Diest, 2013; Tylka & Wood-Barcalow, 2015a).

Many studies have revealed that body appreciation is related to lower BMI (e.g., Satinsky et al., 2012; Tylka & Kroon Van Diest, 2013; Tylka & Wood-Barcalow, 2015a; Webb et al., 2014). However, BMI is an imprecise and flawed measure of physical health (see Tylka et al., 2014). Interestingly, researchers have found that body acceptance by others completely accounts for the relationship between BMI and body appreciation (Augustus-Horvath & Tylka, 2011). In other words, the extent to which women feel that their body is accepted by significant others is more closely related to body appreciation than is their BMI, emphasizing the need to eradicate weight stigma to preserve body appreciation.

Protection against Media Exposure

Evidence suggests that positive body image is protective against exposure to sociocultural appearance ideals. Halliwell (2013) found that women high in body appreciation did not place increased importance on their appearance discrepancies (i.e., differences between how they would like to look and how they actually look) after viewing thin female models – their appearance discrepancies were similar in size to a control group who did not view thin models. In contrast, women low in body appreciation placed increased importance on their appearance discrepancies after viewing thin female models, compared to the control group. Further, Halliwell uncovered that the protective effect of high body appreciation extends to women who have internalized the thin ideal. Among women who endorsed the thin ideal, those high in body appreciation downplayed the importance of their appearance discrepancies after viewing thin female models, whereas those low in body appreciation reported larger appearance discrepancies and placed more importance on these discrepancies after viewing thin female models. Similarly, Andrew, Tiggemann, and Clark (2015c) found that women with low body appreciation experienced increased body dissatisfaction following exposure to thin-ideal advertisements of women, whereas those with high body appreciation did not. This effect remained when controlling for participants' state self-objectification, appearance comparison, and previous media consumption and literacy. Collectively, these studies represent a "convincing case that body appreciation in young adult women serves a protective function against negative impacts from thin-ideal media exposure" (Andrew et al., 2015c, p. 103).

Additionally, certain interventions highlight the protective effects of positive body image against media exposure of appearance ideals. As an illustration, Alleva et al. (2015) developed *Expand Your Horizon*, a body image-improvement program involving fifteen-minute structured writing assignments designed to train women with a negative body image to focus on the functions that their body performs and why these functions are personally important and meaningful. Women in the program experienced higher appearance satisfaction and functionality satisfaction, lower self-objectification, and greater body appreciation when compared to women in an active control program from pre-test to post-test and at a one-week follow-up. In a subsequent study, after exposure to thin-ideal media images of women, women in the *Expand Your Horizon* program experienced greater functionality satisfaction and body appreciation compared to control participants (Alleva, Veldhuis, & Martijn, 2016).

Summary

Positive body image is associated with numerous well-being, self-care, and physical health measures in a positive direction, as well as distress and disturbance in an inverse direction. It also is protective against exposure to media appearance ideals. Positive body image is clearly an adaptive perspective of the body that needs to be, and can be, cultivated.

Future Directions in Positive Body Image Research

To review, positive body image is a novel construct, its major components can be assessed via psychometrically sound scales, and it is associated in an adaptive, and even protective, manner with a plethora of psychological and physical health indices. This is where we are in the study of positive body image. Where do we go from here?

Plenty of research remains to be done. The FAS and BCBS are new, demonstrate excellent psychometric properties, and assess novel components of positive body image – thus, they are ripe for research into the benefits of functionality appreciation and broadly conceptualizing beauty. Researchers need to identify features that promote the ability to bounce back to positive body image during and after perceived body-related threats – a measure of protective filtering would facilitate this research. Protective filtering may be easier to achieve and maintain for some, whereas it may be more effortful for others. Thus, in addition to exploring individual differences in protective filtering, it would be useful to understand which intentional activities promote it. Furthermore, researchers need to examine how various contextual factors shape moment-to-moment experiences of positive body image. The state version of the BAS-2 (SBAS-2) could facilitate these lines of research.

Researchers also need to ensure that current and future models of positive body image can be replicated, and work toward extending these models to arrive at a more nuanced understanding of this construct. Although correlational and cross-sectional investigations have provided basic examinations of positive body image theory and revealed the adaptiveness and novelty of the construct, longitudinal and experimental investigations of model paths are needed to further refine the theory and construct. As reviewed in this chapter, many mediational paths have been investigated in models of positive body image, yet investigations of mediational paths in cross-sectional research may generate biased estimates (Maxwell & Cole, 2007). Therefore, positive body image needs to be explored over a period of years to provide a clearer picture of its development, stability, and transience. It is possible to begin these investigations in children as young as age nine using the recently developed CBAS-2.

Additionally, it is imperative that researchers investigate the interaction, or attunement, of positive body image components. Efforts could be directed toward exploring "upward spirals," or combinations of adaptive variables that trigger self-perpetuating cycles and trajectories of positive psychological growth (Garland et al., 2010). Researchers could use this reciprocal-influence design to study, for instance, whether initial levels of body appreciation predict subsequent body appreciation through embodied activities (e.g., yoga, belly dance), self-care, and intuitive eating (Tylka & Kroon Van Diest, 2015). Further, the line between what is considered adaptive and maladaptive appearance investment is blurred at present. Logically, benign appearance investment would honor self-care, physical health, psychological well-being, and the person's physical qualities (e.g., a new hairstyle), whereas maladaptive appearance investment would entail attempting to change the physical qualities in ways that could be harmful to health and/or well-being (e.g., cosmetic procedures and surgery, use of tanning beds). Researchers therefore need to investigate appearance investment's roles in promoting versus suppressing self-care. Overall, the connections between positive body image and embodied experiences (Piran, 2016) need to be examined.

Another important question for researchers is whether existing body image and disordered eating interventions promote positive body image (Piran, 2015). Positive body image scales could be incorporated into existing and future interventions to more thoroughly evaluate the efficacy and effectiveness of these interventions. Halliwell, Jarman, McNamara, Risdon, and Jankowski (2015) included the BAS-2 when examining the impact of a one-hour cognitive dissonance-based intervention whereby secondary school girls voiced opposition to the thin ideal body type through various activities. The intervention group reported increased body appreciation from pre- to post-intervention, whereas the control group experienced no change. Positive body image components elucidated in qualitative studies and validated in quantitative studies can guide the development of positive body image-specific interventions.

In conclusion, the study of positive body image is rather young, yet it is flourishing. Much remains to be discovered. *New* insights will invariably lead to *more* insights, continuing the "positive trajectory" of positive body image scholarship. This trajectory appropriately parallels the path psychology is taking in general – toward examining not only the pathological but also the positive, and holding hope for learning how to encourage the optimization of psychological well-being and physical health.

References

Albertson, E. R., Neff, K. D., & Dill-Shackleford, K. E. (2015). Self-compassion and body dissatisfaction in women: A randomized controlled trial of a brief meditation intervention. *Mindfulness, 6*, 444–454. doi:10.1007/s12671-014-0277-3

Alleva, J. M., Martijn, C., Van Breukelen, G. J., Jansen, A., & Karos, K. (2015). Expand Your Horizon: A programme that improves body image and reduces self-objectification by training women to focus on body functionality. *Body Image, 15*, 81–89. doi:10.1016/j.bodyim.2015.07.001

Alleva, J. M., Tylka, T. L., & Kroon Van Diest, A. M. (2017). The Functionality Appreciation Scale: Development and psychometric evaluation in U.S. community women and men. *Body Image 23*, 28–44. doi:10.1016/j.bodyim.2017.07.008

Alleva, J. M., Veldhuis, J., & Martijn, C. (2016). A pilot study investigating whether focusing on body functionality can protect women from the potential negative effects of viewing thin-ideal media images. *Body Image, 17*, 10–13. doi:10.1016/j.bodyim.2016.01.007

Andrew, R., Tiggemann, M., & Clark, L. (2015a). Predictors of intuitive eating in adolescent girls. *Journal of Adolescent Health, 56*, 209–214. doi:10.1016/j.jadohealth.2014.09.005

(2015b). The protective role of body appreciation against media-induced body dissatisfaction. *Body Image, 15*, 98–104. doi:10.10166/j.bodyim.2015.07.005

(2016a). Positive body image and young women's health: Implications for sun protection, cancer screening, weight loss and alcohol consumption behaviours. *Journal of Health Psychology, 21*, 28–39. doi: 10.1177/1359105314520814

(2016b). Predicting body appreciation in young women: An integrated model of positive body image. *Body Image, 18*, 34–42. doi:10.1016/j.bodyim.2016.04.003

(2016c). Predictors and health-related outcomes of positive body image in adolescent girls: A prospective study. *Developmental Psychology, 52*, 463–474. doi:10.1037/dev0000095

Augustus-Horvath, C. L., & Tylka, T. L. (2011). The acceptance model of intuitive eating: A comparison of women in emerging adulthood, early adulthood, and middle adulthood. *Journal of Counseling Psychology*, *58*, 110–125. doi:10.1037/a0022129

Avalos, L. C., & Tylka, T. L. (2006). Exploring a model of intuitive eating with college women. *Journal of Counseling Psychology*, *53*, 486–497. doi:10.1037/0022-1067.53.4.486

Avalos, L. C., Tylka, T. L., & Wood-Barcalow, N. (2005). The Body Appreciation Scale: Development and psychometric evaluation. *Body Image*, *2*, 285–297. doi:10.1016/j.bodyim.2005.06.002

Bailey, K. A., Cline, L. E., & Gammage, K. L. (2016). Exploring the complexities of body image experiences in middle age and older adult women within an exercise context: The simultaneous existence of negative and positive body images. *Body Image*, *17*, 88–99. doi:10.1016/j.bodyim.2016.02.007

Bailey, K. A., Gammage, K. L., van Ingen, C., & Ditor, D. S. (2015). "It's all about acceptance": A qualitative study exploring a model of positive body image for people with spinal cord injury. *Body Image*, *15*, 24–34. doi:10.1016/j.bodyim.2015.04.010

Brown, T. A., Cash, T. F., & Mikulka, P. J. (1990). Attitudinal body image assessment: Factor analysis of the Body-Self Relations Questionnaire. *Journal of Personality Assessment*, *54*, 213–230. doi:10.1207/s15327752jpa5501&2_13

Cash, T. F. (2000). *User's manual for the Multidimensional Body Self-Relations Questionnaire.* Available from the author at www.body-images.com

(2004). Body image: Past, present, and future. *Body Image*, *1*, 1–5. doi:10.1016/S1740-1445(03)00011-1

Cash, T. F., & Pruzinsky, T. (2002). Future challenges for body image theory, research, and clinical practice. In T. F. Cash & T. Pruzinsky (Eds.), *Body image: A handbook of theory, research, and clinical practice* (pp. 509–516). New York: Guilford Press.

Cash, T. F., & Smolak, L. (Eds.) (2011). *Body image: A handbook of science, practice, and prevention* (2nd ed.). New York: Guilford Press.

Chrisler, J. C., Marván, M. L., Gorman, J. A., & Rossini, M. (2015). Body appreciation and attitudes toward menstruation. *Body Image*, *12*, 78–81. doi:10.1016/j.bodyim.2014.10.003

Cook-Cottone, C. P. (2015). Incorporating positive body image into the treatment of eating disorders: A model for attunement and mindful self-care [Special series]. *Body Image*, *14*, 158–167. doi:10.1016/j.bodyim.2015.03.004

Dalley, S. E., & Vidal, J. (2013). Optimism and positive body image in women: The mediating role of the feared fat self. *Personality and Individual Differences*, *55*, 465–468. doi:10.1016/j.paid.2013.04.006

Dumitrescu, A. L., Zetu, L., Teslaru, S., Dogaru, B. C., & Dogaru, C. D. (2008). Is it an association between body appreciation, self-criticism, oral health status, and oral health-related behaviors? *Romanian Journal of Internal Medicine*, *46*, 343–350.

Frisén, A., & Holmqvist, K. (2010). What characterizes early adolescents with a positive body image? A qualitative investigation of Swedish girls and boys. *Body Image*, *7*, 205–212. doi:10.1016/j.bodyim.2010.04.001

Garland, E. L., Fredrickson, B., Kring, A. M., Johnson, D. P., Meyer, P. S., & Penn, D. L. (2010). Upward spirals of positive emotions counter downward spirals of negativity: Insights from the broaden-and-build theory and affective neuroscience on the treatment of emotional dysfunctions and deficits in psychopathology. *Clinical Psychology Review*, *30*, 849–864. doi:10.1016/j.cpr.2010.03.002

Gillen, M. M. (2015). Associations between positive body image and indicators of men's and women's mental and physical health. *Body Image*, *13*, 67–74. doi:10.1016/j.bodyim.2015.01.002

Hahn Oh, K., Wiseman, M. C., Hendrickson, J., Phillips, J. C., & Hayden, E. W. (2012). Testing the acceptance model of intuitive eating with college women athletes. *Psychology of Women Quarterly*, *36*, 88–98. doi:10.1177/0361684311433282

Halliwell, E. (2013). The impact of thin idealized media images on body satisfaction: Does body appreciation protect women from negative effects? *Body Image*, *10*, 509–514. doi:10.1016/j.bodyim.2013.07.004

Halliwell, E., Jarman, H., McNamara, A., Risdon, H., & Jankowski, G. (2015). Dissemination of evidence-based body image interventions: A pilot study into the effectiveness of using undergraduate students as interventionists in secondary schools. *Body Image*, *14*, 1–4. doi:10.1016/j.bodyim.2015.02.002

Halliwell, E., Jarman, H., Tylka, T. L., & Slater, A. (2017). Adapting the Body Appreciation Scale-2 for children: A psychometric analysis of the BAS-2C. *Body Image*, *21*, 97–102. doi:10.1016/j.bodyim.2017.03.005

Heinberg, L. J., Thompson, J. K., & Matzon, J. L. (2001). Body image dissatisfaction as a motivator for healthy lifestyle change: Is some distress beneficial? In R. H. Striegel-Moore & L. Smolak (Eds.), *Eating disorders: Innovative directions in research and practice* (pp. 215–232). Washington, DC: American Psychological Association.

Holmqvist, K., & Frisén, A. (2012). "I bet they aren't that perfect in reality": Appearance ideals viewed from the perspective of adolescents with a positive body image. *Body Image*, *9*, 388–395. doi:10.1016/j.bodyim.2012.03.007

Homan, K. J. (2016). Factor structure and psychometric properties of a state version of the Body Appreciation Scale-2. *Body Image*, *19*, 204–207. doi:10.1016/j.bodyim.2016.10.004

Homan, K. J., & Tylka, T. L. (2014). Appearance-based exercise motivation moderates the relationship between exercise frequency and positive body image. *Body Image*, *11*, 101–108. doi:10.1016/j.bodyim.2014.01.003

(2015). Self-compassion moderates body comparison and appearance self-worth's inverse relationships with body appreciation. *Body Image*, *15*, 1–7. doi:10.1016/j.bodyim.2015.04.007

Iannantuono, A. C., & Tylka, T. L. (2012). Interpersonal and intrapersonal links to body appreciation in college women: An exploratory model. *Body Image*, *9*, 227–235. doi: 10.1016/j.bodyim.2012.01.004

Jeffers, A. J., & Benotsch, E. G. (2014). Non-medical use of prescription stimulants for weight loss, disordered eating, and body image. *Eating Behaviors, 15,* 414–418. doi:10.1016/j.eatbeh.2014.04.019

Kelly, A. C., & Stephen, E. (2016). A daily diary study of self-compassion, body image, and eating behavior in female college students. *Body Image, 17,* 152–160. doi:10.1016/j.bodyim.2016.03.006

Kroon Van Diest, A. M., & Tylka, T. L. (2010). The Caregiver Eating Messages Scale: Development and psychometric investigation. *Body Image, 7,* 317–326. doi:10.1016/j.bodyim.2010.06.002

Langdon, S. W., & Petracca, G. (2010). Tiny dancer: Body image and dancer identity in female modern dancers. *Body Image, 7,* 360–363. doi: 10.1016/j.bodyim.2010.06.005

Mahlo, L., & Tiggemann, M. (2016). Yoga and positive body image: A test of the embodiment model. *Body Image, 18,* 135–142. doi:10.1016/j.bodyim.2016.06.008

Maxwell, S. E., & Cole, D. A. (2007). Bias in cross-sectional analyses of longitudinal mediation. *Psychological Methods, 12,* 23–44. doi:10.1037/1082-989X.12.1.23

McHugh, T. L., Coppola, A. M., & Sabiston, C. M. (2014). "I'm thankful for being Native and my body is part of that": The body pride experiences of young Aboriginal women in Canada. *Body Image, 11,* 318–327. doi:10.1016/j.bodyim.2014.05.004

Neff, K. D. (2003). Self-compassion: An alternative conceptualization of a healthy attitude toward oneself. *Self and Identity, 2,* 85–101. doi:10.1080/15298860309032

Parker, S., Nichter, M., Nichter, M., Vuckovic, N., Sims, C., & Ritenbaugh, C. (1995). Body image and weight concerns among African American and White adolescent females: Differences that make a difference. *Human Organization, 54,* 103–114.

Pellizzer, M., Tiggemann, M., & Clark, L. (2016). Enjoyment of sexualization and positive body image in recreational pole dancers and university students. *Sex Roles, 74,* 35–45. doi:10.1017/s11199-015-0562-1

Piran, N. (2015). New possibilities in the prevention of eating disorders: The introduction of positive body image measures [Special series]. *Body Image, 14,* 146–157. doi:10.1016/j.bodyim.2015.03.008

  (2016). Embodied possibilities and disruptions: The emergence of the Experience of Embodiment construct from qualitative studies with girls and women. *Body Image, 18,* 43–60. doi:10.1016/j.bodyim.2016.04.007

Pope, M., Corona, R., & Belgrave, F. Z. (2014). Nobody's perfect: A qualitative examination of African American maternal caregivers' and their adolescent girls' perceptions of body image. *Body Image, 11,* 307–317. doi:10.1016/j.bodyim.2014.04.005

Robbins, A. R., & Reissing, E. D. (2017). Appearance dissatisfaction, body appreciation, and sexual health in women across adulthood. *Archives of Sexual Behavior.* Advance online publication. doi:10.1017/s10508-017-0982-9

Rubin, L. R., & Steinberg, J. R. (2011). Self-objectification and pregnancy: Are body functionality dimensions protective? *Sex Roles, 65,* 606–618. doi:10.1007/s11199-011-9955-y

Satinsky, S., Reece, M., Dennis, B., Sanders, S., & Bardzell, S. (2012). An assessment of body appreciation and its relationship to sexual function in women. *Body Image*, *9*, 137–144. doi:10.1016/j.bodyim.2011.09.007

Seligman, M. E. P., & Csikszentmihalyi, M. (2000). Positive psychology: An introduction. *American Psychologist*, *55*, 5–14. doi:10.1037/0003-066X.55.1.5

Smolak, L., & Cash, T. F. (2011). Future challenges for body image science, practice, and prevention. In T. F. Cash & L. Smolak (Eds.), *Body image: A handbook of science, practice, and prevention* (2nd ed., pp. 471–478). New York: Guilford Press.

Swami, V. (2009). Body appreciation, media influence, and weight status predict consideration of cosmetic surgery among female undergraduates. *Body Image*, *6*, 315–317. doi:10.1016/j.bodyim.2009.07.001

(2017). Sketching people: Prospective investigations of the impact of life drawing on body image. *Body Image*, *20*, 65–73. doi:10.1016/j.bodyim.2016.12.001

Swami, V., Barron, D., Weis, L., & Furnham, A. (2016). Bodies in nature: Associations between exposure to nature, connectedness to nature, and body image in U.S. adults. *Body Image*, *18*, 153–161. doi: 10.1016/j.bodyim.2016.07.002

Swami, V., Begum, S., & Petrides, K. V. (2010). Associations between trait emotional intelligence, actual-ideal weight discrepancy, and positive body image. *Personality and Individual Differences*, *49*, 485–489. doi:10.1016/j.paid.2010.05.009

Swami, V., & Harris, A. S. (2012). Dancing toward positive body image? Examining body-related constructs with ballet and contemporary dancers at different levels. *American Journal of Dance Therapy*, *34*, 39–52. doi:10.1007/s10465-012-9129-7

Swami, V., & Tovée, M. J. (2009). A comparison of actual-ideal weight discrepancy, body appreciation, and media influence between street-dancers and non-dancers. *Body Image*, *6*, 304–307. doi:10.1016/j.bodyim.2009.07.006

Swami, V., Tran, U. S., Stieger, S., Voracek, M., & The YouBeauty.com Team. (2015). Associations between women's body image and happiness: Results of the YouBeauty.com Body Image Survey (YBIS). *Journal of Happiness Studies*, *16*, 705–718. doi:10.1007/s10902-014-9530-7

Swami, V., Weis, L., Barron, D., & Furnham, A. (2017). Associations between positive body image, sexual liberalism, and unconventional sexual practices in U.S. adults. *Archives of Sexual Behavior*. Advance online publication. doi:10.1017/s10508-016-0924-y

Tiggemann, M. (2015). Considerations of positive body image across various social identities and special populations [Special series]. *Body Image*, *14*, 168–176. doi:10.1016/j.bodyim.2015.03.002

Tiggemann, M., Coutts, E., & Clark, L. (2014). Belly dance as an embodying activity? A test of the embodiment model of positive body image. *Sex Roles*, *71*, 197–207. doi:10.1007/s11199-014-0408-2

Tiggemann, M., & McCourt, A. (2013). Body appreciation in adult women: Relationships with age and body satisfaction. *Body Image*, *10*, 624–627. doi:10.1016/j.bodyim.2013.07.003

Tylka, T. L. (2011). Positive psychology perspectives on body image. In
   T. F. Cash & L. Smolak (Eds.), *Body image: A handbook of science, practice, and prevention* (2nd ed., pp. 56–64). New York: Guilford Press.
   (2015). No harm in looking, right? Men's pornography consumption, body
   image, and well-being. *Psychology of Men & Masculinity, 16*, 97–107.
   doi:10.1037/a0035774
Tylka, T. L., Annunziato, R. A., Burgard, D., Daníelsdóttir, S., Shuman, E.,
   Davis, C., & Calogero, R. M. (2014). The weight-inclusive vs. weight-
   normative approach to health: Evaluating the evidence for prioritizing well-
   being over weight loss. *Journal of Obesity.* doi:10.1155/2014/983495
Tylka, T. L., Calogero, R. M., & Daníelsdóttir, S. (2015). Is intuitive eating the
   same as flexible dietary control? Their links to each other and well-being
   could provide an answer. *Appetite, 95*, 166–175. doi:10.1016/j.
   appet.2015.07.004
Tylka, T. L., & Homan, K. J. (2015). Exercise motives and positive body image
   in physically active college women and men: Exploring an expanded
   acceptance model of intuitive eating. *Body Image, 15*, 90–97. doi:10.1016/j.
   bodyim.2015.07.003
Tylka, T. L., & Kroon Van Diest, A. M. (2013). The Intuitive Eating Scale-2:
   Item refinement and psychometric evaluation with college women and men.
   Journal of Counseling Psychology, 60, 137–153. doi:10.1037/a0030893
   (2015a). Protective factors in the development of eating disorders. In L.
   Smolak & M. P. Levine (Eds.), *The Wiley-Blackwell handbook of eating
   disorders* (Vol. 1, pp. 430–444). New York: Wiley & Sons, LTD.
   (2015b). You looking at her "hot" body may not be "cool" for me: Integrating
   male partners' pornography use into objectification theory for women.
   Psychology of Women Quarterly, 39, 67–84. doi:10.1177/0361684314521784
Tylka, T. L., & Iannantuono, A. C. (2016). Perceiving beauty in all women:
   Psychometric evaluation of the Broad Conceptualization of Beauty Scale.
   Body Image, 17, 67–81. doi:10.1016/j.bodyim.2016.02.005
Tylka, T. L., & Wood-Barcalow, N. L. (2015a). The Body Appreciation Scale-2:
   Item refinement and psychometric evaluation. *Body Image, 12*, 53–67.
   doi:10.1016/j.bodyim.2014.09.006
   (2015b). A positive complement [Special series]. *Body Image, 14*, 115–117.
   doi:10.1016/j.bodyim.2015.04.002.
   (2015c). What is and what is not positive body image? Conceptual foundations
   and construct definition [Special series]. *Body Image, 14*, 118–129.
   doi:10.1016/j.bodyim.2015.04.001
Wasylkiw, L., & Butler, N. A. (2014). Body talk among undergraduate women:
   Why conversations about exercise and weight loss differentially predict body
   appreciation. *Journal of Health Psychology, 19*, 1013–1024. doi:10.1177/
   1359105313483155
Wasylkiw, L., MacKinnon, A. L., & MacLellan, A. M. (2012). Exploring the link
   between self-compassion and body image in university women. *Body Image,
   9*, 236–245. doi:10.1016/j.bodyim.2012.01.007
Webb, J. B., Butler-Ajibade, P., & Robinson, S. A. (2014). Considering an affect
   regulation framework for examining the association between body

dissatisfaction and positive body image in Black older adolescent females: Does body mass index matter? *Body Image, 11*, 426–437. doi:10.1016/j. bodyim.2014.07.002

Webb, J. B., Wood-Barcalow, N. L., & Tylka, T. L. (2015). Assessing positive body image: Contemporary approaches and future directions [Special series]. *Body Image, 14*, 130–145. doi:10.1016/j.bodyim.2015.03.010

Wood-Barcalow, N. L., Tylka, T. L., & Augustus-Horvath, C. L. (2010). "But I like my body": Positive body image characteristics and a holistic model for young-adult women. *Body Image, 7*, 106–116. doi:10.1016/j. bodyim.2010.01.001

2 Positive Body Image by Gender and Across the Lifespan

*Lina A. Ricciardelli, Marie L. Caltabiano, and
Laura D. D'Antuono*

This chapter provides a review of the research on positive body image and gender, with a focus on adults, adolescents, and children. It complements and builds on the comprehensive review conducted by Tiggemann (2015), which included a focus on positive body image, age, and gender. In the current chapter, we reviewed available research that includes other targeted subgroups that have been impacted by life course events, such as pregnancy and childbirth. Research that specifically examines positive body image among other cultures and minority identities is covered in Chapter 3 of this book, by Viren Swami (see also Coppola, Dimler, Letendre, & McHugh, 2017; Tiggemann, 2015). In addition, in this chapter we discuss whether positive body image is distinct from negative body image.

The focus on positive body image represents a paradigm shift in the field of body image, as acknowledged in the 2011 second edition of the *Body Image Handbook* edited by Cash and Smolak, which includes a chapter on positive body image by Tylka (2011). An entire issue of the international journal *Body Image* was devoted to the construct of positive image in 2015, which included conceptual papers by Halliwell (2015), Piran (2015), Tiggemann (2015), Tylka and Wood-Barcalow (2015a), and Webb, Wood-Barcalow, and Tylka (2015). In addition to the present book, a handbook on positive body image is appearing this year (Tylka & Piran, 2018). Thus, research on positive body image has taken on momentum in the past several years. In contrast, prior to 2005, the main focus in the field was on understanding the development and consequences of the *negative* aspects of body image (e.g., body dissatisfaction and overvaluation of the importance of physical appearance).

Positive body image is understood to *not be the absence or the opposite of negative body image* (Tylka, 2011). It is not easy to find a simple definition of positive body image, as it is viewed as multifaceted (Grogan, 2017), but the majority of researchers have used the Body Appreciation Scale, which was first developed in 2005 by Avalos, Tylka, and Wood-Barcalow, to measure it. This scale was originally devised to assess: (1) the extent to which women hold positive views of their bodies; (2) the degree to which women accept their bodies in spite of their weight, body shape, and imperfections; (3) the level to which women respect their bodies by attending to their body's needs and engaging in healthy behaviors; and (4) the extent to which women protect their body image by rejecting unrealistic images of the thin-ideal as portrayed in the media.

Another conceptualization of positive body image includes taking a broader view of what it means to be beautiful, as assessed by a new instrument called the Broad Conceptualization of Beauty Scale (Tylka & Iannantuono, 2016). Other researchers have used qualitative methods to study positive body image, which have often complemented the Body Appreciation Scale. This research has uncovered gaps in the literature that need further study and has highlighted other dimensions of positive body image such as body acceptance (Bailey, Gammage, van Ingen, & Ditor, 2015), body confidence (Wood-Barcalow, Tylka, & Augustus-Horvath, 2010), body connection (Piran, 2016a), body functionality (Alleva, Veldhuis, & Martijn, 2016), body pride (Coppola et al., 2017), physical freedom (Piran, 2016a), and body self-compassion (Berry, Kowalski, Ferguson, & McHugh, 2010). The degree to which these constructs are independent or overlap remains to be tested.

Most research on positive body image has been conducted with college women from the United States (see Tiggemann, 2015); fewer studies have been conducted with men, especially older men. Further, studies have primarily focused on the negative aspects of body image among men. In our review of the literature, we found limited research that has specifically focused on positive body image among men. Therefore, we will review some of the main body image studies undertaken with men, although they do not focus on positive body image in particular, to show where more research is needed and to highlight gaps in existing knowledge.

Finally, an important question that will be addressed in this chapter is the extent to which positive body image reflects a construct that is independent from other components of body image. The jury is still out. Some of the evidence reviewed in this chapter shows that there is a large degree of overlap between body image as assessed by the Body Appreciation Scale and other measures which include the Appearance subscale of the Body Esteem Scale for Children (Mendelson & White, 1993). Correlations between these measures were .67 for boys and .81 for girls among children aged 9–11 years, thus suggesting the two scales are measuring a similar construct (Halliwell, Jarman, Tylka, & Slater, 2017). However, the nature of the positive body image construct as reflected in qualitative studies does appear to be distinct from some negative dimensions of body image (e.g., body shame; McKinley & Hyde, 1996). In addition, there is increasing evidence that the positive dimensions of body image among adolescents and adults, such as body appreciation and body respect, are qualitatively different from – and add incremental predictive validity beyond – the negative dimensions (Halliwell, 2015). The evidence which shows that positive body image is distinct from the negative aspects of body image is reviewed in each of the following sections.

Adults

This section will examine two measures, the Body Appreciation Scale and the Broad Conceptualization of Beauty Scale, that have been used to operationalize positive body image. It will also examine qualitative research on positive body image.

Body Appreciation Scale

Most of the studies that have explicitly examined the construct of positive body image have included adult women, and this research has primarily used the Body Appreciation Scale. The first version of the Body Appreciation Scale was developed and validated specifically for women, with a sample of 424 women aged 17–55 years (Avalos, Tylka, & Wood-Barcalow, 2005). This new scale was correlated with other measures of body image, including Franzoi and Shield's Body Esteem (1984) subscales, the Body Surveillance and Body Shame subscales from the Objectified Body Consciousness Scale (McKinley & Hyde, 1996), the Appearance Evaluation subscale of the Multi-Dimensional Body Self-Relations Questionnaire (Brown, Cash, & Mikulka, 1990), the Body Shape Questionnaire-Revised (Mazzeo, 1999), and the Body Dissatisfaction subscale of the Eating Disorder Inventory-2 (Garner, 1991). Correlations ranged from moderate (.50) to high (–.79), suggesting overlap with these existing dimensions of body image. However, the Body Appreciation Scale predicted women's well-being as assessed by self-esteem, optimism, and proactive coping after taking into account other body image dimensions, thus providing more conclusive evidence for the scale's construct and incremental validity (Avalos et al., 2005).

The Body Appreciation Scale-2 was refined and validated among 820 women and 767 men, aged 18–56 years (Tylka & Wood-Barcalow, 2015b). As with the earlier version, this revised scale correlated with other existing measures of body image, including the Appearance Evaluation subscale of the Multi-Dimensional Body Self-Relations

Questionnaire for women and men (Brown et al., 1990), the Body Shape Questionnaire-Revised for women (Mazzeo, 1999), the Male Body Attitudes Scale for men (Tylka, Bergeron, & Schwartz, 2005), and the Body Surveillance subscale from the Objectified Body Consciousness Scale for both women and men (McKinley & Hyde, 1996). Correlations ranged between −.49 and .80 for women and between −.43 and .75 for men, showing again a moderate to high degree of overlap with other body image constructs. However, incremental validity was also demonstrated, as the Body Appreciation Scale-2 predicted unique variance in intuitive eating, self-esteem, and proactive coping after high levels of appearance evaluation and low levels of body dissatisfaction were taken into account. In addition, incremental validity was demonstrated among women with eating disorder symptoms, but it did not reach significance for men once adjustments were made to avoid a Type 1 error (Tylka & Wood-Barcalow, 2015b). However, eating problems among men are often misdiagnosed or undetected (Ricciardelli & McCabe, 2015).

Other research using the Body Appreciation Scale has highlighted how this construct can help us better understand women's and men's mental and physical health. For example, body appreciation among women has been found to be correlated with intuitive eating (Augustus-Horvath & Tylka, 2011; Iannantuono & Tylka, 2012) and better sexual functioning (Satinsky, Reece, Dennis, Sanders, & Bardzell, 2012). Andrew, Tiggemann, and Clark (2016a) found that body appreciation was positively associated with sun protection, skin cancer screening, and seeking medical attention when needed, and was negatively related to weight-loss behavior in 256 adult women aged 18–29 years. In another study, Gillen (2015) found that body appreciation among 284 undergraduate students (60 percent women; aged 18–59 years) was associated with fewer depressive symptoms, higher self-esteem, fewer unhealthy dieting behaviors, and lower drive for muscularity among men and women; among women (only), it was also associated with greater intention to protect their skin from UV exposure and damage.

Although construct and incremental validity have been demonstrated for the Body Appreciation Scale, its high correlations with several negative dimensions of body image suggest that these constructs may be measuring a general latent factor about body image. The correlation between the Body Appreciation Scale and body dissatisfaction as assessed by the Body Areas Satisfaction subscale of the Multidimensional Body-Self Relations Questionnaire (Brown et al., 1990) was −.81 among 101 Australian university students aged 18–56 years (Tiggemann, Coutts, & Clark, 2014). Similarly, a recent unpublished study with 457 women aged 18–87 years, conducted by Bruce (2017), included the Body Appreciation Scale as well as the Appearance Evaluation and Body Areas Satisfaction subscales from the Multidimensional Body-Self Relations Questionnaire (Brown et al., 1990). Examining the underlying latent structure of these three measures using exploratory factor analysis, Bruce showed that the Body Appreciation Scale loaded highly on a single factor with the other two measures. In Bruce's study the three body image measures were strongly interrelated ($r = .80$ to .87) and accounted for 83 percent of the variance of the single factor (Bruce, 2017). Thus, the degree to which positive body image does not represent the opposite of negative body image is not clear, as the negative dimensions were not separable from the positive dimensions. In addition, as concluded by Halliwell et al. (2017, p. 97), we need more evidence that the new generation of positive body image measures "tap into a more complex and nuanced understanding of this construct."

Broad Conceptualization of Beauty Scale

Another more recently devised scale – the Broad Conceptualization of Beauty Scale (Tylka & Iannantuono, 2016), which assesses another facet of positive body image – was validated with 1,086 women aged 18–68 years. The authors of this scale maintain that individuals who broadly conceptualize beauty perceive a wide range of physical appearances as beautiful, irrespective of whether they are changeable or not. Beauty also includes drawing from inner characteristics, such as confidence and self-acceptance, as opposed to physical appearance. Specific items from this scale include "I think that a wide variety of body shapes are beautiful for women," "I think that women of all body sizes can be beautiful," and "I appreciate a wide range of different looks as beautiful." Exploratory and confirmatory factor analysis demonstrated that the scale is unidimensional; it has high internal consistency and high test–retest reliability, as well as convergent, incremental, discriminant, and criterion-related validity (Tylka & Iannantuono, 2016). Especially notable is its modest association with the Body Appreciation Scale, with correlations ranging between .24 and .29 in four different samples, thus showing that it is measuring a different aspect of positive body image (Tylka & Iannantuono, 2016). However, as yet there has been no empirical examination of how it compares to negative aspects of body image. In addition, whether the construct is relevant to men remains unknown (cf Ricciardelli & Williams, 2012). As concluded by Tylka and Iannantuono (2016), "researchers need to explore whether broadly conceptualizing beauty is a feature of men's positive body image" (p. 79).

Qualitative Research

In addition to the development of the above scales, other researchers have utilized qualitative methods, as these can more fully unravel new aspects of any phenomenon and assist researchers in shifting paradigms. Across several qualitative studies, the main themes depicting positive body image are body appreciation, body acceptance, caring for one's body, and a broader conceptualization of beauty.

In between the large validation studies of the two versions of the Body Appreciation Scale, Wood-Barcalow, Tylka, and Augustus-Horvath (2010) completed a qualitative study which included fifteen college women aged 19–21 years classified as having positive body image, and five body image experts (at least one of whom was male). Their findings highlighted several unique characteristics of a positive body image (described in the following). Further, the dimension of appreciation found by Wood-Barcalow and colleagues (2010) focused on what the body can do and on gratitude related to the function, health, and features of one's body. Although there is some overlap with the way body appreciation is assessed by the Body Appreciation Scale, this characterization of appreciation is broader. For example, the women noted: "just be grateful that you do have a body that's healthy and working properly" (p. 114).

In addition to appreciating body function, women also talked about "body acceptance," which was viewed as feeling comfortable with their bodies. For example, women reported being "comfortable in their skin and how they are packaged" (p. 110). Another theme, "taking care of the body via health behaviors," was also important for the women. All fifteen college women reported being proud of listening to their body's needs and making healthy rather than appearance-based decisions. They regularly engaged in moderate exercise, chose nutrient-dense foods, ensured they ate when hungry, and articulated adaptive methods for stress relief.

The participants in Wood-Barcalow et al.'s (2010) study also reported "filtering information in a body-protective manner." All were aware of pressures to be thin, how unrealistic these pressures are, and the importance of not internalizing them. In addition, the women noted how being positive on the inside affected one's appearance for the better. Another dimension reported by Wood-Barcalow et al. (2010) is broadly conceptualizing beauty (as assessed by the Broad Conceptualization of Beauty Scale; Tylka & Iannantuono, 2016). The importance of having a broader conceptualization of beauty was clearly explained by one woman, who reported: "No one defines beauty. You can't look at one person and say 'now that is beauty' and if you're not that, then you're not beautiful. Everybody is beautiful in one way or another. I appreciate different looks, even different skin tones" (p. 115). Women also highlighted how positive body attitudes and body confidence radiate outward. Another dimension of positive body image was being attentive to the body's needs (e.g., "I listen to my body" and "I don't try to overdo it," p. 110). Lastly, women talked about how they maximize their body's assets and minimize their flaws.

Although the majority of studies have focused on women, one unpublished qualitative study focused exclusively on men. The participants were twenty men aged 18–30 years (Russo, 2010). The men were asked questions that assessed beliefs and behaviors associated one's body and muscularity (e.g., "How do you see yourself in terms of body image?"). In line with previous research (e.g., Bottamini & Ste-Marie, 2006; Peat, Peyerl, Ferraro, & Butler, 2011), this study showed that fourteen of the twenty men were highly positive in the evaluations of their bodies, primarily demonstrating body satisfaction rather than dissatisfaction. Almost all of the men – who were asked to rate their attractiveness – rated themselves as more attractive than average, and also described themselves as more attractive than their friends. None of the participants rated their attractiveness as below average. The majority of men also described their appearance with confidence, reporting that they had high self-esteem and were not dissatisfied with their own appearance. As explained by one man, aged twenty-four years, "Well um, I think I'm an attractive guy. I think the way I present myself is pretty attractive, like I like to look good." Similarly, another man, aged twenty-one years, commented: "I am happy with where I am. I am not unhappy with anything about myself, I'm not boasting about anything about myself. I am exactly where I need to be." More research on this positive evaluation of men's body image is needed, as this is very different from that found among women, who do not demonstrate high levels of body satisfaction and high self-esteem.

Other qualitative studies about positive body image have included participants from specific subpopulations, with the main themes being body appreciation, body acceptance, caring for one's body, and a broader conceptualization of beauty. These include adult participants with spinal cord injury (Bailey et al., 2015), Canadian Aboriginal adults (Coppola et al., 2017), and women during pregnancy and the postpartum period (Fox & Neiterman, 2015).

Adults with spinal cord injury. Similar to Wood-Barcalow et al.'s (2010) research, Bailey and colleagues (2015) found body acceptance to be a core aspect of positive body image in a small-scale qualitative study of adult participants with spinal cord injury (five women and four men, aged 21–63 years). As explained by one man, aged forty-eight years:

Having a positive body image means loving yourself and accepting the flaws that you have as well as the positive side so you know just accepting everything that comes with you, that I think is the best way for anybody to have a positive body image is just to accept it and to be the best person you possibly can be. (Bailey et al., 2015, pp. 28–29)

In addition to body acceptance, Bailey and colleagues' participants highlighted body appreciation and gratitude, as noted by seven of the nine participants who were interviewed. This included an appreciation of body function, independence, and health. For example, one female participant, aged thirty-two, explained:

I have started to take better care of my body because I realize that it's so fragile especially now that I am so reliant on my arms to get around like I work out as much as I do and try to eat really healthy and stuff whereas [before her injury] I was a smoker and partier and stuff whereas now I never do that. (p. 29)

Also related to body function and health was the theme of listening to and taking care of the body. This was noted by six of the participants, who talked about eating a healthy, balanced diet and engaging in physical activity for both internal and external benefits.

Two other themes highlighted by Bailey et al., although less salient, were the participants' broad conceptualizations of beauty and how one's inner positivity influences one's outer appearance, both of which were also uncovered by Wood-Barcalow et al. (2010). Broad conceptualization of beauty was mentioned by two participants, both men, which suggests that the construct may be relevant to men as well. Both men stated that all human bodies are beautiful. The focus on inner positivity was mentioned by four participants. For example, one man, aged thirty-five years, noted,

Positive attitude I think is key. If you have a positive attitude then you look at things in a better way and if you are pessimistic then you are going to look at everything like bad. You can be in the best shape and still be like "man, this sucks!" I think a good positive body attitude would be key foundation to positive body image. (p. 30)

Canadian Aboriginal adults. In another recent study, Coppola et al. (2017) investigated the practice of body pride or "loving yourself" with a sample of four female and four adult male Canadian Aboriginal adults aged 20–25 years. This construct was described as an emotion that was not necessarily experienced all the time, but the participants articulated how they experienced body pride by practising humility and recognizing flaws. For example, one woman explained:

Well body pride to me I feel like it would be being comfortable with yourself and loving yourself. I know nobody's perfect, and we may see that we might have flaws, but to almost recognize them and think of them as strengths instead. So body pride is to embrace yourself fully, to be grateful for what you have ... I guess body pride would be just appreciating your body for what it's capable of and taking care of it. (p. 10)

This is very similar to the dimensions of body appreciation, body acceptance, and taking care of one's body as described by Wood-Barcalow and colleagues (2010). However, and interestingly, body pride was also described as a negative experience by one man, who mentioned that "In a sense when you say pride, when you say I'm proud it's got the positive 'cause you're saying I'm proud. But it's also says you are over-coming something, so it also a little bit of a stigma attached to it where people are going to see that there's something that you're having to overcome" (Coppola et al., 2017, p. 10). Overall, this suggests that it is not always easy to focus on the positive aspects of body image without also focusing on the negatives. More research that examines the positives and negatives together is needed, both with other minority groups and with adults of all ages.

Pregnancy and/or postpartum period. Other research undertaken with adult women has focused on how women feel about their bodies during pregnancy and/or the postpartum period (e.g., Bailey, 2001; Fox & Neiterman, 2015; Liechty, Coyne, Collier, & Sharp, 2017; Rubin & Steinberg, 2011). In one study, forty-eight Canadian women aged 17–40 years were interviewed about their perceptions of their pregnant and postpartum bodies (Fox & Neiterman, 2015). The women's feelings about pregnancy were largely contingent on appearance and whether "they looked pregnant or just overweight" (p. 680), and many feelings and attitudes about their body continued to be negative or became even more negative after giving birth. This was especially salient to women when they returned to work, e.g.

I think by the time I go back to work I would want to be able to fit into my work clothes ... I have friends who are exercising, they have more motivation than me ... Body-wise, I am not really a girly girl. But I do need to work on my weight ... [It] may be different for women who work in women's offices with nice, skinny colleagues. (p. 687)

It was only when the women were at home full-time and absorbed in infant care that appearance was less important. Then the focus, for several women, was more on function than appearance. One woman noted about her breasts: "now they have a much greater purpose, and they are good at their job ... And I am proud to be able to do that for my kids ... I like them [her breasts] now a lot better ... I feel more confident in myself, and physically I feel more confident ... I am doing a good job training my boys" (p. 680). Similarly, another woman noted:

I think I just respect it [her body] a little bit more now, like, after seeing what it's capable of doing. Like before, I probably was harder on myself and I expected more of myself ... I guess it's a societal pressure and you feel that you need to look a certain way ... But now that I've got two kids ... I just feel that I respect my body a lot more because of what it's done for me. It built me a family ... I have a better relationship with my body. (p. 680)

Overall, as noted by Bailey (2001), the focus for women during the postpartum period is more on functionality and less on appearance. However, appearance concerns persist during this period, especially when women consider returning to work.

Survey studies of pregnant women have been conducted; however, the main focus has been on body dissatisfaction (e.g., Skouteris, Carr, Wertheim, Paxton, & Duncombe, 2005), and not on body appreciation and body acceptance. However, one study by Rubin and Steinberg (2011) surveyed awareness and appreciation of body functionality among 156 pregnant women aged 18–40 years. Overall, awareness and appreciation of body functionality were associated with fewer depressive symptoms and less unhealthy eating behaviors during pregnancy, whereas body surveillance was associated with more depressive symptoms and less healthy eating. A major strength of this study was that the researchers employed measures specifically designed for pregnant women. Measures designed for the whole popu- lation often do not capture nuances of women's body image during pregnancy.

Age Differences among Adults

The studies reviewed in the previous section did not specifically examine age differences among participants. However, some studies have exam- ined age or specifically focused on women who are in their middle or later years (e.g., Augustus-Horvath & Tylka, 2011). One argument is that as women age, body image may become more positive: Older women are less likely to be influenced by idealized images of beauty because media images are usually of younger women (Bessenoff & Del Priore, 2007; Jankowski, Diedrichs, Williamson, Christopher, & Harcourt, 2016; Tiggemann, 2015). This view was also promoted by

Shakespeare in his description of Cleopatra, a woman who was considered older for the time, in his play *Antony and Cleopatra*: "Age cannot wither her, nor custom stale her infinite variety."

The other argument is that the internalization of Western ageist attitudes coupled with changes in body shape, weight gain, and the development of wrinkles may dispose older women toward a more negative body image (Becker, Diedrichs, Jankowski, & Werchan, 2013; Tiggemann, 2015). A general negative view of aging and bodily changes is also well captured in another of Shakespeare's plays, *As You Like It* – "Sans teeth, sans eyes, sans taste, sans everything" – and such a view was the focus of a recent article from the *Weekend Australian Magazine*, issue dated May 20–21, 2017. As explained by Mimi Spencer, who had recently had her fiftieth birthday, "There are Pilates classes, not because it makes you feel long and stretchy like a puma, but it stops you folding in on yourself like a garden chair, collapsing in the middle so that – what do you know? – one day your belly button disappears" (p. 22).

Survey Studies

In one survey study, Augustus-Horvath and Tylka (2011) found that the body appreciation of 245 women in middle adulthood (aged 40–60 years) was lower than that of 318 women in emerging adulthood (aged 18–25 years). However, body appreciation of 238 women in early adulthood (aged 26–39 years) did not differ from either the younger or the older women. It may be that women in the middle age group are at different life stages and so further studies are needed to more fully evaluate the trajectory of body appreciation across the lifespan to verify if and when there are age-related changes.

Another survey study, by Tiggemann and McCourt (2013), with 158 Australian women aged 18–75 years, showed a positive linear relationship between age and body appreciation, in that older women had higher levels of body appreciation than younger women. However, scores on the Body Appreciation Scale correlated positively with the Body Areas Satisfaction subscale of the Multidimensional Body-Self Relations Questionnaire (Brown et al., 1990), but this relationship became weaker with age. Specifically, the correlation was 0.78 among women aged 18–34 years, 0.69 among women aged 35–49 years, and 0.52 among women aged 51–75 years. Taken together, these findings indicate that older women were more able to appreciate their body for attributes other than physical appearance, while still experiencing body dissatisfaction. Other studies support the stable nature of body dissatisfaction across the lifespan for women (see a review by Tiggemann & Slevec, 2012) and confirm the positive relationship between age and body appreciation (e.g., Bruce, 2017; Swami, Tran, Stieger, Voracek, & the YouBeauty. com Team, 2014). However, more studies that examine body appreciation across the lifespan and longitudinal studies that focus on the development of body appreciation and other dimensions of positive body image are needed.

Survey studies with middle-aged and older men have focused on body dissatisfaction rather than positive body image (Davison & McCabe, 2005; McCabe & Ricciardelli, 2004). This work indicates that the majority of adult men are more preoccupied with losing weight than with gaining muscle and/or weight (McCabe & Ricciardelli, 2004), and the sociocultural appearance pressures experienced by adult men are similar to those experienced by preadolescent and adolescent boys and women across all age groups (McCabe & McGreevy, 2011; McCabe & Ricciardelli, 2004). A negative body image has also been found to be associated with problems in social and sexual functioning among middle-aged men (n = 153, aged 30–49 years), and with depression and anxiety among older men (n = 145, aged 50–86 years; Davison & McCabe, 2005).

Qualitative Studies

One qualitative study has highlighted how women experience their bodies in both positive and negative ways as they age. On a radio program, Rodgers, Paxton, McLean, and Damiano (2016) posed the question "Does the voice in your head get kinder as you get older?" and then content analyzed responses on a Facebook thread from eighty-seven women who identified as being in midlife. Four themes emerged, including physical changes with aging, the reduced importance of physical appearance with age, sociocultural influences on appearance, and the invisibility of women in midlife. Women's comments also showed a shift in focus away from appearance concerns, with more importance being placed on health, fitness, and physical function. Internal qualities and wisdom acquired with age were viewed by these women as more relevant than physical appearance.

Over half of the comments by the women in Rodgers et al.'s (2016) study contained some positive evaluations of body image in midlife, including comments about greater body acceptance or generally positive attitudes toward body image. Women commented on being comfortable with their shape or feeling kinder toward themselves (e.g., "body is good and much more comfortable with it now than I was in my 20s" and "definitely, as I've got older, I'm much kinder with my thinking of my own self than when I was younger": p. 397). Overall, there was growing acceptance and a transition away from the more critical and exacting self-evaluations of one's youth. However, about 40 percent of the comments contained some negative evaluation of body image at this stage of life, or a feeling of increased body dissatisfaction, and the "voices" in the respondents' heads did not get kinder. Finally, 9 percent of women's comments contained both positives and negatives and another 9 percent of comments were neither positive nor negative (Rodgers et al., 2016).

Another qualitative study has also shown that positive and negative body image can coexist in older women. Bailey, Cline, and Gammage (2016) interviewed ten women, aged 56–75 years, from an exercise facility. These women were asked about their feelings and views about their body in general; situations that made them either feel comfortable or uncomfortable about their body; and their emotions, thoughts, and behavioral responses to such situations. The main themes that emerged from the interviews included positive body image, body dissatisfaction, body satisfaction despite ageist stereotypes, and neutral body image. Regarding positive body image, these older women described: unconditional acceptance and support from others as important to how they viewed their bodies; the influence of religion as a positive coping strategy; acceptance of their bodies as well as gratitude for what their bodies were still able to do; being media-literate so they could ignore sociocultural pressures about the ideal body; and listening to and taking care of their bodies. Acceptance was another theme: As mentioned by one woman, "I think I've developed enough so that I'm ok in my own skin to say well this is the way I am" (p. 93). The women also separated "inner" from "outer beauty" but they acknowledged that both were important and interdependent (e.g., "I think internal [body image] is more important sometimes than the external but like I said if you look, if you look good on the outside and people will comment you know and it makes you feel good inside as well": p. 95). In addition, importance was placed on listening to and taking care of the body (e.g., "I try to take good care of it . . . I take care of my body for sure, look after it . . . So if I'm going to live a long time, I'm certainly going to live healthy. I want to live and feel good and I do feel good": p. 95). Overall, Bailey et al. (2016) found no support for the suggestion that older adult women place less importance on appearance with age. In contrast, the women remained highly invested in their appearance. However, what had changed was their higher level of acceptance or gratitude towards their body as they aged, coupled with their increased investment in the physical function of the body.

The findings of Bailey et al. (2016) also mirror findings from earlier studies that focused primarily on negative dimensions of body image. For example, Liechty (2012) reported the dual existence of both satisfaction with body image and a desire for physical change in her sample of thirteen women aged 60–69. The majority of these women believed that it is important to look one's best. Although many of the women were dissatisfied with certain aspects of physical appearance, such as sagging skin, thinning hair, and weight gain, they still felt content with their bodies. As one woman said, "I don't know whether I am satisfied or dissatisfied. I think it's just – this is who I am" (p. 81). Positive self-evaluations occurred when the women took their age into consideration and focused on other aspects of themselves which made them feel good, and aspects which they could control (e.g., wearing stylish clothing). For example, as one woman said, "I think appearance is very important for me ... I usually try to look as stylish as I can even if it is ultra-casual ... It's what's on my body that I'm thinking about, not what my body is," p. 80).

"Looking attractive at any age" was also one of the main themes to emerge in the study by Montemurro and Gillen (2013), who conducted interviews with ninety-six women aged between twenty and sixty-eight years. Overall, Montemurro and Gillen (2013) found that women in their fifties and sixties were more accepting of their bodies and did not aspire to look younger or like Hollywood celebrities. Moreover, looking sexually appealing became less important to women as they aged; however, looking attractive was important at all ages.

The focus placed on physical appearance was stronger for women than for men; however, "presenting well" was important for both men and women. One study that included focus groups with older adults aged 66–92 years showed that both women ($n = 16$) and men ($n = 12$) believed that being neat and tidy, bathing, brushing one's teeth, and wearing clean clothes conveyed personal competence and identity (Jankowski et al., 2016). In addition, both men and women reported that being healthy and physically able was more important than appearance, but they experienced sociocultural pressures to look age-appropriate. Lastly, these older adults acknowledged that older women were more invested in physical appearance than older men.

Earlier studies also highlighted the importance placed by men on the functional and healthy body rather than on appearance concerns. In one study, Drummond (2003) interviewed six retired men aged 58–85 years who were participating in a regular exercise or walking program. Findings highlighted the men's focus on their functional body and the importance they placed on engaging in physical activity for health and movement. As one man explained: "I think as long as you exercise and you do as much as you can and the best that you can, then that's all you can do. I mean, even gardening. At least then you feel like your body is working. It feels like you have done something, and that makes you feel good" (p. 193). Thus, it seems as if for men, a focus on the functional body continues throughout their lives.

In another early study, Halliwell and Dittmar (2003) interviewed twenty men and twenty-two women aged 22–62 years. The researchers asked participants about their current feelings about their bodies, how they had felt about their bodies in the past, and expectations and concerns about age-related changes in their bodies. As with other studies, one theme found in all men's narratives but in none of the women's was the importance of a functional body. In addition, fourteen of the men but none of the women reported that age-related changes in appearance were not a problem. In contrast, all women mentioned that aging had a negative impact on their appearance, but only five of the men reported that this was an issue.

In a more recent study, Liechty, Ribeiro, Sveinson, and Dahlstrom (2014) interviewed fifteen men aged 60–70 years. The men were asked how they defined body image and what physical characteristics they prioritized. Interestingly, the findings were similar to those of the studies conducted more than ten years ago. One of the main themes that summarized the men's narratives was termed by the researchers "what you see is what you get." This theme captured statements about the men's physical attributes and how they were often happy with their bodies. In addition, men often commented that concern over appearance was something they perceived to be a women's issue, which is consistent with findings from other studies (e.g., Halliwell & Dittmar, 2003). Function was viewed as more important than appearance. Moreover, acceptance was another important theme, termed by Liechty et al. (2014) as "I'm not going to look like I'm 30 and I can accept that." For example, one man commented: "We all age, our bodies are going to change and you've got to accept that, you've got to accept basically most of the way you are ... I've gotten to the point over the years where I don't really concern myself ... I really don't care what somebody else thinks" (p. 13). However, this does not mean that older men have only positive perceptions of their bodies. In fact, much of the work on older men's body image concerns has found that men focus on how the body declines, in terms of appearance and function, with age (e.g., Lodge & Umberson, 2013).

Piran (2016b) conducted life-history interviews with thirty-one women aged 50–70 years. The focus was broadly on women's embodied journeys or how women experienced their bodies in relation to the world. These interviews showed that older women were able to recapture physical agency where this had been denied and become more attuned to personal needs rather than being objectified and existing for the care of others. As described by one woman: "I think of my body as the temple that holds my soul. So I have to take care of it and treat it with respect" (p. 186). Similarly, another woman used yoga for self-care and reported: "I love going to yoga and not to the gym. I like being at peace with myself and being in the moment ... I want to be who I am a woman in her 60s, grow old gracefully without [Botox] injections. I don't need people to admire me" (p. 191). In addition, this woman commented on how she now listens to her body: "if you're tired rest, if you are feeling worn out then nurture yourself in some way" (p. 197). Similar research on embodiment needs to be conducted with men, and more research is needed to better understand the processes that may assist older adults to more fully engage with their physical environment in ways that lead them to take better care of their bodies and their health.

Finally, it needs to be noted that none of the located studies on older men's body image have specifically examined the positive dimensions of body image as outlined by Wood-Barcalow et al. (2010). This means that we do not yet know whether men's positive body image differs from that of women's across the lifespan. Moreover, we need longitudinal and qualitative studies that examine older men's experiences of both negative and positive body image, and how their body perceptions relate to other life domains (e.g., intimate relationships, friendships, grandparent roles). To date, this kind of research has been conducted only with women.

Across all ages, body dissatisfaction may coexist with body appreciation. Women place more emphasis on other inner qualities (such as wisdom or caring) or achievements (career, having raised a family) rather than on physical attractiveness in defining themselves in older age. Men instead emphasize their bodies' physical functionality. Despite the effects of aging, both men and women believe that presentation in terms of cleanliness and age-appropriate dress are important in creating a good impression.

Children and Adolescents

There has been little research specifically examining the nature of positive body image among children and adolescents. However, one qualitative study with adolescents was conducted by Frisén and Holmqvist (2010) with fifteen Swedish girls and fifteen Swedish boys, aged 10–13 years, who were recruited based on their high scores on the Body Esteem Scale for Adolescents and Adults (Mendelson, Mendelson, & White, 2001). These adolescents were interviewed about aspects of their body with which they were particularly satisfied as well as parts of their body with which they were not satisfied. Two main themes were uncovered that reflect positive dimensions of body image, including acceptance of one's imperfections and having a functional view of the body. Both of these themes have been noted among adults as discussed earlier in this chapter. Illustrating acceptance, one girl who was dissatisfied with her legs explained: "I'm a little bow-legged. Sometimes it bothers me. It doesn't show when I wear shoes but sometimes when I stand in a certain position it does. It just annoys me. It's nothing that I would like to change. It will have to be like that" (p. 207). Another girl clearly articulated what she liked about her legs: "I run fast. Many people think like 'Oh, my God, my legs are so fat' and so on, but that's just muscles and it's great to have muscles. They say like 'Oh, it wobbles so much' but, well, if it wouldn't wobble at all then you wouldn't have any muscles and you wouldn't be able to walk" (p. 208). For these adolescents, positive body image was determined by the functions that the body could perform, regardless of perceived bodily imperfections.

Piran (2016a) conducted extensive qualitative work with twenty-seven girls aged 9–14 years over a five-year period. The girls were from a range of socioeconomic and cultural backgrounds and all lived in Canada. As with young adult women (aged 20–27 years) and older women (aged 50–68 years), these girls reported both positive and negative lived experiences of the body. These experiences were conceptualized along five dimensions ranging from very positive to very negative, but also included responses that reflected a middle position on this continuum. It also needs to be noted that the dimensions were not independent of one another, thus an interview response could be coded into more than one dimension.

The first dimension was body connection and comfort (e.g., "Well, I like movement . . . My body feels like 'you're ruling! Go. Keep going. You can do it!'") versus disrupted body connection and discomfort (e.g., "Why did you [body] have to change? I kinda feel weird and it's hard, having like big breasts, cause you'd catch, like, guys staring at them": p. 49). The second dimension was agency and functionality (e.g., "I'm the best on my team. I'm the only one who can jump up high enough to block a goal like this") versus restricted agency and restraint (e.g., "Like when you play sports . . . If you're as muscular as the guys, then that's kinda creepy. It's just weird having a guy friend with the same muscles": pp. 49–50). The third dimension was experience and expression of desire (e.g., "I like eating. I like pasta and broccoli . . . I like eating healthy because I want to be fit for soccer and swimming") versus disrupted connection to desire (e.g., "So my body is not wanting the food. I have to be in the mood to want to eat": p. 50). The fourth dimension was attuned self-care (e.g., "I love soccer. Swimming, I love . . . The songs encourage me to sing ... I want to be a singer") versus disrupted attunement, neglect, and self-harm (e.g., "Like when you play sport and you get more competitive ... like a jock, but when you're not, you're like: oh my god! you are girlie": p. 52). The fifth dimension was inhabiting the body as a subjective site (e.g., in reference to a self-drawing, one girl commented: "I am the best on my team. I'm the only one who can jump up high enough to block a goal like this") versus an objectified site (e.g., in reference to a self-drawing, another girl commented: "dress and high heels, purse. I saw that I looked so plain so like put lip gloss, eye shadow, and mascara": p. 53). Although the dimensions were similar between girls, middle-aged women, and older women, the findings indicated a tendency for girls to have more negative experiences as compared with young adult women and older adult women (Piran, 2016a). This may be due to the range of pressures and developmental issues during puberty that adolescents deal with at this stage of life (Ricciardelli & Yager, 2016). However, given that these patterns were based on small samples, Piran notes that studies with larger samples are needed.

In addition to the above qualitative studies, two recent surveys have examined how adolescent girls with higher body appreciation engage in self-care behaviors that benefit physical health and actively avoid behaviors that could physically harm their body (Andrew, Tiggemann, & Clark, 2015, 2016b). In one Australian study, body appreciation was found to predict intuitive eating among 400 adolescent girls (Andrew et al., 2015). In another study of 298 Australian adolescent girls, Time 1 body appreciation predicted a decrease in dieting and alcohol and cigarette use and an increase in physical activity at Time 2 one year later (Andrew et al., 2016b). However, body appreciation did not predict changes in fruit, vegetable, or takeaway food (i.e., fast food) consumption; sun protection use; weekly sleep; or getting medical attention when they have a concern. Similar studies are now needed with adolescent boys, as we do not know whether these findings generalize to boys.

Another recent survey study has examined positive body image among both girls and boys (54.4 percent girls) in the UK by adapting the Body Appreciation Scale-2 for children aged 9–11 years (Halliwell et al., 2017). As with the adult version, the scale was found to reflect a single factor (as assessed by exploratory factor analysis) among both girls and boys. The scale was internally consistent, with high test–retest reliability, and it was strongly related to the appearance subscale of the Body Esteem Scale for Children (Mendelson & White, 1993). It correlated moderately to strongly with other related constructs including body surveillance, awareness of media influence, internalization of media influence, and media influence pressure. In addition, the Body Appreciation Scale-2 for children was positively related to positive affect and negatively related to negative affect. Incremental validity was demonstrated for girls in predicting positive affect, over and above that predicted by appearance concerns. No incremental validity was demonstrated for boys, however. It may be that more work is needed on the scale to ensure that it fully assesses aspects of body image among boys, which have clearly been shown to be different from girls (Ricciardelli & Yager, 2016). More work is now needed that examines how body appreciation among children longitudinally predicts physical and mental health.

Moreover, in order to more fully understand children's body image, it needs to be studied in relation to everyday experiences that are meaningful for them, and that are likely to have a bearing on their body image. Children's physical activity, including sport, active play, and incidental activity, provides such a context (Ricciardelli & Yager, 2016). Physical activity naturally draws children's attention to their bodies, so the study of children's body image alongside their experiences of physical activity may help us to more fully understand how children view and experience their bodies and, in turn, how children can become more connected, comfortable, and satisfied with their bodies.

The existing research on positive body image in children and adolescents indicates that those with body appreciation are better able to resist media influences and internalization of media messages. For some adolescents, positive body image is equated with acceptance of imperfections and having a functional view of the body. Those with body appreciation are also more likely to engage in health protective behaviors. Overall, more work is needed with both children and adolescents, as there are too few studies with these age groups. Further qualitative studies with children and adolescents will assist researchers in better understanding the nature of positive body image among youth and how this differs from other constructs such as body dissatisfaction, appearance concerns, and weight preoccupation. In addition, longitudinal studies are needed, as these will show how positive body image develops in line with changes in puberty, peer and parental relationships, and attitudes toward school and sports (Ricciardelli & Yager, 2016).

Conclusion

Much of the research on positive body image has been done using the Body Appreciation Scale, and in line with the field of positive psychology, the focus is on individuals' strengths and not their weaknesses (Frisén & Holmqvist, 2010). However, body appreciation is only one dimension of positive body image. More work is needed to develop and validate new instruments for assessing other aspects of positive body image that have only been examined qualitatively to date (e.g., body connection and physical freedom).

In addition, most of the research on positive body image has been conducted with women, in line with an accepted but flawed view that body image is a primary focus of women and not men. This view persists despite a notable increase in research on men's body image during the past two decades. A comprehensive study of the dimensions of positive body image has yet to be conducted among boys and men. Similarly, we need more work that examines positive body image among children and adolescents. As with studies on men, much of the focus of research with youth has been on body dissatisfaction. Although approximately 50 percent of children aged 8–10 years are dissatisfied with their bodies (Holt & Ricciardelli, 2008), the other 50 percent are not. Without understanding children's experiences of their body beyond aspects of body dissatisfaction, we have only a limited picture of their body image. Lastly, we need to more fully address how both women and men, across the lifespan, can experience both positive and negative body image concurrently. This is difficult to capture by existing quantitative measures and may explain the unexpectedly high correlations among positive and negative dimensions of body image. More qualitative studies will help us better understand the complex nature of body image by gender and age.

References

Alleva, J. M., Veldhuis, J., & Martijn, C. (2016). A pilot study investigating whether focusing on body functionality can protect women from the potential negative effects of viewing thin-ideal media images. *Body Image, 17*, 10–13. doi:10.1016/j.bodyim.2016.01.007

Andrew, R., Tiggemann, M., & Clark, L. (2015). Predictors of intuitive eating in adolescent girls. *Journal of Adolescent Health, 56*, 209–214. https://dx.doi.org/10.1016/j.jadohealth.2014.09.005

(2016a). Positive body image and young women's health: Implications for sun protection, cancer screening, weight loss and alcohol consumption behaviours. *Journal of Health Psychology, 21*, 28–39. doi:10.1177/1359105314520814

(2016b). Predictors of health-related outcomes of positive body image in adolescent girls: A prospective study. *Developmental Psychology, 52*, 463–474. doi:http://dx.doi.org/10.1037/dev0000095

Augustus-Horvath, C. L., & Tylka, T. L. (2011). The acceptance model of intuitive eating: A comparison of women in emerging adulthood, early adulthood and middle adulthood. *Journal of Counseling Psychology, 58*, 110–125. doi:10.1037/0022-0167.53.4.486

Avalos, L., Tylka, T. L., & Wood-Barcalow, N. L. (2005). The Body Appreciation Scale: Development and psychometric evaluation. *Body Image, 2*, 285–297. doi:10.1016/j.bodyim.2005.06.002

Bailey, L. (2001). Gender shows: First time mothers and embodied selves. *Gender and Society, 15*, 110–129. https://dx.doi.org/10.1177/089124301015001006

Bailey, K. A, Cline, L. E., & Gammage, K. L. (2016). Exploring the complexities of body image experiences in middle age and older adult women with an exercise context: The simultaneous existence of negative and positive body images. *Body Image, 17*, 88–99. doi:10.1016/j.bodyim.2016.02.007

Bailey, K. A., Gammage, K. L., van Ingen, C., & Ditor, D. S. (2015). "It's all about acceptance": A qualitative study exploring a model of positive body image for people with spinal cord injury. *Body Image, 15*, 24–34. doi:10.1016/j.bodyim.2015.04.010

Becker, C. B., Diedrichs, P. C., Jankowski, G., & Werchan, C. (2013). I'm not just fat, I'm old: Has the study of body image overlooked "old talk"? *Journal of Eating Disorders, 1*, 6–12. https://doi.org/10.1186/2050-2974-1-10

Berry, K., Kowalski, K. C., Ferguson, L. J., & McHugh, T. F. (2010). An empirical phenomenology of young adult women exercisers' body self-compassion. *Qualitative Research in Sport and Exercise, 2*, 293–312. https://dx.doi.org/10.1080/19398441.2010.517035

Bessenoff, G. R., & Del Priore, R. E. (2007). Women, weight, and age: Social comparison to magazine images across the lifespan. *Sex Roles, 56*, 215–222. doi:10.1007/s11199-006-9164-2

Bottamini, G., & Ste-Marie, D. M. (2006). Male voices on body image. *International Journal of Men's Health, 5*, 109–132.

Brown, T. A., Cash, T. F., & Mikulka, P. J. (1990). Attitudinal body-image assessment: Factor analysis of the Body–Self Relations Questionnaire. *Journal of Personality Assessment, 55*, 135–144.

Bruce, L. J. (2017). Intuitive eating in relation to other eating patterns and psychosocial correlates. PhD dissertation, Deakin University, Melbourne, Australia.

Coppola, A. M., Dimler, A. J., Letendre, T. S., & McHugh, T. F. (2017). "We are given a body to walk this earth": The body pride experiences of young Aboriginal men and women. *Qualitative Research in Sport, Exercise and Health, 9*, 4–17. doi:10.1080/2159676X.2016.1174727

Davison, T. E, & McCabe, M. P. (2005). Relationships between men's and women's body image and their psychological, social, and sexual functioning. *Sex Roles, 52*, 463–475. doi:10.1007/s11199-005-3712-z

Drummond, M. (2003). Retired men and retired bodies. *International Journal of Men's Health, 2*, 183–199.

Fox, B., & Neiterman, E. (2015). Embodied motherhood: Women's feelings about their postpartum bodies. *Gender and Society, 29*, 670–693. https://doi.org/10.1177/0891243215591598

Franzoi, S. L., & Shields, S. A. (1984). The Body Esteem Scale: Multidimensional structure and sex differences in a college population. *Journal of Personality Assessment, 48*, 173–178. doi:10.1207/s15327752jpa4802_12

Frisén, A., & Holmqvist, K. (2010). What characterizes early adolescents with a positive body image? A qualitative investigation of Swedish girls and boys. *Body Image*, *7*, 205–212. doi:10.1016/j.bodyim.2010.04.001

Garner, D. M. (1991). *Eating Disorder Inventory-2 Professional Manual*. Odessa, FL: Psychological Assessment Resources.

Gillen, M. M. (2015). Associations between positive body image and indicators of men's and women's mental and physical health. *Body Image*, *13*, 67–74. https://dx.doi.org/10.1016/j.bodyim.2015.01.002

Grogan, S. (2017). *Body image: Understanding body dissatisfaction in men, women and children*. Abingdon: Routledge.

Halliwell, E. (2015). Future directions for positive body image research. *Body Image*, *14*, 177–189. https://dx.doi.org/10.1016/j.bodyim.2015.03.003

Halliwell, E., & Dittmar, H. (2003). A qualitative investigation of women's and men's body image concerns and their attitudes toward aging. *Sex Roles*, *49*, 675–684. http://dx.doi.org/10.1023/B:SERS.0000003137.71080.97

Halliwell, E., Jarman, H., Tylka, T. L., & Slater, A. (2017). Adapting the Body Appreciation Scale-2 for Children: A psychometric analysis of the BAS-2C. *Body Image*, *21*, 97–102. doi:10.1016/j.bodyim.2017.03.005

Holt, K. E., & Ricciardelli, L. A. (2008). Weight concerns among elementary school children: A review of prevention programs. *Body Image*, *5*, 233–243. https://doi.org/10.1016/j.bodyim.2008.02.002

Iannantuono, A. C., & Tylka, T. L. (2012). Interpersonal and intrapersonal links to body appreciation in college women: An exploratory model. *Body Image*, *9*, 227–235. http://dx.doi.org/10.1016/j.bodyim.2012.01.004

Jankowski, G. S., Diedrichs, P. C., Williamson, H., Christopher, G., & Harcourt, D. (2016). Looking age-appropriate while growing old gracefully: A qualitative study of ageing and body image among older adults. *Journal of Health Psychology*, *21*, 550–561. http://dx.doi.org/10.1177/1359105314531468

Liechty, T. (2012). "Yes, I worry about my weight … but for the most part I'm content with my body": Older women's body dissatisfaction alongside contentment. *Journal of Women and Aging*, *24*, 70–88. doi:10.1080/08952841.2012.638873

Liechty, T., Coyne, S. M., Collier, K. M., & Sharp, A. D. (2017). "It's just not very realistic": Perceptions of media among pregnant and postpartum women. *Health Communication*. doi:10.1080/10410236.2017.1315680

Liechty, T., Ribeiro, N. F., Sveinson, K., & Dahlstrom, L. (2014). It's about what I can do with my body. *International Journal of Men's Health*, *13*, 3–21.

Lodge, A. C., & Umberson, D. (2013). Age and embodied masculinities: Midlife gay and heterosexual men talk about their bodies. *Journal of Aging Studies*, *27*, 225–232. doi:10.1016/j.jaging.2013.03.004

Mazzeo, S. E. (1999). Modification of an existing measure of body image preoccupation and its relationship to disordered eating in female college students. *Journal of Counseling Psychology*, *46*, 42–50. doi:10.1186/1479-5868-8-75

McCabe, M. P., & McGreevy, S. J. (2011). Role of media and peers on body change strategies among adult men: Is body size important? *European Eating Disorders Review*, *19*, 438–446. doi:10.1002/erv:1063

McCabe, M. P., & Ricciardelli, L. A. (2004). Body image dissatisfaction among males across the lifespan: A review of past literature. *Journal of Psychosomatic Research, 56*, 675–685. doi:10.1016/S0022-3999(03)00129-6

McKinley, N. M., & Hyde, J. S. (1996). The Objectified Body Consciousness Scale. *Psychology of Women Quarterly, 20*, 181–215. https://doi.org/10.1111/j.1471–6402.1996.tb00467.x

Mendelson, B. K., Mendelson, M. J., & White, D. R. (2001). Body Esteem Scale for Adolescents and Adults. *Journal of Personality Assessment, 76*, 90–106. doi:10.1207/S15327752JPA7601_6

Mendelson, B. K., & White, D. R. (1993). Manual for the Body-Esteem Scale for Children. *Concordia University Research Bulletin, 12*, 1–10.

Montemurro, B., & Gillen, M. M. (2013). Wrinkles and sagging flesh: Exploring transformations in women's sexual body image. *Journal of Women and Aging, 25*, 3–23. http://dx.doi.org/10.1080/08952841.2012.720179

Peat, C. M., Peyerl, N. L., Ferraro, R., & Butler, M. (2011). Age and body image in Caucasian men. *Psychology of Men & Masculinity, 12*, 195–200. doi:10.1037/a0021478

Piran, N. (2015). New possibilities in the prevention of eating disorders: The introduction of positive body image measures. *Body Image, 14*, 146–157. http://dx.doi.org/10.1016/j.bodyim.2015.03.008

(2016a). Embodied possibilities and disruptions: The emergence of the experience of embodiment construct from qualitative studies with girls and women. *Body Image, 18*, 43–60. doi:10.1016/j.bodyim.2016.04.007

(2016b). Embodied paths in aging: Body journeys towards enhanced agency and self-attunement. *Women and Therapy, 39*, 186–201. doi:10.1080/02703149.2016.1116853

Ricciardelli, L. A., & McCabe, M. P. (2015). Eating disorders in boys and men. In L. Smolak & M. P. Levine (Eds.), *The Wiley handbook of eating disorders: Volume 1: Basic concepts and foundational research* (pp. 492–502). Chichester: John Wiley & Sons.

Ricciardelli, L. A., & Williams, R. J. (2012). Beauty over the centuries – Male. In T. Cash (Ed.), *Encyclopedia of body image and human appearance* (pp. 50–55). Amsterdam: Academic Press.

Ricciardelli, L. A., & Yager, Z. (2016). *Adolescence and body image: From development to preventing dissatisfaction*. London: Routledge.

Rodgers, R. F., Paxton, S. J., McLean, S. A., & Damiano, S. R. (2016). "Does the voice in your head get kinder as you get older?" Women's perceptions of body image in midlife. *Journal of Women and Aging, 28*, 395–402. doi:10.1080/08952841.2015.1018034

Rubin, L. R., & Steinberg, J. R. (2011). Self-objectification and pregnancy: Are body functionality dimensions protective? *Sex Roles, 65*, 606–618. https://doi.org/10.1007/s11199–011-9955-y

Russo, S. D. (2010). *Body image, drive for muscularity and social comparisons in men*. PhD dissertation, Deakin University, Melbourne, Australia.

Satinsky, S., Reece, M., Dennis, B., Sanders, S., & Bardzell, S. (2012). An assessment of body appreciation and its relationship to sexual function in women. *Body Image, 9*, 137–144. doi:10.1016/j.bodyim.2011.09.007

Skouteris, H., Carr, R., Wertheim, E. H., Paxton, S.J., & Duncombe, D. (2005). A prospective study of factors that lead to body dissatisfaction during pregnancy. *Body Image, 2*, 347–361. doi:10.1016/j.bodyim.2005.09.002

Spencer, M. (2017, May 20–21). First I'll need a little rest: The indignities – amusing and otherwise – of middle age. *The Weekend Australian*, pp. 20–23.

Swami, V. (2018). Considering positive body image through the lens of culture and minority social identities. In E. A. Daniels, M. M. Gillen, & C. H. Markey (Eds.), *Body positive: Understanding and improving body image in science and practice* (in press). Cambridge University Press.

Swami, V., Tran, U. S., Stieger, S., Voracek, M., & The YouBeauty.com Team. (2014). Associations between women's body image and happiness: Results of the YouBeauty.com Body Image Survey (YBIS). *Journal of Happiness Studies*. doi:10.1007/s10902-014-9530-7

Tiggemann, M. (2015). Considerations of positive body image across various social identities and special populations. *Body Image, 14*, 168–176. http://dx.doi.org/10.1016/j.bodyim.2015.03.002

Tiggemann, M., Coutts, E., & Clark, L. (2014). Belly dance as an embodying activity? A test of the embodiment model of positive body image. *Sex Roles, 71*, 197–207. doi:10.1007/s11199-014-0408-2

Tiggemann, M., & McCourt, A. (2013). Body appreciation in adult women: Relationships with age and body satisfaction. *Body Image, 10*, 624–627. http://dx.doi.org/10.1016/j.bodyim.2013.07.003

Tiggemann, M., & Slevec, J. (2012). Appearance in adulthood. In N. Rumsey & D. Harcourt (Eds.), *The Oxford handbook of the psychology of appearance* (pp. 142–159). Oxford: Oxford University Press.

Tylka, T. L. (2011). Positive psychology perspectives on body image. In T. F. Cash, & L. Smolak (Eds.), *Body image: A handbook of science, practice, and prevention* (pp. 55–64). New York: The Guilford Press.

Tylka, T. L., Bergeron, D., & Schwartz, J. P. (2005). Development and psychometric evaluation of the Male Body Attitudes Scale (MBAS). *Body Image, 2*, 161–175. doi:10.1016/j.bodyim.2005.03.001

Tylka, T. L., & Iannantuono, A. C. (2016). Perceiving beauty in all women: Psychometric evaluation of the Broad Conceptualization of Beauty Scale. *Body Image, 17*, 67–81. doi:10.1016/j.bodyim.2016.02.005

Tylka, T. L., & Piran, N. (Eds.). (in press). *Handbook of positive body image and embodiment: Constructs, protective factors, and interventions.* New York: Oxford University Press.

Tylka, T. L., & Wood-Barcalow, N. L. (2015a). What is and what is not positive body image? Conceptual foundations and construct definition. *Body Image, 14*, 118–129. doi:10.1016/j.bodyim.2015.04.001

(2015b). The Body Appreciation Scale-2: Item refinement and psychometric evaluation. *Body Image, 12*, 53–67. doi:10.1016/j.bodyim.2014.09.006

Webb, J. B., Wood-Barcalow, N. L., & Tylka, T. L. (2015). Assessing positive body image: Contemporary approaches and future directions. *Body Image, 14*, 130–145. doi:10.1016/j.bodyim.2015.03.010

Wood-Barcalow, N. L., Tylka, T. L., & Augustus-Horvath, C. L. (2010). "But I like my body": Positive body image characteristics and a holistic model for young adult women. *Body Image, 7*, 106–116. doi:10.1016/j.bodyim.2010.01.001

3 Considering Positive Body Image through the Lens of Culture and Minority Social Identities

Viren Swami

When writing about positive body image, scholars typically highlight a distinction between a historical focus of body image research on pathological aspects and a more contemporary focus on positive aspects (e.g., Tylka & Wood-Barcalow, 2015a). This distinction helps to draw attention to the similarities and differences in the developmental trajectories of research on negative and positive body image. Like the study of negative body image (Cash, 2004), initial work on positive body image was limited to samples of young (typically college) women in the United States. Unlike its counterpart, however, research on positive aspects has branched out very rapidly to include a wide range of different social groups and individuals (Tiggemann, 2015).

Much of this work draws, albeit implicitly, on the notion of "identity" being something that is routinely coconstructed and sustained by the activities of an individual within local social worlds (Bourdieu, 1984; Giddens, 1991). In her seminal work, for example, Becker (2004, p. 535) suggested that identities in postmodern societies are increasingly "constructed as a process of competitively positioning oneself through the savvy manipulation of cultural symbols," such as through the consumption of material goods, adorning the body to demonstrate cultural capital, or attempts to reconfigure the body. In Becker's view, the illusion that the self can be "reshaped and remade" invariably leads to body- and self-disparagement, as individuals struggle to reconcile their actual selves with culturally prescribed ideals of appearance.

There is no denying the importance of this viewpoint in explaining the prevalence of negative body image, but one can also draw on this perspective to better understand how individuals resist unrealistic appearance ideals and creatively use cultural capital to construct social identities that promote positive body image. That is, by focusing on local social worlds and the social identities constructed therein, scholars can (and have) gained a better understanding of the nature and extent of positive body image. Of course, not all research on positive body image has fully adopted this identities perspective; instead, much of the extant research has only scratched at the surface of this approach, hinting at – rather than fully interrogating – the ways in which social identities shape positive body image. Nevertheless, what is clear from the available research is that social identities *do* matter when thinking about positive body image.

In this chapter, I aim to review research that has adopted this identities perspective, even if implicitly, to examine positive body image in different cultural and social groups (with the exception of gender, which has been reviewed in Chapter 2). I begin by focusing on attempts to understand positive body image at a macro level (i.e., in different national and linguistic groups), before delving into more micro levels of identity (e.g., ethnic and socioeconomic differences *within* specific cultural groups). In both cases, my review of the literature is followed by a consideration of research that still needs to be conducted to better understand the nature of positive body image in different groups.

Positive Body Image in Different Cultural Groups

Research examining the effects of cultural identities on positive body image has followed a very similar pattern: In the vast majority of cases, scholars have begun by examining the factorial validity of existing measures of positive body image in different national or linguistic groups. Here, factorial validity refers to the extent to which the underlying putative structure of a scale is recoverable in a set of scores produced by different cultural, national, or linguistic groups. Establishing factorial validity is important for two reasons: (1) it helps to determine the degree to which measures of positive body image are cross-culturally equivalent (i.e., to the extent that scores on a scale produce the same dimensionality in different groups, scholars can assume that the scale is likely tapping the same underlying construct in those different groups); (2) cross-cultural equivalence of dimensionality on a scale allows scholars to compare latent scores on that scale across different groups.

To date, almost all of this research has focused on two scales in particular: the Body Appreciation Scale (BAS; Avalos, Tylka, & Wood-Barcalow, 2005) and its revision, the Body Appreciation Scale-2 (BAS-2; Tylka & Wood-Barcalow, 2015b). This focus on body appreciation is perhaps unsurprising given that the BAS was one of the earliest scales developed to specifically measure a facet of positive body image. In this section, I begin by reviewing the literature that has examined the factor structures of the BAS and the BAS-2 in different cultural and linguistic groups. Later in this section, I suggest that the almost exclusive focus on body appreciation also has drawbacks, notably the lack of attention paid to other facets of positive body image and an incomplete understanding of the "meaning" of positive body image in different cultural groups.

The Body Appreciation Scale

Based on a review of the available literature focused on promoting body acceptance and protecting the self from sociocultural influences, Avalos et al. (2005, p. 287) proposed a definition of body appreciation as the extent to which women "hold favorable opinions of their bodies ... accept their bodies in spite of their weight, body shape, and imperfections ... respect their bodies by attending to their body's needs and engaging in healthy behaviors, and ... protect their body image by rejecting unrealistic images of the thin-ideal portrayed in the media." Based on this definition, Avalos et al. (2005) developed a sixteen-item measure of body appreciation and, through exploratory and confirmatory factor analyses with primarily White college women in the United States, retained thirteen items that loaded onto the same latent dimension. In a later study, Tylka (2013) reported that the one-dimensional structure of BAS scores was invariant across college women and men in the United States.

Beginning in 2008, scholars began to report on the factor structure of BAS scores in other cultural groups. Several of these studies found support for the factor structure reported in the parent study: Studies with samples of Austrian community women and men (Swami, Stieger, Haubner, & Voracek, 2008), Spanish boys and girls (Lobera & Rios, 2011), and Turkish college women (Swami, Özgen, Gökçen, & Petrides, 2015) all upheld the one-dimensional factor structure of BAS scores using exploratory factor analysis (EFA). In contrast, other studies found that BAS scores have a two-dimensional factor in some cultural groups, consisting of facets that tap a general body appreciation construct and a separate construct that may be more closely aligned to body image investment. Thus, studies conducted with adults in Brazil, Hong Kong, Indonesia, Iran, Malaysia, Poland, South Korea, Poland, and Zimbabwe all found support for the two-factor structure of BAS scores (see Table 3.1). As further indicated in Table 3.1, several studies have also assumed the unidimensionality of BAS scores in the absence of factor analytic investigations.

In addition, studies within the same linguistic group have sometimes reported difficulty confirming earlier reported factor structures. For example, in a sample of older Brazilian adults, it was reported using confirmatory factor analysis (CFA) that a two-dimensional model had better fit than all other tested models (Ferreira, Neves, & Tavares, 2014), which contrasts with Swami et al.'s (2011) findings supporting a

Table 3.1 *Translations and examinations of the factorial validity of the Body Appreciation Scale*

Reference	Language	Country	Sample type	N	Data reduction method	Dimensionality	Cronbach α	Mean (SD)
Avalos, Tylka, and Wood-Barcalow (2005, Study 1)	English	United States	College	181 women	EFA	Single dimension	.94	3.84 (0.79)
Avalos, Tylka, and Wood-Barcalow (2005, Study 2)	English	United States	College	327 women	CFA	Single dimension	Not reported	3.45 (0.68)
Swami, Stieger, Haubner, and Voracek (2008)	German	Austria	Community	156 women, 144 men	EFA	Single dimension	.85–.90	Women = 3.74 (0.62); Men = 3.90 (0.59)
Swami and Chamorro-Premuzic (2008)	Bahasa Malaysia (Malay)	Malaysia	Community	591 women	EFA and CFA	CFA of one-dimensional structure showed poor fit; EFA extracted two factors (eight-item GBA and three-item BII) and confirmed by CFA	GBA = .95; BII = .71–.74	GBA = 3.68 (0.86); BII = 3.46 (0.98)
Dumitrescu, Zetu, Teslaru, Dogaru, and Dogaru (2008)	Romanian	Romania	College	127 women, 51 men	N/A	Not examined (one-dimensional assumed)	0.83	Total sample = 3.42 (0.60)

Study	Language	Country	Sample	Sample size	Analysis	Dimensions	Reliability	Means
Llobera and Ríos (2011)	Spanish	Spain	Adolescents	148 girls, 164 boys	EFA	Single dimension	0.91	Sum girls = 49.18 (10.25); boys = 52.01 (9.39)
Swami, Campana, Ferreira, Barrett, Harris, and Tavares (2011)	Brazilian Portuguese	Brazil	College staff and students	195 women, 115 men	EFA	Two dimensions (ten-item GBA and three-item BII)	GBA = .89; BII = .67	GBA women = 3.90, 0.67; men = 4.11 (0.57); BII women = 3.37 (0.75); men = 3.35 (0.81)
Swami and Jaafar (2012)	Bahasa Indonesia (Indonesian)	Indonesia	Community	262 women, 278 men	EFA	Two dimensions (ten-item GBA and three-item BII)	GBA = .90–.93; BII = .72–.68	GBA women = 3.32 (0.86); men = 3.67, 0.78); BII not reported
Swami, Mada, and Tovée (2012)	English	Zimbabwe	Community	140 women	EFA	Two dimensions (ten-item GBA and one-item BII)	GBA = .90	GBA = 4.08 (0.63)
Swami, Hwang, and Jung (2012)	Korean	South Korea	College	200 women, 67 men	EFA	Two dimensions (ten-item GBA and three-item BII)	GBA = .93; BII = 0.55	GBA women = 3.44 (0.78); men = 3.74 (0.82); BII not examined
Tylka (2013)	English	United States	College	527 women, 403 men	CFA	Single dimension	.92–.94	Women = 3.49 (0.79); men = 3.82 (0.70)
Lunde (2013)	Swedish	Sweden	Adolescents	50 girls, 60 boys	N/A	Not examined (one dimension assumed)	.88	Girls = 3.48 (0.69); boys = 3.98 (0.65)
Taylor, Szpakowska, and Swami (2013)	Polish	Poland and United Kingdom	Community	306 women	EFA	Two dimensions (ten-item GBA and three-item BII)	GBA = .83; BII = .62	Poland = 3.24 (0.85); United Kingdom = 3.60 (0.72)

Table 3.1 (cont.)

Reference	Language	Country	Sample type	N	Data reduction method	Dimensionality	Cronbach α	Mean (SD)
Pisitsungkagarn, Taephant, and Attasaranya (2014)	Thai	Thailand	College	302 women	N/A	Not examined (one dimension assumed)	0.89	3.81 (0.59)
Ferreira, Neves, and Tavares (2014)	Brazilian Portuguese	Brazil	Community of older adults	424 women, 182 men	CFA	One dimension with all thirteen items had poor fit; two-factor structure with 4 items each had best fit	Body Valorization = .78; Body care = .82	Not reported
Ng, Barron, and Swami (2015)	Cantonese	China (Hong Kong)	College	1,319 women, 1,084 men	CFA	One dimension with all thirteen items had poor fit; two-factor with GBA (seven items) and BII (two items) had best fit	GBA = .90–.92, BII = .61–.64	GBA women = 3.20 (0.67), men = 3.32 (0.91)
Atari, Akbari-Zardkhaneh, Mohammadi, and Soufiabadi (2015)	Persian	Iran	College	206 women	EFA	Two dimensions (ten-item GBA and three-item BII)	GBA = 0.92, BII = Not reported	Not reported

Study	Language	Country	Setting	Sample	Analysis	Dimensionality	α	Mean (SD)
Swami, Özgen, Gökçen, and Petrides (2015)	Turkish	Turkey	College	501 women	EFA	One dimension	.88	3.23 (0.89)
van den Brink, Smeets, Hessen, and Woertman (2016)	Dutch	The Netherlands	College	399 women	N/A	Not examined (one dimension assumed)	.88	3.62 (0.50)
Bakalim and Tasdelen-Karçkay (2016)	Turkish	Turkey	College	431 women, 310 men	CFA	Two-factor with GBA (seven items) and BII (two items) had best fit	GBA = .89–.90; BII = .62–.65	Not reported
Jain and Tiwari (2016)	Hindi	India	College	37 women, 30 men	N/A	One-dimension factor structure assumed	Not reported	Sum women = 50.03 (7.07) men = 50.00 (8.27)

one-dimensional model. Ferreira et al. (2014) went on to draw a distinction between what they termed "body valorization" (the construct most closely related to body appreciation) and "body care" (more akin to body image investment). Similarly, in a sample of Turkish college women and men, one study found, using CFA, that the previously reported one-dimensional structure had poor fit; a two-factor model consisting of general body appreciation and body image investment had better fit (Bakalim & Tasdelen-Karçkay, 2016).

From a theoretical point of view, the equivocal nature of factor structure of BAS scores is important because it is possible that there are cross-cultural differences in the lower-order facets that contribute to positive body image generally and body appreciation specifically (Swami & Chamorro-Premuzic, 2008). That is, social identities developed in different cultural contexts may lead to different self–body relationships, divergent bodily ideals, and varying attitudes toward the body and the importance of appearance, which in turn result in different localized conceptions of body appreciation. In addition, from a practical point of view, the equivocal factorial validity of the BAS prevents effective comparisons of latent scores on the measure across cultural groups (i.e., cross-cultural comparisons may not be statistically appropriate if the latent dimensionality of BAS scores differs across groups).

Nevertheless, a handful of studies have conducted such cross-cultural comparisons, suggesting that group differences in body appreciation may be small. For example, one study that compared BAS scores between women in the United States ($n = 8,925$) and women in Canada, the United Kingdom, and Australia ($n = 3,508$) reported no significant between-group differences in BAS scores (Swami, Tran, Stieger, Voracek, & the YouBeauty.com Team, 2015). Similarly, a comparison of BAS scores between undergraduates in the United States and South Korea found that US participants had significantly higher body appreciation, although the effect size was small (Jung & Hwang, 2016). The statistical basis of this comparison, however, is unclear given that a previous study with South Korean adults indicated that a two-factor model of the BAS should be extracted (Swami, Hwang, & Jung, 2012), which prevents a direct comparison with US samples, where a one-factor model is preferred. More broadly, the conclusion that cross-cultural differences in body appreciation are small or negligible should be considered preliminary at best, given the difficulties of making such comparisons due to the possible lack of cultural equivalence of BAS scores.

One general conclusion that might be drawn on the basis of the existing BAS data is that the construct of body appreciation may not be cross-culturally equivalent. That is, while all thirteen scale items tap into the construct of body appreciation in some groups, as was the case with US college women and men (Avalos et al., 2005; Tylka, 2013), only some of these items directly tap into the same construct in other cultural groups. In the latter, it would seem that some items of the BAS tap into a different construct, more closely aligned with body image investment or body care. One possible interpretation of these data is that the BAS does not adequately measure the construct of body appreciation in different cultural groups. A more problematic interpretation is that the meaning and experience of body appreciation varies across cultural groups, a point to which I will return presently.

The Body Appreciation Scale-2

Tylka and Wood-Barcalow (2015b) argued that, in the decade since the BAS was first published, scholarly understanding of the concept of body appreciation has evolved. To account for these developments, they developed a revised version of the BAS, called the Body Appreciation Scale-2 (BAS-2). More specifically, they deleted one sex-specific item and several items that had poor factor loadings (including all items that typically loaded onto the body image investment component in some cultural groups). This revised measure consists of ten items, five of which were retained from the parent scale and five of which were newly devised. Across three studies with college and community adults from the United States, Tylka and Wood-Barcalow (2015b) confirmed the BAS-2's one-dimensional factor structure, which was invariant across participant sex.

As with the BAS, scholars have been quick to examine the factorial validity of the BAS-2 in different cultural groups. Thus, using EFA, the one-dimensional factor structure of the BAS-2 has been upheld in college samples from Hong Kong (Swami & Ng, 2015), the Netherlands (Alleva, Martijn, Veldhuis, & Tylka, 2016), and Iran (Atari, 2016), as well as a community sample in Serbia (Jovic, Sfroza, Jovanovic, & Jovic, 2016). In addition, using CFA, the one-dimensional factor structure of the BAS-2 has been confirmed in a mixed college staff-and-student sample from mainland China (Swami, Ng, & Barron, 2016); college samples from France (Kertechian & Swami, 2017) and Romania (Swami, Tudorel, Goian, Barron, & Vintila, 2017); and community samples from Spain (Swami, García, & Barron, 2017), Portugal (Marta-Simões, Mendes, Trindade, Oliveira, & Ferreira, 2016), and Poland (Razmus & Razmus, 2017). With the exception of the Romanian study, these CFA studies have reported that BAS-2 scores are invariant across participant sex, suggesting that the latent construct is stable across sex in most studied populations.

The cross-cultural equivalence of the factor structure of the BAS-2 is important because it could facilitate effective between-group comparisons of latent body appreciation scores. To date, however, only two studies have conducted such comparisons. Swami and Ng (2015) compared BAS-2 scores between their sample of adults from Hong Kong and the mean body appreciation scores reported by Tylka and Wood-Barcalow (2015b). They reported that women and men in Hong Kong had significantly higher body appreciation than their U.S. counterparts, although the effect size of the difference was small (ds = 0.17–0.33). Similarly, Swami, Ng, and Barron (2016) compared BAS-2 scores between their sample of adults from mainland China (who completed a Modern Standard Mandarin version of the scale) and a sample of adults in Hong Kong (who completed a Cantonese version of the BAS-2; Swami & Ng, 2015). They found that participants from mainland China had significantly higher body appreciation scores than their counterparts from Hong Kong, although the effect size of the difference was negligible (η_p^2 = .01).

Cross-cultural comparisons of body appreciation remain in their infancy, but should be facilitated by the one-dimensional factor structure of the BAS-2 that has been reported in diverse cultural groups. More broadly, one liberal interpretation of the above factor-analytic findings is that the construct of body appreciation, as measured using the BAS-2, is similar across cultural groups. However, caution should be applied when drawing this conclusion. For one thing, given that the development of BAS-2 excluded those items that proved cross-culturally problematic, it is possible that BAS-2 scores are masking cultural heterogeneity. To put it differently, the finding that scores on a given measure is one-dimensional in a specific cultural context cannot be used as evidence that the underlying construct itself is one-dimensional in that group. More specifically, it is still possible that the BAS-2 is failing to tap into the multidimensional nature of body appreciation in some cultural contexts. I return to discussing the "meaning" of positive body image after first reviewing attempts to examine the factorial validity of other measures of positive body image.

Other Measures of Positive Body Image

In their review, Webb, Wood-Barcalow, and Tylka (2015) identified a range of other quantitative measures developed by Western researchers that tap into constructs related to positive body image. To date, however, none of these measures has received the same sort of treatment in cultural research as the BAS and the BAS-2. In this section, I briefly review the limited attention that has been paid to establishing the factorial validity of several other measures in different cultural groups, so as to highlight cultural experiences of different elements of positive body image.

Body Image Coping Strategies Inventory. The Body Image Coping Strategies Inventory (BICSI; Cash, Santos, & Williams, 2005) is a twenty-nine-item measure of coping response styles to manage body image-related threats or challenges. Webb et al. (2015) have suggested that, of the three factors identified in the parent study with US college students, one – the nine-item Positive Rational Acceptance subscale – can be used as a measure of positive body image, as it taps into positive rational acceptance and engagement in self-care and rational self-talk in the face of a distressing event. Doğan, Sapmaz, and Totan (2011) examined the factor structure of a Turkish translation of the BICSI in a sample of college students. Using CFA, these authors confirmed the three-factor structure from the parent study and reported that Positive Rational Acceptance scores had adequate internal consistency. Likewise, Dhurup and Nolan (2014) reported that, using EFA, the three-factor structure of the BICSI was upheld in a college sample from South Africa, although they did not indicate whether the measure had been translated. The BICSI also appears to have been translated into Japanese (Yeung & Fukutomi, 2008) and Persian (Farid & Akbari-Kamrani, 2016), although its factor structure has not been investigated in these studies.

Body Image-Acceptance and Action Questionnaire. The Body Image-Acceptance and Action Questionnaire (BI-AAQ; Sandoz, Wilson, Merwin, & Kellum, 2013) is a twelve-item measure that taps into a compassionate response to embrace rather than avoid, escape, or alter the content or form of aversive body-related thoughts and feelings. In its current form, the BI-AAQ measures the degree of negative body-related thoughts, behaviors, and affect. However, Webb et al. (2015) have suggested that a version in which all items are reverse-coded could provide a preliminary measure of body image flexibility. In the parent study with US college students, Sandoz et al. (2013) developed a forty-six-item scale, which was reduced through EFA to a twelve-item scale with a one-dimensional factor structure.

In a study with a community sample, Ferreira, Pinto-Gouviea, and Duarte (2011) translated the original forty-six-item version of the scale into Portuguese. Using EFA, these authors reported that twenty-nine items loaded on to a primary factor and seventeen items loaded on to a secondary factor. They elected to eliminate the second factor because of problems associated with "wording issues" and retained, through a second EFA, twelve items with a one-dimensional structure and adequate internal consistency. In addition, two studies have examined the factor structure of the English version of the BI-AAQ using CFA. In the first study, Kurz, Flynn, and Bordieri (2016) confirmed that the English version of the scale had a one-dimensional factor structure in a sample of Hispanic college students in the United States. More recently, however, it was reported that the BI-AAQ had poor fit in a clinical sample of women and girls in the United States; a modified, eleven-item version of the scale also had poor fit (Lee, Smith, Twohig, Lensegrav-Benson, & Roberts, 2017). Finally, the BI-AAQ has also been used with a sample of Malaysian college students (Manaf, Saravanan, & Zuhrah, 2016), though the authors did not report whether the scale had been translated into Bahasa Malaysia (Malay), nor did they examine the scale's factor structure.

Internal Body Orientation. The eight-item Body Surveillance subscale of the Objectified Body Consciousness Scale (OBCS; McKinley & Hyde, 1996) measures the degree to which women view their bodies as an outside observer would (i.e., an "external body orientation"). Webb et al. (2015) have suggested that this subscale could instead be used as a measure of positive body image if it were scored to measure "internal body orientation" (i.e., a focus on how the body feels rather than how it looks). In the parent study with primarily White U.S college women, McKinley and Hyde (1996) reported that OCBS scores demonstrated good factorial validity and that subscales scores were internally consistent. When scored to measure internal body orientation, the Body Surveillance subscale has been found to have good convergent and discriminant validity in US adults (Augustus-Horvath & Tylka, 2011; Avalos & Tylka, 2006; Homan & Tylka, 2014).

Knauss, Paxton, and Alsaker (2008) prepared a German translation of the scale, but added three novel items to the Body Surveillance subscale and changed the scale's response format. In an EFA with college students (sex unspecified), Knauss et al. (2008) extracted a single Body Surveillance factor with eleven items. Chinese (Fang, Chang, & Shu, 2014), Dutch (Alleva, Martijn, van Breukelen, Jansen, & Karos, 2015), Korean (Forbes & Jung, 2008), and Spanish (Breitkopf, Littleton, & Berenson, 2007; Forbes et al., 2012) translations of the OCBS have also been prepared, but in all cases the authors have neglected to examine the scale's factor structure. Until the factor structure of the OCBS is carefully examined in different national and linguistic groups, caution should be applied when interpreting previous findings in different linguistic groups.

Other Scales. Other scales that have been developed to measure facets of positive body image include the Embodied Image Scale

(Abbott & Barber, 2010), the Body Responsiveness Scale (Daubenmier, 2005), the Authentic Pride subscale of the Body and Appearance Self-Conscious Emotions Scale (Castonguay, Sabiston, Crocker, & Mack, 2014), the Body Acceptance by Others Scale (Avalos & Tylka, 2006), and the Broad Conceptualization of Beauty Scale (Tylka & Iannantuono, 2016), but translations of these scales for use outside English-speaking populations have not been prepared to date.

Summary of Quantitative Measures of Positive Body Image

A range of measures have been developed to measure positive body image (Webb et al., 2015), but the psychometric properties of only a small minority of these scales have received systematic attention outside English-speaking samples. Although the factor structure of the BAS appears problematic across cultures, the BAS-2 holds promise as a suitable measure of a facet of positive body image that retains its one-dimensional factor structure in different cultural groups. Likewise, the available evidence suggests that the BICSI may retain its parent factor structure in non-English samples, but much more work needs to be done to examine the factor structure of the measure in different cultural contexts. Conversely, of the range of other measures of positive body image reviewed by Webb et al. (2015), few have been translated for use in non-English samples and those that have require further investigation of their factor structures before being held up as adequate measures of positive body image in different cultural groups.

This also points to a broader concern with the manner in which cross-cultural research on positive body image has developed. In the case of body appreciation, for example, research has begun with measurement tools designed by scholars in a particular cultural context (the United States) based on an understanding of the nature of body appreciation within that particular cultural context. Next, researchers have sought to examine the factor structure of those measures in a diverse range of cultural groups and, in the case of BAS-2, concluded that the construct is equivalent across groups. This is problematic because scholars may be neglecting culture-specific facets of body appreciation specifically or positive body image generally. That is, because the measures of body appreciation were developed in a particular cultural milieu, they may not fully capture the meaning and lived experience of the construct of body appreciation in other cultural groups. To truly understand the nature and meaning of body appreciation in different cultural groups, different methods are required.

Qualitative Research

One useful way of extending our knowledge of the nature of positive body image in different cultural groups is through qualitative research. To date, however, such research has been extremely limited and has not kept pace with the quantitative research reviewed earlier in the chapter. In a sample of US college women of mixed ethnicities and White body image experts, Wood-Barcalow, Tylka, and Augustus-Horvath (2010) identified a range of characteristics of positive body image through one-on-one interviews. Themes generated through grounded theory included an appreciation of the unique beauty and functionality of one's body, a filtering of information in a protective manner, a broad definition and conceptualization of beauty, and a focus on the body's positive qualities rather than its imperfections. These themes have proved important in contemporary definitions of positive body image, but it should be noted that they are based on interviews with a culturally homogenous group of individuals.

Similar themes emerged in qualitative research with adolescent girls and boys in Sweden who had been identified as having high levels of positive body image in earlier longitudinal research (Frisén & Holmqvist, 2010). Specifically, in this sample, adolescents' appearance satisfaction was characterized by a functional view of the body and an acceptance of bodily imperfections. In addition, participants had also learned to minimize the importance of negative appearance comments from peers and family and to filter appearance information in a body-protective manner. A second study with Swedish adolescents with positive body image revealed that they took a critical approach to societal appearance ideals, viewing them as unnatural and unrealistic (Holmqvist & Frisén, 2012). Instead, these adolescents adopted broader and more flexible definitions of beauty and stressed the importance of looking like "oneself."

Although these studies would seem to suggest that the concept of positive body image is similar across cultural groups, other qualitative research points to characteristics that may be unique to particular cultural groups. For example, one research group conducted one-on-one interviews with Aboriginal young women in Canada about how they conceptualize body pride (McHugh, Coppola, & Sabiston, 2014). This study, too, highlighted the importance of accepting the body despite its imperfections as a central aspect of positive body image. However, other aspects of positive body image that were identified developed from the particular cultural identities of this group of women. For example, all participants in the study explained how body pride was something that emerged from the "inside" but could be expressed through various cultural symbols, such as dance regalia, makeup, and tattoos.

More than simply "showing" body pride in ways that reflect their Aboriginal identity, participants in the study also described how culture shaped their body pride (McHugh et al., 2014; see also Coppola, Dimler, Letendre, & McHugh, 2017). For example, some participants described how their cultural activities such as dance and traditional ceremonies helped to foster a sense of pride in their bodies. For McHugh et al. (2014), these descriptions highlight the complex relationships between body pride and cultural identity. Aboriginal identity was seen as underlying participants' experiences of body pride, but also facilitated participation in cultural activities and the navigation of others' negative perceptions. More broadly, the participants described that, in order to experience body pride, young Aboriginal women had to first be proud of their cultural identities.

Thus, the available qualitative research on positive body image suggests that there may be some core features of positive body image that are stable across cultural groups, such as acceptance of the body despite its imperfections and a focus on the body's functionality. However, it also seems likely that local social identities give rise to elements of positive body image that are unique to particular groups. This highlights the importance of trying to understand the different ways in which immersion in local social and cultural identities can sometimes promote more positive body image. At present, however, the available qualitative research is limited to cultural groups in North America and Europe, and an important future step for researchers will be to extend this work to cultural groups in other parts of the world. Webb et al. (2015, pp. 138–139) have provided a guide that scholars are encouraged to adopt in conducting such research.

Positive Body Image within Cultures

Thus far, this review has examined aspects of positive body image as they manifest in different macro-level cultural groups. Conversely, the social identities approach can also be applied to micro-level cultural identities *within* cultures. This perspective is based on the notion that localized cultural identities that are constructed within broader cultural milieus can sometimes result in changes to body image that are either protective or detrimental. The available research that has focused on such within-culture groups is broad-ranging and in this section I focus on differences in positive body image as a function of race/ethnic identity, socioeconomic status and migration, sexual orientation and gender identity, and religious identity.

Race/Ethnic Identity

Historically, studies of women in North America have indicated that there are marked racial/ethnic differences in rates of negative body image. For example, compared to White women, it has been suggested that ethnic minority – and particularly Black – women may be less likely to internalize mainstream standards of appearance and beauty, particularly the thin ideal (for a review, see Grogan, 2016). Instead, ethnic minority women may be more likely to adopt culture-specific beauty ideals or place less importance on appearance than White women (Rubin, Fitts, & Becker, 2003). Consistent with these suggestions, studies have shown that Black women have lower levels of body dissatisfaction than White women (Franko & Roehrig, 2011), are more accepting of larger body sizes (Aruguete, Nickleberry, & Yates, 2004), and have more flexible conceptions of beauty and attractiveness (Latner, Stunkard, & Wilson, 2005). However, more recent studies have also highlighted shifts in Black women's body image, with meta-analyses concluding that Black–White differences in body dissatisfaction are narrowing (Grabe & Hyde, 2006; Roberts, Cash, & Johnson, 2006).

Although these studies are informative, relatively little research has examined ethnic/racial differences in positive body image specifically. However, one early study with US college women indicated that Black participants were more likely than White participants to have positive body image (Williams, Cash, & Santos, 2004). Qualitative research with White and Black college students in the United States would seem to support this general conclusion. One study found that African American adolescents were more flexible than their White counterparts in their conceptions of beauty, and spoke about "making what you've got work for you" (Parker et al., 1995). Another, more recent qualitative study found that Black women were more likely than their White counterparts to express high levels of body acceptance and resistance of a singular body size as ideal (Webb, Warren-Findlow, Chou, & Adams, 2013). The authors concluded that embracing positive body image may be one way through which members of a historically marginalized group could maintain psychological well-being and cultural pride.

Other qualitative research suggests a more complex picture of the impact of ethnocultural identities on positive body image. Through interviews with Black women attending predominately White colleges in the United States, one group of researchers described how some participants had a self-concept with a contingency of self-worth associated with Black cultural identity (Hesse-Biber, Livingstone, Ramirez, Barko, & Johnson, 2010). In turn, this heightened acceptance of Black cultural identity helped to foster a degree of body confidence and increased body satisfaction. However, it was not only identification with one's cultural identity that conferred a protective effect on body image. In the same study, Hesse-Biber and colleagues (2010) also described how participants with a cultural identity of diversity (due to identification as mixed-race or circumstances of growing up in racially diverse environments) also developed a more positive body image, possibly because they did not "hyperidentify" with either Black or White culture. That is, these "bridge builders" were less likely to be highly influenced by the prescriptive beauty ideals of any specific cultural group.

Other studies with college students in the United States hint at more equivocal findings. For example, in a sample of US college students, Gillen and Lefkowitz (2012) reported that Black participants were more satisfied with areas of their body than White and Latino/a participants. Another study found that the one-dimensional factor structure of the BAS had adequate fit in a sample of Black college women (Cotter, Kelly, Mitchell, & Mazzeo, 2013) and that this sample had higher mean body appreciation scores than the predominantly White college sample from Avalos et al. (2005) (although a direct comparison of scores was not conducted). However, a later study with a sample of US college students found that participant race (Black versus other ethnic groups) was not significantly associated with body appreciation scores, as measured using the BAS (Gillen, 2015). Nevertheless, difficulties in interpreting this finding are that "other" ethnic groups included a range of distinct identities (e.g., White, Asian American, etc.) and the relatively small sample size of Black participants may mean that the association was underpowered. In short, available studies examining ethnic/racial differences in positive body image in the United States suggest that ethnic minority women may have more positive body image than their White counterparts, although more in-depth research is needed.

A handful of studies have examined ethnic differences in positive body image outside the United States. For example, one study examined ethnic differences in body appreciation (measured using the BAS) in White, South Asian, African Caribbean, and Hispanic female undergraduates in the United Kingdom (Swami, Airs, Chouhan, Padilla Leon, & Towell, 2009). Controlling for participant age, these authors found that Hispanic participants had the highest body appreciation scores, followed by African Caribbean and White women. South Asian women had the lowest body appreciation scores. Swami et al. (2009) also found that Hispanic and African Caribbean women had the lowest scores on internalization of media ideals, and concluded that women from these ethnic minority groups may be more likely to adopt ethnocentric ideals of

appearance that allow for greater body diversity or minimize the importance of appearance altogether. They also suggested that the higher self-
esteem reported by these groups may be related to increased body
appreciation. Conversely, the finding that South Asian women reported
the lowest body appreciation scores was attributed to their higher levels
of parental conflict and parental overprotection (particularly in terms of
socializing and one's choice of friends; see Furnham & Husain, 1999),
which may diminish body-protective work.

Two other studies are noteworthy for examining ethnic differences in
positive body image in a non-United States context. In a community
sample from Malaysia, Swami and Chamorro-Premuzic (2008) examined differences on the truncated Malay BAS between ethnic Malay and
Chinese women and reported no significant between-group differences.
Likewise, in neighboring Indonesia, Swami and Jaafar (2012) examined
ethnic differences between Javanese, Sundanese, and Chinese women
and men on a truncated, ten-item version of the BAS. These authors also
reported no significant differences between the three ethnic groups and
no significant ethnicity by gender interaction. Swami and Chamorro-
Premuzic (2008) have suggested that, in countries such as Malaysia,
ethnic differences may be less salient than other social identities in terms
of body appreciation. One such aspect that may be of relevance when
considering positive body image in developing countries is socioeconomic status.

Socioeconomic Status and Transcultural Migration

Studies of negative body image now indicate that the biggest differences
globally are no longer found between countries, but rather between sites
within countries that differ in terms of socioeconomic development (e.g.,
Swami et al., 2010). Swami (2015) has attributed this to a range of
differences between sites that differ in socioeconomic status, including
variation in body size ideals (with heavier bodies being more accepted in
contexts of low socioeconomic status), gender roles and opportunities for
women, and exposure to Western media. Based on this general perspective, Swami, Kannan, and Furnham (2011) hypothesized that variation
in socioeconomic status should also lead to differences in positive body
image. More specifically, they argued that cultural identities developed in
rural, low socioeconomic status contexts may promote more positive
body image; conversely, residing in urban, high socioeconomic status
sites may have a detrimental effect on positive body image.

To test this hypothesis, Swami et al. (2011) administered the truncated
version of the Malay BAS to participants in Sabah, Malaysia, a location

with marked intrastate differences in socioeconomic status. More specifically, they recruited female participants from rural and urban sites in Sabah; their sample also varied in ethnicity, with the inclusion of Kadazan-Dusun, Bajau, and Murut participants. Their analyses indicated that there were no significant ethnic differences and no significant interaction between ethnicity and socioeconomic status. However, they did find that rural participants had significantly higher body appreciation compared with urban participants once the effects of body mass index had been controlled for. Further analyses indicated that the socioeconomic development of the participants' living context was a stronger predictor of body appreciation in this sample than exposure to Western media.

Related to socioeconomic status, two studies have examined the impact of transcultural migration on positive body image. First, Swami, Mada, and Tovée (2012) compared scores on a truncated version of the BAS between Zimbabwean women in Harare, Zimbabwe, and Zimbabwean migrants in London, United Kingdom. They found that the migrant group had significantly lower body appreciation than their counterparts in Zimbabwe. In the migrant group, length of residence in the United Kingdom was not significantly associated with body appreciation, although there was a significant and negative correlation between body appreciation and exposure to Western media. Swami et al. (2012) concluded that the process of transcultural migration may bring antecedent changes (e.g., exposure to Western media that heighten a requirement to work on the body's appearance) that have a detrimental effect on positive body image. It is also possible that migration has an indirect effect on positive body image: For example, the stress of migration may mean that migrants have less time or inclination to engage in body-protective behaviors and attitudes (Swami, 2016).

In the second study, Taylor et al. (2013) compared body appreciation scores (measured using a truncated version of the BAS) between Polish women in Warsaw, Poland, and London, United Kingdom. Unlike Swami et al. (2012), however, the authors of this study reported that the migrant Polish women had significantly higher body appreciation than their counterparts in Poland, even after controlling for subjective social status. In explanation, Taylor et al. (2013) suggested that Polish women in Poland may experience heightened cultural pressure to attain thinness as cultural capital in a context where the introduction of a market economy has brought widespread and rapid sociocultural changes (e.g., changes in the roles of women). That is, as women negotiate new social identities in a rapidly evolving national context, one cost might be a dampening effect on positive body image.

Taken together, these studies suggest that the effects of socioeconomic status and transcultural migration may not be straightforward or linear. Although we might expect elevated positive body image in contexts of low socioeconomic status, actual outcomes may require a closer appreciation of localized national, cultural, and subcultural identities. In a similar vein, the available studies on transcultural migration only point to between-group differences, but they have not been able to determine whether migration specifically dampens or elevates positive body image. To be able to do so, scholars will need to conduct prospective and longitudinal studies that specifically examine the effects of moving between cultures that differ not only in socioeconomic status but also in other related variables, such as exposure to Western media that promotes unrealistic appearance ideals.

Sexual Orientation, Gender Identity, and Gender Ideology

To date, only a handful of studies have examined associations between sexual orientation and positive body image (e.g., Winter, Satinsky, & Jozkowski, 2015). In one study, heterosexual and sexual minority women in the United States were asked to complete the BAS (Winter et al., 2015). Between-group analyses indicated that heterosexual women had significantly lower body appreciation than sexual minority women. On the other hand, there were no significant differences between bisexual and sexual minority women in terms of body appreciation. It has been suggested that sexual minority women experience less pressure to comply with heterosexist norms of appearance, which in turn has a protective effect in terms of body image (Tiggemann, 2015). The greater acceptance of diverse body types among lesbians may also promote healthier body image (VanKim, Porta, Eisenberg, Neumark-Sztainer, & Laska, 2016), although the normalization of homosexuality places pressure on lesbians to attain heteronormative standards of appearance (Smith, Telford, & Tree, 2017).

In contrast, sexual minority status in men may have a detrimental effect on positive body image. For example, one qualitative study of sexual minority college men in the United States documented the pressure that gay men in particular experience with regard to attaining subcultural ideals of appearance, which may blunt any positive body work (VanKim et al., 2016). Moreover, gay men may experience heightened pressure to be both muscular and thin. Unlike lesbians, for whom the broader sexual minority community may facilitate healthier body image, gay men reported that the male sexual minority community offered few resources with which to develop positive body image. Among sexual minority men, the experience of heterosexism has also been found to be negatively associated with body appreciation (Simpson, Sutter, & Perrin, 2016). Further work is necessary to generalize these findings, particularly as the available quantitative evidence base to date is limited to small samples of US participants.

Beyond sexual orientation, two qualitative studies have focused specifically on gender identity and positive body image. The first study, with low-income and ethnically diverse young transgender women in the United States, found that they employed a range of strategies to promote positive body image (Gordon, Austin, Krieger, Hughto, & Reisner, 2016). For example, some women employed critical perspectives of the media to distance themselves from unrealistic femininity ideals, while others relied on gender-affirming support from intimate partners, friends, and community members. In addition, some participants who were taking hormones reported increased body satisfaction, which was attributed to gender-affirming effects (i.e., developing a more feminine physique). The latter finding is consistent with the results of another qualitative study with transgender youth in the United States, which found that those further along in the process of consolidating gender identity described gaining a sense of body satisfaction that reflected resilience (McGuire, Doty, Catalpa, & Ola, 2016).

On the other hand, studies examining associations between body appreciation and gender role ideology remain piecemeal. One early study suggested that, in a sample of British women and men, higher body appreciation was significantly associated with greater internalized male-stereotypic (instrumental) traits but not female-stereotypic (expressivity) traits, although the associations were weak (Swami, Hadji-Michael, & Furnham, 2008). A second study with British women reported that stronger endorsement of traditional femininity ideology – particularly the belief that women should maintain a physical appearance that is consistent with societal ideals – was significantly associated with lower body appreciation (Swami & Abbasnejad, 2010). These studies would seem to suggest that adopting nontraditional gender role ideologies may have a positive impact on positive body image, but again much more in-depth research is needed to better understand these relationships.

Religious Identity

Another set of factors that may offer a protective effect in terms of body image is religiosity or religious identity. Reviews of the literature have concluded that religious beliefs are associated with lower levels of negative body image and disordered eating (Akrawi, Bartrop, Potter,

& Touyz, 2015; Boyatzis & Quinlan, 2008). Moreover, it has been suggested that religious principles may help individuals develop a sense of self-worth that challenges prescriptive standards of appearance and may also help promote positive body image (Kim, 2006). For example, studies of US college women have found that a perceived warm relationship with God was significantly associated with more positive body appreciation (Homan & Cavanaugh, 2013; Homan & Lemmon, 2016). It seems that to the extent that religiosity promotes unconditional acceptance from a higher power despite one's imperfections, it may be a trait that promotes more positive body image (Wood-Barcalow et al., 2010).

Similarly, in Israel, one study found that ultra-Orthodox Jewish women had significant higher body appreciation compared with Modern Orthodox and secular Jewish women (Handelzalts, Geller, Levy, Vered, & Fisher, 2017). Ultra-Orthodox women were also found to have significantly more positive attitudes regarding body care. The authors suggested that positive body image in Israeli Jewish women may vary along a continuum, with greater religiosity being associated with more positive body image. In addition, one study of Protestant Christians found that greater belief in radical dualism (which sees the body as corrupt and separate from oneself) was negatively associated with body appreciation, whereas stronger belief in sanctification (which sees the body as holy, worthy of respect, and integral to the self) was associated with higher body appreciation (Jacobson, Hall, Anderson, & Willingham, 2016).

One subset of this literature has focused on the way in which religiosity impacts body image through sanctification of the body, primarily through modesty in terms of clothing. For example, one study compared scores of body appreciation between British Muslim women who did and did not wear the hijab, or Islamic head and face cover (Swami, Miah, Noorani, & Taylor, 2014). This study found that those who wore the hijab had significantly higher body appreciation, possibly because the hijab protects Muslim women from appearance-based public scrutiny (Mussap, 2009) and sexual objectification (Odoms-Young, 2008). Use of the hijab may also afford some Muslim women the space to challenge prescriptive standards of appearance, which can be experienced as empowering (Al Wazni, 2015). More broadly, the hijab may allow some Muslim women to visibly identify with the wider Muslim community, especially when faced with stressful societal conditions (e.g., the experience of Islamophobia), which may in turn facilitate social support that helps to buffer against threats to body image (Gulamhussein & Eaton, 2015). However, these findings urgently need to be replicated in other national contexts (e.g., see Kertechian & Swami, 2016).

Other Social Identity Groups

Most of the studies reviewed in the preceding section have suggested that there may be some social identities that are associated with more positive body image. However, identification with some social identity groups may have the opposite effect in dampening positive body image. For example, identification with goth youth subculture typically involves transgressive forms of stylistic appearance displays and negotiations of established understandings of appearance (particularly slimness, tight clothing, and makeup). Such expectations, along with appearance competitiveness between members of the goth community, may stimulate dysfunctional cognitions about the importance of appearance and blunt body-protective work. Consistent with this perspective, Swami (2017) reported that young women who identified with goth subculture in the United Kingdom had significantly lower body appreciation than a matched control sample.

Another group in which it might be expected that positive body image will be attenuated is fashion models. Indeed, scholars have frequently commented that – by promoting an extremely slender ideal and through its excessive focus on appearance and body weight, extreme competition, and the use of underweight models – the fashion industry creates a "toxic" environment that increases the incidence of negative body image (Treasure, Wack, & Roberts, 2008). There may be some truth to this claim: In a study of professional fashion models and a matched control sample of nonmodels in London, United Kingdom, Swami and Szmigielska (2013) found that the fashion model group had significantly higher levels of drive for thinness and dysfunctional investment in appearance. However, there was no significant between-group difference in body appreciation, and greater duration as a fashion model was in fact associated with more positive body appreciation. One explanation for these discrepant sets of findings is that, because fashion models more closely mirror societal standards of appearance, they may come to be more appreciative of their bodies.

Summary

Although the study of positive body image in social identity groups within cultures is beginning to grow, this research currently remains in its infancy. Much of the theorizing in this literature, for example, has been borrowed from models of negative body image, with an attendant assumption that negative and positive body image are polar opposites. As Tylka and Wood-Barcalow (2015a) have made clear, however, such an assumption is unlikely to be true, even if does help guide research design and hypothesizing. Just as problematic is the fact that very little research has examined issues related to positive body within specific cultural groups, and what little research that does exist is heavily focused on college samples. Clearly, there is much work to be done to better understand the ways in which social identities within cultures influence and shape positive body image.

The Future of Positive Body Image through the Lens of Culture and Social Identity

Research on positive body image has developed very quickly to include a wide range of different social groups and individuals (Tiggemann, 2015). However, this field remains in its infancy and faces a number of challenges going forward. In terms of macro-level identities, the BAS-2 has emerged as an important tool that may facilitate cross-cultural research on positive body image. An important next step will be to assess cultural differences in body appreciation and more fully examine cross-cultural differences (or lack thereof) in body appreciation. In doing so, however, scholars should bear in mind that the BAS-2 taps only a single fact of positive body image and that alternative measures are required to more fully assess the constructs that make up positive body image in different cultural contexts. Qualitative studies may provide an alternative means of fully understanding the nature and "meaning" of positive body image in different cultural groups. In terms of within-culture issues, there is a clear need for carefully designed, large-sample studies that more carefully examine differences between subcultural groups, particularly in terms of ethnicity, socioeconomic status, sexual orientation, and gender identity. This is true of both research in established sites, such as North America, and that with less studied populations in the rest of the world.

In all future research, adopting a clearer identities framework may be beneficial. Such an approach should seek to understand multiple ways in which identities are (re)negotiated within particular cultural or subcultural contexts and, in turn, the ways in which identities can promote or impede the development of positive body image. One specific way in which an explicit identities approach may be beneficial is in highlighting the underlying mechanisms through which positive body image is developed. Another way in which an identities approach may be useful is in highlighting intersections between different salient aspects of identity, such as the intersection between socioeconomic class and ethnicity. As this review has suggested, different aspects of identity may be more salient in some contexts than others, and focusing on intersectionality may help to identify specific routes through which positive body image emerges.

In conclusion, this review has highlighted the ways in which research on positive body image has developed to include a wide range of different social identities, but has also highlighted the fact that much more research is needed in this vein. Future research will undoubtedly begin to provide a fuller picture of the nature and meaning of positive body image in different cultural and subcultural groups. This is important as such research will also help to identify mechanisms that could, in theory, be leveraged to promote healthier body image in multiple groups. The goal of such research remains the promotion of positive body image in all groups and social identities.

References

Abbott, B. D., & Barber, B. L. (2010). Embodied image: Gender differences in functional and aesthetic body image among Australian adolescents. *Body Image*, *7*, 22–31. doi:10.1016/j.bodyim.2009.10.004

Akrawi, D., Bartrop, R., Potter, U., & Touyz, S. (2015). Religiosity, spirituality in relation to disordered eating and body image concerns: A systematic review. *Journal of Eating Disorders*, *5*, 29. doi:10.1186/s40337-015-0064-0

Al Wazni, A. B. (2015). Muslim women in America and the hijab: A study of empowerment, femininity identity, and body image. *Social Work*, *60*, 325–333. doi:10.1093/sw/swv033

Alleva, J. M., Martijn, C., van Breukelen, G. J. P., Jansen, A., & Karos, K. (2015). Expand Your Horizon: A programme that improves body image and reduces self-objectification by training women to focus on body functionality. *Body Image*, *15*, 81–89. doi:10.1016/j.bodyim.2015.07.001

Alleva, J. M., Martijn, C., Veldhuis, J., & Tylka, T. L. (2016). A Dutch translation and validation of the Body Appreciation Scale-2: An investigation with female university students in the Netherlands. *Body Image*, *19*, 44–48. doi:10.1016/j.bodyim.2016.08.008

Aruguete, M. S., Nickleberry, L. D., & Yates, A. (2004). Acculturation, body image, and eating attitudes among Black and White college students. *North American Journal of Psychology*, *6*, 393–404.

Atari, M. (2016). Factor structure and psychometric properties of the Body Appreciation Scale-2 in Iran. *Body Image*, *18*, 1–4. doi:10.1016/j.bodyim.2016.04.006

Atari, M., Akbari-Zardkhaneh, S., Mohammadi, L., & Soufiabadi, M. (2015). The factor structure and psychometric properties of the Persian version of Body Appreciation Scale. *American Journal of Applied Psychology*, *3*, 62–66. doi:10.12691/ajap-3-3-3

Augustus-Horvath, C. L., & Tylka, T. L. (2011). The acceptance model of intuitive eating: A comparison of women in emerging adulthood, early adulthood, and middle adulthood. *Journal of Counseling Psychology, 58,* 110–125. doi:10.1037/a0022129

Avalos, L. C., & Tylka, T. L. (2006). Exploring a model of intuitive eating with college women. *Journal of Counseling Psychology, 53,* 486–497. doi:10. 1037/ 0022-1067.53.4.486

Avalos, L. C., Tylka, T. L., & Wood-Barcalow, N. (2005). The Body Appreciation Scale: Development and psychometric evaluation. *Body Image, 2,* 285–297. doi:10.1016/j.bodyim.2005.06.002

Bakalim, O., & Tasleden-Karçkay, A. (2016). Body Appreciation Scale: Evaluation of the factor structure and psychometric properties among male and female Turkish university students. *Mersin Üniversitesi Egitim Fakültesi Dergisi, 12,* 410–422. doi:10.17860/efd.38032

Becker, A. E. (2004). Television, disordered eating, and young women in Fiji: Negotiating body image and identity during rapid social change. *Culture, Medicine, and Psychiatry, 28,* 533–559. doi:10.1007/s11013-004-1067-5

Bourdieu, P. (1984). *Distinction.* Cambridge: Harvard University Press.

Boyatzis, C. J., & Quinlan, K. B. (2008). Women's body image, disordered eating, and religion: A critical review of the literature. *Research in the Social Scientific Study of Religion, 19,* 183–208. doi:10.1163/ej.9789004166462.i-299.61

Breitkopf, C. R., Littleton, H., & Berenson, A. (2007). Body image: A study in a tri-ethnic sample of low income women. *Sex Roles, 56,* 373–380. doi:10.1007/s11199-006-9177-x

Cash, T. F. (2004). Body image: Past, present, and future. *Body Image, 1,* 1–5. doi:10.1016/S1740-1445(03)00011-1

Cash, T. L., Santos, M. T., & Williams, E. F. (2005). Coping with body-image threats and challenges: Validation of the Body Image Coping Strategies Inventory. *Journal of Psychosomatic Research, 58,* 190–199. doi:10.1016/j.jpsychores.2004.07.008

Castonguay, A. L., Sabiston, C. M., Crocker, P. R. E., & Mack, D. E. (2014). Development and validation of the Body and Appearance Self-Conscious Emotions Scale (BASES). *Body Image, 11,* 126–136. doi:10.1016/j.bodyim.2013.12.006

Coppola, A. M., Dimler, A. J., Letendre, T. S., & McHugh, T.-L. F. (2017). "We are given a body to walk this earth": The body pride experience of young Aboriginal men and women. *Qualitative Research in Sport, Exercise, and Health, 9,* 4–17. doi:10.1080/2159676X.2016.1174727

Cotter, E. W., Kelly, N. R., Mitchell, K. S., & Mazzeo, S. E. (2013). An investigation of body appreciation, ethnic identity, and eating disorder symptoms in Black women. *Journal of Black Studies, 41,* 3–25. doi:10.1177/0095798413502671

Daubenmier, J. J. (2005). The relationship of yoga, body awareness, and body responsiveness to self-objectification and disordered eating. *Psychology of Women Quarterly, 29,* 207–219. doi:10.1111/j.1471-6402.2005.00183.x

Dhurup, N., & Nolan, V. T. (2014). Body image coping strategies among university students and variations in terms of gender in a developing country. *Anthropologist, 18,* 217–225.

Doğan, T., Sapmaz, F., & Totan, T. (2011). Beden İmgesi baş Etme Stratejileri Ölçeğinin Türkçe uyarlaması: Geçerlilik ve güvenilirlik çalışması [Adaptation of the Body Image Coping Strategies Inventory to Turkish: Validity and reliability]. *Anadolu Psikiyatri Dergisi [Anatolian Journal of Psychiatry]*, *12*, 121–129.

Dumitrescu, A. L., Zetu, L., Teslaru, S., Dogaru, B. C., & Dogaru, C. D. (2008). Is it an association between body appreciation, self-criticism, oral health status, and oral health-related behaviors? *Romanian Journal of Internal Medicine*, *46*, 343–350.

Fang, S.-Y., Chang, H.-T., & Shu, B.-C. (2014). Objectified body consciousness, body image discomfort, and depressive symptoms among breast cancer survivors in Taiwan. *Psychology of Women Quarterly*, *38*, 563–574. doi:10.1177/0361684314552652

Farid, M., & Akbari-Kamrami, M. (2016). The relationship between body image coping strategy and eating disorders among Iranian adolescent girls. *Bali Medical Journal*, *5*, 17–22.

Ferreira, L., Neves, A. N., & Tavares, M. C. G. C. F. (2014). Validity of body image scales for Brazilian older adults. *Motriz: Revista de Educação Física*, *20*, 4. doi:10.1590/S1980-65742014000400002

Forbes, G. B., & Jung, J. (2008). Measures based on sociocultural theory and feminist theory as predictors of multidimensional measures of body dissatisfaction among Korean and U.S. college women. *Journal of Social and Clinical Psychology*, *27*, 70–103. doi:10.1521/jscp.2008.27.1.70

Forbes, G. B., Jung, J., Vaamonde, J. D., Omar, A., Paris, L., & Formiga, N. S. (2012). Body dissatisfaction and disordered eating in three cultures: Argentina, Brazil, and the U.S. *Sex Roles*, *66*, 677–694. doi:10.1007/s11199-011-0105-3

Franko, D. L., & Roehrig, J. P. (2011). African American body images. In T. F. Cash & L. Smolak (Eds.), *Body image: A handbook of science, practice, and prevention* (2nd ed., pp. 221–228). New York: Guilford Press.

Frisén, A., & Holmqvist, K. (2010). What characterizes early adolescents with a positive body image? A qualitative investigation of Swedish girls and boys. *Body Image*, *7*, 205–212. doi:10.1016/j.bodyim.2010.04.001

Furnham, A., & Husain, K. (1999). The role of conflict with parents in disordered eating among British Asian females. *Social Psychiatry and Psychiatric Epidemiology*, *34*, 498–505. doi:10.1007/s001270050226

Giddens, A. (1991). *Modernity and self-identity*. Stanford: Stanford University Press.

Gillen, M. M. (2015). Associations between positive body image and indicators of men's and women's mental and physical health. *Body Image*, *13*, 67–74. doi:10.1016/j.bodyim.2015.01.002

Gillen, M. M., & Lefkowitz, E. S. (2012). Gender and racial/ethnic differences in body image development among college students. *Body Image*, *9*, 126–130. doi:10.1016/j.bodyim.2011.09.004

Gordon, A. R., Austin, S. B., Krieger, N., White Hughto, J. M., & Reisner, S. L. (2016). "I have to constantly prove myself, to people, that I fit the bill": Perspectives on weight and shate control behaviors among low-income, ethnically diverse young transgender women. *Social Science and Medicine, 165,* 141–149. doi:10.1016/j.socscimed.2016.07.038

Grabe, S., & Hyde, J. S. (2006). Ethnicity and body dissatisfaction among women in the United States: A meta-analysis. *Psychological Bulletin, 132,* 622–640. doi:10.1037/0033-2909.132.4.622

Grogan, S. (2016). *Body image: Understanding body dissatisfaction in men, women, and children.* London: Routledge.

Gulamhussein, Q., & Eaton, N. R. (2015). Hijab, religiosity, and psychological wellbeing of Muslim women in the United States. *Journal of Muslim Mental Health, 9,* 2. doi:10.3998/jmmh.10381607.0009.202

Handelzalts, J. E., Geller, S., Levy, S., Vered, T., & Fisher, S. (2017). Body image among three denominations of Jewish women in Israel. *International Journal of Culture and Mental Health, 10,* 206–216. doi:10.1080/17542863.2017.1290126

Hesse-Biber, S., Livingstone, S., Ramirez, D., Barko, E. B., & Johnson, A. L. (2010). Racial identity and body image among Black female college students attending predominately White colleges. *Sex Roles, 63,* 697–711. doi:10.1007/s11199-010-9862-7

Holmqvist, K., & Frisén, A. (2012). "I bet they aren't that perfect in reality": Appearance ideals viewed from the perspective of adolescents with a positive body image. *Body Image, 9,* 388–395. doi:10.1016/j.bodyim.2012.03.007

Homan, K. J., & Cavanaugh, B. N. (2013). Perceived relationship with God fosters positive body image in college women. *Journal of Health Psychology, 18,* 1529–1539. doi:10.1177/1359105312465911

Homan, J. K., & Lemmon, V. A. (2016). Perceived relationship with God moderates the relationship between social comparison and body appreciation. *Mental Health, Religion, and Culture, 19,* 37–51. doi:10.1080/13674676.2016.1140372

Homan, K. J., & Tylka, T. L. (2014). Appearance-based exercise motivation moderates the relationship between exercise frequency and positive body image. *Body Image, 11,* 101–108. doi:10.1016/j.bodyim.2014.01.003

Jacobson, H. L., Hall, M. E. L., Anderson, T. L., & Willingham, M. M. (2016). Temple or prison: Religious beliefs and attitudes toward the body. *Journal of Religion and Health, 55,* 2154–2173. doi:10.1007/s10943-016-02660-z

Jain, P., & Tiwari, G. K. (2016). Positive body image and general health: A mixed methods study. *International Journal of Indian Psychology, 4,* article 76.

Jovic, M., Sforza, M., Jovanovic, M., & Jovic, M. (2016). The Acceptance of Cosmetic Surgery Scale: Confirmatory factor analyses and validation among Serbian adults. *Current Psychology, 36,* 707–716. doi:10.1007/s12144-016-9458-7

Jung, J., & Hwang, C. S. (2016). Associations between attitudes toward cosmetic suirgery, celebrity worship, and body image among South Korean and US female college students. *Fashion and Textiles, 3,* article 17. doi:10.1186/s40691-016-0069-6

Kertechian, S., & Swami, V. (2016). The hijab as a protective factor for body image and disordered eating: A replication in French Muslim women.

Mental Health, Religion, and Culture, 19, 1056–1068. doi:10.1080/
13674676.2017.1312322

(2017). An examination of the factor structure and sex invariance of a French
translation of the Body Appreciation Scale-2 in university students. *Body
Image, 21*, 26–29. doi:10.1016/j.bodyim.2017.02.005

Kim, K. H.-C. (2006). Religion, body satisfaction, and dieting. *Appetite, 46*,
285–296. doi:10.1016/j.appet.2006.01.006

Knauss, C., Paxton, S. J., & Alsaker, F. D. (2008). Body dissatisfaction in boys
and girls: Objectified body consciousness, internalization of the media body
ideal ideal, and perceived pressure from media. *Sex Roles, 59*, 633–643.
doi:10.1007/s11199-008-9474-7

Kurz, A. S., Flynn, M. K., & Bordieri, M. J. (2016). How Bayesian estimation
might improve CBS measure development: A case study with body-image
flexibility in Hispanic students. *Journal of Contextual Behavioral Science, 5*,
146–153. doi:10.1016/j.jcbs.2016.07.055

Latner, J. D., Stunkard, A. J., & Wilson, G. T. (2005). Stigmatized students:
Age, sex, and ethnicity effects in the stigmatization of obesity. *Obesity
Research, 13*, 1226–1231.

Lee, E. B., Smith, B. M., Twohig, M. P., Lensegrav-Benson, T., & Quakenbush-
Roberts, B. (2017). Assessment of the Body Image-Acceptance and Action
Questionnaire in a female residential eating disorder treatment facility.
Journal of Contextual Behavioral Science, 6, 21–28. doi:10.1016/j.
jcbs.2016.11.004

Lobera, I. J., & Ríos, P. B. (2011). Spanish version of the Body Appreciation
Scale (BAS) for adolescents. *Spanish Journal of Psychology, 14*, 411–420.
doi:10.5209/rev_SJOP.2011.v14.ni.37

Lunde, C. (2013). Acceptance of cosmetic surgery, body appreciation, body ideal
internalization, and fashion blog reading among late adolescents. *Body
Image, 10*, 632–635. doi:10.1016/j.bodyim.2013.06.007

Manaf, N. A., Saravanan, C., & Zuhrah, B. (2016). The prevalence and inter-
relationship of negative body image perception, depression, and
susceptibility to eating disorders among female medical undergraduate
students. *Journal of Clinical and Diagnostic Research, 10*, VC01–VC04.
doi:10.7860/JCDR/2016/16678.7341

Marta-Simões, J., Mendes, A. L., Trindade, I. A., Oliveira, S., & Ferreira, C.
(2016). Validation of the Body Appreciation Scale-2 for Portuguese women.
BMC Health Services Research, 16, article 92. doi:10.1186/s12913-016-1423-5

McGuire, J. K., Doty, J. L., Catalpa, J. M., & Ola, C. (2016). Body image in
transgender young people: Findings from a qualitative, community based
study. *Body Image, 18*, 96–107. doi:10.1016/j.bodyim.2016.06.004

McHugh, T.-L., Coppola, A. M., & Sabiston, C. M. (2014). "I'm thankful for
being Native and my body is part of that": The body pride experiences of
young Aboriginal women in Canada. *Body Image, 11*, 318–327. doi:10.1016/
j.bodyim.2014.05.004

McKinley, N. M., & Hyde, J. S. (1996). The Objectified Body Consciousness
Scale: Development and validation. *Psychology of Women Quarterly, 20*,
181–215. doi:10.1111/j.1471-6402.1996.tb00467.x

Mussap, A. J. (2009). Strength of faith and body image in Muslim and non-Muslim women. *Mental Health, Religion, and Culture, 12*, 121–127. doi:10.1080/13674670802358190

Ng, S.-K., Barron, D., & Swami, V. (2015). Factor structure and psychometric properties of the Body Appreciation Scale among adults in Hong Kong. *Body Image, 13*, 1–8. doi:10.1016/j.bodyim.2014.10.009

Odoms-Young, A. (2008). Factors that influence body image representations of Black Muslim women. *Social Science and Medicine, 66*, 2573–2584. doi:10.1016/j.socscimed.2008.02.008

Parker, S., Nichter, M., Nichter, M., Vuckovic, N., Sims, C., & Ritenbaugh, C. (1995). Body image and weight concerns among African American and White adolescent females: Differences that make a difference. *Human Organization, 54*, 103–114. doi:10.17730/humo.54.206g663745q650450

Pisitsungkagarn, K., Taephant, N., & Attasaranya, P. (2014). Body image satisfaction and self-esteem in Thai female adolescents: The moderating role of self-compassion. *International Journal of Adolescent Medicine and Health, 26*, 333–338. doi:10.1515/ijamh-2013-0307

Razmus, M., & Razmus, W. (2017). Evaluating the psychometric properties of the Polish version of the Body Appreciation Scale-2. *Body Image, 23*, 45–49. doi:10.1016/j.bodyim.2017.07.004

Roberts, A., Cash, T. F., Feingold, A., & Johnson, B. T. (2006). Are Black–White differences in females' body dissatisfaction decreasing? A meta-analytic review. *Journal of Consulting and Clinical Psychology, 74*, 1121–1131. doi:10.1037/0022-006X.74.6.1121

Rubin, L. R., Fitts, M. L., & Becker, A. E. (2003). "Whatever feels good in my soul": Body ethics and esthetics among African American and Latina women. *Culture, Medicine, and Psychiatry, 27*, 49–75. doi:10.1023/A:1023679821086

Sandoz, E. K., Wilson, K. G., Merwin, R. M., & Kellum, K. K. (2013). Assessment of body image flexibility: The Body Image – Acceptance and Action Questionnaire. *Journal of Contextual and Behavioral Science, 2*, 39–48. doi:10.1016/j.jcbs.2013.03.002

Simpson, C. C., Sutter, M., & Perrin, P. B. (2016). Can community consciousness be a bad thing? A moderated mediation analysis of heterosexism, mental health, and body appreciation in sexual minority men. *Culture, Health, and Sexuality, 18*, 1279–1294. doi:10.1080/13691058.2016.1183047

Smith, M. L., Telford, E., & Tree, J. J. (2018). Body image and sexual orientation: The experiences of lesbian and bisexual women. *Journal of Health Psychology*, in press. doi:10.1177/1359105317694486

Swami, V. (2015). Cultural influences on body size ideals: Unpacking the impact of Westernization and modernization. *European Psychologist, 20*, 44–51. doi:10.1027/1016-9040/a000150

  (2016). Change in risk factors for eating disorder symptomatology in Malay students sojourning in the United Kingdom. *International Journal of Eating Disorders, 49*, 695–700. doi:10.1002/eat.22509

  (2017). Negative body image and eating disorder symptomatology among young women identifying with goth subculture. *Body Image, 21*, 30–33. doi:10.1016/j.bodyim.2017.02.001

Swami, V., & Abbasnejad, A. (2010). Associations between femininity ideology and body appreciation among British female undergraduates. *Personality and Individual Differences, 48,* 685–687. doi:10.1016/j.paid.2009.12.017

Swami, V., Airs, N., Chouhand, B., Padilla Leon, M. A., Towell, T. (2009). Are there ethnic differences in positive body image among female British undergraduates? *European Psychologist, 14,* 288–296. doi:10.1027/1016-9040.14.4.288

Swami, V., Campana, A. N. N. B. C., Ferreira, L., Barrett, S., Harris, A. S., & Tavares, M. C. G. C. F. (2011). The Acceptance of Cosmetic Surgery Scale: Initial examination of its factor structure and correlates among Brazilian adults. *Body Image, 8,* 179–185. doi:10.1016/j.bodyim.2011.01.001

Swami, V., & Chamorro-Premuzic, T. (2008). Factor structure of the Body Appreciation Scale among Malaysian women. *Body Image, 5,* 409–413. doi:10.1016/j.bodyim.2008.004.005

Swami, V., Tudorel, O., Goian, C., Barron, D., & Vintila, M. (2017). Factor structure and psychometric properties of a Romanian translation of the Body Appreciation Scale-2. *Body Image, 23,* 61–68. doi:10.1016/j.bodyim.2017.08.011.

Swami, V., Frederick, D. A., Aavik, T., Alcalay, L., Allik, J., Anderson, D., ... & Zivcic-Becirevic, I. (2010). Body weight ideals and body dissatisfaction in 26 countries across 10 world regions: Results of the International Body Project I. *Personality and Social Psychology Bulletin, 36,* 309–325. doi:10.1177/0146167209359702

Swami, V., García, A. A., & Barron, D. (2017). Factor structure and psychometric properties of a Spanish version of the Body Appreciation Scale-2 (BAS-2). *Body Image, 22,* 13–17. doi:10.1016/j.bodyim.2017.05.002

Swami, V., Hadji-Michael, M., & Furnham, A. (2008). Personality and individual difference correlates of positive body image. *Body Image, 5,* 322–325. doi:10.1016/j.bodyim.2008.03.007

Swami, V., Hwang, C.-S., & Jung, J. (2012). Factor structure and correlates of the Acceptance of Cosmetic Surgery Scale among South Korean university students. *Aesthetic Surgery Journal, 32,* 220–229. doi:10.1177/1090820X11431577

Swami, V., & Jaafar, J. L. (2012). Factor structure of the Body Appreciation Scale among Indonesian women and men: Further evidence of a two-factor solution in a non-Western population. *Body Image, 9,* 539–542. doi:10.1016/j.bodyim.2012.06.002

Swami, V., Kannan, K., & Furnham, A. (2011). Positive body image: Inter-ethnic and rural–urban differences among an indigenous sample from Malaysian Borneo. *International Journal of Social Psychiatry, 58,* 568–576. doi:10.1177/0020764011415208

Swami, V., Mada, R., & Tovée, M. J. (2012). Weight discrepancy and body appreciation of Zimbabwean women in Zimbabwe and Britain. *Body Image, 9,* 559–562. doi:10.1016/j.bodyim.2012.05.006

Swami, V., Miah, J., Noorani, N., & Taylor, D. (2014). Is the hijab protective? An investigation of body image and related constructs among British Muslim women. *British Journal of Psychology, 105,* 352–363. doi:10.1111/bjop.12045

Swami, V., & Ng, S.-K. (2015). Factor structure and psychometric properties of the Body Appreciation Scale-2 among adults in Hong Kong. *Body Image, 15,* 68–71. doi:10.1016/j.bodyim.2014.10.009

Swami, V., Ng, S.-K., & Barron, D. (2016). Translation and psychometric evaluation of a Standard Chinese version of the Body Appreciation Scale-2. *Body Image, 18,* 23–26. doi:10.1016/j.bodyim.2016.04.005

Swami, V., Özgen, L., Gökçen, E., & Petrides, K. V. (2015). Body image among female university students in Turkey: Concurrent translation and validation of three body image measures. *International Journal of Culture and Mental Health, 8,* 176–191. doi:10.1080/17542863.2014.917117

Swami, V., Stieger, S., Haubner, T., & Voracek, M. (2008). German translation and psychometric evaluation of the Body Appreciation Scale. *Body Image, 5,* 122–127. doi:10.1016/j.bodyim.2007.10.002

Swami, V., & Szmigielska, E. (2013). Body image concerns in professional fashion models: Are they really an at-risk group? *Psychiatry Research, 207,* 113–117. doi:10.1016/j.psychres.2012.09.009

Swami, V., Tran, U. S., Stieger, S., Voracek, M., & The YouBeauty.com Team (2015). Associations between women's body image and happiness: Results of the YouBeauty.com Body Image Survey (YBIS). *Journal of Happiness Studies, 16,* 705–718. doi:10.1007/s10902-014-9530-7

Taylor, D., Szpakowska, I., & Swami, V. (2013). Weight discrepancy and body appreciation among women in Poland and Britain. *Body Image, 10,* 628–631. doi:10.1016/j.bodyim.2013.07.008

Tiggemann, M. (2015). Considerations of positive body image across various social identities and special populations. *Body Image, 14,* 168–176. doi:10.1016/j.bodyim.2015.03.002

Treasure, J. L., Wack, E. R., & Roberts, M. R. (2008). Models as a high-risk group: The health implications of a size zero culture. *British Journal of Psychiatry, 192,* 243–244. doi:10.1192/bjp.bp.107.044164

Tylka, T. L. (2013). Evidence for the Body Appreciation Scale's measurement equivalence/invariance between U.S. college women and men. *Body Image, 10,* 415–418. doi:10.1016/j.bodyim.2013.02.006

Tylka, T. L., & Iannantuono, A. C. (2016). Perceiving beauty in all women: Psychometric evaluation of the Broad Conceptualization of Beauty Scale. *Body Image, 17,* 67–81. doi:10.1016/j.bodyim.2016.02.005

Tylka, T. L., & Wood-Barcalow, N. L. (2015a). What is and what is not positive body image? Conceptual foundations and construct definition. *Body Image, 14,* 118–129. doi:10.1016/j.bodyim.2015.04.001

(2015b). The Body Appreciation Scale-2: Item refinement and psychometric evaluation. *Body Image, 12,* 53–67. doi:10.1016/j.bodyim.2014.09.006

van den Brink, F., Smeets, M. A. M., Hessen, D. J., & Woertman, L. (2016). Positive body image and sexual functioning in Dutch female university students: The role of adult romantic attachment. *Archives of Sexual Behavior, 45,* 1217–1226. doi:10.1007/s10508-015-0511-7

VanKim, N. A., Porta, C. M., Eisenberg, M. E., Neumark-Sztainer, D., & Laska, M. N. (2016). Lesbian, gay, and bisexual college student perspectives on disparities in weight-related behaviors and body image: A qualitative analysis. *Journal of Clinical Nursing, 25,* 3676–3686. doi:10.1111/jocn.13106

Webb, J. B., Warren-Findlow, J., Chou, Y.-Y., & Adams, L. (2013). Do you see what I see? An exploration of inter-ethnic ideal body size comparisons among college women. *Body Image, 10*, 369–379. doi:10.1016/j.bodyim.2013.03.005

Webb, J. B., Wood-Barcalow, N. L., & Tylka, T. L. (2015). Assessing positive body image: Contemporary approaches and future directions. *Body Image, 14*, 130–145. doi:10.1016/j.bodyim.2015.03.010

Williams, E. F., Cash, T. F., & Santos, M. T. (2004). *Positive and negative body image: Precursors, correlates, and consequences.* Paper presented at the 38th annual meeting of the Association for Advancement of Behavior Therapy, New Orleans.

Winter, V. R., Satinsky, S., & Jozkowski, K. N. (2015). Does women's body appreciation differ by sexual orientation? A brief report. *Journal of Bisexuality, 15*, 130–141. doi:10.1080/15299716.2014.999903

Wood-Barcalow, N. L., Tylka, T. L., & Augustus-Horvath, C. L. (2010). "But I like my body": Positive body image characteristics and a holistic model for young-adult women. *Body Image, 7*, 106–116. doi:10.1016/j.bodyim.2010.01.001

Yeung, C. Y. L., & Fukutomi, M. (2008). Japanese body image: Body dissatisfaction, body image-related problems, and effects of magazines exposure on body image. *Bulletin of Tokyo Gakugei University, 59*, 199–209.

4 Moving beyond Body Dissatisfaction and Risky Sexual Behavior
A Critical Review of Positive Body Image and Sexual Health Scholarship

Virginia Ramseyer Winter

The quest to understand the association between positive body image and sexual health is critical. The human experience is an embodied experience and most humans are sexual beings from birth until death. Unfortunately, however, both of these constructs – positive body image and sexual health – are complex and challenging to define and measure. Nevertheless, scholars have innovatively pursued research that adds to our understanding of how body image and sexual health are central to the human experience.

Defining positive body image and sexual health is paramount, given the complexity of these concepts and the myriad ways they are operationalized in research. Positive body image has been defined as a complex construct that is distinct from negative body image and is influenced by one's various social identities, e.g., race (Tylka & Wood-Barcalow, 2015b). Sexual health is similarly complex. The World Health Organization (2006) defines it as:

A state of physical, emotional, mental and social well-being in relation to sexuality; it is not merely the absence of disease, dysfunction or infirmity. Sexual health requires a positive and respectful approach to sexuality and sexual relationships, as well as the possibility of having pleasurable and safe sexual experiences, free of coercion, discrimination and violence. For sexual health to be attained and maintained, the sexual rights of all persons must be respected, protected and fulfilled. (p. 5)

These definitions will be applicable throughout this chapter when the terms "positive body image" and "sexual health" are used. It is important to note that the experience of a positive body image is not synonymous with more narrow dimensions of positive body image that focus on body appreciation, for example. Similarly, sexual health is not tantamount to specific components of sexual health, e.g., contraceptive use. This chapter will address the theoretical foundations behind positive body image and sexual health scholarship, review existing measures and literature, critique the existing literature, and end with recommendations for research, practice, and policy.

Theoretical Foundations

Due to its applied nature, the majority of research on positive body image and sexual health is not firmly grounded in theory, but some scholarship does draw on theory. Objectification theory (Fredrickson & Roberts, 1997) is cited in some literature exploring relations between positive body image and sexual health, despite the theory's strong emphasis on pathology and lack of focus on sexual health variables. Fredrickson and Roberts (1997) posit that sexual objectification in women's everyday lived experiences causes them to view themselves as objects, or to self-objectify. This self-objectification, according to object-ification theory, leads to body shame, anxiety, inability to reach peak motivation states, and a lack of internal awareness. In turn, these nega-tive outcomes lead to depression, eating disorders, and sexual dysfunc-tion (Fredrickson & Roberts, 1997). Research supports most paths of the objectification theory model (Moradi & Huang, 2008) and a couple of studies demonstrate support for sexual behaviors as an additional endogenous variable in the objectification theory model (e.g., Ramseyer Winter, 2017).

The sexual health model (Robinson, Bockting, Simon Rosser, Miner, & Coleman, 2002) is also utilized as a framework in some research in this area. The sexual health model, as applied to HIV prevention, works from the assumption that an improvement in sexual health is an outcome of healthy sexual choices. The model includes ten components of healthy human sexuality, all of which have equal weight. One of these components is body image, making this model relevant to positive body image and sexual health research. Robinson et al. (2002) suggest that the ten components of healthy human sexuality are informed and influenced by sociocultural, interpersonal, and individual characteristics.

Measuring Positive Body Image and Sexual Health

Scholars have used a range of scales and items to measure positive body image and sexual health. This section very briefly explores measures used in this area of research, prior to reviewing the literature on positive body image and sexual health.

Positive Body Image Measures

Researchers utilize a number of scales in body image/sexual health scholarship that measure various components of positive body image. Body satisfaction is the most common component of positive body image found in body image and sexual health literature. It is measured with various scales, including the Body Satisfaction Scale (Slade, Dewey, Newton, Brodie, & Kiemle, 1990), the Multidimensional Body–Self Relations Questionnaire – Body Areas Satisfaction Subscale (Cash, 2000), and the Body Esteem Scale (Franzoi & Shields, 1984). Originally published in 2005 (Avalos, Tylka, & Wood-Barcalow) and revised in 2015 (Tylka & Wood-Barcalow, 2015a), the Body Appreciation Scale (BAS) is one of the most used scales in recent positive body image and sexual health scholarship (e.g., Satinsky, Reece, Dennis, Sanders, & Bardzell, 2012). The BAS includes four components of appreciation: (1) respect for one's body, (2) rejection of cultural expectations of women's bodies, (3) holding favorable opinions of one's body, and (4) acceptance of one's body. The BAS was updated in 2015 (the BAS-2) to be more inclusive and eliminate body dissatisfaction-related language (Tylka & Wood-Barcalow, 2015a).

Sexual Health Measures

Measures used to capture sexual health in body image and sexual health scholarship are narrow in nature and most are related to the prevention of unplanned pregnancy and sexually transmitted infections (STIs), but measure sexual behaviors associated with pregnancy and STIs rather than unplanned pregnancy and STI rates. For example, much of this research explores components of sexual health such as condom use, contraceptive use, and number of sexual partners utilizing single items that are not part of a larger sexual behavior scale. In addition to these, some scholars have explored positive body image as it relates to frequency of sex and sexual function, often using the Derogatis Sexual Functioning Inventory (DSFI; Derogatis & Melisaratos, 1979) as a measurement.

Review of Existing Literature

The following review of literature is organized by the aforementioned measures of sexual health: preventive sexual health, likelihood and frequency of sexual activity, and sexual function. This literature review is not exhaustive, but is representative of the larger body of scholarship.

Preventive Sexual Health

The relationship between positive body image and behaviors that either place one at risk of negative sexuality-related outcomes or prevent such outcomes is more extensive than anything found in other areas of body image and sexual health scholarship. From this research, it appears that associations may differ significantly by gender. Gillen, Lefkowitz, and Shearer (2006) found that more positive appearance evaluation was related to more lifetime sexual partners and more lifetime unprotected sex among undergraduate men. Among undergraduate women in the study, more positive appearance evaluation was related to less lifetime unprotected sex (Gillen et al., 2006). Wiederman and Hurst (1998) found that self-rated facial attractiveness was positively associated with number of lifetime sexual partners among a sample of undergraduate women. However, the findings by Wiederman and Hurst (1998) should be interpreted with caution as they used unvalidated items to measure self-rated attractiveness. These studies examined the associations between body image, number of sex partners, and unprotected sex. However, given the disparate results, more research is needed to fully understand how body image is related to these behaviors.

Other studies have explored relations between positive body image, contraceptive use, and communication about sex. In a study of body appreciation and condom use among a sample of adult women, researchers found that relationship status moderated associations between body appreciation and male condom use by a partner (Ramseyer Winter & Satinsky, 2014). More specifically, body appreciation was significantly related to male condom use by partners among participants with more than one current partner, but body appreciation was not a significant predictor of male condom use by partners among those in monogamous relationships or those who identified as being sexually active but whose sexual encounters were not in the context of a relationship (Ramseyer Winter & Satinsky, 2014). In another study of young adult, primarily White women in heterosexual relationships, Ramseyer Winter and Ruhr (2016) found a positive association between body appreciation and male condom use by a partner as well as a positive association between body appreciation and dual contraceptive use (male condom use by a partner and hormonal contraceptive use by female participants). This area of research suggests positive body image among women may be related to greater use of condoms and hormonal contraceptives. However, additional research is warranted to substantiate these findings.

In terms of communication about sex, research on women shows significant positive associations between positive body image and sex communication, including associations between body appreciation and comfort communicating about sex (Ramseyer Winter, Gillen, & Kennedy, 2016), and between body esteem and asking a partner for their sexual history (Brown, Webb-Bradley, Cobb, Spaw, & Aldridge, 2014). Similarly, among both men and women, Gillen and Markey (2014) found a significant association between positive body image and sex-related communication among a sample of undergraduates. More specifically, as appearance evaluation increased, the likelihood of asking a partner's HIV status and asking a partner to be screened for HIV increased. Taken together, these studies suggest that positive body image may be related to an increased likelihood of communication in the context of a sexual relationship.

Only one known study utilized a composite measure of preventive sexual health that included items such as contraceptive use and STI testing, but also communication about sex, breast exams, and pap smears (Ramseyer Winter, 2017). Among young adult partnered heterosexual women, there was a direct significant relation between body appreciation and preventive sexual behaviors, and an indirect significant relation between these variables through quality of the sexual relationship. This study provides additional support for the notion that positive body image may be related to greater preventive sexual health, at least among women.

Likelihood and Frequency of Sexual Activity

Research suggests positive body image is related to being more likely to have ever had sex. In a sample of men who have sex with men, Kraft, Robinson, Nordstrom, Bockting, and Rosser (2006) found those who perceived themselves as more attractive and had higher levels of body acceptance were more likely to report ever having had anal sex than those with less positive body image. Wiederman and Hurst (1998) utilized a sample of young women and found a significant association between perceived attractiveness and ever having received oral sex.

Research also suggests that positive body image is significantly associated with a higher frequency of sexual activity in heterosexually identified individuals. Using a sample of women who responded to a survey in *Shape* magazine, Ackard, Kearney-Cooke, and Peterson (2000) found that, compared to those who were dissatisfied with their bodies, those who were satisfied reported higher frequency of sex. Similarly, in a 1993 survey of women, Koch, Mansfield, Thurau, and Carey (2005) found that women who reported an increase in feeling attractive over the previous ten years also reported higher frequency of sexual activity.

In another study of college women, researchers found a significant, positive relation between body satisfaction and sexual activity (Lemer, Salafia, & Benson, 2013). Prior to drawing definitive conclusions, additional research is needed to determine if these findings can be replicated with representative samples utilizing validated scales.

Similar results have emerged among samples of sexual minority individuals. In a rare study of primarily bisexually identified women, Zamboni, Robinson, and Bockting (2007) found that greater comfort with one's body was correlated with higher frequency of sexual activity during the previous three months. A study of emerging adult sexual minority men produced similar findings. Researchers found that body pride was positively associated with the number of receptive anal intercourse occasions among gay men (Meanley, Hickok, Johns, Pingel, & Bauermeister, 2014).

Although sexual activity most often occurs in the context of interpersonal relationship(s), few studies have explored positive body image and frequency of sex among couples. Zhaoyang and Cooper (2013) found that among primarily White, exclusively heterosexual couples, frequency of sex was higher among couples when one partner's body satisfaction matched their satisfaction with the other partner's body. Goins, Markey, and Gillen (2012) also found that a higher level of sexual intimacy was related to higher levels of body satisfaction among men in heterosexual relationships. More dyadic research is needed to better understand the complex nature of positive body image and sexual health in the context of interpersonal relationships.

Sexual Function

Another sexual health variable that has been examined in relation to positive body image is sexual functioning. According to Rosen (2000), female sexual function includes the following six domains: (1) desire, (2) arousal, (3) lubrication, (4) orgasm, (5) satisfaction, and (6) pain. In a comprehensive review of the literature, Woertman and van den Brink (2012) described support for an association between body image and each of these six domains. A limited number of studies, however, have explored positive body image and overall sexual function, which may give a broad understanding of relations between body image and sexual functioning. For example, in a sample of primarily White adult women, Satinsky et al. (2012) found that body appreciation significantly predicted overall sexual function, specifically arousal, orgasm, and satisfaction. Although this is a limited body of literature, it suggests that positive body image may be associated with healthier sexual functioning, at least among women.

Critique of Existing Literature

Existing research on positive body image and sexual health has moved the field forward, as it has provided a basic level of understanding of these associations. However, we now need to critically evaluate existing scholarship in light of new knowledge (e.g., a refined definition of positive body image; Tylka and Wood-Barcalow, 2015b) in order to move forward in conducting empirical work, informing theory, and developing interventions. The primary critiques of existing literature relate to a lack of theoretical foundation, complexity in the measures used, and diversity of research participants.

Theoretical Foundation

Although some studies are firmly rooted in either objectification theory or the sexual health model, most research exploring positive body image and sexual health is presented as atheoretical. Although it is unlikely that, and unclear if, these studies are actually atheoretical, what is clear is a lack of communication of the theoretical underpinnings of most scholarship in this area. A strong theoretical foundation has much to offer our research, as theory can lead to research questions, drive the inclusion or exclusion of variables, place embodied experiences in context, and provide a framework for understanding findings in relation to findings in other research. As such, without theory, our research questions, study designs, findings, and implications are underdeveloped and insufficient.

Measurement

Positive body image and sexual health are complex constructs, yet existing research treats them as narrow, singular concepts easily measured by one or two unidimensional scales and, in some cases, one or two unvalidated items. Even in studies (e.g., Ramseyer Winter, 2017) that utilized validated scales (e.g., the Body Appreciation Scale), many did not measure all aspects of positive body image. The same is true for sexual health, as most studies reviewed above measured a couple of sexual health behaviors with single-item measures, such as condom use and number of sex partners. Not only is this a narrow focus, but the focus on sexual risk may unintentionally perpetuate the idea that sexual health and sexual behaviors that place individuals at risk for negative sexuality-related outcomes are synonymous. In fact, sexual health is much broader than behaviors that place one at risk and includes sexual function, pleasure, safety, respect, and more.

These measurement concerns are a significant limitation to existing scholarship, as we cannot understand how positive body image and sexual health relate without measures that reflect their complexity and nuanced nature. Furthermore, without a more comprehensive understanding of these associations, we are limited in our ability to develop innovative interventions that aim to improve positive body image and/or sexual health.

Participant Diversity

Body image research has historically focused on women, as women disproportionately experience body dissatisfaction (Fredrickson & Roberts, 1997; Gillen & Markey, 2016). However, men and sexual minority, transgender, and nonbinary individuals experience romantic and sexual relationships and also live embodied lives. In fact, body image may be influenced by gender and sexual orientation (Markey & Markey, 2014). As such, it is valuable and crucial to understand how body image may relate to sexual health among these populations. Additionally, many body image studies rely on undergraduate students for their samples. There are many advantages to using convenient samples such as these and this research adds important contributions to our understanding of these associations, but these samples also have limitations. Few studies include representative numbers of racial and ethnic minorities and when they do, it is often only Black/African American women. Sexual minority women (e.g., women who have sex with women) are also often excluded from samples. Consequently, our understanding of positive body image and sexual health is primarily limited to young, heterosexually identified, White, cisgender women.

Research has established that body image varies by gender, race, ethnicity, age, and sexual orientation. Further, sexual health is also influenced by identity and sociocultural variables. Refer to Table 4.1 for examples of how body image and sexual health vary by several identities. In sum, existing research has added much to our understanding of these associations, but we ultimately do this area of scholarship and marginalized populations a disservice by limiting our samples to White college women.

Recommendations

Research

Recommendations for future research are directly informed by the aforementioned limitations. The recommendations include: (1) utilization of

Table 4.1 *Examples of how body image and sexual health outcomes vary by sociocultural factors*

	Body image	Sexual health
Gender	Women experience body dissatisfaction at disproportionate rates (Fredrickson & Roberts, 1997).	Sexual double standards partially determine appropriate sexual behavior for women and men (Zaikman & Marks, 2014).
	Mastectomy is associated with an improvement in body satisfaction among trans men (van de Grift et al., 2016).	Men experience orgasm more frequently than women (e.g., Garcia, Lloyd, Wallen, & Fisher, 2014).
	Pregnancy can impact a woman's body image (Hodgkinson, Smith, & Wittkowski, 2014).	Transgender individuals experience sexual violence at a disproportionate rate, when compared to nontransgender individuals (James et al., 2016).
Race/Ethnicity	Black women have higher BMIs and higher levels of body satisfaction, on average, when compared to White women (Grabe & Hyde, 2006).	Racial and ethnic minorities experience higher rates of STIs (CDC, n.d.a).
	Belonging to a racial or ethnic minority group is a protective factor against body dissatisfaction (Grabe & Hyde, 2006).	Women who belong to racial minority groups have less access to contraception than White women (Dehlendorf, Rodriguez, Levy, Borrero, & Steinauer, 2010).
	In addition to body image varying between racial/ethnic groups, there is variation within racial and ethnic groups (Grabe & Hyde, 2006).	Racial and ethnic minorities experience disproportionately high rates of unplanned pregnancy (The Guttmacher Institute, 2016).
Age	Children as young as three assign negative attributes to large body sizes (Spiel, Paxton, & Yager, 2012).	Individuals ages 15–24 account for approximately half of new STI infections (CDC, n.d.b.).
	Body image is an issue for individuals across the lifespan (Tiggemann, 2004).	Older adults are often mistakenly viewed as asexual (Bouman & Kleinplatz, 2015).
	Adolescents experience changes in body composition, which can impact body image (Ricciardelli & Yager, 2015).	Menopause can impact sexual desire among women (USDHHS, n.d.).
Sexual Orientation	Sexual minorities are often excluded from body image and sexual health research (Ramseyer Winter et al., under review).	Men who have sex with men experience high rates of STIs, including HIV (CDC, n.d.c.).
	Body norms may vary among sexual minority communities (Morrison & McCutcheon, 2012).	Lesbian and gay youth have a higher rate of unplanned pregnancy (or impregnating someone) than heterosexual youth (Shantz, 2015).
	Gay men may have poorer body image than heterosexual men because they are subjected to the male gaze (Wiseman & Moradi, 2010).	Lesbian women are significantly more likely to experience orgasm than heterosexual or bisexual women (Garcia et al., 2014).

Note: STI = sexually transmitted infection

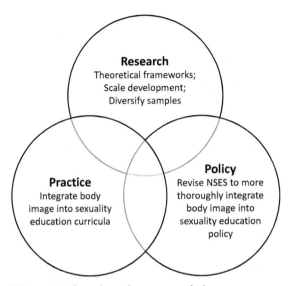

Figure 4.1 Overview of recommendations

existing theoretical frameworks in positive body image/sexual health research; (2) positive body image theory construction; (3) comprehensive positive body image scale development; (4) comprehensive sexual health scale development; and (5) recruitment of diverse samples.

Although there is no specific theory that primarily aims to predict and explain relationships between positive body image and sexual health, there are existing theories that can be useful in informing and making sense of this scholarship. As mentioned previously, objectification theory and the sexual health model have been employed in this research. In addition to these, scholars should consider drawing on or modifying existing theories and models. For example, the tripartite influence model of body image (Thompson, Heinberg, Altabe, & Tantleff-Dunn, 1999) suggests that body image is influenced by parents, media, and peers. It is possible that positive body image in particular is also influenced by these forces. Ecological systems theory (Bronfenbrenner, 1977) could also be used to understand how different systems do and could influence positive body image. Relational–cultural theory (Miller, 1976) is particularly relevant to positive body image and sexual health research as it accounts for relational context, such as romantic relationships. Finally, intersectionality theory (Collins, 1993) has a lot to offer body image research that explores positive body image and sexual health among participants with diverse lived experiences. Furthermore, scholars should utilize existing research to develop and test new theories that aim to explain and predict these relations.

Researchers have used myriad positive body image measures, each measuring different facets of this complex construct. As pointed out in the literature review, some research has relied on unvalidated measures and items that are components of positive body image, but do not fully represent positive body image. The inconsistency in measurement makes it impossible to compare results across studies. To move this research forward, the ability to make these comparisons is essential. Researchers should undertake scale development to create and test the psychometric properties of comprehensive measures of positive body image. However, this task is challenging and will therefore take time. In the meantime, researchers should use several validated measures in their research, aiming to capture as many facets of positive body image as possible. As previously mentioned, there are a number of validated positive body image scales from which to choose. For example, the recently developed Broad Conceptualization of Beauty Scale (Tylka & Iannantuono, 2016) captures a facet of positive body image that was previously overlooked. It should be included in future positive body image/sexual health scholarship.

Like positive body image, sexual health is difficult to measure comprehensively. The ten components of the sexual health model provide a possible framework for a comprehensive measure. The DFSI is likely the most comprehensive existing measure and could be used in combination with other validated scales to thoroughly assess sexual health. The DFSI includes the following subscales: information, experiences, drive, attitudes, psychological symptoms, affect, gender role definitions, fantasy, body image, and sexual satisfaction (Derogatis & Melisaratos, 1979). Otherwise, efforts must be undertaken to develop, validate, and utilize measures of sexual health that encompass the many components of this complex construct.

Finally, future research needs to utilize more diverse samples in terms of gender, gender identity, race, ethnicity, age, and sexual orientation. Representative samples are the gold standard but are not always possible. Nonrepresentative samples can still be inclusive of diverse populations, but this will require researchers to utilize different and sometimes creative recruitment methods. Social media and technology offer opportunities to do just that. For example, researchers can utilize www.reddit.com by posting on relevant subreddits, which are bulletin boards organized by interest/topic. Posting on subreddits requires an account and is a no-cost option for participant recruitment. There are subreddits organized by race, ethnicity, gender, feminism, sexual orientation, and more. By posting on the subreddits of interest, researchers can recruit more diverse samples. Further, Amazon's Mechanical Turk (MTurk; www.mturk.com/mturk/welcome) is a low-cost option that gives researchers access to hundreds of thousands of potential participants across the world. There are also services available to recruit participants. For example, Qualtrics® can recruit a representative sample for a fee. By utilizing these methodologies, researchers' understanding of how positive body image relates to sexual health among diverse samples could be improved.

Defining Sex Education

Sex education is the provision of information about bodily development, sex, sexuality, and relationships, along with skills-building to help young people communicate about and make informed decisions regarding sex and their sexual health. Sex education should occur throughout a student's grade levels, with information appropriate to students' development and cultural background. It should include information about puberty and reproduction, abstinence, contraception and condoms, relationships, sexual violence prevention, body image, gender identity and sexual orientation. It should be taught by trained teachers. Sex education should be informed by evidence of what works best to prevent unintended pregnancy and sexually transmitted infections, but it should also respect young people's right to complete and honest information. Sex education should treat sexual development as a normal, natural part of human development.

Sex education can help young people:

- Avoid negative health consequences
- Communicate about sexuality and sexual health
- Delay sex until they are ready
- Understand healthy and unhealthy relationships
- Understand, value, and feel autonomy over their bodies
- Respect others' right to bodily autonomy
- Show dignity and respect for all people, regardless of sexual orientation or gender identity
- Protect their academic success

Source: www.futureofsexed.org/youthhealthrights.html

Practice and Policy

Given the associations between positive body image and sexual health, the most obvious point of intervention is sexual health education. Comprehensive sexuality education offers an opportunity to provide youth with knowledge and skills related to body image in addition to standard medically accurate sexual health information and associated sexual health skills. Body image is included in some sexual health curricula, but is often an afterthought. Intentionally including body image in sexuality education is an important future direction. Additionally, the Sexual Health Model (Robinson et al., 2002) provides a theoretical foundation for incorporating body image into sexuality education. It is possible that doing this would lead to better sexual health among youth than traditional sexuality education that excludes or includes very limited body image information.

Body image content could include information and skills such as rejecting the thin-ideal, critically evaluating media content, recognizing ways in which individuals perpetuate the thin-ideal, and developing solutions to address these issues. However, this content should not be included without reviewing and learning from existing body image curricula. For example, The Body Project is evidence-based and could inform content included in sexuality education (Stice, Marti, Spoor, Presnell, & Shaw, 2008; Stice, Mazotti, Weibel, & Agras, 2000). However, given the aforementioned limitations in positive body image and sexual health research, such interventions should be rigorously evaluated to provide evidence that including body image in sexuality education curricula leads to better sexual health than is the case for curricula without body image content.

Delivering sexuality education is directly concomitant to sexuality education policy. The National Sexuality Education Standards: Core Content and Skills, K-12 (NSES) were published as part of the Future of Sex Education initiative (Future of Sex Education Initiative [FOSE], 2012). The NSES offers minimum standards of age-appropriate content and skills related to human sexuality and includes the following secondary topic areas: (1) anatomy and physiology, (2) puberty and adolescent development, (3) identity, (4) pregnancy and reproduction, (5) sexually transmitted diseases and HIV, (6) health relationships, and (7) personal safety. The NSES provides standard outcomes for the end of grades 2, 5, 8, and 12. There are no indicators related to body image for the end of second grade, but there are standards for the other three grades. According to the NSES (2012), by the end of fifth grade, students should be able to "describe how friends, family, media, society and culture can influence ideas about body image" (p. 14). The standard is the same for the end of eighth and twelfth grades.

These standards are a great start, but, based on existing scholarship, the minimum education related to body image has not been met. As such, my first recommendation to revise the NSES is to add body image-related indicators to second grade. Children experience body dissatisfaction as early as preschool (Tatangelo, McCabe, Mellor, & Mealey, 2016). Thus, addressing body image in kindergarten and first and second grade is appropriate. Additionally, the NSES should be revised to include skills related to rejecting the thin ideal and promoting body positivity at each grade level. Research suggests that girls as young as elementary school age (6–12 years) internalize the thin ideal seen in the media and girls who rejected objectifying images of women had higher body esteem than those who did not reject the images (Murnen, Smolak, Mills, & Good, 2003). In sum, the NSES provide a starting point for integrating body image into sexuality education curricula, but should be revised to comprehensively improve youth sexual health.

Conclusion

Positive body image and sexual health research has burgeoned in recent years, leading to a collection of scholarship that suggests associations that have significant implications for sexual health. Collectively, this body of research suggests positive body image is related to being more likely to engage in preventive sexual behaviors, being more likely to have ever had sex, having sex more frequently, and better sexual function. Researchers should be applauded for these efforts, but should continue to be engaged in these lines of inquiry, as the existing literature has some important limitations. Based on these limitations, I have made specific recommendations for moving this body of work forward. These include utilizing existing theoretical frameworks, theory construction, positive body image and sexual health scale development, and inclusion of diverse research participants. Incorporating these recommendations will strengthen this area of scholarship but, more importantly, may inform interventions that aim to improve body image and sexual health.

References

Ackard, D. M., Kearney-Cooke, A., & Peterson, C. B. (2000). Effect of body image and self-image on women's sexual behaviors. *International Journal of Eating Disorders, 28*, 422–429. doi:10.1002/1098-108X(200012)28:4<422:: AID-EAT10>3.0.CO;2-1

Avalos, L., Tylka, T. L., & Wood-Barcalow, N. (2005). The Body Appreciation Scale: Development and psychometric evaluation. *Body Image, 2*, 285–297. doi:10.1016/j.bodyim.2005.06.002

Bouman, W. P., & Kleinplatz, P. J. (2015). Moving towards understanding greater diversity and fluidity of sexual expression of older people. *Sexual and Relationship Therapy, 30*, 1–3. doi:10.1080/14681994.2015.990192

Bronfenbrenner, U. (1977). Toward an experimental ecology of human development. *American Psychologist, 32*, 513.

Brown, D. L., Webb-Bradley, T., Cobb, P. D., Spaw, D., & Aldridge, K. N. (2014). African American women's safer sexual practices: The influence of ethnic-racial socialisation and body esteem. *Culture, Health & Sexuality, 16*, 518–532. doi:10.1080/13691058.2014.891048

Cash, T. F. (2000). *The Multidimensional Body-Self Relations Questionnaire user's manual.* Available from the author at www.bodyimages.com

Centers for Disease Control and Prevention (CDC) (n.d.a.). *STDs in racial and ethnic minorities.* Retrieved on April 1, 2017 from www.cdc.gov/std/stats15/minorities.htm

Centers for Disease Control and Prevention (CDC) (n.d.b.). *STDs in racial and ethnic minorities.* Retrieved on April 28, 2017 from www.cdc.gov/std/life-stages-populations/adolescents-youngadults.htm

Centers for Disease Control and Prevention (CDC) (n.d.c.). *Gay, bisexual, and other men who have sex with men (MSM).* Retrieved on April 28, 2017 from www.cdc.gov/std/life-stages-populations/msm.htm

Collins, P. H. (1993). Toward a new vision: Race, class, and gender as categories of analysis and connection. *Race, Sex & Class, 1*, 25–45.

Dehlendorf, C., Rodriguez, M. I., Levy, K., Borrero, S., & Steinauer, J. (2010). Disparities in family planning. *American Journal of Obstetrics and Gynecology, 202*, 214–220. doi:10.1016/j.ajog.2009.08.022

Derogatis, L. R., & Melisaratos, N. (1979). The DSFI: A multidimensional measure of sexual functioning. *Journal of Sex & Marital Therapy, 5*, 244–281. doi:10.1080/00926237908403732

Dyer, A., Borgmann, E., Kleindienst, N., Feldmann Jr, R. E., Vocks, S., & Bohus, M. (2013). Body image in patients with posttraumatic stress disorder after childhood sexual abuse and co-occurring eating disorder. *Psychopathology, 46*, 186–191.

Franzoi, S. L., & Shields, S. A. (1984). The Body Esteem Scale: Multidimensional structure and sex differences in a college population. *Journal of Personality Assessment, 48*, 173–178. doi:10.1207/s15327752jpa4802_12

Fredrickson, B. L., & Roberts, T. A. (1997). Objectification theory. *Psychology of Women Quarterly, 21*, 173–206. doi:10.1111/j.1471-6402.1997.tb00108.x

Future of Sex Education Initiative. (2012). *National sexuality education standards: Core content and skills, K-12* [special publication of the Journal of School Health]. Retrieved on April 28, 2017 from www.futureofsexeducation.org/documents/josh-fose-standards-web.pdf

Garcia, J. R., Lloyd, E. A., Wallen, K., & Fisher, H. E. (2014). Variation in orgasm occurrence by sexual orientation in a sample of U.S. singles. *Journal of Sexual Medicine, 11*, 2645–2652. doi:10.1111/jsm.12669

Gillen, M. M., Lefkowitz, E. S., & Shearer, C. L. (2006). Does body image play a role in risky sexual behavior and attitudes? *Journal of Youth and Adolescence, 35*, 243–255. doi:10.1007/s10964-005-9005-6

Gillen, M. M., & Markey, C. N. (2014). Body image and HIV risk among college students. *American Journal of Health Behavior, 38,* 816–822. doi:10.5993/AJHB.38.6.3

(2016). Body image and mental health. In H. S. Friedman (Ed.), *Encyclopedia of mental health* (2nd ed.) (pp. 187–192). Waltham: Academic Press.

Goins, L. B., Markey, C. N., & Gillen, M. M. (2012). Understanding men's body image in the context of their romantic relationships. *American Journal of Men's Health, 6,* 240–248. doi:10.1177/1557988311431007

Grabe, S., & Hyde, J. S. (2006). Ethnicity and body dissatisfaction among women in the United States: A meta-analysis. *Psychological Bulletin, 132,* 622–640. doi:10.1037/0033-2909.132.4.622

The Guttmacher Institute (2016). *Unintended pregnancy in the United States.* New York: The Guttmacher Institute. Retrieved on April 28, 2017 from www.guttmacher.org/fact-sheet/unintended-pregnancy-united-states

Hodgkinson, E. L., Smith, D. M., & Wittkowski, A. (2014). Women's experiences of their pregnancy and postpartum body image: A systematic review and meta-synthesis. *BMC Pregnancy and Childbirth, 14,* 330. doi:10.1186/1471-2393-14-330

James, S. E., Herman, J. L., Rankin, S., Keisling, M., Mottet, L., & Anafi, M. (2016). *The report of the 2015 U.S. Transgender Survey.* Washington, DC: National Center for Transgender Equality.

Koch, P. B., Mansfield, P. K., Thurau, D., & Carey, M. (2005). "Feeling frumpy": The relationships between body image and sexual response changes in midlife women. *Journal of Sex Research, 42,* 215–223.

Kraft, C., Robinson, B. B. E., Nordstrom, D. L., Bockting, W. O., & Rosser, B. R. S. (2006). Obesity, body image, and unsafe sex in men who have sex with men. *Archives of Sexual Behavior, 35,* 587–595. doi:10.1007/s10508-006-9059-x

Lemer, J. L., Salafia, E. H. B., & Benson, K. E. (2013). The relationship between college women's sexual attitudes and sexual activity: The mediating role of body image. *International Journal of Sexual Health, 25,* 104–114. doi:10.1080/19317611.2012.722593

Markey, C. N. & Markey, P. M. (2014). Gender, sexual orientation, and romantic partner influence on body dissatisfaction: An examination of heterosexual and lesbian women and their partners. *Journal of Social and Personal Relationships, 31,* 162–177. doi:10.1177/0265407513489472.

Meanley, S., Hickok, A., Johns, M. M., Pingel, E. S., & Bauermeister, J. A. (2014). Body mass index, body esteem, and unprotected receptive anal intercourse among young men who have sex with men who seek partners online. *Archives of Sexual Behavior, 43,* 735–744. doi:10.1007/s10508-013-0159-0

Mendelson, B. K., White, D. R., & Mendelson M. J. (1998). Manual for the body-esteem scale for adolescents and adults. Unpublished manuscript, Center for Research in Human Development, Montreal, Quebec, Canada.

Miller, J. (1976). *Toward a new psychology of women.* Boston: Beacon Press.

Moradi, B., & Huang, Y. P. (2008). Objectification theory and psychology of women: A decade of advances and future directions. *Psychology of Women Quarterly, 32,* 377–398. doi:10.1111/j.1471-6402.2008.00452.x

Morrison, T., & McCutcheon, J. (2012). Body image among gay, lesbian, and bisexual individuals. In T. Cash (Ed.), *Encyclopedia of body image and human appearance* (Vol. 1, pp. 103–107). Boston: Academic Press.

Murnen, S. K., Smolak, L., Mills, J. A., & Good, L. (2003). Thin, sexy women and strong, muscular men: Grade-school children's responses to objectified images of women and men. *Sex Roles, 49*, 427–437. doi:10.1023/a:1025868320206

Ramseyer Winter, V. (2017). Toward a relational understanding of objectification, body image, and preventive sexual health. *Journal of Sex Research, 54*, 341–350. doi:10.1080/00224499.2016.1190807

Ramseyer Winter, V., Gillen, M. M., & Kennedy, A. K. (2018). Associations between body appreciation and comfort communicating about sex: A brief report. *Health Communication, 33* (3), 359–362. doi:10.1080/10410236.2016.1255845

Ramseyer Winter, V., & Ruhr, L. R. (2016). Body appreciation and contraceptive use among college women: A brief report. *International Journal of Sexual Health, 29* (2), 168–172. doi:10.1080/19317611.2016.1259707

Ramseyer Winter, V., & Satinsky, S. (2014). Body appreciation, sexual relationship status, and protective sexual behaviors in women. *Body Image, 11*, 36–42. doi:10.1016/j.bodyim.2013.08.004

Ricciardelli, L. A., & Yager, Z. (2015). *Adolescence and body image: From development to preventing dissatisfaction.* New York: Routledge.

Robinson, B. B. E., Bockting, W. O., Simon Rosser, B. R., Miner, M., & Coleman, E. (2002). The Sexual Health Model: Application of a sexological approach to HIV prevention. *Health Education Research, 17*, 43–57. doi:10.1093/her/17.1.43

Rosen, R., Brown, C., Heiman, J., Leiblum, S., Meston, C., Shabsigh, R., … D'Agostino Jr, R. (2000). The Female Sexual Function Index (FSFI): A multidimensional self-report instrument for the assessment of female sexual function. *Journal of Sex & Marital Therapy, 26*, 191–208. doi:10.1080/009262300278597

Satinsky, S., Reece, M., Dennis, B., Sanders, S., & Bardzell, S. (2012). An assessment of body appreciation and its relationship to sexual function in women. *Body Image, 9*, 137–144. doi:10.1016/j.bodyim.2011.09.007

Secord, P. F., & Jourard, S. M. (1953). The appraisal of body-cathexis: Body-cathexis and the self. *Journal of Consulting Psychology, 17*, 343. doi: 10.1037/h0060689

Shantz, K. (2015). *Pregnancy risk among bisexual, lesbian, and gay youth: What does research tell us?* Ithaca: ACT for Youth Center for Excellence.

Slade, P. D., Dewey, M. E., Newton, T., Brodie, D., & Kiemle, G. (1990). Development and preliminary validation of the Body Satisfaction Scale (BSS). *Psychology and Health, 4*, 213–220.

Spiel, E. C., Paxton, S. J., & Yager, Z. (2012). Weight attitudes in 3- to 5-year-old children: Age differences and cross-sectional predictors. *Body Image, 9*, 524–527. doi:http://dx.doi.org/10.1016/j.bodyim.2012.07.006

Stice, E., Marti, C. N., Spoor, S., Presnell, K., & Shaw, H. (2008). Dissonance and healthy weight eating disorder prevention programs: Long-term effects from a randomized efficacy trial. *Journal of Consulting and Clinical Psychology*, *76*, 329–340. doi:10.1037/0022-006X.76.2.329

Stice, E., Mazotti, L., Weibel, D., & Agras, W. S. (2000). Dissonance prevention program decreases thin-ideal internalization, body dissatisfaction, dieting, negative affect, and bulimic symptoms: A preliminary experiment. *International Journal of Eating Disorders*, *27*, 206–217. doi:10.1002/(SICI) 1098-108X(200003)27:2<206::AID-EAT9>3.0.CO;2-D

Tatangelo, G., McCabe, M., Mellor, D., & Mealey, A. (2016). A systematic review of body dissatisfaction and sociocultural messages related to the body among preschool children. *Body Image*, *18*, 86–95. doi:https://doi.org/ 10.1016/j.bodyim.2016.06.003

Thompson, J. K., Heinberg, L. J., Altabe, M., & Tantleff-Dunn, S. (1999). *Exacting beauty: Theory, assessment, and treatment of body image disturbance*. Washington, DC: American Psychological Association.

Tiggemann, M. (2004). Body image across the adult life span: Stability and change. *Body Image*, *1*, 29–41. doi:10.1016/S1740-1445(03)00002-0

Tylka, T. L., & Iannantuono, A. C. (2016). Perceiving beauty in all women: Psychometric evaluation of the Broad Conceptualization of Beauty Scale. *Body Image*, *17*, 67–81. doi:http://dx.doi.org/10.1016/ j.bodyim.2016.02.005

Tylka, T. L., & Wood-Barcalow, N. L. (2015a). The Body Appreciation Scale-2: Item refinement and psychometric evaluation. *Body Image*, *12*, 53–67. doi:10.1016/j.bodyim.2014.09.006

(2015b). What is and what is not positive body image? Conceptual foundations and construct definition. *Body Image*, *14*, 118–129. doi:http://dx.doi.org/ 10.1016/j.bodyim.2015.04.001

United States Department of Health and Human Services Office of Women's Health (USDHHS). (n.d.) *Menopause and menopause treatments*. Retrieved June 14, 2017 from www.womenshealth.gov/a-z-topics/menopause-and-menopause-treatments.

van de Grift, T. C., Kreukels, B. P. C., Elfering, L., Özer, M., Bouman, M.-B., Buncamper, M. E., … Mullender, M. G. (2016). Body image in transmen: Multidimensional measurement and the effects of mastectomy. *The Journal of Sexual Medicine*, *13*, 1778–1786. doi:http://dx.doi.org/10.1016/ j.jsxm.2016.09.003

Wiederman, M., & Hurst, S. (1998). Body size, physical attractiveness, and body image among young adult women: Relationships to sexual experience and sexual esteem. *The Journal of Sex Research*, *35*, 272–281. doi:10.1080/ 00224499809551943

Wiseman, M. C., & Moradi, B. (2010). Body image and eating disorder symptoms in sexual minority men: A test and extension of objectification theory. *Journal of Counseling Psychology*, *57*, 154. doi:10.1037/a0018937

Woertman, L., & van den Brink, F. (2012). Body image and female sexual functioning and behavior: A review. *Journal of Sex Research*, *49*, 184–211. doi:10.1080/00224499.2012.658586

World Health Organization. Sexual and Reproductive Health. www.who.int/ reproductivehealth/topics/gender_rights/sexual_health/en/

Zaikman, Y., & Marks, M. J. (2014). Ambivalent sexism and the sexual double standard. *Sex Roles, 71,* 333–344. doi:10.1007/s11199-014-0417-1

Zamboni, B. D., Robinson, B. B. E., & Bockting, W. O. (2007). Body image and sexual functioning among bisexual women. *Journal of Bisexuality, 6,* 7–26. doi:10.1300/J159v06n04_02

Zhaoyang, R. X., & Cooper, M. L. (2013). Body satisfaction and couple's daily sexual experience: A dyadic perspective. *Archives of Sexual Behavior, 42,* 985–998. doi:10.1007/s10508-013-0082-4

5   Appearance-Related Practices
Can They Be Part of a Positive Body Image?

Kristina Holmqvist Gattario and Carolina Lunde

Today's appearance-focused culture, which is prominent in industrialized countries worldwide, presents people with a plethora of alternatives with which to alter their appearances. Extensive use of cosmetics, skin care products, and fashion clothing, or engagement in activities such as appearance-oriented physical exercise, dieting, tanning, and hair removal, demonstrates the importance that is placed on physical appearance and attractiveness. Consumers worldwide spend $382 billion each year on fragrances, cosmetics, and toiletries alone (Jones, 2010). The scope of appearance-related practices also bears witness to the notions that our physical appearance communicates something important about who we are, that the body is viewed as being malleable, and that people are obliged to invest in their appearance.

As we begin this chapter, we suggest that appearance-related practices can be viewed on a continuum, ranging from casual everyday behaviors in which many people engage (e.g., combing your hair or wearing clothes that make you feel good) to much more extreme practices (e.g., cosmetic surgery). Some practices are culturally specific (e.g., skin bleaching), although as Western body ideals encroach on non-Western cultures through globalization, practices seem to become more homogenous (Walker & Murray, 2012). In line with this observation, Jones (2010) has noted that a country's absolute spending on beauty products grows alongside increased prosperity.

Appearance-related practices are also extremely gendered, and mark constructions of femininity and masculinity (Anderson-Fye, 2012). In many societies, women are more likely (and expected) to wear particular kinds of clothes, pierce their ears, remove leg and axillary hair, and use makeup, while men are more likely to engage in weightlifting to increase the size of their muscles, to groom their beards, or to remove hair from their backs. Many of these appearance-related behaviors are normative, like women's removal of axillary hair, and there are punishments for not adhering to these practices (e.g., stigmatization). In particular for girls and women, engaging in the societal discourse around appearance-related practices, such as fashion and makeup, may be an important way to demonstrate feminine belonging, as investment in appearance is a powerful feminine norm in Westernized societies (Mahalik et al., 2005).

Are Appearance-Related Practices Good or Bad?

From the perspective of the growing multimillion-dollar beauty industry, the fact that people invest in their appearance is highly profitable (Jones, 2010). From the viewpoint of body image research, however, appearance-related behaviors are usually problematized. They are often considered an outward sign of body image concerns or a (too) strong emphasis on physical appearance for self-image and identity. Indeed, physical appearance, and the investments that are made in physical appearance, can become important identity markers. Buying an expensive lipstick or designer apparel means buying something else as well – the symbolic meaning of that object, which constitutes the core of consumer culture. Dittmar (2008), relying on the arguments from Mead's symbolic interactionism, states that material objects and appearance-related investments serve as "imaginary points of view" from which to see the self. The marketing of various appearance-related practices, such as using makeup, tanning, using shapewear, dieting, exercising, and undergoing cosmetic surgery, promises a happy, social, wealthy, skinny, healthy, sexual life. Numerous studies show that the internalization of these ideas and values, equating socially constructed notions of a "perfect" body with a good, fulfilling life, is doubtlessly associated with many adverse body image outcomes (e.g., Cash & Smolak, 2011).

In this chapter, however, we explore the question: Are appearance-related practices and behaviors always "bad," or can they also be associated with healthy outcomes and positive body image? Tentatively, we hypothesize that there may be several ways of expressing a positive body image – for example, by engaging in different behaviors related to the presentation of one's physical self. Indeed, it may be the case that some of the appearance-related practices in which people engage have more benefits than costs. This chapter will explore the potential circumstances for this.

Since research on positive body image began to flourish at the beginning of this decade, positive body image has mostly been associated with mindful, embodying, nonappearance-related activities – such as mindful eating, yoga, or dancing. For instance, body appreciation, one component of positive body image, focuses on body functionality and rejection of stereotypical beauty ideals (Frisén & Holmqvist, 2010;

Holmqvist & Frisén, 2012; Wood-Barcalow et al., 2010). Indeed, these descriptions may not align with high engagement in appearance-related behaviors. If a person appreciates his or her body, focuses more on what the body can do rather than how it looks, and criticizes appearance ideals as unrealistic and unnatural, would that person still invest in his or her appearance?

To provide more nuance to our understanding of positive body image and appearance-related practices, Tylka and Wood-Barcalow (2015) have introduced the concept of *adaptive appearance investment*. This is discussed as one important component of a positive body image. Adaptive appearance investment is defined as "regularly engaging in appearance-related self-care, such as grooming behaviors that protect an individual's sense of style and personality – it is enhancing one's natural features via benign methods" (p. 123). Although the use of well-fitting clothes or mascara may be considered as enhancing one's natural features via benign methods, most people would probably agree that getting breast implants or a nose job is not adaptive appearance investment. Tylka and Wood-Barcalow (2015) underscore that adaptive appearance investment precludes engaging in potentially dangerous behaviors to change one's appearance in order to fit societal beauty standards, basing self-worth on appearance, or being preoccupied with appearance-fixing behaviors. Yet, it may be difficult to draw the line between adaptive and maladaptive appearance investment. Are behaviors that focus on projecting one's style and unique personality always adaptive, given that they are probably influenced by societal norms and ideals? When does self-care shift into preoccupation? Who will be the judge of what behaviors are adaptive versus maladaptive? Or is all appearance investment in fact maladaptive, as it maintains and reinforces restrictive gender stereotypes and body objectification?

In the next section, this chapter will introduce theoretical frameworks and models that may explain why people invest in appearance-related practices, how the meaning and importance of these practices may differ between people, and why. The chapter will continue with a discussion of the complex nature of appearance-related practices, suggesting that describing them as solely bad and related to negative body image may be too simplistic. Based on a review of the existing literature, the associations between appearance-related practices and positive body image will be presented, organized into three patterns. Since most body image research has focused on women's appearance-related practices, women's practices will represent the majority of examples used throughout this chapter. When feasible, men's appearance-related practices will also be discussed.

Why Do People Invest in Appearance at All?

In the current literature, various theoretical frameworks are used to explain why people engage in appearance-related practices. These frameworks yield different answers as to why these practices are common. They tend to differ in scope and the level of analysis, whether focusing on the individual, his or her social environments, or structures in society. One perspective is the evolutionary psychology one. This focuses on humans as a biological organism, thus claiming to be universal rather than cultural-specific. From the viewpoint of this perspective, appearance-related practices may be interpreted as part of a natural, biological process of attracting a partner. The evolutionary perspective suggests that what people find physically attractive is related to what is thought to be beneficial for their reproduction (Swami & Harris, 2012). A person with a symmetrical face, for instance, signals good health and resistance to environmental and genetic stressors; such a face is thus perceived to be more attractive as it enhances reproductive success. This idea may also be applied to considerations that people with a youthful appearance are attractive, as youthfulness may be seen as synonymous with fertility. Having a symmetrical face and looking young, in turn, represent idealized body features that can be pursued through appearance-related practices (e.g., makeup, clothes, cosmetic surgery). From an evolutionary perspective, hence, one might argue that individuals will engage in appearance-related practices to attempt to outrival other competitors in the process of attracting a partner. Common critiques of this perspective are that it is difficult to test, that it is heteronormative, and that it significantly downplays the role of social and cultural forces for the individual.

In contrast, other common perspectives focus on appearance-related practices as a consequence of cognitions and behaviors being internalized from the social environment. According to social learning theory (Bandura, 1977), learning occurs through social modeling and imitation of others. Body image research based on the *tripartite influence model* (Thompson, Coovert, & Stormer, 1999) has identified media, family, and friends as powerful social agents which are imitated, hence highly influencing the extent to which people engage in appearance-related practices. Recent research has shown, for instance, that girls with mothers and friends who try to decrease their body size by dieting, and girls who are more sensitive to media messages, are more likely to start dieting themselves (Balantekin, Birch, & Savage, 2017; Coffman, Balantekin, & Savage, 2016). In addition, the act of obtaining a tattoo, which is an increasingly popular appearance-related practice among young adults (statisticbrain.com), has been found to be more common in individuals who have friends and family that have tattoos (Roberts, Koch, Armstrong, & Owen, 2006). In addition, social learning takes place when family and friends positively comment on individuals' appearances after their having engaged in appearance-related practices, which further reinforces these practices (Hill, Ogletree, & McCrary, 2016).

Finally, feminist perspectives problematize the fact that appearance-related practices are most common among women. Feminists argue that women's appearance investment needs to be understood through the lens of gendered power structures in society, and highlight that appearance practices reinforce female subordination and male dominance (Murnen & Seabrook, 2012). Women's clothing, for example, emphasizes women's submissive, objectified gender role, as it often restricts their physical movements and serves to either hide or accentuate sexualized body parts. Bartky (1990) argues that even though women's engagement in appearance-related rituals may give them a sense of control and positive attention from others, it will lead to little real respect or power in society. Although the most common viewpoint within feminist perspectives is that beauty practices reinforce women's disempowerment, some have instead suggested that women can derive power from beauty practices (Murnen & Seabrook, 2012). In this respect, engaging in beauty practices could be considered a woman's autonomous choice, and an empowering act in terms of deciding for herself on how to treat her own body. One illustration is the American singer Lady Gaga, whom Halberstam (2012), among others, views as inhabiting a new model of feminism. Lady Gaga critiques fixed gender roles, challenging and exposing notions of both femininity and masculinity. One well-known example is her wearing a "meat dress" to the MTV Music Awards in 2010. Although the meat dress was interpreted in many different ways, one suggestion was that it was a statement against women being treated as objects.

Thus, appearance-related practices need not only be understood from one single perspective, as more than one of these frameworks may be "right." Some aspects of the evolutionary framework (e.g., attempting to look young) are likely to be useful but that does not mean that social learning and influences of gendered power structures are not also taking place at the same time. We suggest that these frameworks complement each other and are all required in order to achieve a better understanding of appearance-related practices.

Importance and Meaning of Appearance Investment

To understand the range of existing appearance-related practices and their relation to body image, we need first to understand that the importance and meaning of these practices may differ between people. More than a decade ago, Cash, Melnyk, and Hrabosky (2004) proposed that individuals' appearance investment might mean different things depending on the cognitive-behavioral processes involved in terms of the salience of appearance in their lives. Two central processes have been identified: self-evaluative salience and motivational salience. Self-evaluative salience refers to the extent to which individuals define or measure their self-worth by their physical appearance. High self-evaluative salience has been considered a more maladaptive form of appearance investment as it is associated with more negative body image, quality of life, and self-esteem; more unhealthy eating attitudes; and more negative fluctuations in day-to-day body satisfaction (Melnyk, Cash, & Janda, 2004).

Motivational salience, on the other hand, refers to the extent to which people attend to their appearance and engage in appearance-managing behaviors. These behaviors may be grooming as well as beautifying practices, but they can be done for different reasons. Motivational salience has been found to be unrelated to body image, quality of life, self-esteem, and day-to-day fluctuations in body satisfaction (Melnyk, Cash, & Janda, 2004). However, motivational salience has also been found to be positively related to internalization of current ideals of beauty as well as unhealthy eating attitudes (for women only; Cash, Melnyk, & Hrabosky, 2004). These findings indicate that appearance-related practices are not necessarily negative, and that we need to examine not only the extent to which individuals engage in appearance-related practices, but also the *meanings* and *importance* they attribute to these practices.

People Have Different Motives for Engaging in Appearance-Related Behaviors

Closely related to the meanings and importance attributed to appearance-related practices are individuals' motives for engaging in these. The final theoretical framework that will be presented is called *self-determination theory* (SDT). An adaptation of this framework can be used to understand the motivational dynamics of adaptive and maladaptive appearance investment. This is illustrated in Figure 5.1 and subsequently discussed.

SDT postulates that there are three basic psychological needs that, if satisfied, aid individuals' psychological health and well-being: the needs of *autonomy* (perceiving oneself and one's behavior as an expression of the self), *competence* (a sense of confidence), and *relatedness* (connecting to and

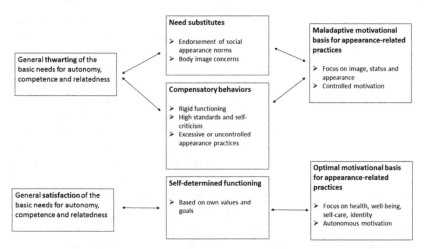

Figure 5.1 Applying SDT and basic needs theory to the dynamics of appearance-related behaviors
Note: Modified from Vertstuyf et al. (2012)

caring for others, being cared for, and belongingness). According to the theory, thwarted basic needs are an important contributor to the pursuit of need substitutes, compensatory behaviors, and maladaptive functioning.

In the context of the present chapter, need substitutes may include a stronger endorsement of social appearance norms. Compensatory behaviors may include setting unrealistically high self-standards for one's appearance. According to the model, these will contribute to a maladaptive motivational basis for appearance-related practices which focuses on image, status, and appearance and is driven by controlled motivation. The latter refers to engaging in appearance-related behaviors due to pressure, such as strong pressure to adhere to appearance norms and ideals. In line with this, Patton et al. (2014), showed that attachment anxiety – which may indicate an insufficiently met relatedness need – rendered girls and young women (aged 12–24) more susceptible to thin-ideal media messages and sociocultural appearance pressures. The authors argued that poorer quality attachment bonds (i.e., attachment anxiety) may be one of the developmental factors predisposing individuals to an attentional bias towards external role models, such as people embodying "successful happy lives" in the media, a heightened fear of negative evaluation and criticism, and thus, appearance preoccupation and body dissatisfaction. We believe that this reasoning bears resemblance to Cash's notion of maladaptive appearance investment, and the hazards of defining one's self-worth by physical appearance.

In contrast, basic needs satisfaction may result in a more optimal motivational basis for appearance-related behaviors. Basic needs satisfaction results in *self-determined functioning*, which in this context would refer to engaging in appearance-related practices as a result of full choice rather than as a result of pressure, and because it reflects one's goals and values. Motives to invest in appearance instead tend to focus on internal benefits (e.g., health, well-being, self-care, identity). An example, as discussed earlier in this chapter, is engaging in appearance self-care for reasons of enjoyment and because it is viewed as an important part of one's self and identity. It should be noted, however, that there is not a clear-cut distinction between controlled and self-determined motivation, and that an individual may be driven by both forms of motivation simultaneously. To be more specific, people may be motivated to exercise both because of its perceived benefits for physical appearance *and* for health reasons. As will be discussed later in this chapter, the issue of "full choice" in relation to different appearance-related practices also deserves further scrutiny.

What Are the Associations between Appearance-Related Practices and Positive Body Image?

Having set out this background, we will now present research focusing on different behaviors on the continuum of appearance-related practices and their links to positive body image. As we reviewed the current literature, it became evident that few studies have viewed people's appearance-related practices from a positive perspective. Instead, the majority have examined the negative factors related to appearance-related practices (e.g., body dissatisfaction, body ideal internalization, decreased self-esteem, excessive exercise, and disordered eating; Walker & Murray, 2012). The studies with a positive perspective which we identified may be presented under three themes, which illustrate how appearance-related practices can be part of positive body image. The studies included either components of positive body image, such as body appreciation and body pride, or increased body satisfaction. Importantly, themes, and the appearance-related practices presented within them, are not mutually exclusive, but instead overlap.

Appearance-Related Practices as Projections of Identity and Personal Style

Russell (2012) suggested that adornment, such as cosmetics use, tattoos, piercing, and clothing, has two primary purposes: "beautification" and "signification." Beautification refers to adornment with the purpose of making the wearer more attractive. This is quite explicitly related to appearance-related practices. Signification, however, has a less apparent relation to such practices. In signification, the adornments are signs that stand for something else – they mark the culture, class, religion, or other social group to which the wearer belongs (e.g., particular clothing, jewelry, or tattoos indicating the wearer's age, socioeconomic status, or cultural affiliation). Also within social groups, adornments can be used to show the wearer's status, rank, or wealth, as well as age and gender. In many cases, cosmetics use, clothing, or a particular hairstyle can have double purposes; they play the role of beautification as well as signification.

The role of signification for positive body image is particularly interesting. A qualitative study of adolescent Aboriginal girls from Canada showed that they conceptualized positive body image (or, more specifically, body pride) as experienced on the "inside," yet expressed outwardly in their choice of style and grooming (McHugh, Coppola, & Sabiston, 2014). The girls emphasized that by using certain dance regalia, makeup, and tattoos that symbolized their Native heritage, they showed pride in who they were. Thus, their inner body pride and outer body appearance were directly linked.

Similarly, a few studies have investigated individuals' "need for uniqueness," that is, their pursuit of differentness relative to others (Tian, Bearden, & Hunter, 2001). This differentness may be achieved through appearance-related practices (such as clothing, cosmetics, tattoos, and piercing) in order to develop and enhance one's personal and social identity. Several studies have shown that individuals with tattoos experience a higher need for uniqueness than individuals without tattoos (Hill, Ogletree, & McCrary, 2016; Swami, 2012; Tiggemann & Golder, 2006; Tiggemann & Hopkins, 2011). Higher need for uniqueness has also been related to greater body appreciation, suggesting a positive relationship between the wish to be unique and having a positive body image (Gillen & Dunaev, 2017; Hill, Ogletree, & McCrary, 2016).

In line with the above reasoning, popular reasons for getting tattoos are to express oneself, to be a unique individual, to be creative, and to demonstrate bonds with friends and family members (Dickson et al., 2015; Hill, Ogletree, & McCrary, 2016). In a short-term longitudinal study, Swami (2011) examined British adults who were obtaining their first tattoo and found that three weeks after obtaining their tattoo, they reported higher body appreciation, self-ascribed uniqueness, and self-esteem. The author related his finding to earlier work by Benson (2000), who argued that, in societies where the body is commercialized and objectified, tattoos may offer individuals a means of reclaiming or stating their ownership over their bodies. In this way, an appearance-related practice such as tattooing may increase body pride and positive body image. In another study, tattooed and nontattooed US college students' levels of body appreciation were compared (Hill, Ogletree, & McCreary, 2016). Contrary to the authors' expectations (that tattooed participants would have lower levels of body appreciation), results showed no differences in body appreciation between the groups.

Clothing style is another appearance-related practice that can be interpreted within the frame of projecting one's identity and personal style. In a study of US college women, participants were asked to write essays about their body satisfaction and appearance-managing behaviors (Rudd & Lennon, 2000). Almost 30 percent of the women wrote about clothing practices. These practices were often motivated as positive forms of self-expression (e.g., "I feel that my clothing represents the type of person I am"). Clothing practices were also motivated to camouflage body imperfections and enhance body assets (e.g., "I like clothes that enhance the features of my body"). The latter motive is consistent with descriptions of positive body image that include emphasizing body assets rather than dwelling on imperfections (Tylka & Wood-Barcalow, 2015).

Other illustrative examples of how engaging in clothing practices can play a role in positive body image can be found within the fat activism movement. Common components within this movement are fashion blogs and web magazines, in which women of size portray their practices of dressing in fashionable clothes – hence occupying space in a marketplace (the fashion industry) that tends to exclude and condemn fat (Sewell, 2010). Researchers who have analyzed the blog posts of fat-activist women have shown that these acts of publicly exposing their nonnormative bodies in fashionable clothes and identifying themselves as fat are ways for the women to refuse and renegotiate current beauty ideals and to accept and embrace their bodies (Afful & Ricciardelli, 2015; Gurrier & Cherrier, 2013).

A final example of a female positive body image context in which several appearance-related practices (makeup, clothing, tattoos, and physical exercise) are used to promote identity and personal style is the Roller Derby sport movement (Eklund & Masberg, 2014; Strübel & Petrie, 2016). Roller Derby is a fast-growing high-contact sport on roller skates, performed mostly by White women aged 18–44 years, in which a strong body is valued (Strübel & Petri, 2016). Participants tend to dress up in a punk/rockabilly style "that satirizes and challenges the boundaries of traditional femininity through the use of short skirts, fishnets, bras and panties, tattoos, fake blood, flaunted injuries (e.g., bruises), and aggressive behavior" (p. 349). Many skaters choose to wear makeup and face paint, ranging from slightly more of this than would be considered usual to a full mask of paint and glitter (Eklund & Masberg, 2014). In a large-scale study, Eklund and Masberg (2014) reported that 97 percent of Roller Derby women indicated that the sport had a positive impact on their body image. A content analysis of open-ended answers showed that the women reported more positive body image for three major reasons: (1) increased body acceptance, (2) adoption of a more athletic perception of the body, and (3) clothing choices. In relation to appearance-related practices, the women's adoption of an athletic perception of their bodies included not only appreciation of increased body functionality but also appreciation of aesthetic aspects related to the increased muscle mass they obtained from performing sports:

One of my derby sisters and I talk about this regularly. We suddenly have muscles in places we never had them before. We find ourselves acting like 16-year-old boys, flexing in mirrors and asking people to feel our muscles. It's silly, but I have found a new love for my body that I never had before and it's really nice. (p. 56)

In relation to the third theme, clothing choices, the women also stated that wearing revealing clothes during Roller Derby practice and competitions increased their confidence. One of the women expressed it in the following way: "I feel more powerful and sexy standing on the tracks in skates, Spanx and fishnets than I ever could have imagined!" (p. 58). In Strubel and Petri's (2016) comparison of Roller Derby women and non-Roller Derby women, they found that Roller Derby women reported higher body esteem concerning their weight and physical condition (but no difference as regards their perceived sexual attractiveness). The authors argued that practicing Roller Derby and thereby engaging in practices that challenge traditional notions of femininity and masculinity can empower women who may be seen as overweight and unfeminine to participate in an alternative, athletic environment that promotes positive body image.

Appearance-Related Practices as Expressions of Self-Care

Another theme illustrating the possible associations between appearance-related practices and a positive body image is the concept of self-care. Cook-Cottone (2015; see also Chapter 6 of this book) stresses the importance of engaging in what she refers to as "mindful self-care" in order to cultivate an active appreciation of, and engagement with, the body. Mindful self-care practices may include engaging in mindfulness and self-compassion, spirituality, and taking care of one's physical health. Mindful self-care practices may also include spending time with others who maintain body-positive attitudes and dealing effectively with negative stereotypical body attitudes and ideals. Importantly, Cook-Cottone argues, mindful self-care practices are performed with an attitude of loving kindness.

Although appearance-related practices are not included in the above examples, women in particular may view their engagement in different kinds of appearance-related practices (e.g., beauty care rituals) as a way of taking care of themselves. Especially in the media, many appearance-related practices (skin and hair care, manicure, pedicure) are often advertised and packaged as acts of self-care. An example is the well-known and long-lived slogan used by L'Oréal Paris, the world's largest cosmetics and beauty company: "Because you're worth it" (first used in the 1970s as "Because *I'm* worth it"; www.youtube.com/watch?v=j6DHRFuCEwA). The slogan insinuates that women, who are the main target for beauty products, should feel that they are precious and valuable and, therefore, worthy of self-care through investment in beauty products.

Perceptions of appearance-related practices as acts of self-care have been found in interviews with women. An ethnographic study at a beauty center was conducted in order to understand older women's (>50 years) experiences of beauty treatments (facials, pedicures, manicures, and body massage; Paulson, 2008). Women in this study reported that these treatments had not only physical benefits in terms of appearance, but also various psychological benefits. Beauty treatments were used to promote a sense of wellbeing and relaxation, or simply as "time for oneself" or "time out" from the problems of growing older. A similar idea of appearance-related practices taking the form of self-care was found in interviews with women with a positive body image (Wood-Barcalow, Tylka, & Augustus-Horvath, 2010). Women reported using manicures as well as healthy eating and exercise to maintain and enhance their appearances. They framed these behaviors as acts of kindness towards their bodies.

One additional example of appearance-related behavior that may be conceptualized as self-care is tanning. Ironically, tanning is perhaps the appearance-related behavior with the best documented negative health effects (e.g., skin cancer; American Cancer Society, 2015). We would not go as far as to refer to tanning as self-care; however, research has shown that tanning is not only motivated by reasons of appearance (Day et al., 2016; Gillen & Markey, 2012) and that many tanners also appreciate its psychological effects, including feelings of relaxation and improved mood (Darlow, Heckman, & Munschi, 2016).

The Positive Feedback Loop between Appearance-Related Practices,
Approximating Body Ideals and Increased Body Satisfaction

Finally, it may be the case that investing in appearance moves individuals closer to body ideals and other appearance norms – even though it should be noted that these norms and ideals are extremely unrealistic. Looking similar to the ideal may in turn evoke affirming social reactions and rewards, which may positively strengthen body satisfaction (see the previous section on social learning theory). Thus, there may be a positive feedback loop between investing in appearance, approaching appearance norms, and heightened or improved body satisfaction.

One appearance-related practice that has the potential to move people closer to the current body ideal is *physical exercise*. This idea has been exploited by gyms and fitness centers, who often market their classes by referring to appearance or the specific area of the body that the class will, supposedly, "fix." By attending a class named "Barre" you may be lured by the idea that you can "get the body of a dancer, without taking a single dancing step" (www.sats.se), or you might attend "ABSolution" or "Shape" and get a "summer ready body" (www.24hourfitness.com). When it comes to the links between exercise and body image, overall positive effects of exercise on men's and women's body image have been well documented (Hausenblas & Fallon, 2006). Exercisers seem to be more satisfied with their bodies than nonexercisers, and exercise seems to improve body satisfaction. The reason for these effects may be that regular engagement in exercise benefits a functional view of the body, which is connected to positive body image (Frisén & Holmqvist, 2010; see also Dunaev and Markey, Chapter 8 in this book). The positive effect between exercise and body satisfaction can also be explained by increases in physical self-efficacy. For example, Burgees, Grogan, and Burwitz (2006) found that adolescent girls who took part in a dance intervention demonstrated immediate improvements in perceived body attractiveness and physical self-worth. These processes may also be applicable in explaining the positive body image reported among Roller Derby women, as discussed earlier.

However, and relying on the arguments from SDT, it is not only exercising per se that matters. Perhaps even more important are people's motives for exercising. Indeed, appearance-related motives are among the most commonly reported reasons to engage in exercise for both men and women – second only to health motives (Strelan & Hargreaves, 2005). Appearance-related exercise motives are less adaptive as they are related to negative body image outcomes, such as body dissatisfaction and self-objectification (Strelan & Hargreaves, 2005;

Strelan, Mehaffney, & Tiggemann, 2003). Exercise motives that relate to health, well-being, and functional views of the body, on the other hand, are associated with positive body image outcomes (Strelan et al., 2003). Homan and Tylka (2014), for instance, demonstrated a significant link between women's higher exercise frequency and body appreciation, but this effect was reduced when taking into account appearance-related exercise motives. In a later study, Tylka and Homan (2015) found that exercise motivated by health and enjoyment was associated with positive embodiment and greater internal body orientation (referring to an attunement to how the body feels and functions) in both men and women. A protective effect of nonappearance-related motives has also been demonstrated in appearance-focused exercise environments (e.g., fitness centers with full-body mirrors, or classes focusing on "fixing" appearance flaws) (O'Hara, Cox, & Amorose, 2014). Focusing on health rather than appearance allows for full engagement in the exercise activity itself instead of worrying about one's appearance. Hence, the positive effects of exercise on body image seem to ensue when exercise is *not* an appearance-related investment, but rather an investment in one's physical health.

We would like to end this section by attending to one of the most extreme and invasive appearance-related practices, namely that of cosmetic surgery. During recent years, rates of cosmetic surgery have skyrocketed in Westernized countries (ASPS, 2016). Cosmetic procedures include breast enlargement, breast reduction, liposuction, rhinoplasty, thigh lift, tummy tuck, gynecomastia (male breast reduction), labioplasty (female genital surgery), neck lift, and body contouring, to name but a few procedures listed on the website plasticsurgery.com (www .plasticsurgery.org/cosmetic-procedures). Minimally invasive procedures, such as Botox and filler injections, have also become increasingly popular. The surge of interest in cosmetic surgery has been confirmed by the American Society of Plastic Surgeons (ASPS, 2016), who reported a 132 percent increase in cosmetic surgery between 2000 and 2016. These statistics bear evidence that cosmetic surgery, as Northrop (2012) argues, "has slipped from marginal to mainstream" (p.12).

On its website, the ASPS states the following about cosmetic surgery:

Cosmetic plastic surgery includes surgical and nonsurgical procedures that enhance and reshape structures of the body to improve appearance and confidence. Healthy individuals with a positive outlook and realistic expectations are appropriate candidates for cosmetic procedures. Plastic surgery is a personal choice and should be done for yourself, not to meet someone else's expectations or to try to fit an ideal image. (www.plasticsurgery.org/cosmetic-procedures)

Indeed, the idea of cosmetic surgery being a personal choice, used as a means to improve appearance and increase self-esteem, is the most widely accepted justification for cosmetic surgery. For example, in one study of young men and women in Sweden, undergoing cosmetic surgery to feel better about oneself was generally accepted, whereas doing it to gain social advantages (e.g., attract a partner, get hired) was less so (Lunde & Gyberg, 2016). In another study examining adolescents, there was an inverse relationship between cosmetic surgery acceptance and age, with younger participants more strongly endorsing the idea of having cosmetic surgery for social reasons (Lunde, 2013). Tentatively, this finding may mirror a greater tendency among younger individuals to consider cosmetic surgery "to meet someone else's expectations."

The quotation from ASPS also highlights the optimal candidates for surgery: "healthy individuals with a positive outlook and realistic expectations." Studies examining whether those who undergo cosmetic surgery are less psychologically healthy than others have produced somewhat mixed results (see e.g. Margraf, Meyer, & Lavallee, 2015; Sarwer, 2006). However, a higher prevalence of body dysmorphic disorder has been identified among cosmetic surgery patients than among the general population. Furthermore, body dissatisfaction and strong appearance investment (comparable to Cash's notion of self-evaluative salience), have been identified as motivators for being interested in and obtaining cosmetic surgery (Markey & Markey, 2009, 2015; Sarwer, 2006).

A few studies have examined associations between positive body image and interest in cosmetic surgery. The lack of studies probably originates from an underlying assumption that individuals with a positive body image would be less likely to consider or pursue cosmetic surgery. In line with this, Swami (2009) found that cosmetic surgery consideration was associated with lower body appreciation in female university students. In a late adolescent sample, on the other hand, there were no links between girls' and boys' body appreciation and consideration of cosmetic surgery (Lunde, 2013). Perhaps this lack of effect is due to the age of the participants, as it could be expected that people who consider cosmetic surgery appreciate their bodies to a lesser extent. However, there is some evidence that cosmetic surgery may be associated with positive increases in body satisfaction (von Soest et al., 2009). Von Soest and colleagues argue that this effect is due to experiences of increased attractiveness and positive appearance-related feedback from others. Indeed, cosmetic surgery is sometimes even referred to as "body image surgery" (Pruzinsky & Edgerton, referred to in Markey & Markey, 2015). Does this indicate that the extreme practice of cosmetic surgery may also have benefits for people's body image?

Here, we would like to refer back to the tenets of SDT and the motivational dynamics of adaptive vs maladaptive appearance-related behaviors, self-determined vs controlled motivation, and the question of full choice. In the statement on its website, the ASPS conveys an idea of free choice, stating that "cosmetic surgery is a personal choice that should be done for oneself, and not because of someone else's expectations." This statement may appear quite straightforward, but is in fact extremely complex. Chambers (2007), a political philosopher, argues that it is not sufficient to rely on "the freedom of choice" to evaluate the ethics of different cultural practices. She argues that cultural practices, such as different appearance-related practices, must always be evaluated in relation to the harm or risk associated with the practice, as well as the amount of influence and pressure affecting individuals' choice to pursue the practice. Cutting one's hair, for example, is a cultural appearance practice associated with little harm or risk. The amount of social influence and pressure involved in cutting one's hair may vary – for instance, there may be greater expectation placed on men to have a short haircut, which may have an influence on their choice to adhere to this norm. Tanning, on the other hand, is an appearance-related practice that is indeed associated with harm and risk. Again, the social pressure to tan may vary.

So what about cosmetic surgery? An individual who undergoes cosmetic surgery may feel that he or she does so of his or her own volition and full personal choice. Yet, aesthetic cosmetic surgery exists as a cultural practice only because of strong societal appearance and gender norms. In addition, it is a cultural practice that is extremely gender-biased, with 90 percent of patients being women (ASPS, 2016). Chambers argues that these facts make cosmetic surgery an even more questionable cultural practice. She claims that women's "free choice" to pursue cosmetic surgery will contribute to their continued subordination in a nongender-equal society, as the pursuit of cosmetic surgery is fueled by a profoundly unequal norm of the importance of female attractiveness. Thus, women's beauty practices per se, and especially those that are harmful, *should* be of concern, because women are coerced to undertake beauty practices. In addition, it should be noted that as appearance norms become internalized, people may derive substantial pleasure from conforming to norms. This constitutes the core of the positive feedback loop between approximating current beauty standards and getting socially rewarded for doing so. In view of this, people may experience increased body satisfaction when engaging in a range of appearance-related practices. However, whether these positive effects are sustained, and whether they really contribute to psychological health in the long term, remain important questions (Markey & Markey, 2015).

Damned if You Do, Damned if You Don't, and the Paradox of "Natural" Beauty

The three themes described above present some of the circumstances under which appearance-related practices can be part of a positive body image. However, although these practices *can* be part of a positive body image, engaging in them is not always unproblematic. Some of this complexity has already been described: Appearance practices can be health-damaging and it is questionable whether they are truly voluntary. However, the complexity also lies in the societal perceptions of people who engage (especially excessively) in appearance-related practices. Indeed, it is not easy to navigate the societal expectations regarding physical appearance. On the one hand, societal norms dictate that women, and increasingly also men, should be beautiful and invest in their appearance to look attractive. On the other hand, people who do invest in their appearance run the risk of being seen as superficial. Attractive individuals – both men and women – are viewed positively, which is known as the "physical attractiveness stereotype" (Rennels, 2012). The "beauty is beastly effect" is a different side of this coin. For example, Paustian-Underdahl and Walker (2016) showed that women who are seen as attractive may be discriminated against, especially in traditionally male domains. For example, attractive women are less likely to be hired for managerial or male-typed jobs. This effect has been explained by stereotypes associating female attractiveness with higher femininity, which in turn is associated with stereotypes of feminine women being less agentic, and thus not suited for male-typed jobs (Johnson, Podratz, Dipboye, & Gibbons, 2010).

Thus, women need to navigate their way through the complexities of being "damned if they do and damned if they don't" in terms of appearance investment. This was illustrated in a recent focus group study of twenty young Swedish women discussing feminine norms (Kling, Frisén, & Holmqvist Gattario, 2017). Sweden is rated as one of the most gender-equal societies in the world (Stavrova, Fetchenhauer, & Shlösser, 2012; United Nations Development Program, 2016), and provides a cultural context of particular interest for examining conceptions of feminine norms and appearance-related behaviors. The women in the study expressed ambivalent thoughts regarding appearance investment, feeling pressured to conform to societal beauty norms, yet worried that someone would view them as being superficial. According to the participants, beauty was supposed to come "naturally" without investment – one should just effortlessly have it (see also the concept of "effortless perfection"; Travers, Randall, Bryant, Conley, & Bohnert, 2015). The women also referred to gender equality in their discussions, saying that women who admit to spending time and effort on their appearance may be considered weak and nongender-equal, and that they themselves felt looked down upon when someone found out they were spending time on their appearance. Consequently, the young women tried to keep up an image of nonadherence to beauty norms, while secretly still trying to conform. For example, a participant reported, on grooming: "I wouldn't say that 'I just spent four hours on fixing my hair'. It should be like 'I just got out of bed'" (p. 6).

Concluding Remarks

Appearance-related practices range from potentially harmless everyday behaviors to radical, extreme behaviors associated with great health risks. On this continuum of appearance-related practices, most behaviors are widespread in Westernized societies, and new ways of enhancing one's appearance are invented constantly. Although people's, and especially women's, engagement in appearance-related behaviors is usually prob-lematized, this chapter has explored whether appearance-related practices and behaviors are always "bad," or if they can also be associated with healthy outcomes and positive body image. The literature on appearance-related practices and positive body image is scarce, but we believe there is enough evidence to conclude that, yes, appearance-related practices can be part of a positive body image. Specifically, we have highlighted three ways in which the research literature has connected appearance-related practices to a positive body image, or increased body satisfaction: (1) appearance-related practices to project one's sense of identity and per-sonal style, (2) appearance-related practices as expressions of self-care, and (3) the positive feedback loop between appearance-related practices, approximating body ideals, and increased body satisfaction.

These themes shed light on the complexities of appearance-related practices as they are used not only to enhance appearance, but also as important, symbolic expressions of who we are and what we experience in life. For many individuals, appearance-related practices are entangled with acts of self-care in a complex way. Engaging in appearance-related practices may be perceived as an act of kindness towards the self and, therefore, may enhance wellbeing. Still, we should not forget that many, if not most, appearance-related practices are conditioned by constrain-ing societal norms. Hence, it is up for debate whether engaging in appearance-related practices can really be an autonomous choice, whether appearance-related practices are empowering or disempower-ing, and for whom this might be the case.

Nonetheless, reducing appearance-related practices to solely bad is too simplistic, and may not be helpful when trying to understand the meanings of appearance-related practices in people's lives. Whether appearance-related practices are good or bad, adaptive or maladaptive, or anywhere in between may depend on many different factors, such as the extent to which people base their self-worth on their appearance, the extent to which they engage and invest in appearance-related practices, which particular practices they engage in, and their motives for engaging in these. We need also to consider the pressures associated with these appearance-related practices – what are the rewards for adhering and the punishments for not adhering? To what extent are the pressures unequally distributed, for instance, between men and women? These questions may guide us toward a greater understanding of individuals' engagement in appearance-related practices and how they relate to positive body image.

Finally, it is debatable whether anyone can actually judge accurately when it comes to adaptive versus maladaptive appearance investment. In her book *Body Work: The Social Construction of Women's Body Image*, Blood (2005) criticized society, and also body image research, for pathologizing women's perceptions of their bodies. She argued that the constant iteration of female body image as negative or flawed oversimplifies women's lived experiences of their bodies – and that the scientific community risks reproducing the dissatisfaction that it wishes to prevent. Although these arguments may be questioned, we note that women risk being penalized no matter what they do: They are pressured to adhere to appearance norms, yet women who invest in their appearance risk being viewed as superficial and are looked down upon. A societal discourse of women as "damned if they do and damned if they don't" is not helpful in promoting empowerment and positive embodiment.

References

Afful, A. A., & Ricciardelli, R. (2015). Shaping the online fat acceptance movement: Talking about body image and beauty standards. *Journal of Gender Studies*, *24*, 453–472. doi:http://dx.doi.org.ezproxy.ub.gu.se/10.1080/09589236.2015.1028523

Anderson-Fye, E. (2012). Anthropological perspectives on physical appearance and body image. In T. F. Cash (Ed.), *Encyclopedia of body image and human appearance* (pp. 15–22). London: Academic Press.

ASPS (2016). 2016 Cosmetic plastic surgery statistics. Retrieved from www.plasticsurgery.org/documents/News/Statistics/2016/cosmetic-procedure-trends-2016.pdf.

Balantekin, K. N., Birch, L. L., & Savage, J. S. (2017). Family, friend, and media factors are associated with patterns of weight-control behavior among adolescent girls. *Eating and Weight Disorders*. Advance online publication. doi:http://dx.doi.org.ezproxy.ub.gu.se/10.1007/s40519-016-0359-4

Bandura, A. (1977). *Social learning theory*. Englewood Cliffs, NJ: Prentice Hall.

Bartky, S. L. (1990). *Femininity and domination: Studies in the phenomenology of oppression*. New York: Routledge.

Benson, S. (2000). Inscriptions of the self: Reflections on tattooing and piercing in contemporary Euro-America. In J. Caplan (Ed.), *Written on the body: The tattoo in European and American history* (pp. 234–254). Princeton: Princeton University Press.

Blood, S. K. (2005). *Body work: The social construction of women's body image*. New York: Routledge.

Burgess, G., Grogan, S., & Burwitz, L. (2006). Effects of a 6-week aerobic dance intervention on body image and physical self-perceptions in adolescent girls. *Body Image*, *3*, 57–66. doi:http://dx.doi.org.ezproxy.ub.gu.se/10.1016/j.bodyim.2005.10.005

Cash, T. F., Melnyk, S. E., & Hrabosky, J. I. (2004). The assessment of body image investment: An extensive revision of the appearance schemas inventory. *International Journal of Eating Disorders*, *35*, 305–316. doi:http://dx.doi.org.ezproxy.ub.gu.se/10.1002/eat.10264

Cash, T. F. & Smolak, L. (2011). *Body image. A handbook of science, practice and prevention*. New York: Guilford Press.

Chambers, C. (2007) Are breast implants better than female genital mutilation? Autonomy, gender equality and Nussbaum's political liberalism. *Critical Review of International Social and Political Philosophy*, *7*, 1–33.

Cook-Cottone, C. (2015). Incorporating positive body image into the treatment of eating disorders: A model for attunement and mindful self-care. *Body Image*, *14*, 158–167. doi:http://dx.doi.org.ezproxy.ub.gu.se/10.1016/j.bodyim.2015.03.004

Coffman, D. L., Balantekin, K. N., & Savage, J. S. (2016). Using propensity score methods to assess causal effects of mothers' dieting behavior on daughters' early dieting behavior. *Childhood Obesity*, *12*, 334–340. doi:http://dx.doi.org.ezproxy.ub.gu.se/10.1089/chi.2015.0249

Darlow, S. D., Heckman, C. J., & Munshi, T. (2016). Tan and thin? Associations between attitudes toward thinness, motives to tan and tanning behaviors in adolescent girls. *Psychology, Health & Medicine*, *21*, 618–624. doi:http://dx.doi.org.ezproxy.ub.gu.se/10.1080/13548506.2015.1093643

Day, A. K., Wilson, C. J., Hutchinson, A. D., & Roberts, R. M. (2016). Australian young adults' tanning behaviour: The role of ideal skin tone and sociocultural norms. *Australian Journal of Psychology*, *69*, 86–94. doi:http://dx.doi.org.ezproxy.ub.gu.se/10.1111/ajpy.12121

Dickson, L., Dukes, R. L., Smith, H., & Strapko, N. (2015). To ink or not to ink: The meaning of tattoos among college students. *College Student Journal*, *49*, 106–120.

Dittmar, H. (2008). *Consumer culture, identity and well-being: The search for the "good life" and the "body perfect."* New York: Taylor & Francis.

Eklund, A., & Masberg, B. A. (2014). Participation in roller derby, the influence on body image. *Clothing & Textiles Research Journal*, *32*, 49–64. doi:http:// dx.doi.org.ezproxy.ub.gu.se/10.1177/0887302X13511295

Frisén, A., & Holmqvist, K. (2010). What characterizes early adolescents with a positive body image? A qualitative investigation of Swedish girls and boys. *Body Image*, *7*, 205–212. doi:http://dx.doi.org.ezproxy.ub.gu.se/10.1016/ j.bodyim.2010.04.001

Gillen, M. M. & Dunaev, J. (2017). Body appreciation, interest in cosmetic enhancements, and need for uniqueness among U.S. college students. *Body Image*, *22*, 136–143.

Gillen, M. M., & Markey, C. N. (2012). The role of body image and depression in tanning behaviors and attitudes. *Behavioral Medicine*, *38*, 74–82. doi:http://dx.doi.org.ezproxy.ub.gu.se/10.1080/08964289.2012.685499

Gurrieri, L., & Cherrier, H. (2013). Queering beauty: Fatshionistas in the fatosphere. *Qualitative Market Research: An International Journal*, *16*, 276–295.

Halberstam, J. J. (2012). Lady Gaga embodies a new model of feminism. Women's e-news. Retrieved from http://womensenews.org/2012/10/lady- gaga-embodies-new-model-feminism/

Hausenblas, H. A., & Fallon, E. A. (2006). Exercise and body image: A meta- analysis. *Psychology & Health*, *21*, 33–47. doi:http://dx.doi.org.ezproxy .ub.gu.se/10.1080/14768320500105270

Hill, B. M., Ogletree, S. M., & McCrary, K. M. (2016). Body modifications in college students: Considering gender, self-esteem, body appreciation, and reasons for tattoos. *College Student Journal*, *50*, 246–252.

Holmqvist, K., & Frisén, A. (2012). "I bet they aren't that perfect in reality:" Appearance ideals viewed from the perspective of adolescents with a positive body image. *Body Image*, *9*, 388–395. doi:http://dx.doi.org.ezproxy.ub.gu.se/ 10.1016/j.bodyim.2012.03.007

Homan, K. J., & Tylka, T. L. (2014). Appearance-based exercise motivation moderates the relationship between exercise frequency and positive body image. *Body Image*, *11*, 101–108. doi:http://dx.doi.org.ezproxy.ub.gu.se/ 10.1016/j.bodyim.2014.01.003

Johnson, S. K., Podratz, K. E., Dipboye, R. L., & Gibbons, E. (2010). Physical attractiveness biases in ratings of employment suitability: Tracking down the "beauty is beastly" effect. *The Journal of Social Psychology*, *150*, 301–318. doi:http://dx.doi.org.ezproxy.ub.gu.se/10.1080/00224540903365414

Jones, G. (2010). *Beauty imagined: A history of the global industry*. New York: Oxford University Press.

Kling, J., Holmqvist Gattario, K., & Frisén, A. (2017). Swedish women's perceptions of and conformity to feminine norms. *Scandinavian Journal of Psychology*, *58*, 238–248. doi:http://dx.doi.org.ezproxy.ub.gu.se/10.1111/ sjop.12361

Lunde, C. (2013). Acceptance of cosmetic surgery, body appreciation, body ideal internalization, and fashion blog reading among late adolescents in Sweden. *Body Image*, *10*, 632–635. doi:http://dx.doi.org.ezproxy.ub.gu.se/10.1016/ j.bodyim.2013.06.007

Lunde, C., & Gyberg, F. (2016). Maternal and paternal influences on young Swedish women's and men's cosmetic surgery acceptance. *Sex Roles, 74*, 242–253. doi:http://dx.doi.org.ezproxy.ub.gu.se/10.1007/s11199-015-0574-x

Mahalik, J. R., Morray, E. B., Coonerty-Femiano, A., Ludlow, L. H., Slattery, S. M., & Smiler, A. (2005). Development of the conformity to feminine norms inventory. *Sex Roles, 52*, 417–435. doi:http://dx.doi.org.ezproxy.ub.gu.se/10.1007/s11199-005-3709-7

Margraf, J., Meyer, A. H., & Lavallee, K. L. (2015). Psychological health and aims of aesthetic surgery seekers. *Clinical Psychological Science, 3*, 877–891. doi:http://dx.doi.org.ezproxy.ub.gu.se/10.1177/2167702614551409

Markey, C. N., & Markey, P. M. (2009). Correlates of young women's interest in obtaining cosmetic surgery. *Sex Roles, 61*, 158–166. doi:http://dx.doi.org.ezproxy.ub.gu.se/10.1007/s11199-009-9625-5

(2015). Can women's body images be "fixed"? Body image and cosmetic surgery. In M. C. McHugh and J. C. Chrisler (Eds.), *The wrong prescription for women: How medicine and media create a "need" for treatments, drugs and surgery* (pp. 221–236). Santa Barbara: Praeger.

McHugh, T. F., Coppola, A. M., & Sabiston, C. M. (2014). "I'm thankful for being native and my body is part of that": The body pride experiences of young aboriginal women in Canada. *Body Image, 11*, 318–327. doi:http://dx.doi.org.ezproxy.ub.gu.se/10.1016/j.bodyim.2014.05.004

Melnyk, S. E., Cash, T. F., & Janda, L. H. (2004). Body image ups and downs: Prediction of intra-individual level and variability of women's daily body image experiences. *Body Image, 1*, 225–235. doi:http://dx.doi.org.ezproxy.ub.gu.se/10.1016/j.bodyim.2004.03.003

Murnen, S. K., & Seabrook, R. (2012). Feminist perspectives on body image and physical appearance. In T. F. Cash (Ed.), *Encyclopedia of body image and human appearance* (pp. 438–443). London: Academic Press.

Northrop, J. M. (2012). *Reflecting on cosmetic surgery: Body image, shame and narcissism*. London/New York: Taylor & Francis.

O'Hara, S. E., Cox, A. E., & Amorose, A. J. (2014). Emphasizing appearance versus health outcomes in exercise: The influence of the instructor and participants' reasons for exercise. *Body Image, 11*, 109–118. http://dx.doi.org/10.1016/j.bodyim.2013.12.004

Patton, S. C., Beaujean, A. A., & Benedict, H. E. (2014). Parental bonds, attachment anxiety, media susceptibility, and body dissatisfaction: A mediation model. *Developmental Psychology, 50*, 2124–2133. doi:http://dx.doi.org.ezproxy.ub.gu.se/10.1037/a0037111

Paulson, S. (2008). "Beauty is more than skin deep." An ethnographic study of beauty therapists and older women. *Journal of Aging Studies, 22*, 256–265. doi:http://dx.doi.org.ezproxy.ub.gu.se/10.1016/j.jaging.2007.03.003

Paustian-Underdahl, S., & Walker, L. S. (2016). Revisiting the beauty is beastly effect: Examining when and why sex and attractiveness impact hiring judgments. *The International Journal of Human Resource Management, 27*, 1034–1058. doi:http://dx.doi.org.ezproxy.ub.gu.se/10.1080/09585192.2015.1053963

Pelletier, L. G., Dion, S., & Lévesque, C. (2004). Can self-determination help protect women against sociocultural influences about body image and reduce their risk of experiencing bulimic symptoms? *Journal of Social and Clinical Psychology*, *23*, 61–88. doi:http://dx.doi.org.ezproxy.ub.gu.se/10.1521/jscp.23.1.61.26990

Rennels, J. L. (2012). Physical attractiveness stereotyping. In T. F. Cash (Ed.), *Encyclopedia of Body Image and Human Appearance* (pp. 636–643). San Diego: Elsevier Academic Press.

Roberts, A. E., Koch, J. R., Armstrong, M. L., & Owen, D. C. (2006). Correlates of tattoos and reference groups. *Psychological Reports*, *99*, 933–934. doi:http://dx.doi.org.ezproxy.ub.gu.se/10.2466/PR0.99.7.933-934

Rudd, N. A., & Lennon, S. J. (2000). Body image and appearance-management behaviors in college women. *Clothing & Textiles Research Journal*, *18*, 152–162. doi:http://dx.doi.org.ezproxy.ub.gu.se/10.1177/0887302X0001800304

Russell, R. (2012). Cosmetics use: Psychological perspectives. In T. F. Cash (Ed.), *Encyclopedia of body image and human appearance* (pp. 366–371). London: Academic Press.

Sarwer, D. (2006). Psychological assessment of cosmetic surgery patients. In D. Sarwer et al. (Eds.), *Psychological aspects of reconstructive and cosmetic plastic surgery* (pp. 267–283). Philadelphia: Lippincott Williams & Wilkins.

Sewell, M. A. (2010). *Ameliorating fat stigma: Resilience as a correlate to self-esteem, body image, and sexual quality of life for internet-savvy big beautiful women.* Retrieved from https://search-proquest-com.ezproxy.ub.gu.se/docview/622194340?accountid=11162

Stavrova, O., Fetchenhauer, D., & Schlösser, T. (2012). Cohabitation, gender, and happiness: A cross-cultural study in thirty countries. *Journal of Cross-Cultural Psychology*, *43*, 1063–1081. doi:http://dx.doi.org.ezproxy.ub.gu.se/10.1177/0022022111419030

Strelan, P., & Hargreaves, D. (2005). Reasons for exercise and body esteem: Men's responses to self-objectification. *Sex Roles*, *53*, 495–503. doi:http://dx.doi.org.ezproxy.ub.gu.se/10.1007/s11199-005-7137-5

Strelan, P., Mehaffey, S. J., & Tiggemann, M. (2003). Self-objectification and esteem in young women: The mediating role of reasons for exercise. *Sex Roles*, *48*, 89–95. doi:http://dx.doi.org.ezproxy.ub.gu.se/10.1023/A:1022300930307

Strübel, J., & Petrie, T. A. (2016). 'Bout time! Renegotiating the body in roller derby. *Sex Roles*, *74*, 347–360. doi:http://dx.doi.org.ezproxy.ub.gu.se/10.1007/s11199-015-0490-0

Swami, V. (2009). Body appreciation, media influence, and weight status predict consideration of cosmetic surgery among female undergraduates. *Body Image*, *6*, 315–317. doi:http://dx.doi.org.ezproxy.ub.gu.se/10.1016/j.bodyim.2009.07.001

(2011). Marked for life? A prospective study of tattoos on appearance anxiety and dissatisfaction, perceptions of uniqueness, and self-esteem. *Body Image*, *8*, 237–244. doi:http://dx.doi.org.ezproxy.ub.gu.se/10.1016/j.bodyim.2011.04.005

Swami, V. & Harris, A. S. (2012). Evolutionary perspectives on physical appearance. In T. F. Cash (Ed.), *Encyclopedia of body image and human appearance* (pp. 404–411). London: Academic Press.

Thompson, J. K., Coovert, M. D., & Stormer, S. M. (1999). Body image, social comparison, and eating disturbance: A covariance structure modeling investigation. *International Journal of Eating Disorders, 26,* 43–51. doi:10.1002/(SICI)1098-108X(199907)26:1<43::AID-EAT6>3.0.CO;2-R

Tian, K. T., Bearden, W. O., & Hunter, G. L. (2001). Consumers' need for uniqueness: Scale development and validation. *Journal of Consumer Research, 28,* 50–66. doi:http://dx.doi.org.ezproxy.ub.gu.se/10.1086/321947

Tiggemann, M., & Golder, F. (2006). Tattooing: An expression of uniqueness in the appearance domain. *Body Image, 3,* 309–315. doi:http://dx.doi.org.ezproxy.ub.gu.se/10.1016/j.bodyim.2006.09.002

Tiggemann, M., & Hopkins, L. A. (2011). Tattoos and piercings: Bodily expressions of uniqueness? *Body Image, 8,* 245–250. doi:http://dx.doi.org.ezproxy.ub.gu.se/10.1016/j.bodyim.2011.03.007

Travers, L. V., Randall, E. T., Bryant, F. B., Conley, C. S., & Bohnert, A. M. (2015). The cost of perfection with apparent ease: Theoretical foundations and development of the effortless perfectionism scale. *Psychological Assessment, 27,* 1147–1159. doi:http://dx.doi.org.ezproxy.ub.gu.se/10.1037/pas0000109

Tylka, T. L., & Homan, K. J. (2015). Exercise motives and positive body image in physically active college women and men: Exploring an expanded acceptance model of intuitive eating. *Body Image, 15,* 90–97. doi:http://dx.doi.org.ezproxy.ub.gu.se/10.1016/j.bodyim.2015.07.003

Tylka, T. L., & Wood-Barcalow, N. (2015). What is and what is not positive body image? conceptual foundations and construct definition. *Body Image, 14,* 118–129. doi:http://dx.doi.org.ezproxy.ub.gu.se/10.1016/j.bodyim.2015.04.001

United Nations Development Program (2016). Table 5: Gender inequality index. Retrieved from http://hdr.undp.org/en/composite/GII

Verstuyf, J., Patrick, H., Vansteenkiste, M., & Teixeira, P. J. (2012). Motivational dynamics of eating regulation: A self-determination theory perspective. *The International Journal of Behavioral Nutrition and Physical Activity, 9,* 16. doi:http://dx.doi.org.ezproxy.ub.gu.se/10.1186/1479-5868-9-21

von Soest, T., Kvalem, I. L., Skolleborg, K. C., & Roald, H. E. (2009). Cosmetic surgery and the relationship between appearance satisfaction and extraversion: Testing a transactional model of personality. *Journal of Research in Personality, 43,* 1017–1025. doi:http://dx.doi.org.ezproxy.ub.gu.se/10.1016/j.jrp.2009.07.001

Walker, D. C., & Murray, A. D. (2012). Body image behaviors: Checking, fixing, and avoiding. In T. F. Cash (Ed), *Encyclopedia of body image and human appearance* (pp. 166–172). London, UK: Academic Press.

Wasylkiw, L., & Butler, N. A. (2014). Body talk among undergraduate women: Why conversations about exercise and weight loss differentially predict body appreciation. *Journal of Health Psychology, 19,* 1013–1024. doi:http://dx.doi.org.ezproxy.ub.gu.se/10.1177/1359105313483155

Wood-Barcalow, N., Tylka, T. L., & Augustus-Horvath, C. (2010). "But I like my body": Positive body image characteristics and a holistic model for young-adult women. *Body Image, 7,* 106–116. doi:http://dx.doi.org.ezproxy.ub.gu.se/10.1016/j.bodyim.2010.01.001

6 Mindful Self-Care and Positive Body Image
Mindfulness, Yoga, and Actionable Tools for Positive Embodiment

Catherine Cook-Cottone

Caring for yourself, bringing support and healing to your own efforts to help
others and the larger world in which we live,
is an essential daily practice –
not a luxury, not some form of self-indulgence
(Siegel, 2010, p. 3)

Cultivating a positive body image is more than a cognitive task (Cook-Cottone, 2016a; Piran, 2015). Our relationship with our bodies is rich and complex with manifestations in the cognitive, physical, emotional, and relational domains (Cook-Cottone, 2016a; Frederickson & Roberts, 1997; Piran, 2015, 2016). Over the past decade, researchers have refined the concept of positive body image. Critically, positive body image is unique from negative body image (Tylka & Wood-Barcalow, 2015). It is multifaceted, holistic, and both stable and malleable (Wood-Barcalow, Tylka, & Augustus-Horvath, 2010). Importantly, positive body image is also protective (Wood-Barcalow et al., 2010). Positive body image has been defined as a love and respect for the body in which an individual: (1) appreciates the unique beauty of his or her body and its functions; (2) accepts and admires his or her body; (3) feels comfortable, confident, and happy with his or her body; (4) emphasizes his or her body's assets rather than dwelling on its imperfections; and (5) interprets incoming information in a body-protective manner (Wood-Barcalow et al., 2010).

Positive body image is also bidirectional (Cook-Cottone, 2016a). That is, individuals tend to feel and think about their bodies in a manner similar to how they experience and treat their bodies, and individuals tend to treat their bodies in ways that are congruent with how they feel and think about their bodies. Positive body image is inextricably linked to, and interdependent with, embodiment (Cook-Cottone, 2016a). Embodiment is the way we live in our bodies, our presence within the physical self, interoceptive awareness, our responsiveness to internal cues, and our decision making in the care and nourishing of our bodies. Embodiment lies in the choices we make that affect the physical self, the food we eat, our physical exercise, sexual decision making, and more.

Further, it is theorized that how we think affects how we experience our embodiment, and how we experience our embodiment affects how we think (Cook-Cottone, 2016a; Siegel, 2009). This is because, phenomenologically, we *are* our bodies (Cook-Cottone, 2015a, 2015b; Douglass & Bottrill, in press; Svenaeus, 2013). As phenomenologists would explain, the everyday way of being with your body is "being as a body" (Svenaeus, 2013, p. 83). That is, how you are *as a body* is reflected in how you conceptualize your body, your body image. In this way, positive body image comes from, in part, the nature of your embodiment (Cook-Cottone, 2016a; Piran & Teall, 2012).

To illustrate, Mathilde, a woman who is positively embodied, wakes in the morning present to the effects of her rest on her body. She notices her energy level. She inhales and takes a deep stretch to engage her muscles and connect with her body. Then, she exhales and releases the activation she just created in her body. Getting up, she runs warm water on a washcloth and places it on her face. She is headed for a run, but takes the time to wash her face and put on some sunblock. Caring for her skin and protecting it from the sun is important to her. She dresses for her run with attention to the weather outside and the needs of her body. Filling up a water bottle, she heads out to meet her friends for their weekly run. In this way, Mathilde is embodied. Her care for and support of her body is intricately linked to her moment-by-moment functioning.

Quite differently, Sarah wakes up and tries to remember how much she drank last night. Her head is pounding and she stumbles out of bed to get some ibuprofen. She takes 800 milligrams, knowing it is too much, but she does not want to feel anything – anything at all. She realizes there is no time for a shower. She is late again. Throwing on her heels from last night, she grabs her coat to head out the door, promising herself she will skip breakfast and lunch to make up for all the drinking calories. She has a big event Friday night and she wants to be at her ideal weight. She runs into the counter on her way out of the door as she is lost in thought. Sarah's relationship with her body is based on cognitive and behavioral attempts to modify her size and shape and ignore or suppress her physical needs, and perhaps her emotions. She often stumbles, runs into things, and stubs toes as she has no sense of her body in space. She drinks alcohol frequently and takes too many over-the-counter painkillers to compensate for the poor manner in which she treats her body.

There is a growing field of research documenting the protective power of positive embodiment (Cook-Cottone, 2015a, 2015b; Piran, 2015, 2016). To be positively embodied, like Mathilde, means to feel a sense of connection with your body, experience agency and functionality as related to your body, have your body available to you to experience and express desire, inhabit the body as a subjective (rather than objective) site, and practice attuned self-care (i.e., self-care based on the felt needs of your body; Piran, 2015). What crosses all of these domains (i.e., connection, agency, functionality, the experience and expression of desire, subjective inhabitation, and attuned self-care) is that they are subjective, embodied actions and experiences. They are things you do with and for your body. Subjective inhabiting of the body presents like Mathilde. She is actively engaged in her life in a way that comes from a deep connection with her self and what she is hoping for and working toward in life. Mathilde loves her body for what it can do (e.g., go running with friends) and respects and has compassion for her body in what challenges it (e.g., she is lactose intolerant and avoids dairy as an act of self-care). She is the subject of her story in an empowered and self-supported manner. In fact, she recently stopped dating someone because that person seemed overly focused on appearance. Further, Mathilde is a powerful advocate for her own sexual decision-making. She appreciates sexual intimacy as an important part of a relationship. She knows that she must feel emotionally safe in a relationship and allows only those relationships in her life that honor her body and her sexuality as much as she does. She is engaged in attuned self-care that is based on the needs of her body rather than a narrative that has been internalized by a cultural script. She listens to her body and rests when she needs rest. Mathilde eats when she is hungry and notices when she is craving specific nutrients or foods. In these ways, Mathilde exemplifies positive embodiment.

Recent research suggests that the more one positively inhabits one's body in nourishing, nurturing, and healthy activities, the more positively one tends to think about one's body (Cook-Cottone, 2016a; Piran, 2015; Piran & Teall, 2012). Conversely, when not positively embodied, an individual may experience a sense of disconnection, disturbance of body image or body dissatisfaction, substance use problems, and disordered eating (Cook-Cottone, 2015a; Homan & Tylka, 2014). Given that embodiment can be a preconscious experience, there is limited prescriptive information on how to become positively embodied. However, mindful self-care gives form to positive embodiment integrating mindful awareness, active mindful practices, and mindful care of each aspect of the self (Cook-Cottone, 2015b; Cook-Cottone & Guyker, 2017). This chapter will review positive embodiment and mindful self-care as constructs, and their relationships with positive body image. In addition, mindful self-care and yoga will be explicated as actionable practices for the enhancement of positive embodiment and body image.

Positive Embodiment

According to philosophers, the embodied character of experience stays in the subconscious background, seemingly unknown to us; this is "being-in-the-world normally" (Heidegger, 1927/1996; Svenaeus, 2013, p. 83). Being-in-the-world normally and being positively embodied are akin to the experience of the young child within the context of a safe, supportive, and nourishing environment. That is, the child plays, eats, engages with others from and with the body. Laughter, tears, hugs, and locomotion are spontaneous. There is an absence of consciousness, overt awareness, or judgment of the body. For some, as they develop and age, something changes. For example, Piran (2015, 2016) describes how, when girls go through puberty, they may lose vital embodied experiences of engaging in the world in a positive manner. For example, they may begin to dress for appearance rather than comfort, evaluate their bodies by form not function, and struggle to maintain relationships that prioritize self-worth over acceptance by others (Piran, 2015, 2016).

Barbara Fredrickson, Tomi-Ann Roberts, and Niva Piran are pioneers in the operationalization of positive embodiment. In 1997, Frederickson and Roberts proposed objectification theory. This theory is a paradigm-shifting framework for understanding women's experiences within a sociocultural context that sexually objectifies the female body and tends to value women according to their appearance and sexuality. In other words, women are viewed and valued through the lens of another's objectifying gaze. According to the theory, there is an internalization of the sociocultural objectification, a process by which the body is separated out from the person, reduced to the status of a mere instrument, and regarded as if it was capable of representing the whole person. Piran (2016) detailed the early work of Simone de Beauvoir (1952), a philosopher specializing in the phenomenology of the feminine body, who described the experience of the adolescent female's loss of embodiment as the body getting away from her, no longer serving as a straightforward expression of the adolescent girl's individuality. Specifically, earlier in development, a girl's body is personally experienced with a sense of implicit ownership and as a preconscious vehicle through which she explores the world. Her embodiment is an expression of who she is. In contrast, as a girl moves into adolescence, her embodiment may become a shared expression of the girl and the culture. How she is in and with her body takes on a cultural expression that sometimes silences the individual expression of self. For example, social norms for appearance and behavior, such as wearing tight clothing that restricts movement, may take hold and over-power her embodied way of engaging in the world. For some, there may be little or no insight or discernment regarding the proportional expression of self and culture as embodiment becomes a sociocultural phenomena. For example, Sarah is lost in what others might like or not like about her body, the current trends in the ideal body shape, and being the right kind of sexy for the person she is hoping to date. Despite how much she hates it, she has been working out. Sarah has been targeting her glutes and has eased off arm workouts, for appearance's sake. Sarah experiences her sense of self almost wholly unaware of any internal physiological, emotional, and cognitive experiences manifesting her own wants, likes, and needs. Instead, her thoughts and behaviors are driven by cultural expectations of what her body should look like.

Some believe that it is this internalization of the objectifying gaze that can lead to a sense of the *body uncanny* (Svenaeus, 2013, p. 84), in which the body is viewed and judged as distinct from the self (Fredrickson & Roberts, 1997; Piran, 2015). When this happens, the body is alienated and seen as an obstacle or problem that needs to be corrected (Svenaeus, 2013). The self is no longer unconsciously embodied as the individual interacts with the world, and body image now instead reflects internalized distortions and iconic ideals of the culture (Fredrickson & Roberts, 1997). As detailed in an extensive qualitative study of female embodiment across the lifespan, for some girls and women, there is a disconnection from the body and a sense of discomfort in the body (Piran, 2016). The consequences are substantial. In their groundbreaking theory article, Fredrickson and Roberts (1997) described the disembodied experience of the self as untenable, resulting in shame, attenuated and interrupted motivational states, reduced awareness of internal bodily states, and increased risk of anxiety, depression, sexual dysfunction, and eating disorders.

In contrast, positive embodiment arises from inhabiting the body in a positive manner (Piran, 2015). According to Piran and Teall's (2012) Developmental Theory of Embodiment, there are three domains of protective factors that maintain or enhance positive embodiment: physical (physical freedom), mental (mental freedom), and social (social power). Specifically, this model identifies the physical domain protective factors as: (1) pleasurable engagement in physical activities, (2) safe social environments, (3) social experiences that support attuned self-care, and (4) a pleasurable connection to desires. The emotional domain protective factors include: (1) freedom of voice and engagement in activities unrelated to appearance, (2) freedom from stereotypes or gendered appearance standards, and (3) freedom from constraining stereotypes. Last, the social power domain protective factors are: (1) freedom from exposure to discrimination related to social identities, (2) a social environment that provides social power and equity unrelated to appearance, (3) empowering relationships, and (4) a positive connection to one's embodied social location (e.g., social class, place in community and cultural systems). The scope of intervention here is broad, with substantial cultural and societal implications. Addressing each of the domains in the positive embodiment model, as well as engaging in mindful self-care and embodied practices such as yoga, are actions in which an individual can engage while he or she works toward a shift in broader familial, social, and societal pressures that create risk factors for poor body image.

Mindful Self-Care and Its Connection to Positive Embodiment

Mindful self-care is a set of active, daily behaviors that operationalize what it means to take care of and appreciate the self (e.g., hydrating, planning meals and snacks, exercising, engaging in supportive relationships, practicing mindful awareness and self-compassion, cultivating a sense of purpose, and maintaining supportive routine and structure in daily life; Cook-Cottone, 2015b, 2016a; Cook-Cottone & Guyker, 2017). Critically, mindful self-care can create a sense of agency, which has been identified in qualitative research as a key aspect of positive embodiment (Piran, 2016). Emerging research supports the notion that if you mindfully take care of yourself, you may be more likely to appreciate your body (Cook-Cottone & Guyker, 2017). Moreover, if you appreciate your body, you may be more likely to take care of it (Homan & Tylka, 2014; Wood-Barcalow et al., 2010). Mindful self-care practices are intended to promote positive embodiment, a way of being connected to and expressing the inner and outer experiences of self in a mindful way. Whereas traditionally self-care has been operationalized as a set of tasks known to be associated with various outcomes (e.g., following a meal plan to stabilize sugar levels as a self-care plan for diabetes), mindful self-care is more than a set of prescribed behaviors performed to attain an externally constructed objective (e.g., increased health according to various medical markers; Cook-Cottone & Guyker, 2017). It is a way of mindfully inhabiting the body with practices reflecting qualities such as relaxation, self-compassion, meaning, and mindful awareness (Cook-Cottone, 2015a; Piran, 2015; Piran & Teall, 2012).

Consistent with theoretical models of positive embodiment, the Attuned Representational Model of Self (ARMS) views the self as a system integrating internal experiences (i.e., physiological, emotional, and cognitive) and external experiences (i.e., familial, community, and

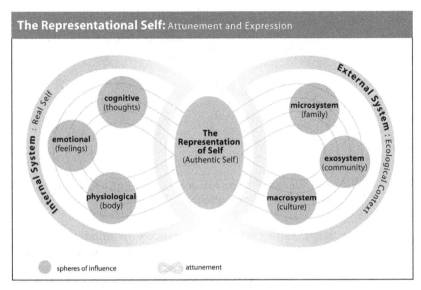

Figure 6.1 The Attuned Model of Self (ARMS)
Note: Adapted from Cook-Cottone, C. P. (2015b).

cultural – see Figure 6.1; Cook-Cottone, 2015a, 2015b). The authentic experience of self is nested in the center of these two domains (i.e., internal and external). It is theorized that in order to maintain a healthy and positive experience of the self, an individual must do two things: (1) maintain positive attunement with and regulation of each of the internal aspects of self, and (2) engage effectively in one's relationships across each of the ecological domains, from family to culture (Cook-Cottone, 2015a; Cook-Cottone & Guyker, 2017; Piran, 2015, 2016; Piran & Teall, 2012). As an individual grows and develops, internal dysregulation and external demands and stressors can disrupt and/or challenge attunement and integration, contributing to a less effective and more negative experience of the self (Cook-Cottone & Guyker, 2017; Piran, 2015, 2016). In action, mindful self-care allows an individual to meet personal needs while staying effectively connected to his or her outer experience. For more on this model, see Cook-Cottone (2006, 2015a, 2015b, 2017; Piran, 2016).

Consistent with a larger body of theoretical work on self-regulation, mindful self-care is seen as the foundation required for physical and emotional well-being (Cook-Cottone, 2015a, 2015b; Cook-Cottone & Guyker, 2017; Linehan, 1993, 2015; Piran, 2016; McCusker et al., 2015; Riegel et al., 2012). Depending on the source, program, or

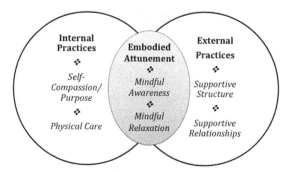

Figure 6.2 Mindful self-care practices and the experience of self
Note: Adapted from Cook-Cottone, C. P. (2017)

theory, there are a variety of potential aspects to mindful self-care: mindful awareness (i.e., nonjudgmental present-moment awareness of internal and external experiences), mindful relaxation (i.e., use of mindfulness meditations and activities to relax), nutrition, hydration, exercise, self-soothing, rest, medical care, self-compassion, supportive relationships, environmental structure (e.g., routine, a manageable schedule, soothing and healthy office and home spaces), and spiritual practices (Cook-Cottone, 2015a; Linehan, 1993; Norcross, 2007; McCusker et al., 2015; Piran, 2016; Riegel et al., 2012). There is emerging qualitative and quantitative research indicating that mindful self-care may support positive embodiment (Cook-Cottone, Keddie, Guyker, & Talebkah, 2017; Cook-Cottone & Guyker, 2017; Piran, 2016).

Measuring mindful self-care. The Mindful Self-Care Scale (MSCS), developed to measure mindful-self-care activities that promote positive embodiment and well-being, appears promising (Cook-Cottone & Guyker, 2017). Specifically, in the first phase of the study, the MSCS was developed using exploratory and confirmatory factor analyses, resulting in a six-factor structure: Physical Care, Supportive Relationships, Mindful Awareness, Self-compassion and Purpose, Mindful Relaxation, and Supportive Structure (descriptions below; Cook-Cottone & Guyker, 2017). The six MSCS factors map well onto the ARMS model (see Figure 6.2).

Mindful and Actionable Tools for Positive Body Image

Mindful self-care is a set of actionable behaviors that include yoga and other practices of positive embodiment (e.g., engaging in supportive relationships, healthy eating to nourish the body, meditation, relaxation through listening to soothing music; Cook-Cottone, 2016a; Cook-Cottone & Guyker, 2017). To provide a prescriptive guide, mindful self-care will be reviewed next. In addition, the benefits of a mindful yoga practice will be discussed specifically as they relate to positive embodiment.

Mindful Self-Care

Mindful self-care practices will be reviewed in accordance with six domains that have been identified through research, including physical care, self-compassion and purpose, supportive relationships, supportive structure, mindful awareness, and mindful relaxation (see Figures 6.1 and 6.2). Consistent with the theory supporting the Mindful Self-Care Scale (MSCS), Riegel et al. (2012) describe mindful self-care as having two layers: (1) mindful awareness within self-care practices, and (2) an overall monitoring and a reflection upon the sufficiency of self-care. For the specific MSCS items associated with each domain, see the appendix of the chapter.

Physical self-care. Physical self-care addresses the physical needs of the self and reflects an active, positive physical embodiment. This aspect of self-care is aligned with Piran and Teall's (2012) physical domain protective factor of pleasurable engagement in physical activities, as well as with findings from Piran's (2016) qualitative study detailing the physical aspects of attuned self-care such as addressing physical needs. Physical self-care involves basic nutrition, hydration, and exercise practices (Benelam & Wyness, 2010; Beydoun, 2014; Brown & Gerbarg, 2015; Cook-Cottone, 2015b; Cook-Cottone & Guyker, 2017; Davis, Eshelman, & McKay, 2008; Hopkins, Davis, VanTieghem, Whalen, & Bucci, 2012; Norcross & Guy, 2007). Specifically, physical self-care includes exercising for 30–60 minutes a day (which may include yoga or other physical practices), planning daily exercise, engaging in a mind/body practice such as yoga, adequately hydrating, eating nutritional foods, and planning meals and snacks (Cook-Cottone & Guyker, 2017).

According to Norcross and Guy (2007), nutrition and hydration are critical aspects of self-care. Research suggests that a healthy body responds to unavoidable stresses in life better than an unhealthy body does (Cook-Cottone & Guyker, 2017; Davis et al., 2008). Nutrition and hydration self-care behaviors include eating a healthy amount of nourishing foods (Cook-Cottone & Guyker, 2017). This also includes the planning needed to make that happen (Cook-Cottone, 2015b; Cook-Cottone & Guyker, 2017). Research indicates that lack of nutritional self-care can cause problems. For example, drops in sugar levels, insufficient or excessive energy intake, and nutrient deficits (e.g., low iron intake, low vitamin

D and B12 levels) have all been identified as related to mood and sense of well-being and can be dysregulating (e.g., Beydoun, 2014; Brown & Gerbarg, 2015; Cook-Cottone & Guyker, 2017). Similarly, it is well accepted that water is essential for a positive experience of the body and maintaining recommended levels of hydration (i.e., 1–2 liters a day, or about 6–8 glasses) is critical to healthy functioning (Benelam & Wyness, 2010; Cook-Cottone, 2015b, 2017; Cook-Cottone & Guyker, 2017). If hydration does not occur within the context of self-care and water loss is not replaced, dehydration occurs. Consequently, positive embodiment can be difficult to achieve. For example, even mild dehydration (around 2 percent loss of body weight) can result in headaches, fatigue, and reduced physical and mental performance (Benelam & Wyness, 2010).

Exercise is a critical component of self-care and contributes to positive embodiment (Cook-Cottone & Guyker, 2017; Piran, 2015; Piran & Teall, 2012). The association between exercise and well-being has been well documented (Cook-Cottone, 2015b; Cook-Cottone & Guyker, 2017; Norcross & Guy, 2007). The World Health Organization (2017) recommends that adults aged 18–64 should exercise for at least 150 minutes a week. This should entail activity of moderate intensity, including strength training and aerobic physical exercise, throughout the week, with sessions of at least ten minutes in duration to reduce health risks. For children the recommendation is higher: sixty minutes per day of aerobic exercise, with additional muscle and bone strengthening workouts (CDC, 2015). Exercise should be done in service of health and well-being and should include pleasurable activities such as playing a sport with friends, running at a pace that feels good to the body, or walking along the beach with a good friend or a beloved dog. When exercise is compulsory or compensatory (e.g., "I ate five pieces of pizza and now I am exercising to burn off 1,000 calories"), it is not in service of well-being, is not attuned to physical health, and can be considered a risk indicator for overexercising or eating disorder. When working with those at risk of overexercising or disordered eating, practitioners should follow individual medical recommendations for exercise.

The likelihood of positive embodiment is increased with exercise: Exercise reduces stress by releasing endorphins into the bloodstream, decreases muscle tension, and increases alpha wave activity (Cook-Cottone & Guyker, 2017). It also improves strength and flexibility, lessens fatigue, increases resting metabolism, rids the body of toxins, and improves blood flow to the brain (Cook-Cottone & Guyker, 2017; Davis et al., 2008). Overall, the beneficial effects of regular exercise include improvements on measures of cognition and psychological well-being in healthy individuals (note, "healthy" refers to individuals who are not diagnosed with a medical or mental health disorder requiring a distinct set of exercise recommendations; Cook-Cottone & Guyker, 2017; Hopkins et al., 2012).

Self-compassion and purpose (mindful grit). The practices of self-compassion and intentional, purposeful action address the needs of the emotional and cognitive self (see Figures 6.1 and 6.2). According to Neff, self-compassion entails "treating oneself with kindness, recognizing one's shared humanity, and being mindful when considering negative aspects of oneself" (2011, p. 1). Self-compassion allows for positive embodiment, is associated with positive body image, and is protective against eating pathology (Braun, Park, & Gorin, 2016). Specifically, the practice of self-compassion allows an individual to maintain a growth mindset and remain embodied in the face of struggle and failure (Cook-Cottone, 2015b; Neff, 2011). A growth mindset involves believing that abilities, like intelligence, can be developed through hard work and practice (Dweck, 2015). The practice of self-compassion includes the acceptance of failure and challenge as part of the process of living (Cook-Cottone & Guyker, 2017). Further, the practice of self-compassion includes the ability to engage in supportive and comforting self-talk and permission to experience feelings (Cook-Cottone & Guyker, 2017; Neff, 2011). For example: During a recent argument with a friend, Mathilde lost her temper and said something potentially hurtful. As she thought over what happened, she reminded herself that everyone gets upset and sometimes says things that they regret. She allowed herself to feel the regret related to her actions, breathing through the achy and heavy feelings in her stomach and chest. She gave herself permission to cry as she felt her feelings. Cook-Cottone and Guyker (2017) argue that such self-compassionate thoughts may help an individual keep going in the face of difficulty and allow for ongoing positive embodiment.

A sense of purpose may also contribute to positive embodiment (Cook-Cottone & Guyker, 2017). In her 2016 qualitative study, Piran found that women engaged in attuned self-care feel a need to engage in meaningful pursuits. A sense of purpose or mission may function some-what like a spiritual, long-term goal aligning a person's behaviors and intentions (Cook-Cottone, 2015b; Cook-Cottone & Guyker, 2017; Norcross & Guy, 2007; Sayrs, 2012). In this way, what one does on a daily basis is aligned with what one intends to do in the longer term and across one's life. This creates a sense of personal congruence. Purpose can be a source of strength and meaning during difficult and challenging times, giving an individual a reason to pick her or himself up by the proverbial bootstraps and persevere (Cook-Cottone & Guyker, 2017; Norcross & Guy, 2007). There is a growing body of theoretical work that aligns meaning and purpose with well-being. For example, Ryan and Deci (2001) suggest that happiness and well-being may be found via an eudaimonic approach in which an individual focuses on meaning and self-realization, in contrast to a hedonic approach in which happiness is pursued via a search for pleasure and the avoidance of pain. The former allows for a sustainable approach to positive embodiment (Cook-Cottone & Guyker, 2017). In contrast, those who pursue happiness based on the fleeting pleasures of a neurological or physical reward experience the ephemeral nature of such rewards. For example, the pleasure that comes from drinking alcohol, the high associated with gambling, or the relief that comes with hitting the snooze button to avoid getting up in the morning might last minutes or hours; although these experiences may feel good, they lack meaning. In contrast, the sense of well-being that results from good works has a hardier, lasting effect. For example, the difficult work and challenges involved in parenting a child from a place of reflective and intentional loving kindness (as opposed to yelling and reacting in the moment); founding a nonprofit organization; helping build homes for those in need; or supporting individuals during a disaster are more easily tolerated because they have meaning and the positive aftereffects last longer.

Cook-Cottone and Guyker (2017) theorized that self-compassion and purpose may be related to a concept termed *grit*, the ability to work hard toward a chosen goal with persistence and perseverance (Duckworth & Gross, 2014). The research on grit explores determinants of success, such as the ability to self-regulate attention, emotion, and behaviors, within the context of the tenacious pursuit of a superordinate goal despite setbacks (Cook-Cottone & Guyker, 2017; Duckworth & Gross, 2014). That is, grit keeps a person going, even during hard times (Cook-Cottone & Guyker, 2017). There is, however, risk involved in pushing toward goals without paying attention to physical and emotional needs or a sense of meaning. In contrast to this, self-compassion and purpose can combine to create *mindful grit*, a more sustainable form of grit in which a sense of purpose and meaning is combined with the practice of self-compassion (Cook-Cottone & Guyker, 2017).

Self-care in relationships. Researchers of positive embodiment agree that positive embodiment occurs within the context of relationships (Piran, 2015; Piran & Teall, 2012). In terms of relationships, self-care practices that are aligned with positive embodiment include spending time with people who are good to you, feeling supported by people in your life, feeling like you have people who will be there for you when you are distraught, spending time with people who listen to and respect your limits, and having a group of people in your life who are special to you.

This aspect of self-care is aligned with all of Piran and Teall's (2012) protective factors: the physical domain protective factors of a safe social environment and social experiences that support self-care; the mental domain protective factor of freedom of voice and assertive action; and the social power domain protective factor detailing empowering relationships (Piran & Teall, 2012). The importance of engagement in self-care in relationships was also found in Piran's (2016) qualitative study described earlier. Participants in that study reported relationships in which their emotional needs were met and described how they sought validating relational forums (i.e., social groups in which one feels seen, heard, and supported).

Generally, supportive relationships are theorized to enhance well-being (Cook-Cottone, 2015b; Cook-Cottone & Guyker, 2017; McCusker et al., 2015; Norcross & Guy, 2007; Sayrs, 2012). According to Cook-Cottone and Guyker (2017), however, it is important to make a distinction between simply having relationships and engaging in healthy and supportive relationships. An example of a supportive relationship is having a friend who supports you when you are engaged in positive and healthy behaviors (Cook-Cottone & Guyker, 2017; McCusker et al., 2015). In contrast, a relationship that is not supportive or adaptive is a relationship in which an individual feels as if she or he cannot say "no" or set a limit (Cook-Cottone & Guyker, 2017). Self-care in this area is related to the notion that an important aspect of healthy relationships is appropriate boundaries (Norcross & Guy, 2007; Sayrs, 2012).

Supportive structure in self-care. Positive embodiment involves a supportive relationship with one's environment in terms of physical space, routine, and schedule (Cook-Cottone & Guyker, 2017). Within this domain, self-care is found in how one manages one's physical space as well as one's time. It involves a commitment to organizing one's space as well as creating a pleasing and comforting environment that is supportive of one's daily functioning. It also involves a balanced schedule that supports both work and well-being.

Research suggests that an individual's physical environment can affect well-being (Cook-Cottone, 2015b; Cook-Cottone & Guyker, 2017; Norcross & Guy, 2007). Specifically, the comfort and appeal of lighting, furniture, decorations, flooring, and windows can make a difference to the overall tone of a space, which may play a role in a person's sense of comfort throughout the day (Norcross & Guy, 2007). Indeed, environmental *microstressors* (e.g., a doorknob that never works) can aggregate, whittling away at an individual's resiliency and ability to cope (Cook-Cottone, 2015b; Cook-Cottone & Guyker, 2017). Conversely, a supportive environment, such as an organized workplace that offers water close to one's desk and soothing and relaxing music in the waiting room, can bolster positive embodiment by reducing environmental stressors (Cook-Cottone & Guyker, 2017).

Structure in self-care also means creating a balance between the demands of others and one's own needs, including maintaining a manageable work schedule (Cook-Cottone & Guyker, 2017). Positive embodiment is facilitated by a schedule that allows for sufficient rest and restoration (Cappuccio, 2011; Cook-Cottone, 2015b; Cook-Cottone & Guyker, 2017; Lim & Dinges, 2010; Norcross & Guy, 2007). For some, this may mean scheduling patients in a way that leaves breaks for one's own recovery between sessions. For others, it may mean balancing work that requires physical exertion with seated tasks. It can also mean taking adequate vacation or family leave time, or taking a respite break when caring for an aging parent.

Mindful awareness as self-care. The literature indicates that mindful awareness is a fundamental and unique feature of mindful self-care (Cook-Cottone & Guyker, 2017; Shapiro, Brown, & Biegel, 2007). Mindfulness awareness is the way a person is embodied from moment to moment (see Figures 6.1 and 6.2; Cook-Cottone & Guyker, 2017). Specifically, to be mindful is to practice calm awareness of thoughts, feelings, and the physical body, as well as the careful and intentional selection of which thoughts and feelings an individual uses to guide his or her actions. Self-awareness and mindfulness self-care practices include formal (i.e., intentional practices such as yoga or seated and walking meditation) and informal practices (i.e., deliberately engaging in mindful awareness during daily activities such as doing dishes or folding laundry). Self-awareness, one-mindedness (i.e., attending to one thing at a time), and active practices such as meditation and yoga are increasingly acknowledged for their effectiveness as self-care practices (Cook-Cottone & Guyker, 2017; Linehan, 1993; Norcross & Guy, 2007; Sayrs, 2012; Shapiro & Carlson, 2009).

Mindful relaxation as self-care. Mindful relaxation practices can be described as techniques for self-soothing, calming, and relaxation. Self-soothing is believed to be an effective tool in emotional regulation (Linehan, 1993). It can be a positive, healthy response to feeling stressed, being in distress, or having an intense emotional reaction (Cook-Cottone & Guyker, 2017; Davis et al., 2008; Norcross & Guy, 2007). Self-soothing includes structured relaxation techniques (e.g., progressive muscle relaxation), deep breathing and other types of breath work (e.g., yogic breathing, extended exhale breathing, three-part breaths), and pursuit of stimuli or activities that are calming and relaxing (e.g, listening to music, aromatherapy; Cook-Cottone, 2015b; Cook-Cottone &

Guyker, 2017; McCusker et al., 2015). Self-soothing and relaxation can also be achieved via other behaviors, such as reading, writing, and cultivating sensory awareness (Cook-Cottone, 2015b; Davis et al., 2008; Norcross & Guy, 2007).

Yoga as a Self-Care Practice for Positive Embodiment

Yoga can be a pathway to positive embodiment (Cook-Cottone, 2016b). Yoga is a mind/body practice that combines breath work, physical practice (asanas, which are structured physical poses), relaxation, and meditation designed to enhance self-regulation (Büssing, Michalsen, Khalsa, Telles, & Sherman, 2012; Cook-Cottone, 2015a, 2015b, 2016a; Klein & Cook-Cottone, 2013). Yoga is believed to address three primary mechanisms, all key to positive body image: (1) mind and body integration, (2) self-regulation, and (3) nonjudgmental awareness of experience (Büssing et al., 2012; Cook-Cottone, 2016a). Yoga provides dedicated time for awareness of and attention to the body (Cook-Cottone, 2016b). It allows time for the yoga practitioner to get comfortable with the uncomfortable, both physical and emotional, and to stay present and engaged with and in the body (Cook-Cottone, 2016b). The implications are substantial in terms of opportunities to practice being with cravings, difficult feelings, and struggles with self-regulation, which can all be obstacles to positive embodiment (Cook-Cottone, 2016b). Yoga also allows the practitioner the opportunity to explore the uncomfortable safely and on their own terms (Cook-Cottone, 2015b, 2016b). Being present and allowing oneself the opportunity to feel physical and emotional experiences can be a very corrective and healing experience within the context of one's relationship with the body (Cook-Cottone, 2016b). In addition, yoga is fairly accessible in the United States and is relatively low cost (Neumark-Sztainer, 2014), although for those in rural or impoverished areas, access to in-person yoga classes can be an obstacle, and although a growing number of studios offer free or sliding scale classes, the fee per session – at $10–$25 – may reduce access for some. Online classes by subscription and free online videos are increasingly available, thus alleviating some barriers to access.

Emerging research supports yoga as a protective, embodied practice that may be beneficial to body image and reduced eating disorder symptoms (Douglass & Bottrill, in press; Klein & Cook-Cottone, 2013; Neumark-Sztainer, 2014). In a review of the effects of yoga on eating disorder symptoms and correlates, Klein and Cook-Cottone (2013) found that, although more well-controlled studies are needed, yoga appears to play a positive role in the prevention and treatment of eating disorders. Yoga's basic tenants – to work toward a mind–body connection and to do so with loving kindness, compassion, equanimity – and joy, align with positive embodiment (Cook-Cottone, 2016b). Indeed, Mahlo and Tiggemann (2016) recently found that adult yoga practitioners (n = 193), when compared to nonyoga participants (n = 127), scored higher on measures of positive body image and embodiment and lower on self-objectification. However, other research has found no impact of yoga on body image. Specifically, Mitchell, Mazzeo, Rausch, and Cooke (2007) compared the effectiveness of a yoga program to a dissonance program and a passive control group on body image outcomes among women who were dissatisfied with their bodies. There was no significant postintervention difference between the yoga and the control groups. In fact, at postintervention, the dissonance group participants had significantly lower scores than both of the other groups on measures of disordered eating, drive for thinness, body dissatisfaction, alexithymia, and anxiety. This study, however, has been criticized for not integrating a high enough dosage of yoga (Klein & Cook-Cottone, 2013; Cook-Cottone, 2013). Some evidence suggests that yoga practice two or three times a week is required to promote and maintain positive outcomes (Cook-Cottone, 2013).

Yoga may play an important role in the prevention of body dissatisfaction, negative body image, and eating disorders in children as well as adults. For example, eating disorder prevention programs that include concrete, embodied components (e.g., active yoga practice and relaxation strategies) have been found to be effective for younger children (e.g., grades five and six; Cook-Cottone, 2016a; Cook-Cottone, Kane, Keddie, & Haugli, 2013; Scime & Cook-Cottone, 2008; Scime, Cook-Cottone, Kane, & Watson, 2006). For a step-by-step manual of a school-based eating disorder prevention program, see *Girls Growing in Wellness and Balance: Yoga and Life Skills to Empower* (Cook-Cottone et al., 2013). This program was the first yoga-based eating disorder prevention program to be studied in schools and has been found to be effective across a range of studies, reducing body dissatisfaction, drive for thinness, and eating disorder symptoms while increasing physical self-concept and self-care (e.g., Cook-Cottone, Jones, & Haugli, 2010; Cook-Cottone, Keddie, Guyker, & Talebkah, 2017; Norman, Sodana, & Cook-Cottone, 2014; Scime & Cook-Cottone, 2008; Scime et al., 2006).

Several randomized controlled trials (RCTs) involving yoga conducted among eating disordered populations suggest some efficacy. First, Caraei, Fyfe-Johnson, Breuner, and Brown (2010) examined the effect of individualized yoga on adolescents in treatment for eating disorders. Participant in the yoga group showed significantly lower scores on measures of eating disorder behavior at follow-up as compared to participants in the standard treatment group. Second, McIver, O'Halloran, and McGartland (2009) assessed the effect of yoga on binge eating disorder with a community-based sample of adult women. Compared to the control group, the yoga group showed statistically significant decreases in binge eating scores at the end of the program and at the three-month follow-up. Women reported moving from a feeling of estrangement from their bodies to one of empowerment in their bodies, experiencing increased sensations of satiation and showing greater feelings of connection with their body over time, suggesting yoga increases positive embodiment. Most recently, Pacanowski, Diers, Crosby, and Neumark-Sztainer (2017) investigated the effects of yoga on negative affect, a known eating disorder risk factor, among individuals in a residential eating disorder treatment program. Findings demonstrated that yoga significantly reduced premeal negative affect compared to treatment as usual. However, the effect was attenuated postmeal, i.e., the positive impact on affect did not persist after eating.

Yoga also seems to be beneficial as an adjunct to traditional eating disorder therapies (Cook-Cottone, Beck, & Kane, 2006; Klein & Cook-Cottone, 2013; Neumark-Sztainer, 2014). In the first study of its kind, Cook-Cottone et al. (2006) found that patients in treatment for eating disorders benefited from engagement in a yoga-based program, showing reductions in drive for thinness, body dissatisfaction, and eating disordered behaviors.

Although early results on yoga's effectiveness on eating disorders are promising, more research is needed to detail the specific mechanisms responsible for positive outcomes, the potential risks, and the teaching and yoga styles that may be most effective for individuals with particular eating pathologies (Neumark-Sztainer, 2014). Further, Neumark-Sztainer (2014) has noted that to date there has been no systematic study of potential harm caused by yoga for practitioners with eating disorders – for example, focusing more on the ability to do a pose than on a person's experience in a pose, or on an emphasis on weight or shape rather than on breath and present moment experience. To that end, Cook-Cottone and Douglass (2017) recently detailed the first specific protocol for yoga studios to create a body positive yoga environment.

Conclusion: It's a Practice

Being positively embodied requires practice (Cook-Cottone, 2016a). To counter societal and cultural pressures that lead to self-objectification, one must be in subjective action in her or his life. Specifically, we determine our own embodiment through presence, choice, and action rather than through internalizing sociocultural norms. Douglass and Bottrill (in press) beautifully articulate the embodiment of our felt lives in saying: "Our deepest desires and fears are communicated through a flush of our face, the turning of our shoulders or a tightening of our jaw" (p. 5). Our embodied reaction to the world is our main tool for the experience of felt emotion, the generation of meaning, the organization of experience, and the shape of our identities (Douglass & Bottrill, in press). To be embodied is a practice (Cook-Cottone, 2016b). It has been said that Aristotle once mused: "We are what we repeatedly do." Mindful self-care and yoga are promising, actionable tools to positive embodiment and can provide a pathway to positive body image and all of the protections and life satisfaction that follow.

Appendix   Mindful Self-Care Scale (MSCS)

The MSCS is free to use. Permission is not required with correct citation of the source. However, the authors request that you notify the corresponding author via email if you use the MSCS in research (contact Catherine Cook-Cottone, PhD at cpcook@buffalo.edu). Please cite:

Cook-Cottone, C. P., & Guyker, W. M. (2017). The development and validation of the Mindful Self-Care Scale (MSCS): An assessment of practices that support positive embodiment. *Mindfulness*. Advance online publication. Retrieved from https://link.springer.com/article/10.1007/s12671–017–0759–1

Directions for Administration

Check the box that reflects the frequency of your behavior (how much or how often) within past week (7 days): never (0 days), rarely (1 day) sometimes (2–3 days), often (4–5 days), and regularly (6–7 days). Note, one item is reverse scored (see Physical Care*).

Physical Care (8 items)

1. I drank at least 6–8 cups of water
2. I ate a variety of nutritious foods (e.g., vegetables, protein, fruits, and grains)
3. I planned my meals and snacks
4. I exercised at least 30–60 minutes
5. I took part in sports, dance or other scheduled physical activities (e.g., sports teams, dance classes)
6. I did sedentary activities instead of exercising (e.g., watched tv, worked on the computer) – reversed score*
7. I planned/scheduled my exercise for the day
8. I practiced yoga or another mind/body practice (e.g., Tae Kwon Do, Tai Chi)

Supportive Relationships (5 items)
9. I spent time with people who are good to me (e.g., support, encourage, and believe in me)
10. I felt supported by people in my life
11. I felt that I had someone who would listen to me if I became upset (e.g., friend, counselor, group)
12. I felt confident that people in my life would respect my choice if I said "no"
13. I scheduled/planned time to be with people who are special to me

Mindful Awareness (4 items)
14. I had a calm awareness of my thoughts
15. I had a calm awareness of my feelings
16. I had a calm awareness of my body
17. I carefully selected which of my thoughts and feelings I used to guide my actions

Self-Compassion and Purpose (6 items)
18. I kindly acknowledged my own challenges and difficulties
19. I engaged in supportive and comforting self-talk (e.g., "My effort is valuable and meaningful")
20. I reminded myself that failure and challenge are part of the human experience
21. I gave myself permission to feel my feelings (e.g., allowed myself to cry)
22. I experienced meaning and/or a larger purpose in my _work/school_ life (e.g., for a cause)
23. I experienced meaning and/or larger purpose in my _private/personal_ life (e.g., for a cause)

Mindful Relaxation (6 items)
24. I did something intellectual (using my mind) to help me relax (e.g., read a book, wrote)
25. I did something interpersonal to relax (e.g., connected with friends)
26. I did something creative to relax (e.g., drew, played instrument, wrote creatively, sang, organized)
27. I listened to relax (e.g., to music, a podcast, radio show, rainforest sounds)
28. I sought out images to relax (e.g., art, film, window shopping, nature)
29. I sought out smells to relax (lotions, nature, candles/incense, smells of baking)

Supportive Structure (4 items)
30. I kept my work/school area organized to support my work/school tasks
31. I maintained a manageable schedule
32. I maintained balance between the demands of others and what is important to me
33. I maintained a comforting and pleasing living environment

General (3 items – not to be averaged)
G1. I engaged in a variety of self-care strategies
G2. I planned my self-care
G3. I explored new ways to bring self-care into my life

References

Benelam, B., & Wyness, L. (2010). Hydration and health: A review. *Nutrition Bulletin, 35*, 3–25. doi:10.1111/j.1467–3010.2009.01795.x

Beydoun, M. A. (2014). The interplay of gender, mood, and stress hormones in the association between emotional eating and dietary behavior. *The Journal of Nutrition, 144*, 1139–1141. doi:10.3945/jn.114.196717

Braun, T. D., Park, C. L., & Gorin, A. (2016). Self-compassion, body image, and disordered eating: A review of the literature. *Body Image, 17*, 117–131. doi:10.1016/j.bodyim.2016.03.003

Brown, R. P., & Gerbarg, P. L. (2015). Nutrients, phytomedicines, and mind–body treatments for substance abuse. In R. P. Bruwn & P. L. Gerbarg (Eds.), *Textbook of addiction treatment: International perspectives* (pp. 747–772). New York: Wiley.

Büssing, A., Michalsen, A., Khalsa, S. B. S., Telles, S., & Sherman, K. J. (2012). Effects of yoga on mental and physical health: A short summary of reviews. *Evidence-Based Complementary and Alternative Medicine: eCAM, 2012*, 165410. doi:10.1155/2012/165410.

Cappuccio, F. P., Cooper, D., D'Elia, L., Strazzullo, P., & Miller, M. A. (2011). Sleep duration predicts cardiovascular outcomes: A systematic review and meta-analysis of prospective studies. *European Heart Journal, 32*, 1484–1492. doi.org/10.1093/eurheartj/ehr007

Carei, T. R., Fyfe-Johnson, A. L., Breuner, C. C., & Brown, M. A. (2010). Randomized controlled clinical trial of yoga in the treatment of eating disorders. *Journal of Adolescent Health, 46*, 346–351. doi:10.1016/j.jadohealth.2009.08.007

Center for Disease Control [CDC] (2015, June 4). Physical activity basics. Retrieved from www.cdc.gov/physicalactivity/basics/adults/index.htm.

Cook-Cottone, C. (2013). Dosage as a critical variable in yoga therapy research. *International Journal of Yoga Therapy, 23*, 11–12.

Cook-Cottone, C. P. (2015a). Incorporating positive body image into the treatment of eating disorders: A model for attunement and mindful self-care. *Body Image, 14,* 158–167. doi:10.1016/j.bodyim.2015.03.004

(2015b). *Mindfulness and yoga for self-regulation: A primer for mental health professionals.* New York: Springer.

(2016a). Embodied self-regulation and mindful self-care in the prevention of eating disorders. *Eating Disorders, 24,* 98–105. doi: 10.1080/10640266.2015.1118954

(2016b). Yoga for the re-embodied self: The therapeutic journey home. *Yoga Therapy Today,* Winter, 40–48.

(2017). *Mindfulness and yoga for schools: A guide for teachers and practitioners.* New York: Springer.

Cook-Cottone, C. P., Beck, M., & Kane, L. (2006). Manualized-group treatment of eating disorders: Attunement in mind, body, and relationship (AMBR). *Journal for Specialists in Group Work, 33,* 61–83. doi:10.1080/01933920701798570

Cook-Cottone, C. P., & Douglass, L. L. (2017). Yoga communities and eating disorders: Creating safe space for positive embodiment. *International Journal of Yoga Therapy.* Advance online publication. doi: 10.17761/IJYT2017.

Cook-Cottone, C. P., & Guyker, W. M. (2017). The development and validation of the Mindful Self-Care Scale (MSCS): An assessment of practices that support positive embodiment. *Mindfulness.* Advance online publication. Retrieved from https://link.springer.com/article/10.1007/s12671–017–0759–1

Cook-Cottone, C. P., Jones, L. A., & Haugli, S. (2010). Prevention of eating disorders among minority youth: A matched-sample repeated measures study. *Eating Disorders, 18,* 361–376. doi: 10.1080/01933920701798570

Cook-Cottone, C. P., Kane, L., Keddie, E., & Haugli, S. (2013). *Girls growing in wellness and balance: Yoga and life skills to empower.* Onalaska: Schoolhouse Educational Services, LLC.

Cook-Cottone, C. P., Keddie, E., Guyker, W., & Talebkah, K. (2017). A controlled study of a yoga-based eating disorder prevention program: Working toward attunement and self-care. *Eating Disorders Journal of Treatment and Prevention, 25,* 392–405. doi:10.1080/10640266.2017.1365562.

Davis, M., Eshelman, E. R., & McKay, M. (2008). *The relaxation and stress reduction workbook* (6th ed.). Oakland: New Harbinger Publications.

de Beauvoir, S. (1952). *The second sex* (H. Parshley, Trans). New York: Knopf.

Douglass, L. L., & Bottrill, S. (in press). Yoga as a tool for emotional regulation in individual with eating disorders. In H. Mason & K. Birch (Eds.), *Yoga for mental health.* Scotland, UK: Handspring Publishing.

Duckworth, A., & Gross, J. J. (2014). Self-control and grit related but separable determinants of success. *Current Directions in Psychological Science, 23,* 319–325. doi:10.1177/0963721414541462

Duyff, R. L. (2011). *American dietetic association complete food and nutrition guide.* New York: Houghton Mifflin Harcourt.

Dweck, C. (2015). Carol Dweck revisits the "growth mindset." *Education Week*, *35*(5), 20–24.

Homan, K. J., & Tylka, T. L. (2014). Appearance-based exercise motivation moderates the relationship between exercise frequency and positive body image. *Body Image*, *11*, 101–108. doi: 10.1016/j.bodyim.2014.01.003

Hopkins, M. E., Davis, F. C., VanTieghem, M. R., Whalen, P. J., & Bucci, D. J. (2012). Differential effects of acute and regular physical exercise on cognition and affect. *Neuroscience*, *215*, 59–68. doi:10.1016/j.neuroscience.2012.04.056

Fredrickson, B. L., & Roberts, T. (1997). Objectification theory: Toward understanding women's lived experiences and mental health risks. *Psychology of Women Quarterly*, *21*, 173–206. doi: 10.1111/j.1471–6402.1997.tb00108.x

Klein, J., & Cook-Cottone, C. P. (2013). The effects of yoga on eating disorder symptoms and correlates: A review. *International Journal of Yoga Therapy*, *23*, 41–50.

Lim, J., & Dinges, D. F. (2010). A meta-analysis of the impact of short-term sleep deprivation on cognitive variables. *Psychological Bulletin*, *136*, 375–389. doi: 10.1037/a0018883

Linehan, M. M. (1993). *Skills training manual for treating borderline personality disorder*. New York: Guilford Press.

Neff, K. D. (2011). Self-compassion, self-esteem, and well-being. *Social and Personality Psychology Compass*, *5*, 1–12. doi:10.1111/j.1751–9004.2010.00330.x

Norcross, J. C., & Guy, J. D. (2007). *Leaving it at the office: A guide to psychotherapist self-care*. New York: The Guildford Press.

Norman, K., Sodano, S. M., & Cook-Cottone, C. P. (2014). An exploratory analysis of the role of interpersonal styles in eating disorder prevention outcomes. *Journal for Specialists in Group Work*, *39*, 301–315. doi:10.1080/01933922.2014.948234

Neumark-Sztainer, D. (2014). Yoga and eating disorders: Is there a place for yoga in the prevention and treatment of eating disorders and disordered eating behaviours? *Advances in Eating Disorders: Theory, Research and Practice*, *2*, 136–145. doi:10.1080/21662630.2013.862369

Mahlo, L., & Tiggemann, M. (2016). Yoga and positive body image: A test of the Embodiment Model. *Body Image*, *18*, 135–142. doi:10.1016/j.bodyim.2016.06.008

McCusker, J., Cole, M. G., Yaffe, M., Strumpf, E., Sewitch, M., Sussman, T., Ciampi, A., Lavoie, K., Platt, R., & Belzile, E. (2015). A randomized trial of a depression self-care toolkit with or without lay telephone coaching for primary care patients with chronic physical conditions. *General Hospital Psychiatry*, *37*, 257–265. doi: 10.1016/j.genhosppsych.2016.02.004

McIver, S., O'Halloran, P., & McGartland, M. (2009). Yoga as a treatment for binge eating disorder: A preliminary study. *Complementary Therapies in Medicine*, *17*, 196–202. doi:10.1016/j.ctim.2009.05.002

Mitchell, K. S., Mazzeo, S. E., Rausch, S. M., & Cooke, K. L. (2007). Innovative interventions for disordered eating: Evaluating dissonance-based and yoga interventions. *International Journal of Eating Disorders, 40*, 120–128. 10.1002/eat.20282

Pacanowski, C. R., Diers, L., Crosby, R. D., & Neumark-Sztainer, D. (2017). Yoga in the treatment of eating disorders within a residential program: A randomized controlled trial. *Eating Disorders, 25*, 37–51. doi:10.1080/10640266.2016.1237810

Piran, N. (2015). New possibilities in the prevention of eating disorders: The introduction of positive body image measures. *Body Image, 14*, 146–157. doi:10.1016/j.bodyim.2015.03.008

(2016). Embodied possibilities and disruptions: The emergence of the experience of embodiment construct from the qualitative studies with girls and women. *Body Image, 18*, 43–60. doi:10.1016/j.bodyim.2015.03.008

Piran, N., & Teall, T. (2012). The developmental theory of embodiment. In G. McVey, M. Levine, N. Piran, & B. Ferguson (Eds.), *Preventing eating-related and weight-related disorders: Collaborative research, advocacy, and policy change* (pp. 169–198). Waterloo: Wilfrid Laurier University Press.

Riegel, B., Jaarsma, T., & Stromberg, A. (2012). A middle-range theory of self-care of chronic illness. *Advances in Nursing Science, 35*, 194–204. doi:10.1097/ANS.0b013e318261b1ba

Ryan, R. M., & Deci, E. L. (2001). On happiness and human potential: A review of research on hedonic and eudaimonic well-being. *Annual Review of Psychology, 52*, 141–166. doi:10.1146/annurev.psych.52.1.141

Sayrs, J. H. (2012). Mindfulness, acceptance, and values-based interventions for addiction counselors: The benefits of practicing what we preach. In S. C. Hayes & M. Levine (Eds.), *Mindfulness and acceptance for addictive behaviors: Applying contextual CBT to substance abuse and behavioral addictions* (pp. 187–215). Oakland: Context Press of New Harbinger Press.

Scime, M., & Cook-Cottone, C. P. (2008). Primary prevention of eating disorders: A constructivist integration of mind and body strategies. *International Journal of Eating Disorders, 41*, 134–142. doi:10.1002/eat.20480

Scime, M., Cook-Cottone, C. P., Kane, L., & Watson, T. (2006). Group prevention of eating disorders with fifth grade females: Impact on body dissatisfaction, drive for thinness, and media influence. *Eating Disorders, 14*, 143–155. doi:10.1080/10640260500403881

Shapiro, S. L., Brown, K. W., & Biegel, G. M. (2007). Teaching self-care to caregivers: Effect of mindfulness-based stress reduction on the mental health of therapists in training. *Training and Education in Professional Psychology, 1*, 105–115. doi:10.1037/1931–3918.1.2.105

Shapiro, S. L., & Carlson, L. E. (2009). *The art and science of mindfulness: Integrating mindfulness into psychology and the helping professions.* Washington, DC: American Psychological Association. doi: 10.1037/11885–000

Siegel, D. J. (2009). Mindful awareness, mindsight, and neural integration. *The Humanistic Psychologist, 37*, 137–158. doi: 10.1080/08873260902892220

(2010). *The mindful therapist: A clinician's guide to mindsight and neural integration.* New York: WW Norton & Company.

Svenaeus, F. (2013). Anorexia nervosa and the body uncanny:
A phenomenological approach. *Philosophy, Psychiatry, and Psychology, 20,*
81–91. https://muse.jhu.edu/article/511263.

Wood-Barcalow, N. L., Tylka, T., & Augustus-Horvath, C. L. (2010). "But I like
my body": Positive body image characteristics and a holistic model for
young-adult women. *Body Image, 7,* 106–116. doi: 10.1016/j.
bodyim.2010.01.001

7 The Health At Every Size® Paradigm
Promoting Body Positivity for All Bodies

Patti Lou Watkins, Dawn Clifford, and Brian Souza

> I can only hope that in the future, I will be more forgiving, tolerant, and above all accepting of myself, much less others. Regardless of a person's shape and size, we are all beautiful, and while I'm just beginning to understand this, it can only get better from here.
> (College student response to Health At Every Size® curriculum)

This chapter will introduce readers to the Health At Every Size® (HAES) paradigm, reviewing treatment-outcome research and illustrating its applications in clinical, fitness, and educational settings. In doing so, it will highlight the potential role that the HAES paradigm might play in promoting body positivity. Programs to promote body positivity and prevent eating disorders have proliferated in recent years (Tylka & Wood-Barcalow, 2015). These programs, largely based on media literacy and dissonance induction, have made great strides toward improving body image, reducing negative affect, and alleviating thoughts and behaviors associated with disordered eating (Khanh-Dao Le, Barendregt Hay, & Mihalopoulos, 2017). However, some researchers contend that these interventions are limited in their ability to sustain such changes. For example, Piran (2015) notes that, while cognitive dissonance and media literacy programs have resulted in fewer clinically significant cases, they often have small effect sizes and fail to maintain improvements over time.

Wright and Leahy (2016) critique these psychoeducational approaches to improving body image because they place too much emphasis on individual change while skirting around societal stigmatization of fat.[1] These scholars contend that, although media literacy programs routinely address messages about the thin ideal, they rarely address messages about fat bodies – not only messages communicated through popular

---

[1] Fat Studies scholars prefer use of the word "fat" versus the word "obese" as the latter represents a medicalized, pathologizing term. The word "fat" signifies a reclaiming of a pejorative label in the same vein as the LGBTQ community has reclaimed the word "queer."

160

culture, but also messages espoused through medical, educational, and governmental institutions about the "obesity epidemic." LaMarre, Rice, and Jankowski (2017) offer a similar critique, noting that the lived experiences of fat people are commonly neglected in programs that aim to promote body positivity. LaMarre and colleagues also lament that existing interventions are overly focused on the individual. For instance, the attempt to minimize dissonance between actual and ideal bodies overlooks the reality that some people's bodies are truly ostracized in today's society.

A recent popular press article in *Revelist*, an online publication geared toward millennial women, echoes these scholarly critiques. Author Evette Dionne (2017) contends that, as the body positivity movement has become more mainstream, visibly fat and otherwise marginalized bodies are no longer an integral part of the conversation. Rather, she explains, the body positivity movement is centered on people whose bodies are already deemed acceptable by society. Thus, it neglects to address the widespread societal bias against fat bodies, as well as the ways in which such bodies intersect with other diverse identities.

In response to these shortcomings, Wright and Leahy (2016) advocate for sociocritical, social justice-oriented approaches that directly address weight bias and discrimination, as a more comprehensive and lasting means of enhancing body positivity than the current cognitive dissonance and media literacy programs. Similarly, LaMarre et al. (2017) contend that eating disorder-prevention efforts must examine not only societal oppression of fat, but also intersections with oppression based on other identities such as gender, race, ethnicity, sexual orientation, age, and disability status. Halliwell (2015) acknowledges that while research has begun to consider ethnicity in relation to positive body image, it has not yet addressed how sexual identity or visible physical difference and disability impact positive body image. Thus, rather than simply focusing on individual change, LaMarre and colleagues assert that interventions must strive to create equitable environments that challenge biases and support body diversity.

Proponents of sociocritical approaches acknowledge that "while teaching for positive body image has always been difficult, the dominant 'obesity' discourse in contemporary times makes this work even more difficult, if not impossible" (Wright & Leahy, 2016, p. 144). For example, Wright and Cliff (2010) identified confusing and contradictory messages inherent in a high school health curriculum that attempted to prevent both obesity and eating disorders, leading them to speculate that obesity prevention programs may have dangerous repercussions in terms of eating disorders as they normalize a fear of fat and undermine concurrent messages about body positivity. Alberga, Russell-Mayhew, von Ranson, and Mclaren (2016) concur with this sentiment, quoting an interviewee in an article in the *New York Times*: "My therapist tells me not to talk about my weight and that my body is fine. But my doctor keeps weighing me and says that I need to lose weight" (para. 1). Thus, individuals routinely receive conflicting messages about weight from various sources.

Given the cross-purposes of the obesity and eating disorder prevention agendas, Russell-Mayhew and Grace (2016) call for a social justice approach to health that eschews interventions targeting weight loss. Instead, they endorse wellness-based approaches that focus on promoting health for individuals of all shapes and sizes. Such efforts would aim to modify sociocultural factors, such as cultural attitudes about ideal bodies, rather than placing the onus for change solely on the individual. Their vision includes fostering critical thinking skills to develop positive body image, challenging societal appearance standards, embracing size diversity, reducing weight bias, and promoting both nutrition and physical activity without a focus on weight.

The HAES paradigm invoked by Russell-Mayhew and colleagues (Nutter et al., 2016) is a sociocritical approach that holds great promise. As O'Hara and Taylor (2014) explain, the HAES approach underscores the value of critical awareness "enacted through the principles of challenging scientific and cultural assumptions, valuing people's body knowledge and their lived experiences, and acknowledging social injustice and the role of disadvantage and oppression as health hazards" (p. 276). Indeed, Tylka and Wood-Barcalow (2015) recognize HAES as a framework that can contribute to body positivity research and interventions.

This chapter will first present the background of the HAES paradigm and delineate its guiding principles. Subsequently, it will provide a review of HAES intervention research. It will then consider the HAES model's utility within clinical, fitness, and college classroom settings, accentuating its potential for promoting body positivity. The chapter will conclude by sharing resources for implementing the HAES approach across these locales.

The Health At Every Size Paradigm

In 1999, the *Journal of Social Issues* released a special volume entitled "Dying to Be Thin in the Name of Health: Shifting the Paradigm," in which scholars spanning the behavioral and biomedical sciences critiqued the traditional weight-centric or weight-normative approach to health. Based on the research literature at the time, articles in this issue presented data challenging the widely accepted idea that body weight is the cause of disease and early mortality. For instance, Ernsberger and Koletsky (1999) postulated that, instead, higher weight may simply be a correlate of poor health habits that cause disease, or that weight cycling and weight loss interventions may themselves impair health.

Other authors reviewed data documenting the ineffectiveness of weight-loss approaches and the range of harmful physical and psycho-social side effects that often accompany these efforts, including dis-ordered eating, negative affect, and lowered self-esteem (e.g., Berg, 1999; McFarlane, Polivy, & McCabe, 1999). Given these data, authors in this issue proposed a paradigm shift away from the traditional weight-centric approach and toward what was termed a "wellness" or "nondieting" approach to health. This new paradigm would decentralize weight as an intervention target, eliminating it as an outcome variable. Instead, it would promote health behavior change, assessing effects on both metabolic and psychosocial health.

This same year, Robison (1999) expounded on the need for a changed approach to weight and health. His alternative paradigm incorporated the ideas that individual variations in body shape and size are natural and that thin bodies are not intrinsically healthy or aesthetically appealing, nor are fat bodies intrinsically unhealthy or unappealing. Considering the deleterious effects of weight-loss approaches, his approach endorsed body self-acceptance, eating in response to hunger rather than externally imposed regimens, and physical activity for pleasure-based versus calorie-burning purposes. In sum, the goal was to empower individuals to lead healthy, fulfilling lives caring for the bodies they presently have, regardless of size.

Two decades later, contemporary research continues to expose short-comings and problems associated with the weight-centric health para-digm (e.g., Bacon & Aphramor, 2011; O'Hara & Taylor, 2014; Tylka et al., 2014). These ongoing challenges to the traditional weight-centric model have evolved into what is today known as the HAES movement (Bruno, 2017), a weight-neutral paradigm for promoting holistic well-being. The movement was formally articulated by the Association for Size Diversity and Health (ASDAH, 2017) in 2003, with the term HAES trademarked by this organization in 2012.

Based on its initial set of tenets, Burgard (2009) explains that the HAES paradigm is about enhancing physical, emotional, and spiritual health without focusing on weight loss. In doing so, it promotes eating based on internal hunger cues, satiety, appetite, nutrition, and enjoyment rather than externally imposed rules, such as following a rigid diet. It also promotes physical activity for pleasure and health benefits rather than regimented exercise for the primary purpose of weight loss. As in earlier versions of the nondieting, wellness paradigm, body self-acceptance is a central HAES tenet. According to O'Hara and Taylor (2014), this entails "making peace with our bodies and celebrating their rich diversity" (p. 276). However, the HAES framework additionally stresses acceptance of others' bodies and, concomitantly, an end to the bias associated with negative judgments of others' physiques. Weight inclusivity, which is respect for the inherent variety of body shapes and sizes, is indisputably a primary principle of this approach.

The HAES model has continued to evolve since its initial conceptualization. In 2013, ASDAH (2017) modified its principles, moving beyond a largely individualistic framework to one that acknowledges broader sociocultural determinants of health. It has thus become an approach to both policy and individual decision making, taking on a stronger social justice orientation and paying greater attention to intersectionality. Specifically, the amended tenets urge practitioners to disseminate services with an understanding that socioeconomic status, race, gender, sexual orientation, age, and other identities might impact weight stigma. The new tenets further state that HAES advocates should support environments that address inequities based on social group memberships.

Burgard (2010) explains that the HAES model focuses on individuals' choices as well as changes in sociocultural and ecological environments to support well-being. She cites the Academy for Eating Disorders' rejection of weight-centric policies in favor of a weight-neutral stance as an example of institutional change. Tylka et al. (2014) describe ways in which HAES principles might be enacted at the policy and individual level as well as within a variety of health care settings. The revised HAES model prompts professionals working in these settings to acknowledge their biases surrounding weight and intersecting identities and to actively work on eliminating stigma and discrimination in their own practices. Perhaps a primary difference between a HAES approach and traditional body positivity programs is that the former aids people in developing resilience and the capacity to cope with distress associated with living in a weight-biased world (O'Hara & Taylor, 2014), whereas the latter typically does not challenge the bias inherent in weight-centric approaches to health. In fact, some eating disorder prevention programs concomitantly seek to prevent obesity (Khanh-Dao Le et al., 2017) – a clear indication that fat bodies are unacceptable. Burgard (2010) observes that many larger individuals have not entertained the idea that poor treatment based on their weight, by professionals and laypersons alike, is undeserved. The HAES model illuminates the role of weight bias in well-being.

The following section reviews existing research studies that have evaluated the efficacy of HAES interventions. More often than not, researchers compared participants in a HAES condition to participants in weight loss interventions rather than eating disorder prevention programs. Nevertheless, a number of these studies included measures of body image and/or disordered eating behavior, as highlighted here.

HAES Intervention Research

An increasing number of experimental and quasiexperimental studies have been conducted to assess the effectiveness of HAES-based interventions compared to weight loss interventions and control groups. One of the first studies investigating the efficacy of a nondiet program was a randomized controlled trial conducted by Bacon, Stern, Van Loan, and Keim (2005) on 30–45-year-old female chronic dieters with BMI scores greater than 30. The intervention group received education on the HAES model of body acceptance, exercise for enjoyment, and intuitive eating, while the control group received a traditional weight management program (e.g., counting calories, weighing in, monitoring intensity and duration of exercise). At a two-year follow-up, the HAES group maintained their weight while the diet group regained weight lost during the intervention. However, the HAES group experienced statistically significant improvements in self-esteem, reductions in dietary restraint, and reductions in body dissatisfaction from baseline to follow-up compared to the diet group. The HAES group displayed increases in reported time spent in moderate, hard, and very hard activity compared to the diet group. Finally, the HAES group experienced statistically significant improvements in cholesterol as well as systolic blood pressure from pre- to posttest. This was a landmark study for the HAES movement as it constituted a randomized controlled trial demonstrating that mental and physical health improvements were possible irrespective of weight status.

Since this initial study, two systematic reviews have been conducted reporting overall findings from research on HAES or other nondiet interventions. The first systematic review included programs that promote attending to internal cues (e.g., hunger, fullness, cravings, etc.) and reported results from twenty studies (Schaefer & Magnuson, 2014). Of the twenty studies, ten found significant improvements in body dissatisfaction, body image avoidance, self-acceptance, body image dissatisfaction, body satisfaction, or body shape concern in participants engaged in HAES or other nondiet interventions compared to participants in diet or control conditions.

The second systematic review on nondiet approaches by Clifford et al. (2015) included findings from sixteen studies. Of these, five included measurements of body image, body image avoidance, body esteem, body satisfaction/dissatisfaction, or body preoccupation, with three reporting improvements from pre- to postintervention in these areas. In terms of overall findings, both research groups concluded that HAES-oriented interventions have consistently superior effects on mental and emotional health compared to diet programs or control groups. Furthermore, no HAES-oriented intervention worsened participants' physical condition. Both groups of researchers also concluded that HAES-oriented interventions have significantly lower attrition rates compared to diet interventions, suggesting that they may be more enjoyable and sustainable than traditional programs.

Since the publication of these reviews, new studies evaluating HAES-based interventions have been published. For example, Mensinger, Calogero, Stranges, and Tylka (2016) conducted a six-month trial in which they randomized eighty women aged 30–45 into a weight-neutral program or a weight loss program. The weight-neutral intervention employed the Health-Focused, Understanding Lifestyle, Group Supported, and Self-Esteem Building Program for Better Health. This program emphasizes the principles of eating for well-being and pleasure, size acceptance, and the importance of engaging in physical activity for personal enjoyment and fulfillment. This study did not include body image outcome measures. However, researchers measured blood pressure, blood lipids, blood glucose, anthropometric variables, distress, self-esteem, quality of life, dietary intake, physical activity and intuitive eating at baseline, postintervention, and two years postrandomization. The weight-neutral group experienced significant improvements in LDL cholesterol and intuitive eating scores at both postintervention and follow-up compared to the weight loss group. In both the weight-neutral and weight loss programs, participants experienced increases in physical activity, fruit and vegetable intake, self-esteem, and quality of life from baseline through follow-up. These study results confirm the findings from Bacon et al.'s (2005) study that interventions grounded in a weight-neutral, HAES model do not worsen health outcomes or health-related behaviors as compared to weight loss programs, and HAES participants experienced some improved cardiometabolic functioning in the form of reduced LDL cholesterol at follow-up, which was not seen in the weight loss program participants.

In another recent study, Carbonneau and colleagues (2017) conducted a quasiexperimental research study comparing 216 Canadian women in a HAES intervention group to 110 in a waitlist control group.

Their thirteen-week program focused on making dietary and physical activity changes for the purpose of health promotion with an emphasis on body acceptance and intuitive eating. These researchers also did not assess changes in body image, but did measure changes in BMI, intuitive eating, and diet quality at baseline, postintervention (four months), and one-year follow-up. The HAES intervention group experienced improvements in intuitive eating scores compared to the control group at both postintervention and follow-up. Dietary quality, as measured by the Healthy Eating Index scores from food frequency questionnaire data, improved at four months compared to the control group, but was not sustained at one-year follow-up. However, at one-year follow-up, a significant positive association between intuitive eating scores and Healthy Eating Index scores emerged for the intervention group alone, suggesting that individuals who eat in response to internal cues of hunger, fullness, and cravings are more likely to consume a higher quality diet. Skeptics of the HAES movement believe that a nondiet approach in which individuals give themselves full permission to eat pleasurable foods will lead to poor diet quality. Carbonneau and colleagues' findings call into question this assumption. While there were no sustained improvements in Healthy Eating Index scores in the HAES group, there were no declines in these scores either. Despite what some might think, adopting an eating pattern that is based on internal hunger and fullness cues while honoring cravings does not result in poorer diet quality.

Overall, the studies reviewed support the notion that HAES-based programs provide equal or better physiological and psychological outcomes compared to control conditions largely composed of weight loss interventions. Although not all of these studies assessed variables related to body positivity, the majority of those that did found that HAES-informed programming reduced body dissatisfaction and improved body image and self-esteem (Clifford et al., 2015; Schaefer & Magnuson, 2014). Furthermore, in twenty-four cross-sectional studies, intuitive eating, which is one of the components of a HAES approach, was associated with a more positive body image (Bruce & Ricciardelli, 2016). Based on the promising results of HAES-informed research, therapeutic techniques based on this model have made their way into clinical settings.

Clinical Settings

Practitioners have implemented HAES principles with clients in both nutrition and psychological settings. In both of these fields, the traditional medical model dictates that practitioners prescribe weight loss interventions despite their aforementioned ineffectiveness and the propensity for side effects associated with this weight-centric approach, including body image distress and disordered eating (Raynor & Champagne, 2016; Watkins & Gerber, 2016).

In nutrition settings, a variety of approaches are used to address clients' weight concerns. In one study, researchers sought to understand how dietitians approached nutrition counseling sessions with adults seeking assistance with weight management. Chapman et al. (2005) conducted fifteen focus groups with Canadian dietitians. Some reported advocating for moderate weight loss, while others promoted a HAES approach. Most dietitian participants promoted an "all foods can fit" dietary mindset, meaning that moderation is better than elimination, as is encouraging clients to make small lifestyle changes gradually over time. The dietitians agreed that they perceive themselves as inadequately skilled to address psychological problems associated with weight concerns. The researchers concluded that there is a need within nutrition settings to move away from functioning as "nutrition educators" and toward more of a "nutrition therapist" role.

Client-centered behavior-change counseling techniques such as motivational interviewing are replacing education-oriented sessions within nutrition settings. These techniques are especially useful when addressing clients' weight and body image concerns from a HAES perspective (Glovsky, 2014; Clifford & Curtis, 2016). Nutritionists and dietitians, however, feel that they have inadequate training in such counseling techniques, which presents a significant barrier in addressing body-related issues in applied settings (MacLellan & Berenbaum, 2007; Rapoport & Perry, 2000). In one study of 4,202 dietitians, only 25 percent reported receiving counseling skills-based training (Rapoport & Perry, 2000). Also lacking is training to support clients in improving body image. A practice paper on eating disorders by the American Dietetic Association does mention the need to assess body image when working with patients with eating disorders, but there is no mention of addressing body image when intervening, nor is this topic mentioned in their position paper on adult overweight and obesity (Cline, Diekman, & Lachawicz-Morrison, 2011). Therefore, it is clear that more training is needed for nutrition practitioners to support their clients in developing a positive body image.

Some nutrition practitioners have navigated this area on their own. In an article titled "Tips on Improving Patients' Body Image" (Peregrin, 2007), a few dietitians proposed suggestions on addressing body image in clinical settings. Registered dietitian Roberta Anding stated: "If you look at the cover of popular magazines, many of the celebrities meet the weight criteria for anorexia nervosa. Young girls are bombarded with messages of thinness in a world that is super-sized. It is important to help people, especially adolescents, challenge these unrealistic images portrayed by the media" (Peregrin, 2007, p. 1721). She went on to explain that education is key in clinical settings so that patients realize that beauty and health can come in a variety of shapes and sizes. Whereas media education is one useful strategy to support clients in developing a positive body image, more research and tools are needed to best equip nutrition practitioners in this area, including connecting professionals to the HAES paradigm. Registered dietitians Leslie Schilling and Rebecca Scritchfield founded Registered Dietitians 4 Body Confidence (2017) in 2015 to spur conversation among dietitians about the valuable role they might play in helping to improve clients' body image. They have attempted to organize, connect, and equip professionals who are committed to improving the body image of their clients through using HAES-oriented resources.

Another area that has been overlooked in the training of nutrition professionals is weight bias. Weight bias among dietitians is well documented (Harvey, Summerbell, Kirk, & Hill, 2002; Swift, Hanlon, El-Redy, Puhl, & Glazebrook, 2013). Puhl and Brownell (2006) surveyed 2,449 overweight and obese women and found that 37 percent reported receiving inappropriate comments from dietitians about their weight. Importantly, weight stigma is associated with depression, anxiety, lower self-esteem, poor body image, and disordered eating (Greenleaf, Petrie, & Martin, 2014; Puhl & Heuer, 2009; Puhl & Latner, 2007). Therefore, dietitians may be inadvertently creating psychological distress in their clients.

Weight stigma is also quite prevalent in psychology practice settings, including among therapists who specialize in treating eating disorders (Puhl, Latner, King, & Luedicke, 2014). Furthermore, higher-weight clients often experience intersecting oppression around both their weight and psychiatric diagnosis (Mizock, 2015). Mizock attributes increasing weight stigma among therapists to recent mental health initiatives urging them to address weight among clients in the higher BMI ranges and to prescribe weight loss interventions for this perceived problem, regardless of the reason(s) other than weight for which clients may be seeking therapy. She explains that these initiatives now tend to equate higher weight with both physical and mental disorder. Burgard (2010, p. 22) laments: "In the realm of 'obesity' treatment, the solution to being stigmatized is seen as weight loss" rather than addressing and eliminating the stigma itself.

Both Burgard (2010) and Mizock (2015) maintain that the HAES model should replace a weight-centric approach in working with psychotherapy clients, offering specific suggestions ranging from individual behavior (e.g., soliciting from clients their preferred terminology for size, such as "fat," "overweight," "large," etc.) to environmental modification (e.g., ensuring that furniture in the treatment setting can accommodate larger-sized bodies). Burgard's chapter in Maine and McGilley's (2010) text *Treatment of Eating Disorders: Bridging the Research–Practice Gap* does just that, offering numerous concrete suggestions for working with higher-weight clients and illustrating these with examples from her practice. Burgard lists misconceptions that therapists typically have about weight (e.g., that fat people's food intake must be pathological), explaining that one cannot judge what a client is doing with food and exercise simply based on his or her body size. She encourages therapists to treat fat people presenting with depression or trauma as one would persons in lower BMI ranges, rather than prescribing weight loss as the treatment for these presenting complaints. She also details a number of stereotype management skills that she teaches clients because they must continually contend with a fatphobic environment outside of the therapy setting.

Burgard makes a vitally important point when she asks therapists to refrain from prescribing for fat people the same beliefs (e.g., obsession with weight) and behaviors (e.g., restrictive eating) that therapists view as evidence of an eating disorder that needs to be treated in thinner clients. Alarmingly, in an article titled "Long-Term Maintenance of Weight Loss in Obesity: Possible Insights from Anorexia Nervosa" that recently appeared in the *International Journal of Eating Disorders*, Gianini, Walsh, Steinglass, and Mayer (2017) imply that therapists should do this very thing, noting similarities between individuals with anorexia nervosa and those on the National Weight Control Registry (NWCR), which studies individuals who have lost and kept off thirty or more pounds for a year. In a reaction piece to this article, "Is Anorexia the Latest Treatment for Obesity?," clinical psychologist Alexis Conason (2017) states:

Rather than viewing anorexia nervosa as a tool to help fat people lose weight, the rigid restrictive dieting and preoccupation with weight and shape evidenced by people on the NWCR may signal widespread eating disordered symptoms among people at higher weights. Instead of devoting resources to trying to increase this eating disordered behavior, the real need is for more resources dedicated to the identification and treatment of eating disorders across the weight spectrum. (para. 12)

As in the field of nutrition, mental health professionals should examine their own biases and work to overcome these in order to promote a sense of wellness rather than an obsession with weight among their clients of every weight status. In contrast to a weight-centric clinical approach,

Be Nourished (2017) exemplifies a HAES-based practice setting that employs therapists specializing in both nutrition and psychotherapy. The founders describe their commitment to the HAES approach on their website: "After many years of helping women let go of their preoccupation with food and weight, we know that Body Trust® is the beating heart behind the cultivation of Health at Every Size® and Intuitive Eating practices." The organization offers a variety of therapeutic modalities to help clients attain long-term body acceptance via the HAES model. The five core competencies of the Body Trust® program that they share with their clients and the health care professionals who complete their training include: (1) practice weight-neutral self-care, (2) eat intuitively, (3) move your body joyfully, (4) nurture self-compassion, and (5) redefine success. Be Nourished is not alone in offering HAES-based treatment: An international Health At Every Size Registry (2017) reveals a growing number of practitioners who operate within this framework.

Fitness Settings

With its emphasis on life-enhancing movement, the HAES paradigm is quite germane to fitness environments. Although physical activity may take place in other contexts, fitness centers have become increasingly popular sites for physical activity (International Health, Racquet, and Sportsclub Association, 2016). Fitness centers are contexts in which cultural norms, social interactions, and physical environment influence body perceptions (Cardinal, Whitney, Narimatsu, Hubert, & Souza, 2014). In other words, fitness centers are neutral sites that can nurture or thwart positive body image depending on the atmosphere. Thus, an exploration of how a HAES approach might be integrated into these environments is warranted.

The HAES paradigm advocates for physical activity enacted for the intrinsic motives of health and enjoyment rather than extrinsic, appearance-related motives related to weight loss (Burgard, 2010). Physical activity is more strongly associated with positive body image when people are active for health and enjoyment rather than appearance motives (Homan & Tylka 2014). The HAES model encourages individuals to discover pleasurable activities, tuning into their immediate psychosocial benefits, with the understanding that weight may or may not change as a result. Indeed, physical activity has been associated with improvements in metabolic and psychosocial health, including positive body perceptions and body image, independent of weight status or weight change (Hausenblas, & Fallon, 2006; Homan & Tylka, 2014; McAuley et al., 2016).

Unfortunately, typical fitness settings operate in accordance with a weight-centric rather than a weight-neutral paradigm. That is, fitness professionals regularly perceive weight loss as the primary goal of physical activity and achieving a certain BMI as imperative to health. Furthermore, they tend to view clientele who do not lose weight as lacking willpower or otherwise personally deficient (Chambliss, Finley, & Blair, 2004; Fernández-Balboa & González Calvo, 2017). Donaghue and Allen (2016) reported that personal fitness trainers often endorse the belief that anyone can lose weight if they are willing. Such beliefs perpetuate stigma and discriminatory behavior toward larger people. In fact, numerous studies have shown that weight bias is particularly prevalent among fitness staff (Cardinal et al., 2014).

Weight bias is also prevalent among frequent exercisers (Flint & Reale, 2016). Thus, people whose bodies are perceived as deviant from the norm may experience bias from both fitness staff and fellow members, which may discourage larger people from exercising at fitness centers. People do not want to be physically active in contexts where they feel ridiculed or do not feel accepted and supported (Lewis et al., 2011). Vartanian and Novak (2011) found that perceived weight bias and stigma surrounding exercise lead people to avoid physical activity. For many of those who continue to access these settings, negative body image and psychosocial distress rather than body positivity might be the result.

In line with a HAES approach, it is essential to understand how to best create environments, from the individual to the policy level, that promote body positivity. Because the HAES model suggests that physical activity should be enjoyable and personally meaningful, self-determination theory (Ryan & Deci, 2002) can help guide these efforts. Consistent with the sociocritical nature of the HAES model, self-determination theory emphasizes the importance of the social context when developing strategies that facilitate the internalization of motivation and promotion of well-being. Education regarding self-determination theory can help fitness professionals recognize that people enjoy physical activity and become internally motivated when the basic needs of competence, autonomy, and relatedness are met (see Chapter 5). The social climate of fitness centers can promote basic needs by providing diverse fitness opportunities that allow members to explore their interests and find an activity which they enjoy and feel competent performing.

Another strategy that fitness centers could employ to facilitate body positivity is to create a culture that focuses on the health and fitness benefits of physical activity rather than aesthetic motives. Self-determination theory scholars Ingledew and Markland (2008) contend that physical activity contexts should promote health, fitness, and social motives rather than disparaging weight loss motives. Pickett and Cunningham (2017) concur, advocating for a HAES-based model in physical activity settings where people can exercise simply as a means to holistic health, rather than achievement of an arbitrary aesthetic ideal.

The HAES model also advocates for acceptance of all bodies irrespective of size, ability, or disease status. Accepting the uniqueness of the body can have a greater ability to enhance positive body perceptions compared to a focus on weight or aesthetics (Homan & Tylka, 2014). Tylka and Wood-Barcalow (2015) suggest positive body image is linked to perceived body acceptance by others. Therefore, when fitness center personnel are genuinely accepting of their clients' bodies, these clients may experience body positivity themselves. Such acceptance could occur within a caring climate, which Noddings (2005) describes as a social context that involves empathetic communication and genuine interest in learning about others. Brown and Fry (2014) report that caring physical activity climates are associated with greater intention to be active, prosocial behaviors, and well-being. It is fair to say, then, that caring climates satisfy the basic need of relatedness outlined in self-determination theory, and that relatedness should be associated with positive body image.

Some research has investigated ways to transform fitness centers into more welcoming spaces for individuals in larger bodies. In a study using concept mapping, Souza and Ebbeck (2018) prompted current and past members of fitness centers, as well as employees of such centers, to identify strategies that can increase positive attitudes toward larger members of fitness centers. Participants endorsed many of the strategies described here. For instance, they called for programming geared toward healthy living without a focus on weight and a fitness culture that recognized the achievements of all members regardless of weight. Additionally, they asked that fitness staff demonstrate warm regard and sincere concern for all members and that fitness centers implement and enforce zero tolerance policies for harmful language from staff and members. Participants also called for a wide variety of fitness opportunities and equipment suited to larger bodies, as well as other changes to the physical environment including the removal of scales, mirrors, and fashion magazines promoting the thin ideal. Whereas traditional body positivity programs would help individuals reject damaging messages communicated via these magazines, a HAES approach would replace such magazines with media featuring positive images of people of all shapes and sizes. Participants further recommended that exercise classes and descriptions such as "fat burning cardio" or "abs, butt, and thighs" be renamed using more body positive terminology such as "energizing cardio" or "total body fitness." Finally, they asked that fitness leaders refrain from aesthetic-related comments and focus on the experiential aspects of physical activity.

Thus far, few studies have evaluated the efficacy of such an approach to physical activity. However, Hsu, Buckworth, Focht, and O'Connell (2013) compared an eight-week integrated HAES/Self-Determination Theory intervention to an exercise-only group in a randomized controlled trial. The control participants received two individualized and supervised forty-five-minute exercise sessions per week that consisted of aerobic and resistance exercises prescribed according to established guidelines. The intervention participants received a one-hour weekly group meeting focused on behavior change followed by thirty minutes of individualized and supervised exercise. The group meetings covered strategies to identify meaningful physical activity opportunities, self-regulatory skills, the HAES principles, and means of facilitating social support. The researchers designed and conducted the intervention in a manner consistent with self-determination theory that supported the basic human needs of autonomy, competence, and relatedness. For example, by deemphasizing weight loss, the intervention supported autonomous motivation. Appropriate goal setting and a focus on health provided competence, and relatedness was supported through various forms of social support. At the end of the study, both groups showed improvements in physical activity levels. However, physical activity levels declined for the control group at the four-week follow-up, while physical activity levels in the intervention group increased during that time. This finding was perhaps due to large increases in autonomy and competence in the intervention group, which were maintained at follow-up. Autonomy and competence are also inversely associated with negative body perceptions (Thøgersen-Ntoumani & Ntoumanis, 2007). Thus, it is worth exploring the possibility that autonomy and competence, and perhaps relatedness, positively correlate with positive body perceptions.

In addition to this experimental study, a few clinical case studies of HAES-based fitness centers have been published (Ernst, 2005; Watkins, Ebbeck, & Levy, 2005). Watkins et al. describe a community-based fitness center, Feel WonderFull Fitness, tailored for larger women that embraced the HAES philosophy by specifically targeting multiple aspects of the social and physical environment to promote body acceptance and reduce weight bias. The physical environment was purposely positioned in a private location, mirrors and scales were absent, magazines available to attendees included women of larger sizes, and equipment was specifically designed for larger bodies. Social support was provided by hiring larger fitness professionals and training them in the HAES principles, providing group outings such as hikes, and providing feedback by acknowledging and reinforcing controllable behavioral factors (e.g., attendance) rather than weight loss. Women attending Feel WonderFull reported experiences of weight bias at traditional community fitness centers, contrasting their experience in those venues to the accepting climate of Feel WonderFull. Subsequently, Watkins, Ebbeck, and Levy (2014) published a quantitative quasiexperimental study assessing client outcomes in this setting compared to control groups solicited from the community who engaged in low or moderate levels of physical activity. After three months, and without changes in BMI, Feel WonderFull participants experienced improvements in perceived body attractiveness and disordered eating as well as depression and physical activity. Clients' anecdotal remarks reflected the HAES-based milieu of the club (p. 194): "This facility is just not as intimidating as other clubs in town I've been to, especially for plus size women. It provides a comfortable atmosphere and you don't feel so self-conscious working out here."

Finally, Feel WonderFull participants reported a high level of client satisfaction with this program, underscoring the notion that HAES programs are more palatable than traditional weight-centric approaches (Bacon & Aphramor, 2011). Based on theory-driven research as well as clinical case studies, fitness centers might consider implementing HAES strategies in order to boost body positivity and enhance the exercise experience for clients of all sizes.

Classroom Settings

Introducing college students to the HAES paradigm seems warranted on two accounts. First, college students represent a high-risk population for body dissatisfaction and disordered eating practices (Eisenberg, Nicklett, Roeder, & Kirz, 2011). Second, weight bias is also quite common among college students. In their largescale study of college students' attitudes toward obese persons, Ambwani, Thomas, Hopwood, Moss, and Grillo (2014) found that both women and men, regardless of weight or disordered eating status, endorsed stigmatizing beliefs with considerable frequency.

Although weight bias has become the norm on college campuses, students majoring in behavioral health fields tend to have particularly strong antifat attitudes (Watkins & Concepcion, 2014). Various researchers have argued that the weight-centric curriculum which these students typically experience is responsible for engendering and reinforcing stigmatizing beliefs toward those on the higher end of the weight spectrum (e.g., McHugh & Kasardo, 2012; O'Brien, Hunter, & Banks, 2007). Watkins and Gerber (2016) add that these weight-centric messages could also adversely impact the way that students perceive their own bodies and urge educators to integrate the HAES paradigm into their teaching.

Instructors in the behavioral health sciences, among other academic disciplines, have recently begun to offer college courses that integrate the HAES model into their curricula (Watkins, Farrell, & Doyle-Hugmeyer, 2012). For instance, Lewis & Clark College offers the course Fat Studies and Health At Every Size as part of their graduate eating disorders certificate training. According to the catalogue description, this course:

Explores the interdisciplinary field of scholarship in Fat Studies that aims to debunk weight-centric misconceptions and countering mainstream narratives. Examines fat bias, fat shame, and weight-based oppression as a social justice issue that intersects with other systems of oppression. Introduction to the paradigm of Health at Every Size, a weight-neutral approach to health promotion that emphasizes size diversity, intuitive eating, and joyful movement. HAES is also an important paradigm in working with people who have experienced disordered eating.

Similarly, the clinical psychology doctoral program at Alliant International University – San Francisco offers the course Body Image: Health At Every Size, with the following syllabus description:

This class will address body size and weight issues from a social constructionist perspective. Body ideals and people's experiences of their own bodies have been culturally constructed in very much the same way as race, gender, and sexuality. We will use feminist and constructionist theory to deconstruct the dominant discourse on body size and weight. The class will deal with issues ranging from the importance of language and micro-interaction to structural and institutional sizeism, all of which serve to create negative body image among the entire population and marginalize fat people. Topics include medical and psychological abuses, the impact of media representations, gender, sexuality, racial/ethnic differences, body images, who is profiting from dieting culture and the "war on 'obesity,'" and the fat liberation movement. Discussion will include clinical application of "Health at Every Size" rather than weight-focused approaches in working with clients with "weight issues."

While such courses are on the rise, little research yet exists as to their impact on students' body-related beliefs and behaviors. However, several recent studies point to HAES-based pedagogy positively impacting student health behaviors, weight bias, and body image.

Two quasiexperimental studies have investigated the effects of a HAES-infused curriculum on college students' psychosocial functioning, including body image. Humphrey, Clifford, and Neyman-Morris (2015) compared an undergraduate course titled "Health at Every Size: A Non-Diet Approach to Wellness" to a basic nutrition course with some HAES content and a traditional basic nutrition course without HAES content. They found that the HAES class produced significant improvements from pre- to posttest on measures of weight bias and eating behavior, as well as all three subscales (i.e., Appearance, Weight, and Attribution) of the Body Esteem Scale (BES; Mendelson, Mendelson, & White, 2001). The course with some HAES content produced significant changes in weight bias and some aspects of eating behavior, but not body esteem, whereas the course with no HAES content produced no significant changes in any of the variables across time. At posttest, students in the HAES course exhibited significantly better scores on measures of weight bias and eating behavior, along with the BES Appearance and Weight subscales, compared to both control classes.

Watkins, Gerber, Krieger, Pham, and Bauman (2016) achieved similar results in their study comparing an undergraduate/graduate Fat Studies course that incorporated teaching about the HAES model with control psychology courses. Compared to the control condition, composed of students from Psychology of Gender, Psychotherapy, and Social Cognition classes, Fat Studies produced significant improvements over time on measures of weight bias and sociocultural attitudes toward appearance, as well as on four subscales (Appearance Evaluation, Appearance Orientation, Overweight Preoccupation, and Self-Classified Weight) of the Multidimensional Body–Self Relations Questionnaire-Appearance Scale (MBSRQ-AS; Cash, 2000). Posttest scores on measures of weight bias and sociocultural appearance were significantly better for students in the Fat Studies class. Although there were no significant differences between Fat Studies and the control condition at posttest on the MBSRQ-AS scales, scores trended toward better body image for students who had experienced the HAES-based curriculum.

In a mixed methods study, Christel (2016) evaluated the impact of a Plus-Size Swimwear Design class that incorporated education in the HAES model. Although the study did not include quantitative measures of body image, it revealed significant improvements across the term on a self-report measure of weight bias among the senior fashion students in this class. Qualitative data based on students' written critical reflections throughout the course revealed that they gained compassion toward others as well as themselves, in concert with a greater understanding of weight bias and thin privilege discussed through the HAES model.

Finally, qualitative data from several other studies further illustrate the impact of HAES-infused curricula on students' attitudes toward weight. Based on written reflections, Cameron (2016) found that graduate students in the Obesity Discourses in Society, Education, and Health Care class gained a critical understanding of the dominant weight-centric health standard while shifting their thinking toward a weight-neutral paradigm. These data also revealed that students acquired greater acceptance of their own bodies as well as others' bodies, including those of their clients in health care settings.

Similarly, Watkins has examined student writings in both Women, Weight, and Body Image (Watkins & Doyle-Hugmeyer, 2013) and Fat Studies (Watkins, 2015, 2016) courses, both of which are undergraduate/graduate courses cross-listed between Psychology and Women, Gender, and Sexuality Studies. Watkins and Doyle-Hugmeyer describe the evolution of the former class from one that reflected traditional psychological approaches to body image and weight to one that now highlights weight bias as a social justice issue and as a major contributor to body image distress. As such, the course incorporates HAES education. For instance, students review the Body Positive® (2017) website – tag line "Boosting body image at any weight" – administered by Deb Burgard, a licensed clinical psychologist who treats clients with eating disorders using the HAES model. Students' written responses to this website illustrate the overall trend toward body positivity that they experienced throughout the class. For instance, one student stated: "I have found it better just to accept that this is my body and I will be living with it for a long time, rather than try to change it and be very unhappy for failing in my attempts" (Watkins & Doyle-Hugmeyer, 2013, p. 83). In response to the class, students also described behavioral changes such as weighing themselves less often, replacing dieting with intuitive eating, and replacing regimented exercise routines with more enjoyable forms of physical activity, in addition to becoming more accepting of others' bodies as well as their own. Watkins found similar results based on a Fat Studies class in which the HAES model is prominent. The following excerpts from student assignments illustrate these transformations:

Health At Every Size has changed my life. I used to wake up every morning and weigh myself and get so angry when I didn't see the number I wanted to see. I used to work out hardcore just to lose weight. I wasn't really happy with my body or my life. I no longer exercise because I feel I have to. I exercise now to make me feel good. Working out doesn't have to be going to the gym. Working out can be snowboarding, hiking, playing basketball. I have stopped weighing myself every morning. I put the scale in the storage closet so I don't have to look at it. I even encouraged my roommate to stop weighing herself too. I will never go on another diet. The material in this class has taught me I can be happy with my body just the way it is. (Watkins, 2016, p. 166)

I never thought this class would change my life, almost save my life. Through studies shown in class and real life people following their dreams, it made my mind completely change about how I view my body and myself. (Watkins, 2015, para. 22)

Given these – albeit preliminary – findings, educators might consider incorporating material on the HAES paradigm into their curricula not only as a means of promoting body positivity and related health behaviors, but also as a means of mitigating students' weight bias toward others.

Conclusion

Research based on both experimental and quasiexperimental designs has demonstrated the ability of HAES-based interventions to improve both metabolic and psychosocial health. Qualitative research and case studies support these outcomes as well as illustrate the use of HAES strategies in clinical, fitness, and college classroom settings. Because researchers have viewed the HAES model as an alternative to the weight-centric model of health, they have typically compared HAES to weight loss interventions, relying on a variety of dependent measures to assess effects. While not all of these studies have included measures of body image, body perceptions, and disordered eating, findings from those that have suggest that HAES-based programs have much to offer by way of bolstering body positivity.

The HAES paradigm constitutes a sociocritical approach to body positivity, encompassing a broader array of bodies, especially those that have been marginalized by society based on weight and/or other diverse identities. It also actively challenges this marginalization by addressing weight bias from individual through policy levels in ways that many existing body positivity programs do not. Thus, scholars and practitioners might draw on the HAES philosophy along with techniques derived from this model in efforts to improve body positivity and prevent disordered eating for people of all shapes and sizes.

Resources

The Association for Size Diversity and Health (2017) is a repository for information about the HAES model. Their website includes webinars that guide practitioners in the implementation of HAES in clinical settings, including working with clients who have eating disorders. Other webinars advise instructors on the integration of HAES concepts into their teaching. The site also contains a HAES curriculum comprising three PowerPoint presentations, with the option of an audio lecture to accompany these presentations. Drawing from twenty-six instructors who challenge dominant obesity discourses in their college classrooms, Cameron (2015) compiled a list of resources, including readings, blogs, videos, and assignments related to the field of Fat Studies, which encompasses the HAES paradigm.

Linda Bacon (2017), a HAES scholar, runs a website containing videos that explain various aspects of this approach, as well as information about her books *Health At Every Size: The Surprising Truth about Your Weight* (Bacon, 2008) and *Body Respect: What Conventional Health Books Get Wrong, Leave Out, and Just Plain Fail to Understand about Weight* (Bacon & Aphramor, 2014), geared to a general audience wishing to learn how to integrate HAES principles into their lives. The National Association to Advance Fat Acceptance (2017) contains information about the HAES model as well. For instance, among its educational materials is a HAES School Toolkit. This entire site is devoted to ending size discrimination, with many other materials informed by a HAES perspective, including guidelines for therapists, fitness professionals, healthcare providers, and nutritionists and dieticians.

Other resources exist to guide professionals in practicing from a HAES perspective (Clifford & Curtis, 2016; Willer, 2013). Registered dietitian Ellen Glovsky (2014) has published a book, *Wellness, Not Weight: Health at Every Size and Motivational Interviewing*, that provides scientific information on the HAES paradigm, along with information to help practitioners communicate these concepts to their clients. Licensed social workers Judith Matz and Ellen Frankel (2014) wrote a useful book for those in clinical settings titled *Beyond a Shadow of a Diet*. The authors present research showing that dietary restrictions can trigger overeating. They explain the HAES paradigm to practitioners, and their book includes a chapter on body image counseling in which they outline activities that would be appropriate in both group and individual counseling settings. A 2015 article by Souza in *ACSM's Health & Fitness Journal* offers suggestions for adopting the HAES approach for health and fitness professionals.

In addition, many organizations offer continuing education training to teach professionals how to practice from a HAES perspective. For instance, Be Nourished (2017) offers online courses and in-person training on their Body Trust® Wellness program. While this is not an exhaustive listing of resources, it might serve as a starting point for scholars, practitioners, and instructors to explore the HAES paradigm as a means of promoting body positivity in the context of holistic health.

References

Alberga, A. S., Russell-Mayhew, S., von Ranson, K. M., & McLaren, L. (2016). Weight bias: A call to action. *Journal of Eating Disorders, 34*, 1–6. doi:10.1186/s40337-016-0112-4

Ambwani, S., Thomas, K. M., Hopwood, C. J., Moss, S. A., & Grillo, C. M. (2014). Obesity stigmatization as the status quo: Structural considerations and prevalence among young adults in the U.S. *Eating Behaviours, 15*, 366–370.

Association for Size Diversity and Health. (2017). Retrieved July 13, 2017 from www.sizediversityandhealth.org/.

Bacon, L. (2008). *Health At Every Size: The surprising truth about your weight.* Dallas, TX: BenBella Books.

(2017). Website. Retrieved July 13, 2017 from https://lindabacon.org/.

Bacon, L., & Aphramor, L. (2011). Weight science: Evaluating the evidence for a paradigm shift. *Nutrition Journal, 9*, 1–13. doi:10.1186/1475-2891-10-9.

(2014). *Body respect: What conventional health books get wrong, leave out, and just plain fail to understand about weight.* Dallas: BenBella Books.

Bacon, L., Stern, J. S., Van Loan, M. D., & Keim, N. L. (2005). Size acceptance and intuitive eating improve health for obese, female chronic dieters. *Journal of the American Dietetic Association, 105*(6), 929–936. doi:10.1016/j.jada.2005.03.011

Be Nourished. (2017). Retrieved July 13, 2017 from http://benourished.org/.

Berg, F. M. (1999). Health risks associated with weight loss and obesity treatment programs. *Journal of Social Issues, 55*, 277–297.

Body Positive ®. (2017). Retrieved July 13, 2017 from www.bodypositive.com/.

Brown, T. C., & Fry, M. D. (2014). Motivational climate, staff and members' behaviors, and members' psychological well-being at a national fitness franchise. *Research Quarterly for Exercise and Sport, 85*(2), 208–217. doi:10.1080/02701367.2014.893385

Bruce, L. J., & Ricciardelli, L. A. (2016). A systematic review of the psychosocial correlates of intuitive eating among adult women. *Appetite, 96*, 454–472.

Bruno, B. A. (2017). Health At Every Size and me. *Fat Studies, 6*, 54–66.

Burgard, D. (2009). What is "Health At Every Size"? In E. Rothblum & S. Solovay (Eds.), *The fat studies reader* (pp. 41–53). New York: NYU Press.

(2010). What's weight got to do with it? Weight neutrality in the Health At Every Size paradigm and its implications for clinical practice. In M. Maine & B. H. McGilley (Eds.). *Treatment of eating disorders: Bridging the research–practice gap* (pp. 17–33). London: Academic Press.

Cameron, E. (2015). Teaching resources for post-secondary educators who challenge dominant "obesity" discourse. *Fat Studies, 4*, 212–226.

(2016). Learning to teach every body: Exploring the emergence of a critical "obesity" pedagogy. In E. Cameron & C. Russell (Eds.), *The fat pedagogy reader: Challenging weight-based oppression in education* (pp. 172–178). New York: Peter Lang Publishing.

Carbonneau, E., Bégin, C., Lemieux, S., Mongeau, L., Paquette, M. C., Turcotte, M., . . . Provencher, V. (2017). A Health at Every Size intervention improves intuitive eating and diet quality in Canadian women. *Clinical Nutrition, 36*(3), 747–754. doi:10.1016/j.clnu.2016.06.008

Cardinal, B. J., Whitney, A. R., Narimatsu, M., Hubert, N., & Souza, B. J. (2014). Obesity bias in the gym: An under-recognized social justice, diversity, and inclusivity issue. *Journal of Physical Education, Recreation and Dance, 85*, 3–6.

Cash, T. F. (2000). *MBSRQ users' manual*. Norfolk, VA: Old Dominion University.

Chambliss, H. O., Finley, C. E., & Blair, S. N. (2004). Attitudes toward obese individuals among exercise science students. *Medicine & Science in Sports & Exercise, 36*(3), 468–474. doi:10.1249/01.MSS.0000117115.94062.E4

Chapman, G. E., Sellaeg, K., Levy-Milne, R., Ottem, A., Barr, S. I., Fierini, D., . . . Thiele, K. (2005). Canadian dietitians' approaches to counseling adult clients seeking weight-management advice. *Journal of the American Dietetic Association, 105*(8), 1275–1279.

Christel, D. (2016). Obesity education as an intervention to reduce weight bias in fashion students. *Journal of Education and Learning, 5*, 170–179.

Clifford, D., & Curtis, L. (2016). *Motivational interviewing in nutrition and fitness*. New York: Guilford Press.

Clifford, D., Ozier, A., Bundros, J., Moore, J., Kreiser, A., & Neyman Morris, M. (2015). Impact of non-diet approaches on attitudes, behaviors, and health outcomes: A systematic review. *Journal of Nutrition Education and Behavior, 47*, 143–155. doi:10.1016/j.jneb.2014.12.002

Cline, A., Diekman, C.B., & Lachawicz-Morrison, E. (2011). Practice paper of the American Dietetic Association: Nutrition intervention in the treatment of eating disorders. *Journal of the American Dietetics Association, 111*(8), 1261–1273.

Conason, A. (2017, April 27). Is anorexia the latest treatment for obesity? Retrieved from www.psychologytoday.com/blog/eating-mindfully/201704/is-anorexia-the-latest-treatment-obesity.

Dionne, E. (2017, January 24). Fat acceptance activists explain why body positivity is becoming meaningless: It's complicated. Retrieved from www.revelist.com/ideas/fat-acceptance-body-positivity/6632.

Donaghue, N., & Allen, M. (2016). "People don't care as much about their health as they do about their looks": Personal trainers as intermediaries between aesthetic and health-based discourses of exercise participation and weight management. *International Journal of Sport and Exercise Psychology, 14*(1), 96–118. doi:10.1080/1612197X.2015.1016086

Eisenberg, D., Nicklett, E. J., Roeder, K., & Kirz, N. E. (2011). Eating disorder symptoms among college students: Prevalence, correlates, and treatment-seeking. *Journal of American College Health, 59*, 700–707.

Ernsberger, P., & Koletsky, R. J. (1999). Biomedical rationale for a wellness approach to obesity: An alternative to a focus on weight loss. *Journal of Social Issues, 55*, 221–260.

Ernst, C. (2005). A day in the life of a HAES fitness trainer. *Health At Every Size, 19*, 83–88.

Fernández-Balboa, J. M., & González Calvo, G. (2017). *A critical narrative analysis of the perspectives of physical trainers and fitness instructors in relation to their body image, professional practice and the consumer culture.* Sport, Education and Society, online edition, 1–13. doi:10.1080/13573322.2017.1289910

Flint, S. W., & Reale, S. (2016). Weight stigma in frequent exercisers: Overt, demeaning and condescending. *Journal of Health Psychology,* online edition, 1–10. doi:10.1177/1359105316656232

Gianini, L. M., Walsh, B., Steinglass, J., & Mayer, L. (2017). Long-term weight loss maintenance in obesity: Possible insights from anorexia nervosa? *International Journal of Eating Disorders, 50,* 341–342. doi:10.1002/eat.22685

Glovsky, E. (2014). *Wellness, not weight: Health at Every Size and motivational interviewing.* San Diego: Cognella.

Greenleaf, C., Petrie, T., & Martin, S. (2014). Relationship of weight-based teasing and adolescents' psychological well-being and physical health. *Journal of School Health, 84,* 49–55.

Halliwell, E. (2015). Future directions for positive body image research. *Body Image, 14,* 177–189. doi.org/10.1016/j.bodyim.2015.03.003

Harvey, E. L., Summerbell, C. D., Kirk, S. F., & Hill, A. J. (2002). Dietitians' views of overweight and obese people and reported management practices. *Journal of Human Nutrition and Dietetics, 15*(5), 331–347.

Hausenblas, H. A., & Fallon, E. A. (2006). Exercise and body image: A meta-analysis. *Psychology and Health, 21*(1), 33–47. doi:10.1080/14768320500105270

Health At Every Size Registry. (2017) Retrieved July 13, 2017 from www.haescommunity.com/haes/search_registry.php.

Homan, K. J., & Tylka, T. L. (2014). Appearance-based exercise motivation moderates the relationship between exercise frequency and positive body image. *Body Image, 11*(2), 101–108. doi:10.1016/j.bodyim.2014.01.003

Hsu, Y., Buckworth, J., Focht, B. C., & O'Connell, A. A. (2013). Feasibility of a self-determination theory-based exercise intervention promoting Health at Every Size with sedentary overweight women: Project CHANGE. *Psychology of Sport and Exercise, 14*(2), 283–92. doi:10.1016/j.psychsport.2012.11.007

Humphrey, L., Clifford, D., & Neyman Morris, M. (2015). Health At Every Size college course reduces dieting behaviors and improves intuitive eating, body esteem, and anti-fat attitudes. *Journal of Nutrition Education, and Behavior, 47,* 354–360.

Ingledew, D. K., & Markland, D. (2008). The role of motives in exercise participation. *Psychology and Health, 23*(7), 807–828. doi:10.1080/08870440701405704

International Health, Racquet, & Sportsclub Association. (2016). *About the industry.* Retrieved from www.ihrsa.org/about-the-industry.

Khanh-Dao Le, L., Barendregt, J. J., Hay, P., & Mihalopoulos, C. (2017). Prevention of eating disorders: A systematic review and meta-analysis. *Clinical Psychology Review, 53,* 46–58.

LaMarre, A., Rice, C., & Jankowski, G. (2017). Eating disorder prevention as biopedagogy. *Fat Studies.* www.tandfonline.com/doi/full/10.1080/21604851.2017.1286906.

Lewis, S., Thomas, S. L., Blood, R. W., Castle, D. J., Hyde, J., & Komesaroff, P. A. (2011). How do obese individuals perceive and respond to the different types of obesity stigma that they encounter in their daily lives? A qualitative study. *Social Science & Medicine, 73*(9), 1349–1356. doi:10.1016/j.socscimed.2011.08.021

MacLellan, D., & Berenbaum, S. (2007). Canadian dietitians' understanding of the client-centered approach to nutrition counseling. *Journal of the American Dietetic Association, 107*(8), 1414–1417.

Maine, M., & McGilley, B. H. (2010). *Treatment of eating disorders: Bridging the research-practice gap*. London: Academic Press.

Matz, J., & Frankel, E. (2014). *Beyond a shadow of a diet: The comprehensive guide to treating binge eating disorder, compulsive eating, and emotional overeating*. New York: Routledge.

McAuley, P. A., Blaha, M. J., Keteyian, S. J., Brawner, C. A., Al Rifai, M., Dardari, Z. A., . . . Al-Mallah, M. H. (2016). Fitness, fatness, and mortality: The FIT (Henry Ford Exercise Testing) Project. *The American Journal of Medicine, 129*(9), 960–965. doi:10.1016/j.amjmed.2016.04.007

McFarlane, T., Polivy, J., & McCabe, R. E. (1999). Help, not harm: Psychological foundation for a nondieting approach toward health. *Journal of Social Issues, 55,* 261–276.

McHugh, M. C., & Kasardo, A. E. (2012). Anti-fat prejudice: The role of psychology in explication, education, and eradication. *Sex Roles, 66,* 617–627.

Mendelson, B. K., Mendelson, M. J., & White, D. R. (2001). Body-esteem scale for adolescents and adults. *Journal of Personality Assessment, 76*(1), 90–106.

Mensinger, J. L., Calogero, R. M., Stranges, S., & Tylka, T. L. (2016). A weight-neutral versus weight-loss approach for health promotion in women with high BMI: A randomized-controlled trial. *Appetite, 105,* 364–374.

Mizock, L. (2015). The double stigma of obesity and serious mental illnesses: Promoting health and recovery. *Stigma and Health, 1,* 86–91. doi:10.1037/2376-6972.1.S.86

National Association to Advance Fat Acceptance. (2017). Retrieved from www.naafaonline.com/dev2/.

Noddings, N. (2005). *Caring in education*. Retrieved from http://infed.org/mobi/caring-in-education/.

Nutter, S., Russell-Mayhew, S., Alberga, A. S., Arthur, N., Kassan, A., Lund, D. E., . . . Williams, E. (2016). Positioning of weight bias: Moving towards social justice. *Journal of Obesity.* doi:10.1155/2016/3753650

O'Brien, K. S., Hunter, J. A., & Banks, M. (2007). Implicit anti-fat bias in physical educators: Physical attributes, ideology, and socialization. *International Journal of Obesity, 31,* 308–314.

O'Hara, L., & Taylor, J. (2014). Health At Every Size: A weight-neutral approach for empowerment, resilience, and peace. *Journal of Social Work and Human Services Practice, 2,* 272–282.

Peregrin, T. (2007). Tips on improving patients' body image. *Journal of the American Dietetic Association, 107*(10), 1712–1714.

Pickett, A. C., & Cunningham, G. B. (2017). Physical Activity for Every Body: A model for managing weight stigma and creating body-inclusive spaces. *Quest, 69*(1), 19–36. http://dx.doi.org/10.1080/00336297.2016.114512

Piran, N. (2015). New possibilities in the prevention of eating disorders: The introduction of positive body image measures. *Body Image, 14,* 146–157.

Puhl, R. M., & Brownell, K. D. (2006). Confronting and coping with weight stigma: An investigation of overweight and obese adults. *Obesity, 14*(10), 1802–1815.

Puhl, R. M., & Heuer, C. A. (2009). The stigma of obesity: A review and update. *Obesity, 17,* 941–964.

Puhl, R. M., & Latner, J. (2007). Stigma, obesity, and the health of the nation's children. *Psychological Bulletin, 133*(4), 557–580.

Puhl, R. M., Latner, J. D., King, K. M., & Luedicke, J. (2014). Weight bias among professionals treating eating disorders: Attitudes about treatment and perceived patient outcomes. *International Journal of Eating Disorders, 47,* 65–75. doi:10.1002/eat.22186

Rapoport, L., & Perry, K. N. (2000). Do dietitians feel that they have had adequate training in behaviour change methods? *Journal of Human Nutrition and Dietetics, 13*(4), 287–298.

Raynor, H. A., & Champagne, C. M. (2016). Position of the Academy of Nutrition and Dietetics: Interventions for the treatment of overweight and obesity in adults. *Journal of the Academy of Nutrition and Dietetics, 116*(1), 129–147.

Registered Dietitians 4 Body Confidence. (2017). Retrieved July 13, 2017 from www.rd4bc.com

Robison, J. I. (1999). Weight, health and culture: Shifting the paradigm for alternative health care. *Alternative Health Practitioner, 5,* 45–69.

Russell-Mayhew, S., & Grace, A. D. (2016). A call for social justice and best practices for the integrated prevention of eating disorders and obesity. *Eating Disorders, 24,* 54–62.

Ryan, R. M., & Deci, E. L. (2002). An overview of self-determination theory. In E. L. Deci & R. M. Ryan (Eds.), *Handbook of self-determination research* (pp. 3–33). Rochester: University of Rochester Press.

Schaefer, J. T., & Magnuson, A. B. (2014) A review of interventions that promote eating by internal cues. *Journal of the Academy of Nutrition and Dietetics, 114*(5), 734–760.

Souza, B. J. (2015). A weight-neutral approach to health and fitness instruction. *ACSM's Health & Fitness Journal, 19*(3), 17–22.

Souza, B. J. & Ebbeck, V. (2018). Perspectives on increasing positive attitudes toward larger members in fitness centers. *Journal of Applied Sport Psychology, 30*(1), 96–118. http://dx.doi.org/10.1080/10413200.2017.1337822

Swift, J. A., Hanlon, S., El-Redy, L., Puhl, R. M., & Glazebrook, C. (2013). Weight bias among UK trainee dietitians, doctors, nurses and nutritionists. *Journal of Human Nutrition and Dietetics, 26*(4), 395–402.

Thøgersen-Ntoumani, C., & Ntoumanis, N. (2007). A self-determination theory approach to the study of body image concerns, self-presentation and self-perceptions in a sample of aerobic instructors. *Journal of Health Psychology, 12*(2), 301–315. https://doi.org/10.1177/1359105307074267

Tylka, T. L., Annunziato, R. A., Burgard, D., Daníelsdóttir, S., Shuman, E., Davis, C., & Calogero, R. M. (2014). The weight-inclusive versus weight-normative approach to health: Evaluating the evidence for prioritizing well-being over weight loss. *Journal of Obesity*, online edition, 1–18. doi.org/10.1155/2014/983495.

Tylka, T. L., & Wood-Barcalow, N. L. (2015). What is and what is not positive body image? Conceptual foundations and construct definition. *Body Image*, *14*, 118–129. doi:10.1016/j.bodyim.2015.04.001

Vartanian, L. R., & Novak, S. A. (2011). Internalized societal attitudes moderate the impact of weight stigma on avoidance of exercise. *Obesity*, *19*(4), 757–762. doi:10.1038/oby.2010.234

Watkins, P. L. (2015). Fat Studies 101: Learning to have your cake and eat it too. *Media/Culture Journal*, *18*(3). Retrieved from http://journal.mediaculture.org.au/index.php/mcjournal/article/view Article/968.
   (2016). Inclusion of fat studies in a Difference, Power, and Discrimination curriculum. In E. Cameron & C. Russell (Eds.), *The fat pedagogy reader: Challenging weight-based oppression in education* (pp. 161–169). New York: Peter Lang Publishing.

Watkins, P. L., & Concepcion, R. Y. (2014). Teaching Health At Every Size to health care professionals and students. In E. Glovsky (Ed.), *Wellness not weight: Motivational interviewing and Health At Every Size* (pp. 159–169). San Diego: Cognella Academic Publishing.

Watkins, P. L., & Doyle-Hugmeyer, A. (2013). Teaching about eating disorders from a Fat Studies perspective. *Transformations*, *23*, 147–158.

Watkins, P. L., Ebbeck, V., & Levy, S. S. (2005). Feel WonderFull Fitness: A tailored exercise program for larger women. *Health At Every Size*, *19*, 101–120.

Watkins, P. L., Ebbeck. V., & Levy, S. S. (2014). Overcoming weight bias: Promoting physical activity and psychosocial health. *Ethnicity and Inequalities in Health and Social Care*, *7*(4), 187–197. http://dx.doi.org/10.1108/EIHSC-11-2013-0043

Watkins, P. L., Farrell, A., & Doyle-Hugmeyer, A. (2012). Teaching Fat Studies: From conception to reception. *Fat Studies*, *1*, 180–194.

Watkins, P. L., & Gerber, M. R. (2016). Weight-centrism in psychology: Implications and new directions. *Fat Studies*, *5*, 57–72.

Watkins, P. L., Gerber, M. R., Krieger, K., Pham, H., & Bauman, L. (2016, March). In J. Chrisler (Chair). Women's weight in the world. Quantitative effects of a Fat Studies curriculum. Paper presented at the Association for Women in Psychology annual meeting, Pittsburgh, PA.

Willer, F. (2013) *The non-diet approach guidebook for dietitians: A how to guide for applying the non-diet approach to individual dietetic counselling*. Queensland: NutritionSense Allied Health.

Wood-Barcalow, N. L., Tylka, T. L., & Augustus-Horvath, C. L. (2010). "But I like my body": Positive body image characteristics and a holistic model for young-adult women. *Body Image*, *7*(2), 106–116. doi:10.1016/j.bodyim.2010.01.001

Wright, J., & Cliff, K. P. (2010). Confusing and contradictory: Considering obesity discourse and eating disorders as they shape body pedagogies in HPE. *Sport, Education and Society, 15*(2), 221–233. doi:10.1080/13573321003683893

Wright, J., & Leahy, D. (2016). Moving beyond body image: A socio-critical approach. In E. Cameron & C. Russell (Eds.), *The fat pedagogy reader: Challenging weight-based oppression in education* (pp. 141–150). New York: Peter Lang Publishing.

8   Better than Before

Individual Strategies for Body Image Improvement

Jamie L. Dunaev and Charlotte H. Markey

We all have thoughts and feelings about our bodies. They are complex, dynamic, and in some cases even seemingly contradictory. These thoughts and feelings – referred to as our body image – have the potential to shape not only our general sense of self, but also our interactions with others and our psychological and behavioral health. Body image has become a vibrant area of scholarly study and has garnered a great deal of popular interest due to the large number of people, especially adolescent girls and women, who are dissatisfied with their bodies (Cash, 2002; Gillen & Markey, 2015; Markey & Gillen, 2017). At the extreme, body dissatisfaction has been shown to predict eating disorders (Stice, 2002), depression (Gillen, Markey, & Markey, 2012), and impaired social functioning (e.g., anxiety, compromised sexual interactions; Cash & Fleming, 2002; Goins, Markey, & Gillen, 2012; Wiederman, 2002). Although body image is often investigated in terms of body *dissatisfaction*, recent research has illuminated the utility of a similar, but distinct, construct: positive body image.

Positive body image is described as the extent to which one experiences love, confidence, respect, appreciation, and acceptance of one's physical appearance and abilities (Wood-Barcalow, Tylka, & Augustus-Horvath, 2010). People who have a high positive body image are apt to accept their physical selves, and focus on the functionality rather than just the aesthetics of their body (Andrew, Tiggemann, & Levina, 2016; Bailey, Gammage, van Ingen, & Ditor, 2015; Wood-Barcalow et al., 2010). It has also been suggested that positive body image may help individuals engage in "protective filtering," wherein negative information about appearance and the body is rejected and positive information is accepted (Andrew, Tiggemann, & Clark, 2015; Wood-Barcalow et al., 2010). In other words, positive body image includes affective, cognitive, and behavioral characteristics and is not merely the absence of body dissatisfaction (Andrew et al., 2016; Tylka, 2011).

Positive body image is conceptualized as having various facets and has been measured using a variety of new assessments that tap into these facets. Perhaps the most often used measure is the Body Appreciation

Scale (BAS and BAS-2; Avalos, Tylka, & Wood-Barcalow, 2005; Tylka & Wood-Barcalow, 2015), which assesses body acceptance and respect for and favorable opinions toward the body. Body functionality (Rubin & Steinberg, 2011) refers to recognition of the functions the body provides and includes capabilities ranging from athletic endeavors to interpersonal communication. The Embodied Image Scale (EIS; Abbott & Barber, 2010) is one assessment tool that allows for consideration of the body's positive capacities, not just negative attributes (Alleva, Martijn, Van Breukelen, Jansen, & Karos, 2015). Another element of positive body image is body gratitude (Dunaev, Brochu, & Markey, 2017). Gratitude can be defined as a "wider life orientation towards noticing and appreciating the positive in the world" (Wood, Froh, & Geraghty, 2010, p. 2), and has most often been assessed using qualitative approaches (e.g., "list characteristics of your body that you are grateful for"). Finally, body image flexibility has been assessed using the Body Image Acceptance and Action Questionnaire (BI-AAQ; Sandoz, Wilson, Merwin, & Kellum, 2013). Flexibility refers to a self-compassionate approach to the body in that individuals are encouraged to embrace their physical selves and work to alter their negative thoughts and feelings about their bodies.

This discussion of measures is not comprehensive, but is relevant to our discussion of intervention research that follows. It is also important to note that research suggests individuals may hold both positive and negative views of their bodies (e.g., different aspects of their physical selves) simultaneously; this is not easily captured by a single assessment tool. For example, in one study (Bailey, Kline, & Gammage, 2016) composed of analyses of middle-aged and older women's body images, results suggest that women experienced negative and positive body image simultaneously. That is, they were capable of feeling satisfied with their bodies while wishing they were younger and believing that youth contributed to beauty. They also often reported feeling positively about one aspect of their bodies while being dissatisfied with another. And they made relative evaluations of their bodies: "[I'm] grateful that I'm not out of shape so I think for my age it's not bad but I'm always trying to make it better" (Bailey et al., 2016, p. 93).

With the complexity of body image being increasingly acknowledged (Andrew et al., 2016), and research examining positive body image attracting more attention in the past decade (Webb, Wood-Barcalow, & Tylka, 2015), interventions aiming to improve different facets of positive body image have begun to emerge (e.g., appreciation, functionality, gratitude; Alleva et al., 2015; Dunaev et al., 2017). Although education and intervention efforts to *decrease* body *dissatisfaction* have proliferated across the past thirty years, the integration of positive body image into this area of study and practice is relatively new. Similar to other scholars' discussions on this topic (Tylka & Wood-Barcalow, 2015; Webb et al., 2015), we contend that decreasing body dissatisfaction and increasing positive body image are not synonymous. Yet they *can* be viewed as two sides of the same coin. For instance, there is some preliminary evidence to suggest that interventions that have been effective at reducing negative body image may also be useful for enhancing positive body image (Halliwell, Jarmna, McNamara, Risdon, & Jankowski, 2015). Thus, in order to flesh out our discussion of interventions aimed at enhancing positive body image, we include relevant research that has examined efforts to decrease body dissatisfaction as well.

Further, many previously implemented efforts tend to rely on educational and community settings (Alleva et al., 2015). Our purpose in this chapter is to describe interventions that may aid *individuals* in improving their body image on their own. We define "individual efforts" as those in which a single individual can take part, separate from social settings and (usually) without the aid of a researcher or clinician. Individual-level strategies provide a unique opportunity to engage individuals in positive body image enhancement outside the confines of a professional or formal setting, allowing users greater privacy and more flexibility in accessing these programs. This can include activities such as engaging in prespecified writing activities (e.g., reflections or keeping a diary), exercising or participating in some other type of physical activity, or completing various therapies that could be adapted for computer-based delivery (e.g., cognitive behavioral therapy, mindfulness training, media literacy). Considering the amount of time and effort required to implement societal-level changes (e.g., requiring disclaimers on photos, banning underweight runway models), it is important that we investigate strategies which individuals can use now and implement for themselves. This is not to say that individual efforts could not be pursued following some instruction from a clinician, an educator, or even a book. Individual efforts aimed at improving elements of positive body image may be initiated in clinical and community settings or even schools, and then practiced within individuals' homes.

Interventions for Individual-Level Body Image Improvement

Writing Exercises for Positive Body Image Enhancement

Writing-based interventions have been used to address a number of mental and physical health concerns, including those related to body image. These writing exercises can be long-term, for instance keeping daily diary entries for a number of weeks, or short-term, such as responding to a single writing prompt for an experimental study. One potential approach to enhancing positive body image may be through using writing activities to actively cultivate appreciation for the body by focusing on its more positive aspects (e.g., functionality, health).

In one recent study, Alleva and colleagues (2015) randomly assigned eighty-one women to either a body functionality treatment group ($n = 41$) or a control group ($n = 40$). Participants in the treatment condition completed three fifteen-minute writing assignments over the course of roughly a week, with each writing assignment focusing on different aspects of body functionality (e.g., physical capabilities, health, self-care). Participants in the control condition did similar writing assignments on the topic of creativity. Results indicated that when compared to participants in the control group, participants in the body functionality group reported higher body functionality satisfaction, higher appearance satisfaction, lower self-objectification, and greater body appreciation (Alleva et al., 2015).

In a follow-up study, Alleva, Veldhuis, and Martijn (2016) examined whether focusing on body functionality could buffer against the negative effects of thin, idealized media models. In this experiment, seventy undergraduate women were randomly assigned to either a treatment ($n = 35$) or control ($n = 35$) group. Participants in the treatment group were given a description of body functionality and were asked to write about the functions of their body and why those functions are meaningful. Participants in the control group were asked to write about the details of routes they frequently travel. All participants were then shown a series of fifteen images, twelve of which contained images of thin, idealized female models. The results of this study showed the women in the functionality group reported higher levels of functionality satisfaction and body appreciation when compared to the control group. No significant effects were found for appearance appreciation or self-objectification, suggesting that a focus on body functionality may buffer against the negative effects of thin-ideal imagery for some aspects of body image (e.g., body appreciation) but not others (e.g., appearance satisfaction; Alleva et al., 2016).

In addition to focusing on body functionality, writing interventions can also be used to foster a sense of gratitude toward life in general and one's body in particular. A growing body of research has found robust associations between gratitude and well-being, including improvements in depression, generalized anxiety, drug and alcohol dependence, relationship quality, positive affect, and stress (Wood et al., 2010). One suggested reason for this is that gratitude exercises may enhance well-being by encouraging individuals to focus on assets rather than deficits and to recognize things they might have otherwise taken for granted (Seligman, Steen, Park, & Peterson, 2005). When applied to body image, focusing on things for which one is grateful may encourage individuals to consider positive things about their body that they might frequently overlook.

Three studies have examined the effect of writing-based gratitude interventions on body image. In the first of these studies, Geraghty and colleagues (2010) randomly assigned British men and women to a gratitude diary group ($n = 40$), a thought monitoring and restructuring group ($n = 22$), or a waitlist control group ($n = 120$). Participants in the gratitude condition were given diaries and instructed to list six things they felt grateful for (in general) each day for two weeks. Participants in the thought monitoring and restructuring condition were given workbooks and instructed to record and positively restructure negative body thoughts. Results indicated that participants in the gratitude condition reported significantly lower levels of body dissatisfaction when compared to a control waitlist condition, and similar levels compared to the thought monitoring and restructuring group. Furthermore, participants in the gratitude condition were significantly more likely to complete the two-week intervention when compared to the monitoring and restructuring condition (Geraghty, Wood, & Hyland, 2010).

In a replication study, Wolfe and Patterson (2017) found that undergraduate female participants assigned to a general gratitude diary condition ($n = 35$) experienced more marked increases in body esteem and decreases in body dissatisfaction when compared to control (education about body image; $n = 45$) and cognitive restructuring diary ($n = 28$) conditions. The authors also found that participants in the gratitude condition were more likely to complete the study and reported significant increases in positive mood and decreases in depressive symptoms when compared to the cognitive restructuring condition. However, the authors found no differences in changes in body appreciation between the groups (Wolfe & Patterson, 2017).

In one additional study, Dunaev, Brochu, and Markey (2017) tested the effects of a body-specific gratitude writing exercise on body image. In this study, young men and women were randomly assigned to either a body gratitude ($n = 185$) or control ($n = 184$) condition. Participants in the body gratitude condition were instructed to think about and write down (at least) three aspects of their body that they were grateful for, including the health, physical appearance, or functionality of their body. Participants in the control condition were instructed to think and write about their ideal vacation. Following this brief intervention, participants in the body gratitude condition reported significantly higher appearance esteem and lower body dissatisfaction when compared to participants in the control condition (Dunaev et al., 2017).

Conclusions and Recommendations Writing-based interventions are relatively simple, require less time and effort than many societal and institutional interventions, and are easily accessible to individuals. Previous research in the area of writing-based interventions and body image suggests that paradigms such as Pennebaker and Beall's (1986) expressive writing exercises may not be optimal if they require participants to ruminate on negative body-related thoughts and experiences (Earnhardt, Martz, Ballard, & Curtin, 2002; Lafont & Oberle, 2014; O'Connor, Hurling, Hendrickx, & Wood, 2011). Instead, based on the limited data available, it appears that approaches focused on cultivating body appreciation and highlighting positive body attributes may be a better direction for improving body image overall. This area of research is in its infancy, however. Although some studies used positive body image constructs (Alleva et al., 2015, 2016; Wolfe & Patterson, 2017), most of what is known about body image and writing-based interventions is based on research using measures of negative body image (i.e., body dissatisfaction).

Tentative findings provide support for the notion that writing-based interventions can successfully be used to both decrease negative body image and improve positive body image. Specifically, evidence suggests writing about body functionality can improve body appreciation and functionality satisfaction (Alleva et al., 2015, 2016), and writing about gratitude (general or body-specific) can decrease body dissatisfaction and increase body esteem (Dunaev et al., 2017; Geraghty et al., 2010; Wolfe & Patterson, 2017). Additionally, writing-based interventions that focus on positive aspects of one's body or life (e.g., gratitude) may result in lower intervention attrition rates when compared to writing about negative aspects (e.g., restructuring negative body thoughts; Geraghty et al., 2010; Wolfe & Patterson, 2017). Thus, a gratitude intervention may be more sustainable over time compared to other types of interventions.

Beyond the sheer dearth of studies in the area of writing-based interventions and positive body image, there are other limitations that should be addressed. First, because few studies employed pre- and postintervention measurements alongside control and comparison groups, little is known about the presence, magnitude, or endurance of these effects. Second, no work has examined the potential boundary conditions of these effects. For instance, we do not know how long (e.g., five minutes, daily, weekly) or how structured a writing intervention has to be in order to improve body image. We also do not know what types of individuals (e.g., women, individuals high in body dissatisfaction) may respond more positively to these types of interventions. Thus, much more research is needed in this area to determine the potential efficacy of writing-based interventions for positive body image enhancement.

Exercise-Based Positive Body Image Enhancement

The physical benefits of regular exercise (e.g., walking, aerobic exercise, weightlifting, sports) are well established and discussed, yet less attention is focused on the potential mental health benefits of exercise, particularly as they relate to body image. However, the link between exercise and body image is relatively clear – exercise can contribute to the acquisition of the thin and muscular bodies that are idealized and promoted in Western media (Markey, 2014). Many individuals may thus engage in exercise for the purpose of reshaping their bodies – whether the end goal is weight loss or muscle gain – to more closely approximate these body ideals (Hausenblas & Fallon, 2006). Although it is typically not the case that individuals are able to achieve these body ideals via exercise alone, as actual objective changes in body size and shape are not an inevitable result (Markey, 2014), the extant literature suggests that engaging in physical activity may have a positive impact on body image.

Meta-analyses of hundreds of correlational and experimental studies provide strong empirical support for the small-to-moderate negative association between exercise and body dissatisfaction (Campbell & Hausenblas, 2009; Hausenblas & Fallon, 2006; Reel et al., 2007), yet there are far fewer studies exploring the association between exercise and *positive body image constructs* (e.g., body appreciation, body functionality). A handful of studies have qualitatively approached this question. For instance, Wood-Barcalow and colleagues (2010) interviewed college-aged women ($N = 15$) who had been identified as having positive body image and found that many of these women reported exercising regularly. Frisén and Holmqvist (2010) found similar results in interviews with body positive Swedish adolescent boys and girls ($N = 30$) who reported being physically active and enjoying exercise. Finally, Krane and colleagues (2004) found that female college athletes ($N = 21$) reported feeling empowered by and proud of their strong bodies.

At least two quantitative studies have specifically looked at the association between exercise and positive body image (Béres, Czeglédi, & Babusa, 2017; Homan & Tylka, 2014). The first study found that college-aged women ($N = 321$) who frequently engaged in moderate exercise also reported greater body appreciation, internal body orientation, and body functionality satisfaction. Further, these effects were weaker for women who reported exercising for reasons of appearance (Homan & Tylka, 2014). The second study used an experimental design to examine the effects of a single-exercise session on body appreciation. A total of 322 Hungarian women were randomly assigned to complete either one hour of aerobic exercise in a fitness class ($n = 155$) or one hour of aerobic exercise at home using an exercise video ($n = 167$). Results indicated that women in both groups showed a moderate improvement in body appreciation following the one-hour exercise session. Further, no significant differences in body appreciation were found between the two groups (Béres et al., 2017). These two studies provide preliminary evidence for the positive association between exercise and positive body image.

Conclusions and Recommendations Exercise-based positive body image interventions may be a particularly promising avenue for future research, as they have the capacity to confer both physical and mental health benefits. Based on the limited evidence, it appears that exercise has the potential both to reduce negative body image (Campbell & Hausenblas, 2009; Hausenblas & Fallon, 2006) and to enhance positive body image (Béres et al., 2017). Furthermore, it appears to be the case that exercise can be beneficial whether it is performed in a gym setting or at home (Béres et al., 2017). Researchers interested in positive body image should thus consider their work as an extension of the already well-developed literature on exercise and body image by including measures of both positive and negative body image.

In addition to the need for more studies that demonstrate the effects of exercise on positive body image (e.g., randomized control trials with pre- and postintervention measurements), there are a number of other under-explored topics in this area. In particular, few studies have tested for mediators and moderators of these effects. Understanding the characteristics of the exerciser (e.g., gender, age, reason for exercising) and the exercise program (e.g., duration, type of exercise, intensity) that might result in the most body image benefits, or why exercise improves body image (e.g., improvements in self-efficacy, objective physical fitness changes), is important for developing more effective and efficient exercise-based interventions (Martin Ginis, Bassett-Gunter, & Conlin, 2012).

Online Positive Body Image Enhancement

Widespread access to smartphones, tablets, and computers makes online dissemination of interventions a viable option for body image enhancement. The online body image-related intervention that has been subject to the greatest degree of empirical testing, *StudentBodies*, is a structured cognitive behavioral online intervention designed for adolescent girls and women that addresses risk factors for eating disorders (e.g., body image, drive for thinness, nutritional and exercise knowledge and attitudes; Winzelberg & Taylor, 1998). This program requires that participants log in (at least) weekly for eight weeks, read the content for that week (e.g., nutrition basics, cultural images of beauty), and complete an assignment related to that content (e.g., self-monitoring exercises to promote cognitive restructuring). Based on a meta-analysis of ten randomized controlled trials (six in the United States and four in Germany), this intervention has been shown to be moderately effective for reducing negative body image and other eating disorder-related attitudes (Beintner, Jacobi, & Taylor, 2011).

Various other, less empirically tested programs have also been developed. For instance, *Food, Mood, and Attitude* is a computer-based program also designed to address risk factors for eating disorders (e.g., body dissatisfaction). Following two one-hour sessions of computer-based activities (e.g., media images and thin-ideal internalization; coping strategies), female undergraduate ($n = 118$) students showed decreases in weight and shape concern and thin-ideal internalization when compared to a control group ($n = 115$; Franko et al., 2005). Another program, *BodiMojo*, focuses on body image enhancement for adolescents. Participants in this intervention completed an online four-week program, including games, quizzes, videos, and tailored feedback on topics ranging from media literacy and physical appearance comparisons to exercise and nutrition. This program was effective for improving body appearance satisfaction and decreasing body dissatisfaction for girls ($n = 113$) when compared to a control group (normal health classes). However, these effects had disappeared when measured three months later, and furthermore the program had no significant effects for boys ($n = 65$) when compared to the control group (Franko, Cousineau, Rodgers, & Roehrig, 2013).

Although only a limited number of online or computer-based programs have been developed and tested to reduce negative body image, many interventions to enhance positive body image could be adapted for online delivery. For instance, Gledhill and colleagues (2017) developed a program to train women to more accurately judge the body sizes of computer-developed 3D female figures. After four daily laboratory-based training sessions, participants across two studies showed reduced weight and shape concerns when compared to a control group (Gledhill et al., 2017). Further, interventions aimed at improving media literacy, which have been shown to be particularly effective for improving body image in school settings (Yager, Diedrichs, Ricciardelli, & Halliwell, 2013), could potentially be adapted into self-guided online activities. Finally, techniques that encourage mindfulness have been shown to improve body image (Alberts, Thewissen, & Raes, 2012; see Chapter 6 in this book by Cook-Cottone) and are amenable to online delivery (Krusche, Cyhlarova, & Williams, 2013). For instance, breathing exercises, simple meditation exercises, self-care, yoga postures, and stretching could all be directed via online sources. These are actually already available online through YouTube, but have not been tested for online positive body image enhancement to date. Each of these potential positive body image enhancement intervention strategies – the ability to accurately judge body sizes and evaluate media information and the focus on self-care – could improve individuals' ability to engage in protective filtering and focus on positive embodiment.

Beyond specific programming, online spaces can also be used to access body image-relevant content (e.g., photos, inspirational stories) and discussion groups. For instance, although research suggests that social media use (e.g., Facebook, Instagram) may increase body *dissatisfaction* (Manago, Ward, Lemm, Reed, & Seabrook, 2015; Meier & Gray, 2014; Tiggemann & Slater, 2013; Tiggemann & Zaccardo, 2015), less is known about how social media may be used to improve body image and cultivate positive body image specifically. The recent proliferation of social media hashtags related to body positivity and acceptance (e.g., #bodypositive, #lovetheskinyourein; Marcus, 2016) makes this an important area for future body image research. It may be the case the individuals can learn to intentionally curate their online spaces in a way that allows for exposure to positive body image enhancing content (e.g., photos, quotes) with the touch of a button. In the future, interventions that educate individuals to make social media a source of positive body image enhancement may be particularly appealing.

Conclusions and Recommendations Online interventions have been successfully used in the field of public health (e.g., promoting sexual health among adolescents; see Stevens, Dunaev, Malven, Bleakley, & Hull, 2016), yet remain underutilized in body image research. The paucity of body image research in the area of this particular modality is striking given that internet-based interventions are highly customizable and thus amenable to various approaches to body image improvement (e.g., cognitive behavioral, dissonance-based, mindfulness). They also allow participants relative anonymity while discussing sensitive topics, are accessible from virtually anywhere, and may provide a more actively engaging experience than some more traditional school- or community-based programs (Yager & O'Dea, 2008). Further, there is abundant empirical support for the use of self-help techniques to improve body image and address various other psychosocial issues (e.g., depression, anxiety; Gould & Clum, 1993; Hrabosky & Cash, 2007; Yager & O'Dea, 2008).

Current evidence suggests that previously tested online and computer-based programs have been useful for decreasing body dissatisfaction (e.g., weight concerns, shape concerns; Beintner et al., 2011; Franko et al., 2005, 2013), yet these programs have yet to specifically focus on positive body image constructs. Further, there is good evidence to suggest that a number of strategies may enhance body image (e.g., media literacy, perceptual training, mindfulness training), yet have not been tested for online-delivered positive body image enhancement interventions. As can be seen, additional research is needed to understand how the internet, including professionally designed programming and preexisting content (e.g., photos, hashtags, social networking sites), might affect positive body image.

Future Directions

Correlates of Positive Body Image

There are a variety of known correlates and predictors of positive body image that may serve as targets for interventions to increase positive body image. The logic is that if the predictor (e.g., self-esteem) is improved or enhanced, positive body image may be as well. Although not all of these correlates and predictors have been empirically examined in an intervention context, we review them to assist future researchers as they consider designing interventions and studies to examine their efficacy.

Body image research in general (e.g., Groesz, Levine, & Murnen, 2002), and research focusing on positive body image in particular (e.g., Andrew et al., 2015), points to the negative impact of appearance-driven media consumption. Thus, limiting media consumption may be one potential way to improve positive body image, but may prove extremely difficult in an increasingly digital world. As mentioned above, one approach to limiting the deleterious effects of the media is through education and media literacy programming. An example of one such program is Wilksch and Wade's (2009) eight-session media literacy program for girls and boys in the eighth grade. Weight and shape concerns declined following this program – a finding that may be indicative of positive body image enhancement.

Another avenue that may be conducive to increasing positive body image is the cultivation of perceived appearance acceptance by others (Andrew et al., 2016). Individuals tend to report appreciating their own bodies when they feel that others do as well (Markey, Markey, & Birch, 2004). One way to make salient this perceived acceptance is through communication with valued others (e.g., parents, friends, significant others). Interventions to improve communication among individuals and those closest to them as a means of enhancing positive body image are rare. However, in a recent study (Markey et al., 2017) in which researchers asked romantic couples to discuss their bodies and weight, results suggested that doing so led participants to have more realistic body ideals than they reported before the intervention. Future research should consider the extent to which communication interventions among different types of dyads (e.g., parent–child) may increase positive body image.

Because the link between eating behaviors and body image is undeniable (Markey, 2014), researchers have examined the potential of eating-based interventions as a means of improving positive body image. For example, in a recent intervention targeting preadolescents (McCabe, Connaughton, Tantangelo, Mellor, & Busija, 2017), four sixty-minute educational sessions plus one recap session were capable of improving not only eating behaviors (i.e., fruit and vegetable consumption) but also body esteem. Considering the vast majority of American adults fail to meet recommendations for daily fruit and vegetable intake (Moore & Thompson, 2015), improving body image while simultaneously increasing health behaviors is a laudable goal.

Research dating back to Harter's landmark studies (e.g., Harter, 1999) indicates the correlation between individuals' perception of their appearance and their general sense of self. An implication of this and other work (e.g., Clay, Vignoles, & Dittmar, 2005) is that improving self-esteem, broadly construed, may bolster positive body image. For example, evidence for this comes from O'Dea and Abraham's (2000) *Everybody's Different* intervention among 11–14-year-olds. This study found that improvements in body image and self-esteem were linked and persisted across twelve months. These findings have been replicated by several other studies, suggesting that self-esteem enhancement techniques can increase body image, and potentially positive body image in particular (Steiner-Adair et al., 2002).

Future Research Recommendations and General Conclusions

The purpose of this chapter was to identify published studies that, broadly speaking, might be used to inform individuals on the best means of cultivating or enhancing their positive body image. Perhaps most striking is the overall paucity of research efforts in this area. This research is in its infancy, and many scholars within and outside of the field may be just beginning to embrace positive body image as a distinct construct from negative body image. Nevertheless, the studies reviewed here provide preliminary evidence for effective individual-level strategies for improving positive body image. Although some intervention strategies were able to produce changes in both negative and positive body image (Alleva et al., 2015), others were effective at reducing body dissatisfaction but not at improving body appreciation (Béres et al., 2017; Wolfe & Patterson, 2017). These results provide further evidence for the distinctness of positive body image as a construct and make more salient the need to develop interventions specifically aimed at addressing positive body image.

There are a number of general issues that need to be addressed in order to develop more effective and efficient positive body image enhancement interventions. First, researchers in the area need to adopt more rigorous methods, specifically in terms of study design. In our review, we found very few studies using randomized controlled trials with pre- and posttest measures. Without these types of studies, inferences about causal relationships and the magnitude of change attributable to any particular intervention strategy cannot be made. Additionally, in order to determine the endurance of these effects, interventions should include posttest measures at various time points following the intervention (e.g., one day later, one week later). Finally, researchers conducting these studies should consider adopting open science practices (e.g., preregistration of studies, making data accessible online) to increase the reproducibility and transparency of their work.

Most studies to date that have examined issues of positive body image employ samples of girls and women, and most often comprise undergraduate students. Although girls and women tend to exhibit more negative body image (Gillen & Markey, 2015), recent research suggests that boys and men also report high levels of body dissatisfaction (Bearman, Martinez, Stice, & Presnell, 2006). The development of interventions to improve positive body image and the studies examining these interventions that follow need to include both male and female participants. However, given the distinct body image concerns for girls/women and boys/men – with the former frequently desiring thinness and the latter frequently desiring muscularity – it may be appropriate to develop interventions that are gender specific. Similarly, researchers should design and test interventions aimed at individuals across the lifespan. For instance, because of their different body image concerns, interventions that are appropriate for children and adolescents are unlikely to be effective for middle-aged individuals (Dunaev, Schulz, & Markey, 2016).

If the field is to continue to progress, there also must be more attention paid to theory. Theories help identify important aspects of the attitude or behavior change process, such as mediators and moderators, and as such provide vital information about viable intervention points. For instance, designing an optimal exercise-based intervention requires understanding characteristics of the exerciser (e.g., gender, age), the exercise program (e.g., type of exercise, intensity of exercise), and various other relevant issues (e.g., accessibility). Comprehensive theoretical models will allow researchers to examine how these variables interact to shape attitude and behavior change and ultimately help to improve positive body image.

Future interventions in this area should also incorporate a variety of outcome measures. Although the Body Appreciation Scale is frequently used as a positive body image measure, studies should seek to assess multiple components of positive body image (e.g., body gratitude, body acceptance). Doing so will allow for a more comprehensive assessment of positive body image that encompasses a variety of issues (e.g., aesthetics, functionality). Similarly, if we are to continue to understand what interventions might be effective for both enhancing positive body image and decreasing negative body image, studies must continue to incorporate negative body image constructs alongside positive body image constructs. Finally, interventions should determine what the long-term effects of positive body image enhancement are by utilizing longitudinal designs and behavioral outcomes.

Several decades of research has revealed the deleterious effects of body dissatisfaction and the value of interventions aimed to reduce this dissatisfaction (Gillen & Markey, 2017; McCabe, et al., 2017). However, following the more general trend in the field of psychology, with attention moving from reducing illness and impairment toward an emphasis on optimization of the human experience, the field of body image has begun to move toward an examination of positive body image. This shift signals an appreciation of the value of not just "settling for" one's body, but embracing it (Andrew et al., 2016a). In this chapter, we have presented a variety of potential avenues for intervention to improve positive body image, and preliminary evidence to support them. In particular, writing exercises appear to offer opportunities for self-reflection, appreciation, and gratitude that may encourage positive body image and improvements in mental health more generally. Second, exercise may not only enhance both physical and mental health, but also has the potential to improve positive body image. Exercise can take place in a variety of contexts (e.g., with or without others present), but is inherently self-directed and, when framed positively (i.e., not as obligatory), may have lasting benefits. Finally, online interventions offer privacy, access, and endless opportunities to spread positive messages pertaining to body image, and may enhance body appreciation and focus on functionality and limit the valuation of beauty ideals.

Although we have identified a number of areas that require additional research before firm conclusions can be made about the efficacy of different intervention approaches, we believe this presents an exciting opportunity for body image researchers. We are hopeful that the next decade of body image research will focus not only on positive body image, but also on the individually directed interventions that can improve positive body image. These interventions may be especially valuable to a number of vulnerable populations. For example, individuals without access to or coverage for mental health treatment, young people experiencing their first body image concerns, and individuals who may not believe their body dissatisfaction requires formal treatment may all be amenable to participating in individually directed options for the improvement of positive body image.

References

Abbott, B. D., & Barber, B. L. (2010). Embodied image: Gender differences in functional and aesthetic body image among Australian adolescents. *Body Image, 7,* 22–31. doi:10.1016/j.bodyim.2009.10.004

Alberts, H. J. E. M., Thewissen, R., & Raes, L. (2012). Dealing with problematic eating behavior: The effects of a mindfulness-based intervention on eating behavior, food cravings, dichotomous thinking and body image concern. *Appetite, 58,* 847–851. doi:10.1016/j.appet.2012.01.009

Alleva, J. M., Martijn, C., Van Breukelen, G. J. P., Jansen, A., & Karos, K. (2015). Expand your horizon: A programme that improves body image and reduces self-objectification by training women to focus on body functionality. *Body Image, 15,* 81– 89. doi:10.1016/j.bodyim.2015.07.001

Alleva, J. M., Veldhuis, J., & Martijn, C. (2016). A pilot study investigating whether focusing on body functionality can protect women from the potential negative effects of viewing thin-ideal media images. *Body Image, 17,* 10–13. doi: 10.1016/j.bodyim.2016.01.007

Andrew, R., Tiggemann, M., & Clark, L. (2015). The protective role of body appreciation against media-induced body dissatisfaction. *Body Image, 15,* 98–104. doi: 10.1016/j.bodyim.2015.07.005

Andrew, R., Tiggemann, M., & Levina, C. (2016). Predicting body appreciation in young women: An integrated model of positive body image. *Body Image, 18,* 34–42. doi:10.1016/j.bodyim.2016.04.003

Avalos, L., Tylka, T. L., & Wood-Barcalow, N. (2005). The body appreciation scale: Development and psychometric evaluation. *Body Image*, *2*, 285–297. doi:10.1016/j.bodyim.2005.06.002

Bailey, K. A., Gammage, K. L., van Ingen, C., & Ditor, D. S. (2015). "It's all about acceptance": A qualitative study exploring a model of positive body image for people with spinal cord injury. *Body Image*, *15*, 24–34. doi:10.1016/j.bodyim.2015.04.010

Bailey, K. A., Kline, L. E., & Gammage, K. L. (2016). Exploring the complexities of body image experiences in middle age and older adult women within an exercise context: The simultaneous existence of negative and positive body images. *Body Image*, *17*, 88–99. doi:10.1016/j.bodyim.2016.02.007

Bearman, S. K., Martinez, E., Stice, E., & Presnell, K. (2006). The skinny on body dissatisfaction: A longitudinal study of adolescent girls and boys. *Journal of Youth and Adolescence*, *35*, 217–229. doi:10.1007/s10964-005-9010-9

Beintner, I., Jacobi, C., & Taylor, C. B. (2011). Effects on an internet-based prevention programme for eating disorders in the USA and Germany: A meta-analytic review. *European Eating Disorder Review*, *20*, 1–8. doi:10.1002/erv.1130

Béres, A., Czeglédi, E., & Babusa, B. (2017). Effects of a single aerobic exercise session on body image. *Mentálhigiéné és Pszichoszomatika*, *18*, 84–104. doi:10.1556/0406.18.2017.1.4

Campbell, A., & Hausenblas, H. A. (2009). Effects of exercise interventions on body image: A meta-analysis. *Journal of Health Psychology*, *14*, 780–93. doi:10.1177/1359105309338977

Cash, T. F. (2002). A "negative body image": Evaluating epidemiological evidence. In T. F. Cash & T. Pruzinsky (Eds.), *Body image: A handbook of theory, research, and clinical practice* (pp. 269–276). New York: Guilford Press.

Cash, T. F., & Fleming, E. C. (2002). The impact of body image experiences: Development of body image quality of life inventory. *International Journal of Eating Disorders*, *31*, 455–460. doi:10.1002/eat.10033

Cash, T. F., & Hrabosky, J. I. (2003). The effects of psychoeducation and self-monitoring in a cognitive-behavioral program for body-image improvement. *Eating Disorders*, *11*, 255–270.

Clay, D., Vignoles, L., & Dittmar, H. (2005). Body image and self-esteem among adolescent girls: Testing the influence of sociocultural factors. *Journal of Research on Adolescence*, *15*, 451–477. doi:10.1111/j.1532-7795.2005.00107.x

Dohnt, H. K., & Tiggemann, M. (2008). Promoting positive body image in young girls: An evaluation of 'Shapesville.' *European Eating Disorders Review*, *16*, 222–233. doi: 10.1002/erv.814

Dunaev, J., Brochu, P. M., & Markey, C. H. (2018). An attitude of gratitude: The effects of body-focused gratitude on weight bias internalization and body image. *Body Image*, *7* (25), 9–13. doi:10.1016/j.bodyim.2018.01.006

Dunaev, J., Schulz, J. L., & Markey, C. H. (2016). Cosmetic surgery attitudes among midlife women: Appearance esteem, weight esteem, and fear of negative appearance evaluation. *Journal of Health Psychology*, *23* (1), 1–8. doi: 10.1177/1359105316642249

Earnhardt, J. L., Martz, D. M., Ballard, M. E., & Curtin, L. (2002). A writing intervention for negative body image. *Journal of College Student Psychotherapy*, *17*, 19–35. doi:10.1300/j035v17n01_04

Franko, D. L., Cousineau, T. M., Rodgers, R. F., & Roehrig, J. P. (2013). BodiMojo: Effective internet-based promotion of positive body image in adolescent girls. *Body Image*, *10*, 481–488. doi:10.1016/j.bodyim.2013.04.008

Franko, D. L., Mintz, L. B., Villapiano, M., Green, T. C., Mainelli, D., Folensbee, L.,... Budman, S. H. (2005). Food, mood, and attitude: Reducing risk for eating disorders in college women. *Health Psychology*, *24*, 567–578. doi:10.1037/0278-6133.24.6.567

Frisén, A., & Holmqvist, K. (2010). What characterizes early adolescents with a positive body image? A qualitative investigation of Swedish girls and boys. *Body Image*, *7*, 205–212. doi:10.1016/j.bodyim.2010.04.001

Geraghty, A. W. A., Wood, A. M., & Hyland, M. E. (2010). Attrition from self-directed interventions: Investigating the relationship between psychological predictors, intervention content and dropout from a body dissatisfaction intervention. *Social Science & Medicine*, *71*, 30–37. doi:10.1016/j.socscimed.2010.03.007

Gillen, M. M., & Markey, C. N. (2015). Body image and mental health. In H. S. Friedman (Ed.), *Encyclopedia of mental health* (2nd ed.). New York: Elsevier. (2017). Beauty and the burn: Tanning and other appearance-altering attitudes and behaviors. *Psychology, Health, & Medicine*, *22* (10), 1–7. doi: 10.1080/13548506.2017.1330544

Gillen, M. M., Markey, C. N., & Markey, P. M. (2012). An examination of dieting behaviors among adults: Links with depression. *Eating Behaviors*, *13*, 88–93. doi: 10.1016/j.eatbeh.2011.11.014

Gledhill, L. J., Cornelissen, K. K., Cornelissen, P. L., Penton-Voak, I. S., Munafò, M. R., & Tovée, M. J. (2017). An interactive training programme to treat body image disturbance. *British Journal of Health Psychology*, *22*, 60–76. doi:10.1111/bjhp.12217

Gould, R. A., & Clum, G. A. (1993). Meta-analysis of self-help treatment approaches. *Clinical Psychology Review*, *13*, 169–186. doi:10.1016/0272-7358(93)90039-O

Groesz, L. M., Levine, M. P., Murnen, S. K. (2002). The effect of experimental presentation of thin media images on body satisfaction: A meta-analytic review. *International Journal of Eating Disorders*, *31*, 1–16. doi: 10.1002/eat.10005

Goins, L. B., Markey, C. N., & Gillen, M. M. (2012). Understanding men's body image in the context of their romantic relationships. *American Journal of Men's Health*, *6*, 240–248. doi: 10.1177/1557988311431007

Halliwell, E., Jarman, H., McNamara, A., Risdon, H., & Jankowski, G. (2015). Dissemination of evidence-based body image interventions: A pilot study into the effectiveness of using undergraduate students as interventionists in secondary schools. *Body Image*, *14*, 1–4. doi:10.1016/j.bodyim.2015.02.002

Harter, S. (1999). *The construction of the self: A developmental perspective*. New York: Guilford Press.

Hausenblas, H. A., & Fallon, E. A. (2006). Exercise and body image: A meta-analysis. *Psychology & Health, 21*, 33–47. doi:10.1080/14768320500105270

Homan, K. J., & Tylka, T. L. (2014). Appearance-based exercise motivation moderates the relationship between exercise frequency and positive body image. *Body Image, 11*, 101–108. doi:10.1016/j.bodyim.2014.01.003

Hrabosky, J. I., & Cash, T. F. (2007). Self-help treatment for body-image disturbances. In J. D. Latner & G. T. Wilson (Eds.), *Self-help approaches for obesity and eating disorders: Research and practice* (pp. 118–138). New York: Guilford Press.

Krane, V., Choi, P. Y. L., Baird, S. M., Aimar, C. M., & Kauer, K. J. (2004). Living the paradox: Female athletes negotiate femininity and muscularity. *Sex Roles, 50*, 315–329. doi:10.1023/B:SERS.0000018888.48437.4f

Krusche, A., Cyhlarova, E., & Williams, J. M. G. (2013). Mindfulness online: An evaluation of the feasibility of a web-based mindfulness course for stress, anxiety, and depression. *BMJ Open, 3*, e003498. doi:10.1136/bmjopen-2013-003498

Lafont, J., & Oberle, C. D. (2014). Expressive writing effects on body image: Symptomatic versus asymptomatic women. *Psychology, 5*, 431–440. doi:10.4236/psych.2014.55053

Manago, A. M., Ward, L. M., Lemm, K. M., Reed, L., & Seabrook, R. (2015). Facebook involvement, objectified body consciousness, body shame, and sexual assertiveness in college women and men. *Sex Roles, 72*, 1–14. doi:10.1007/s11199-014-0441-1

Marcus, S. R. (2016). Thinspiration vs. thicksperation: Comparing pro-anorexic and fat acceptance image posts on a photo-sharing site. *Cyberpsychology: Journal of Psychosocial Research on Cyberspace, 10*, online edition. doi:10.5817/CP2016-2-5

Markey, C. H. & Gillen, M. M. (2017). Body image. In R. J. Levesque (Ed.), *Encyclopedia of adolescence* (2nd ed.). New York: Springer.

Markey, C. H., Gillen, M. M., August, K. J., Markey, P. M., & Nave, C. S. (2017). Does "body talk" improve body satisfaction among same-sex couples? *Body Image, 23*, 103–108. https://doi.org/10.1016/j.bodyim.2017.08.004

Markey, C. N. (2014). *Smart people don't diet: How psychology, common sense, and the latest science can help you lose weight permanently*. New York: Da Capo/Lifelong Books.

Markey, C. N., Markey, P. M., & Birch, L. L. (2004). Understanding women's body satisfaction: The role of husbands. *Sex Roles: A Journal of Research, 51*, 209–21. doi:10.1023/B:SERS.0000037764.40569.2b

Martin Ginis, K. A., Bassett-Gunter, R. L., & Conlin, C. (2012). Body image and exercise. In E. O. Acevedo (Ed.), *The Oxford handbook of exercise psychology* (pp. 55–75). Oxford: Oxford University Press.

McCabe, M. P., Connaughton, C., Tantangelo, G., Mellor, D., & Busija, L. (2017). Healthy me: A gender-specific program to address body image concerns and risk factors among preadolescents. *Body Image, 20*, 20–30. doi: 10.1016/j.bodyim.2016.10.007

Meier, E., & Gray, J. (2014). Facebook photo activity associated with body image disturbance in adolescent girls. *Cyberpsychology, Behavior, and Social Networking, 17*, 199–206. doi: org/10.1089/cyber.2013.0305

Moore, L. V., & Thompson, F. E. (2015). Adults meeting fruit and vegetable intake recommendations – United States, 2013. *Centers for Disease Control and Prevention, Morbidity and Mortality Weekly Report, 64*. Retrieved from www.cdc.gov/mmwr/preview/mmwrhtml/mm6426a1.htm.

O'Connor, D. B., Hurling, R., Hendrickx, H., & Wood, H. (2011). Effects of written emotional disclosure on implicit self-esteem and body image. *British Journal of Health Psychology, 16*, 488–501. doi:10.1348/135910710X523210

O'Dea, J. A., & Abraham, S. (2000). Improving the body image, eating attitudes, and behaviours or young male and female adolescents: A new educational approach that focuses on self-esteem. *International Journal of Eating Disorders, 28*, 43–57. doi:10.1002/(SICI)1098–108X(200007)28:1<43:: AID-EAT6>3.0.CO;2-D

Pennebaker, J. W. & Beall, S. K. (1986). Confronting a traumatic event: Toward an understanding of inhibition and disease. *Journal of Abnormal Psychology, 95*, 274–281. doi:10.1037//0021–843X.95.3.274

Raedeke, T. D. (2007). The relationship between enjoyment and affective responses to exercise. *Journal of Applied Sport Psychology, 19*, 105–115. doi:10.1016/j.psychsport.2006.10.005

Reel, J. J., Greenleaf, C., Baker, W. K., Aragon, S., Bishop, D., Cachaper, C., … Hattie, J. (2007). Relations of body concerns and exercise behavior: A meta-analysis. *Psychological Reports, 101*, 927–942. doi:10.2466/pr0.101.3.927–942

Rubin, L. R., & Steinberg, J. R. (2011). Self-objectification and pregnancy: Are body functionality dimensions protective? *Sex Roles, 65*, 606–618. doi:10.1007/s11199-011-9955-y

Sandoz, E. K., Wilson, K. G., Merwin, R. M., & Kellum, K. K. (2013). Assessment of body image flexibility: The body image-acceptance and action questionnaire. *Journal of Contextual Behavioral Science, 2*, 39–48. doi:10.1016/j.jcbs.2013.03.002

Seligman, M. E., Steen, T. A., Park, N., & Peterson, C. (2005). Positive psychology progress: Empirical validation of intervention. *American Psychologist, 60*, 410–421. doi:10.1037/0003–066X.60.5.410

Stiner-Adair, C., Sjostrom, L., Franko, D. L., Pai, S., Tucker, R., Becker, A. E., & Herzog, D. B. (2002). Primary prevention of risk factors for eating disorders in adolescent girls: Learning from practice. *International Journal of Eating Disorders, 32*, 401–411. doi:10.1002/eat.10089

Stevens, R., Dunaev, J., Malven, E., Bleakley, A., & Hull, S. (2016). Social media in the sexual lives of African American and Latino youth: Challenges and opportunities. *Media and Communication, 4*, 60–70. doi:10.17645/mac. v4i3.524

Stice, E. (2002). Risk and maintenance factors for eating pathology: A meta-analytic review. *Psychological Bulletin, 128*, 825–848. doi:org/10.1037/0033–2909.128.5.825

Tiggemann, M., & Slater, A. (2013). NetGirls: The internet, Facebook, and body image concern in adolescent girls. *International Journal of Eating Disorders*, *46*, 630–633. doi:10.1002/eat.22141

Tiggemann, M., & Zaccardo, M. (2015). "Exercise to be fit, not skinny": The effect of fitspiration imagery on women's body image. *Body Image*, *15*, 61–67. doi:10.1016/j.bodyim.2015.06.003

Tylka, T. L. (2011). Positive psychology perspectives on body image. In T. F. Cash & L. Smolak (Eds.), *Body image: A handbook of science, practice, and prevention* (pp. 56–64). New York: Guilford Press.

Tylka, T. L., & Wood-Barcalow, N. L. (2015). What is and what is not positive body image? Conceptual foundations and construct definitions. *Body Image*, *14*, 118–129. doi:10.1016/j.bodyim.2015.04.001

Webb, J. B., Wood-Barcalow, N. L., & Tylka, T. L. (2015). Assessing positive body image: Contemporary approaches and future directions. *Body Image*, *14*, 130–145. doi: 10.1016/j.bodyim.2015.03.010

Wiederman, M. W. (2002). Body image and sexual functioning. In T. F. Cash & T. Pruzinsky (Eds.), *Body image: A handbook of theory, research, & clinical practice* (pp. 287–294). New York: Guilford Press.

Wilksch, S. M., & Wade, T. D. (2009). Reduction of shape and weight concern in young adolescents: A 30-month controlled evaluation of a media literacy program. *Journal of the American Academy of Child & Adolescent Psychiatry*, *48*, 652–661. doi: 10.1097/CHI.0b013e3181a1f559

Winzelberg, A. J., & Taylor, C. B. (1998). Evaluation of a computer-mediated eating disorder intervention program. *The International Journal of Eating Disorders*, *24*, 339–349.

Wolfe, W. L., & Patterson, K. (2017). Comparison of a gratitude-based and cognitive restructuring intervention for body dissatisfaction and dysfunctional eating behavior in college women. *Eating Disorders*, *25* (4), 330–344. doi: 10.1080/10640266.2017.1279908

Wood, A. M., Froh, J. J., & Geraghty, A. W. (2010). Gratitude and well-being: A review and theoretical integration. *Clinical Psychological Review*, *30*, 890–905. doi: 10.1016/j.cpr.2010.03.005

Wood-Barcalow, N. L., Tylka, T. L., & Augustus-Horvath, C. L. (2010). "But I like my body": Positive body image characteristics and a holistic model for young-adult women. *Body Image*, *7*, 106–116. doi:10.1016/j.bodyim.2010.01.001

Yager, Z., Diedrichs, P. C., Ricciardelli, L. A., & Halliwell, E. (2013). What works in secondary schools? A systematic review of classroom-based body image programs. *Body Image*, *10*, 271–281. doi:10.1016/j.bodyim.2013.04.001

Yager, Z., & O'Dea, J. A. (2008). Prevention programs for body image and eating disorders on university campuses: A review of large, controlled interventions. *Health Promotion International*, *23*, 173–189.

9   Programmatic Approaches to Cultivating Positive Body Image in Youth

Elizabeth A. Daniels and Tomi-Ann Roberts

Research on body image prevention and intervention programs with youth has focused nearly exclusively on examining reductions in negative body perceptions and behaviors, such as body dissatisfaction (Yager, Diedrichs, Ricciardelli, & Halliwell, 2013) and/or eating disorders (Fingeret, Warren, Cepeda-Benito, & Gleaves, 2006; Stice, Shaw, & Marti, 2007), as opposed to cultivating positive body image, such as body appreciation. Indeed, since the 1980s, the vast majority of such programs have focused on reducing negative body image (Piran, 2015). This focus is understandable given the relationships between body dissatisfaction and negative health behaviors and attitudes such as the onset of dieting and disordered eating (Neumark-Sztainer, Paxton, Hannan, Haines, & Story, 2006), depression (Stice, Hayward, Cameron, Killen, & Taylor, 2000), cigarette use (Neumark-Sztainer et al., 2006), and risky sexual behaviors (Schooler, 2013). However, as Tylka and Wood-Barcalow (2015a; see also Chapter 1) have observed, reducing negative body image without cultivating positive body image may result in individuals simply holding a neutral or tolerant attitude toward their body. In contrast, fostering positive body image may allow individuals to appreciate, respect, and enjoy their bodies.

The construct of positive body image is multifaceted. It includes: (1) appreciating one's body and its functions; (2) accepting and admiring one's body despite sociocultural appearance pressures; (3) feeling comfortable, confident, and happy with one's body; (4) focusing on the strong points of one's body rather than its perceived flaws; and (5) taking in positive information about one's body while rejecting negative information (Wood-Barcalow, Tylka, & Augustus-Horvath, 2010; see Chapter 1). Since the articulation and development of this construct in the literature, research on positive body image has flourished (Tylka & Wood-Barcalow, 2015a; see Chapter 1). Piran and Teall (2012) outlined a related multifaceted construct termed *positive embodiment*, which includes the following five processes: (1) positive connection to the body via positive self-talk in the face of aversive experiences such as threats to body image;

(2) experiences of functionality and agency related to the body; (3) attuned self-care (i.e., awareness of internal cues, such as hunger, and action based on such cues, e.g., eating); (4) positive experiences and expressions of the body's desires (e.g., sexual desire); and (5) experiencing the body from a subjective rather than an objective position (see Chapter 6). Building on Piran and colleagues' original work, Menzel and Levine (2011) proposed the Embodiment Model of Positive Body Image, which identified participation in embodying activities, such as sport or yoga, as an important mechanism in the development of positive body image. Embodying activities are proposed to increase the frequency of mind–body integration, body awareness and responsiveness, and feelings of physical competence and empowerment; these experiences may, in turn, foster positive body image. Taken together, these conceptual models illuminate the various components of positive body image as well as pathways to cultivating positive body image.

In this chapter, we will review the existing literature on programmatic approaches to cultivating positive body image in youth, typically adolescents. Unfortunately, nearly all body image programs remain disconnected from the theoretical and empirical work on positive body image and positive embodiment. Little if any programmatic emphasis on positive body concepts appears in most prevention/intervention work,[1] and outcome measures tend to focus exclusively on the relief of body dissatisfaction or eating disorder symptomatology, as opposed to assessing positive cognitive, emotional, and experiential elements of the body. However, as Tylka (see Chapter 1) has argued, positive body image is not simply the opposite of negative body image on a continuum, but rather is its own distinct construct, and is therefore worth cultivating separately in programmatic work aimed at enhancing body image in youth.

Indeed, research on coping and emotion regulation provides reason to suspect that enhancing positive feelings and cognitions about the body may be essential to truly successful programmatic body image intervention work. First, research on repressive coping has shown that suppressing negative body-related thoughts and emotions may provide short-term improvements in well-being for some, but for many can, paradoxically, yield a preoccupation with such thoughts, leading to behavioral rebound effects that engender long-term unfavorable outcomes. For example, Barnes and Tantleff-Dunn (2010) found that dieters who suppressed food- and weight-related thoughts and emotions experienced more food cravings and were more likely to engage in binge

---

[1] In this chapter we will use the terms "prevention" and "intervention" interchangeably, as they are used in the literature, to refer to programs that aim to address body image.

eating episodes than those not focused on suppressing unwanted thoughts. This may help explain why immediate postintervention Time 2 reductions in body dissatisfaction or eating disorder symptomatology seen in many body image intervention programs are lost at longer-term Time 3 follow up (e.g., three months later), and even suggests that focusing on reducing negative thoughts and emotions about the body may, paradoxically, yield a preoccupation with negative body image and rebound effects. In contrast, mindfulness techniques that enable individuals to accept unwanted thoughts about food and the body have proven more successful for those attempting to reduce food cravings and intake (Forman et al., 2007).

Second, research on positive emotions shows that they can provide an "undoing" regulatory effect on negative emotions (e.g., Fredrickson, Mancuso, Branigan, & Tugade, 2000). This suggests that cultivating positive feelings about their bodies in youth may provide a way of undoing the negative emotions generated by body dissatisfaction and body image disturbance. Supportive evidence for this undoing effect is provided by work indicating that the constructs of body appreciation and functionality appreciation are negatively correlated with general negative affect and depressive symptomatology (e.g., Iannantuono & Tylka, 2012; Tylka et al., 2015). Third, research has confirmed that positive emotions lead to more broad-minded coping, which can in turn engender "upward spirals" of further positive emotions and sustained well-being (Fredrickson & Joiner, 2002; Garland et al., 2010), suggesting that cultivating positive emotions about one's body may trigger an upward spiral of greater overall health and well-being in youth, above and beyond shorter-term improvements in dissatisfaction with their bodies. Indeed, in samples of college students, body appreciation has been found to be associated with self-esteem, optimism, and proactive coping (Avalos, Tylka, & Wood-Barcalow, 2005; Tylka & Wood-Barcalow, 2015a).

Because nearly all of the body image intervention programs and outcomes in youth are focused on relieving negative body image, these programs will be the focus of this review. However, we will endeavor to highlight the places where positive body image and positive embodiment approaches and outcome measures are used successfully or are implied to have been so used, or where theoretical and measurement concepts related to positive body image and positive embodiment might help explain conceptual shortcomings in existing programs or disappointing long-term outcomes for participants in such programs. Note that we have not provided a comprehensive review of all body image programs with youth. Instead, we have focused on several programs that have the potential to impact aspects of positive body image specifically.

Existing Interventions: Schools

Schools are a convenient and sensible location for administering body image intervention programs to large numbers of young people. School children in the United States generally spend 943–1,025 hours in school every year (Desilver, 2014). Thus, they are physically present in school for large amounts of time. Further, the age-graded system used in most US schools means that body image interventions can be targeted to meet the needs of children at similar stages of development (Levine & Smolak, 2005). Body image curricula can also be incorporated into existing coursework and/or extracurricular activities (Diedrichs & Halliwell, 2012; Levine & Smolak, 2005). In addition, schools provide the opportunity to implement ecological approaches, such as a whole-school approach (McVey, Tweed, & Blackmore, 2007; O'Dea & Maloney, 2000), to foster positive body image. An ecological approach seeks to modify groups, institutions, and other environmental factors that impact body image (Neumark-Sztainer, Levine, Paxton, Smolak, Piran, & Wertheim, 2006).

For example, McVey and colleagues (2007) used an ecological, whole-school approach in an eating disorder intervention aimed at middle school children. This approach involved a focus on curriculum, school climate, and school–community partnerships and included students, teachers, administrators, school personnel, parents, and public health nurses. The intervention involved workshops for teachers and parents, curriculum delivered to students, support groups for students, and a variety of schoolwide activities. The content of the intervention included a range of topics, such as media-driven appearance pressures, physical changes of puberty, and genetic influences on body size. The intervention was effective in reducing the internalization of media ideals and weight loss behaviors in both girls and boys, as well as in reducing disordered eating among girls. Impacts were stronger for children at high risk (defined as currently trying to lose weight or currently trying to gain muscle) versus low-risk participants.

In contrast to a whole-school approach, many intervention programs have used a classroom-based approach. Yager, Diedrichs, Ricciardelli, and Halliwell (2013) reviewed existing classroom-based body image programs for secondary school students (adolescents) (see Holt & Ricciardelli, 2008 for a review of programs with elementary school children). Programs were universal-selective in nature as opposed to targeting at-risk populations and were conducted from 2000 onward. A total of sixteen studies were eligible for inclusion in the review. The theoretical approach for each study was variable and included: psychoeducation for body image; psychoeducation for eating disorders; self-esteem enhancement; healthy weight-control skills; stress and coping skills; body acceptance skills; reducing the impact of peers; enhancing media literacy; cognitive dissonance; and developmental factors. Results indicated that seven programs were effective in improving at least one aspect of body image or body dissatisfaction from pre- to posttest; however, effect sizes were typically small ($d = 0.22$–0.48). The strongest effect sizes were found for participants' knowledge from baseline to posttest, and these effects were large in size ($d = 0.73$–1.63). Effective programs focused on younger adolescents (ages 12–14) and included activities on media literacy, self-esteem, and peers. Of particular relevance to the present chapter, the dependent measures in the reviewed studies assessed body dissatisfaction rather than aspects of positive body image. For example, the body dissatisfaction subscale of the Eating Disorders Inventory (Garner, Olmstead, & Polivy, 1983) and the Shape and Weight Concern subscale of the Eating Disorders Examination Questionnaire (EDE-Q; Fairburn & Cooper, 1993) were the most commonly used measures of body image/body dissatisfaction. Several of the interventions ($n = 6$) had a focus on body acceptance skills – a component of positive body image – in their content, but none specifically measured changes in positive body image.

It is possible that existing interventions, such as those reviewed by Yager et al. (2013) which were designed and implemented before the construct of positive body image was articulated in the research literature, may impact positive aspects of the body perceptions of youth but researchers are not capturing such changes because they primarily use outcome measures that assess *dis*satisfaction, with improvement operationalized as reductions in negative body image. This may be because of the lack of validated scales to assess positive body image with children. Fortunately, the Body Appreciation Scale-2 (Tylka & Wood-Barcalow, 2015b) was recently modified for children as young as age nine (Halliwell, Jarman, Tylka, & Slater, 2017; see Chapter 1).

As mentioned previously, the studies reviewed by Yager and colleagues used a variety of theoretical approaches. Studies taking a body acceptance approach are particularly relevant to the present chapter. Given that research strongly suggests that focusing on alleviating negative thoughts and emotions does not necessarily lead to true well-being (e.g., Seligman, 2011), positive body image interventions likely provide unique contributions to youth and their embodied lives. Accordingly, we next describe those six studies from Yager and colleagues' review and highlight how researchers could assess positive body image, based on Wood-Barcalow et al.'s (2010) conceptualization, in these existing interventions.

Programs that include body acceptance skills. Of the six studies, four were designed for adolescent girls specifically, and examined the effectiveness of prevention programs involving body acceptance skills. Brown, Winzelberg, Abascal, and Taylor (2004) designed an eight-week, online, psychoeducational eating disorder prevention program for adolescent girls. The program entailed four content areas: (1) eating disorders, (2) body image, (3) healthy nutrition, and (4) exercise. The body image unit included a journaling activity in which girls were instructed to explore their own body image concerns and their thoughts about cultural pressure valuing a thin ideal. Girls were also instructed to discuss their current body image and factors that create and sustain negative body perceptions. Changes in drive for thinness, bulimia behaviors, weight concerns, shape concerns, and restraint were measured from pre- to posttest as well as at a three-month follow-up. Participants in the program reported a reduction in eating restraint and an increase in knowledge compared to participants in the control group. These changes, however, were not present at follow-up. It is of note that changes in body acceptance, an aspect of positive body image, were not assessed. It is possible, though, that the journaling activity helps girls make connections between cultural pressures and their own potentially negative feelings about their bodies. Increasing awareness, in turn, could prompt greater acceptance of their own bodies as opposed to unrealistic cultural beauty ideals. Future research is necessary to test this possibility.

Similarly, Steiner-Adair et al. (2002) assessed the effectiveness of an eating disorder prevention program designed for early adolescent girls. The program entailed weekly sessions of 45–90 minutes over an 8–15-week period (depending on the length of sessions). The curriculum encompassed a wide range of activities, including body scans (i.e., directing awareness to each part of the body and observing the sensations in each body part), body appreciation-guided meditation, and physical activity. This program also included a social justice component aimed at educating participants about weightism and providing lessons on how to be an activist. Changes in weight esteem, appearance esteem, dis/satisfaction with specific aspects of one's body and appearance, and awareness and internalization of the thin ideal were measured from pre- to posttest and at a six-month follow-up. Participants in the intervention program reported increased knowledge and weight-related body esteem compared to participants in the control group. Improvements were maintained at follow-up. Similar to the study of Brown and colleagues (2004), aspects of positive body image were not assessed. However, components of positive body image may have been positively impacted by several activities in the intervention, including conducting body scans, participating in body appreciation-guided meditation, and engagement in physical activities. These activities could help girls learn to appreciate their own bodies and the functions their bodies can perform. Education on weightism might also help girls accept their own bodies despite sociocultural appearance pressures. Future research should investigate whether these practices do have such impacts on girls' body attitudes. In addition, state measures may be especially useful for capturing improvements that occur directly following an activity (see Chapter 1 for a discussion of measurement and positive body image).

In a third eating disorder prevention program designed for early adolescent girls, Weiss and Wertheim (2005) assessed the effectiveness of a program that entailed four weekly sessions. The curriculum covered a variety of topics, including sociocultural contributions to body image and developing girls' sense of self- and body esteem. The content tied to these topics encompassed discussion on body image concerns and eating problems as well as ways in which girls can feel good about their bodies and themselves. Changes in bulimic behavior, body dissatisfaction, drive for thinness, interoceptive awareness (i.e., perceptions of internal bodily sensations), weight loss behaviors, perceptions of their current and ideal figures, perceived media influences, and pressures to be thin were measured from pre- to posttest and at a three-month follow-up. Girls at high risk of disordered eating in the intervention group reported improvements in body dissatisfaction, drive for thinness, and interoceptive awareness at posttest; however, these improvements were not maintained at follow-up. There were no improvements in outcomes for girls at low risk for disordered eating. Nevertheless, it is possible that the curriculum on identifying ways in which girls can feel good about their bodies and themselves may generate positive impacts on aspects of positive body image, including fostering body acceptance and appreciation (although aspects of positive body image were not assessed in this study). In addition, if girls learn how to feel good about their bodies, they may become comfortable, confident, and happy with their bodies. Future research should investigate whether these aspects of positive body image improve from pre- to postintervention and whether they persist later.

Finally, in a fourth eating disorder prevention program designed for early adolescent girls, Stewart, Carter, Drinkwater, Hainsworth, and Fairburn (2001) assessed the effectiveness of a program that entailed six weekly forty-five-minute sessions. The curriculum covered a variety of topics, including identifying and developing a positive body image. Girls in the intervention group showed a small reduction in dietary restraint, body shape and eating concerns, and overall eating disorder symptoms compared to participants in the control group from pre- to posttest; however, these changes were largely not maintained at six-month follow-up. Whereas developing a positive body image was a specific component of the intervention program, similar to other prevention studies, aspects of positive body image were not assessed. In addition, the authors did not describe the specific activities they implemented to cultivate positive body image. Therefore, it is not possible to speculate as to whether and how the program could, in fact, positively impact specific components of positive body image.

Just one study assessed the effectiveness of a prevention program aimed at boys. Stanford and McCabe (2005) assessed the effectiveness of a prevention program designed for early adolescent boys. The program entailed two one-hour sessions, one of which focused on understanding that bodies come in different shapes and sizes and are only one aspect of a person. The other session focused on sociocultural messages boys receive about the ideal male body. Changes in body image satisfaction, body image importance, body change strategies to lose weight, body change strategies to increase muscle tone, attitudes toward the use of food supplements, excessive exercise attitudes and behaviors, drive for thinness, and bulimic behaviors were measured from pre- to posttest. Boys in the intervention group reported increased satisfaction with their muscles, increased self-esteem, and reduced negative affect compared to boys in the control condition. Similar to the studies on prevention programs for girls that were reviewed earlier, aspects of positive body image were not assessed in this study. A fruitful path for future research on this program, however, may be to examine whether it increases boys' self-compassion toward their bodies. Neff (2003) articulated the construct of self-compassion and its three main elements, which include: (1) self-kindness, (2) common humanity, and (3) mindfulness. Berry and colleagues subsequently applied self-compassion to the physical self and termed the construct body self-compassion, which entails appreciating one's body as unique, taking ownership of one's body, and engaging in less social comparison (Berry, Kowalski, Ferguson, & McHugh, 2010). It is possible that through the lesson on body diversity, boys may come to understand that, like other people's bodies (common humanity), their body is on a spectrum from short to tall and slight to heavy and there is no one perfect shape or size. Such awareness could also generate aspects of body self-compassion, including body acceptance and appreciation, in boys. Future research is necessary to assess these possibilities.

Last, just one study assessed the effectiveness of a prevention program aimed at both girls and boys. Richardson, Paxton, and Thomson (2009) assessed the effectiveness of a body image and self-esteem program that is widely used in schools throughout the UK and Australia with both girls and boys. The program entails four fifty-minute lessons and encompasses a series of aims, some of which emphasize aspects of positive body image. For example, one aim is to encourage participants to engage in activities that have a positive impact on body image. Program materials are designed to encourage participants to work with each other to develop strategies for improving their own body image and self-esteem. Internalization of the thin ideal, body comparison, appearance teasing, dietary restraint, and bulimic symptoms, as well as body dissatisfaction and body satisfaction, were assessed from pre- to posttest as well as at a three-month follow-up. Girls in the intervention reported increased media literacy and lower internalization of the thin ideal compared to girls in the control group from pre- to posttest; however, lower internalization was not present at follow-up. Boys in the intervention reported increased media literacy and greater body satisfaction compared to boys in the control group from pre- to posttest and at follow-up. It is of note that an aim of this intervention is to have children develop specific practices, including enjoyable physical movement, as well as other strategies that encourage positive views of the body and the self. It is possible that this process fosters body acceptance as well as appreciation for one's body and the functions it performs. However, future research measuring components of positive body image is necessary to assess these possibilities.

The six prevention programs reviewed here likely impact aspects of positive body image. Specifically, appreciation for one's body and its function and accepting one's body despite sociocultural appearance pressures appear to be the two specific components of positive body image that these programs may impact. However, none of the evaluation research on these programs directly assessed positive body outcomes. Therefore, these programs' effectiveness on positive body image components is unknown. Further, limited information about the programs was available in the journal articles, making it difficult to determine if other components of positive body image, including focusing on the strong points of one's body rather than its perceived flaws and taking in positive information about one's body while rejecting negative information, could be affected. A fruitful avenue for future research would be to examine whether and how prevention and intervention programs affect each of the five components of positive body image outlined by Wood-Barcalow and colleagues (2010).

To date, just one small-scale pilot study ($n = 62$ British girls) has examined whether a body image intervention program impacts components of positive body image. Halliwell and colleagues investigated if a one-hour cognitive dissonance body image intervention delivered at school affected adolescent girls' body appreciation, body dissatisfaction, and thin-ideal internalization (Halliwell, Jarman, McNamara, Risdon, & Jankowski, 2015). The intervention included: defining and reviewing the origins of the thin-ideal beauty standards for girls and women; discussion of the cost of pursuing the thin ideal; discussion of appearance compliments and practicing nonappearance-based compliments; role play on convincing a friend to reject the thin ideal; creating a body activism list; and participating in a self-affirmation exercise. Results of the evaluation research demonstrated that body dissatisfaction decreased and body appreciation increased for girls in the intervention group, but not for girls in the control group. Thin-ideal internalization decreased for girls in both intervention and control groups. In addition, the majority of the girls in the intervention program rated it as "somewhat" or "very" relevant and interesting, suggesting that such a program could be well received more broadly. This study will need to be expanded in future research with larger and more diverse samples to lend support to the present findings. In future research, it would be useful to examine why the intervention was effective. For example, it included both discussions and activities. A meta-analysis of eating disorder prevention programs found that interactive programs are more effective than didactic ones (Stice et al., 2007). Stice and colleagues (2007) proposed that interactive programs that entail active participation likely facilitate the acquisition of key concepts that prompt changes in attitudes and behaviors.

In summary, schools are an ideal site for body image prevention programs given the large amount of time youth spend in school and the ability to deliver age-specific content to youth at various stages of development. Most existing body image programs aimed at youth focus on relieving negative body image rather than cultivating positive body image; in addition, evaluation research has primarily assessed programmatic impacts on negative body image. However, as we have outlined in the preceding sections, particular content in existing programs may, in fact, be conducive to fostering positive body image. Researchers, however, need to measure programmatic impacts on positive body image in future studies. In addition, body image researchers should consider incorporating a focus on cultivating positive body image as well as alleviating negative body image in future prevention research.

Existing Interventions: Sport Settings

Children in the United States also spend a significant amount of time in organized sport settings. Indeed, sport is the primary organized activity in which adolescents engage, consuming approximately four hours a week on average, which is more time than all other organized activities combined (Child Development Supplement of the Panel Study for Income Dynamics as cited by Mahoney, Harris, & Eccles, 2006). In the 2015–16 school year, 7,868,900 high school students participated in interscholastic sports (National Federation of State High School Associations [NFSHSA], 2016). Despite the relatively large amount of time that youth spend in sport, there is typically little explicit emphasis on youth development, such as character development or life skills development, in sport settings (Weiss, Stuntz, Bhalla, Bolter, & Price, 2013). In addition, despite evidence that athletes in select sports and at varying levels of competition are at increased risk of eating problems (Smolak, Murnen, & Ruble, 2000) and body image concerns (Varnes, Stellefson, Janelle, Dorman, Dodd, & Miller, 2013), there are few body image intervention programs designed specifically for sport settings.

An exception was a prevention program, "BodySense: A Positive Body Image Initiative for Female Athletes," conducted with 11–18-year-old girls in gymnastics clubs in Canada, their parents, club staff, and coaches (Buchholz, Mack, McVey, Feder, & Barrowman, 2008). The program entailed education on a range of topics including, for example, eating attitudes and beliefs, body health, body diversity, resisting dieting pressures, enjoyable physical activity, positive self-image, and balancing sport and life outside of sport. In addition, posters and other educational materials about body image, disordered eating, and sport nutrition as well as nutritional snacks were provided to the clubs. Newsletters about the topics addressed in the program were mailed to athletes' homes and sport clubs. A program coordinator was also available to athletes, parents, club staff, and coaches by phone or email. Participants were assessed before implementation of the program (Time 1) and after the three-month program (Time 2). Results demonstrated that athletes in the program felt less pressure from their sports clubs to be thin from pre- to postprogram; however, there were no changes in their body esteem, eating attitudes and behaviors, or awareness and internalization of societal standards of appearance. Survey participation at both time points by coaches and fathers was too low to assess possible change in their body-related attitudes. Mothers' body-related attitudes were not affected by the program. Similar to the school-based prevention programs previously described, components of positive body image were not directly assessed in this study. However, it is possible that aspects of positive body image were impacted by the program. For example, the unit on body diversity could have positively affected girls' acceptance of their body's shape and size despite sociocultural appearance pressures. Similarly, the focus on enjoyable physical activity could have increased girls' appreciation of their own body and its function. Future research is necessary to investigate these possibilities, with a focus on an interactive rather than didactic method in program design (Stice et al., 2007).

Other prevention research involving sport and body image has been conducted on a national sports-based positive youth development program for girls. "Girls on the Run" (GOTR) began in 1996 and currently includes 200 councils in all fifty U.S. states and the District of Columbia (Girls on the Run, n.d.). It consists of two afterschool programs, one for girls in grades 3–5 and another for girls in grades 6–8 (called "Girls on the Track" (GOT)). The programs consist of biweekly sessions designed around particular themes, including body image and media literacy as well as self-esteem and positive development more broadly, over the course of 8–12 weeks. Running is incorporated into each session and the season culminates with participation in a five-kilometer run. In a small-scale study ($n = 34$), Waldron (2007) investigated the impact of GOT on sixth-grade girls' self-perceptions. Quantitative results indicated no impact of the program on girls' perceived physical competence or physical appearance competence; however, in interviews girls reported improving their physical skills and physical self-efficacy as well as learning about taking care of their body through healthy eating versus dieting. Rauscher, Kauer, and Wilson (2013) conducted a larger-scale study ($n = 138$ girls, ages 8–14, M age = 10.5) assessing the impact of GOTR/GOT on girls' self-perceptions. Results indicated increased body esteem and reduced objectified body consciousness from baseline to the end of the season. The program thus positively impacted girls' body perceptions. However, the authors also assessed girls' attitudes using open-ended questions. The qualitative data indicated a more complex picture of girls' attitudes. In response to a question asking girls to describe a strong, healthy girl, almost a third of girls listed physical attributes (e.g., "good body," "pretty"), weight (e.g., "skinny," "not fat"), or level of fitness ("toned," "having four- or six-pack muscles"). These findings suggest that these girls had knowledge of and endorsed, at least to a certain extent, cultural beauty standards for women that dictate a toned, thin body ideal. Taken together, these results demonstrate that GOTR has the potential to positively impact girls' body perceptions, but the program may not shift girls' attitudes far enough (i.e., to reject cultural beauty norms). Similar to the other prevention programs reviewed in this chapter, the research on GOTR has not assessed whether the program impacts components of positive body image. It is possible, however, that through their participation in GOTR, girls' body appreciation (including appreciating its functionality), body acceptance, and confidence in their body may be positively impacted. Future research will be necessary to test these possibilities.

Aside from the studies reviewed here, no other research on body image intervention programs in sport was located. However, it is likely that youth and collegiate sport teams include some prevention education, activities, and resources that range in level of formality and expert delivery. For example, The Ohio State University convened a multidisciplinary Body Image and Health Task Force in the mid-1990s to address body image concerns on the campus (Rudd & Carter, 2006). The Task Force is still active and conducts a variety of activities on the campus, including consultations with various sport teams on an annual basis. Given the widespread engagement in sport by young people, body image researchers, including those focused on positive body image specifically, should consider sport contexts as a site for systematic prevention efforts. Researchers should also draw on existing sport-relevant research. For example, Daniels and colleagues have found positive reactions (including positive self-reflections) to media images of athletes performing their sport in adolescent girls, adolescent boys, college women, and college men (Daniels, 2009, 2012; Daniels & Linder, 2017; Daniels & Wartena, 2011), suggesting that such images could usefully be incorporated into body image programs with athletes. A variety of sport-specific issues (described next) will need to be considered in such efforts, however.

In considering ways in which positive body image might be cultivated in sport settings, it is important to understand the specific challenges that female athletes specifically face in terms of body image. From interview studies with female college athletes, Krane and colleagues (Krane, Choi, Baird, Aimar, & Kauer, 2004; Krane, Waldron, Michalenok, & Stiles-Shipley, 2001) articulated a central struggle for female athletes as "living the paradox" (p. 315). This paradox contrasts the feminine ideal body (i.e., ultra-thin), prized in the larger sociocultural context, with the sporting body (i.e., muscular, larger than nonathletes), which is necessary for athletic success. Female athletes often find it difficult to reconcile these opposing ideals (Krane et al., 2001, 2004; Russell, 2004). For example, a female hockey player said: "How many people would rather look like Rachel Hunter [a model] rather than Mia Hamm [a soccer player]? Because Rachel Hunter is this little skinny thing, waif-like person and then Mia Hamm's thicker, and that's not as cool, I still think that's not gonna change" (Krane et al., 2004, p. 319). This clash between body ideals is particularly relevant to levels of muscularity. For example, a softball player reported: "I like the way I feel when I get the muscle … but yet, in the back of my mind I get scared that I'm gonna get big and people are gonna look at me like 'oh my god.' … I get scared of looking too much like a guy, like having too much muscle" (Krane et al., 2004, p. 320). Thus, female athletes are aware that the bodies they need for sport success (performance body) are not valued in the broader culture (social body). Further, quantitative research with adolescent girls (aged 13–18) has demonstrated that female athletes have higher functional body image compared to their nonathletic peers, but do not differ from their nonathletic peers in aesthetic satisfaction, supporting the notion that female athletes have distinct self-perceptions about their performance versus social bodies (Abbott & Barber, 2011). Accordingly, body image intervention programs with female athletes must target both.

In addition to addressing both performance and social body perceptions, body image intervention programs for athletes must consider sport-specific barriers to healthy body image. Petrie and Greenleaf (2012) identified a range of risk factors for poor body image specific to sport culture, including weigh-ins, sport body stereotypes, revealing uniforms, and attitudes of coaches, teammates, and judges. Many coaches in various sports weigh their athletes because of a pervasive, yet not well supported by empirical evidence, belief that a lower weight will lead to a stronger sport performance. Weight monitoring by coaches can create considerable pressure on athletes about eating and weight, and as a result athletes may experience dissatisfaction with their bodies' size. These impacts can be exacerbated by public weigh-ins, posting athletes' weights in a public area such as the locker room, and/or tying playing time to achieving weight goals.

Petrie and Greenleaf (2012) noted that a source of body dissatisfaction in sport might be sport body stereotypes, that is, the belief that certain bodies are better suited to a particular sport than other bodies – for example, female gymnasts should be very small. In order to meet these expectations, athletes may use pathological means, such as disordered eating practices, to modify their bodies. Another barrier to healthy body image in sport is revealing uniforms, more common in women's than in men's sports. This attire (e.g., bikini in women's beach volleyball) reveals the shape and size of the athlete's body and may generate body discomfort and dissatisfaction in players. Finally, coaches, teammates, and judges may cause and/or reinforce negative body attitudes in athletes through direct means (e.g., commenting on an athlete's eating) or indirectly (e.g., awarding scores differentially based on body type in judged sports, such as figure skating).

Petrie and Greenleaf (2012) offered a number of suggestions for overcoming sport-specific barriers to positive body image and cultivating what they termed a "body-healthy sport environment" (p. 163). A central task is dispelling the belief that a lower weight will create a performance gain. In fact, athletes may lose muscle mass rather than fat via dieting. Restrictive eating and fluid intake may also result in insufficient energy for optimal sport performance. A more positive approach would be for coaches and other sport personnel to emphasize the health rather than the weight of an athlete, including educating athletes about healthy eating and nutrition. In addition, educating coaches about the limited effectiveness of weight loss on performance would be useful. Coaches could then be encouraged to focus on more fruitful areas for athlete development, such as skill mastery, increasing physical conditioning and strength, and cultivating psychological skills useful for competition. Finally, coaches need to be better educated about body image concerns and eating disorders, so they can address their own behaviors (e.g., weight-centric comments to athletes) as well as practices (e.g., use of weigh-ins).

In summary, sport settings are opportune sites for body image prevention programs, given the widespread involvement in sport among youth. Sport has the potential to cultivate aspects of positive body image, such as appreciation of one's body and its functionality, as well as increased experiences of embodiment including mind–body integration, body awareness and responsiveness, and feelings of physical competence and empowerment. Despite the utility of addressing body image in sport settings, little body image prevention work has been conducted in sport settings to date. Future research in this area should incorporate a focus on cultivating positive body image as well as reducing negative body image, and should address sport-specific barriers to healthy body image (e.g., weigh-ins, revealing uniforms).

Existing Interventions: Dance Settings

Another important site for body image intervention programming is dance classes. Dance is a very popular activity, particularly among girls (Grieser et al., 2006; O'Neill, Pate, & Liese, 2011), and dance classes contribute to approximately 29 percent of youth physical activity (O'Neill et al., 2011). Langdon (2012) has argued that recent sociocultural developments in dance (e.g., popular television shows such as "Dance Moms") reflect a shift in focus from self-expression to audience-based approval, and this may be why dance is increasingly associated with negative body image. In addition, the nearly universal use of mirrors and detailed commentary on the appearance of specific body parts in particular positions in most dance studios have been shown to induce heightened body self-consciousness, especially among less experienced youth dancers (e.g., Radell, Adame, Cole, & Bluemnkehl, 2011). Dancers have been shown to suffer rates of body image disturbances, such as eating disorders, up to three times higher than the general population (Arcelus, Witcomb, & Mitchell, 2014). Thus, dance studios are likely to have students with fragile body images, and are especially well positioned to offer positive body image interventions.

One way dance can enhance positive body image is via its use as a form of therapy for at-risk populations (Langdon, 2012). Dance movement therapy (DMT) is a long-standing form of body image intervention that focuses on emotion and subjectivity rather than the appearance of the body (e.g., Hornyak & Baker, 1989). Indeed, the American Dance Therapy Association recently celebrated its fiftieth anniversary (Cruz, 2016). The vast majority of studies of the effectiveness of DMT in improving body image have been done with adult populations, including breast cancer and cystic fibrosis patients and larger women with emotional eating. The few studies of the effectiveness of DMT for youth have been conducted in clinical settings, either as single case studies (e.g., an eleven-year-old girl who was a victim of cyber bullying; Hagensen, 2015), or in very small groups (e.g., seven children aged 5–8 in a psychiatric facility; Erfer & Ziv, 2006), and these have shown qualitative improvements in body image. One study of individuals with autism spectrum disorder included youth as young as sixteen years old in its young adult sample (Koch, Mehl, Sobanski, Sieber, & Fuchs, 2015). The participants experienced seven sessions of DMT, each consisting of four elements: warm-up, dyadic movement in partners, mirror movements in a group circle, and finally verbal reflections. Although body image was not explicitly assessed pre- and post-DMT intervention, psychological well-being (including positive affect and coping) and body awareness (the phenomenological sense of where the body is in space, and the relationship between the body and the self) were. Participants in the DMT group showed significant improvements compared to a control group in both psychological well-being and body awareness.

A second way that dance has been used in programmatic efforts to engender improvements in body image in youth is as a form of exercise, with the benefits to body image that occur with any form of physical fitness. For example, Burgess, Grogan and Burwitz (2006) explored the effects of a six-week "aerobic dance" intervention among fifty 13–14-year-old British schoolgirls. The girls were given the Body Attitudes Questionnaire (BAQ), which contains both negative and positive body image-related factors including Disparagement, Feeling Fat, Attractiveness, and Strength (Ben-Tovim & Walker, 1991), and the Children and Youth Physical Self-Perception Profile (CY-PSPP; Whitehead, 1995), with four subscales of Sport Competence, Physical Condition, Body Attractiveness, and

Strength Competence, at three points: preintervention, at the changeover between conditions, and post-study at twelve weeks. A crossover design was employed wherein participants served as their own control, receiving either the six-week aerobic dance intervention followed by a six-week physical education swimming lessons control or vice versa. Results revealed that for these inexperienced dancers, participation in six weeks of aerobic dance significantly enhanced body attitudes and physical self-perceptions. There were significant improvements in Attractiveness, Feeling Fat, Fitness, and Physical Self-Worth. Unfortunately, significant deterioration in nearly all of these measures was seen once the girls were reintroduced to their typical physical education programming, reverting back to pre-test levels. The authors point out that this reinforces the fact that the aerobic dance intervention itself and not some other uncontrolled factor had produced the positive shift in teen girls' feelings about their bodies, but it also highlights the inability of six weeks of aerobic dance to engender sustainable positive body image.

A more recent, comprehensive intervention program that provides dance studios and conventions with body- and self-esteem-enhancing dance education seminars, as well as antisexualization certificate programs for studios, conventions and costume companies, is Youth Protection Advocates in Dance (YPAD; see www.ypad4change.org). Dance has become big business, and studios and individual dancers are increasingly active participants on social media platforms, posting videos on YouTube and "body shots" on Instagram, Snapchat, and Facebook. Often those dance videos and young dancers who are the most sexualized in their movements, costumes, or poses are the ones who garner the most views, "likes," and "shares," such as a YouTube video from 2010 featuring eight- and nine-year-old girls at a dance competition performing a highly sexualized dance in adult lingerie-style costumes to Beyoncé's "Single Ladies (Put a Ring on It)" which has gotten over nine million views (National Center on Sexual Exploitation, 2016). The American Psychological Association's Task Force on the Sexualization of Girls (APA, 2007) provided evidence of the myriad consequences of this sexualized treatment and self-sexualization for girls' body image. In an effort to cultivate more positive body image in the environment of sexualization via dance social media, YPAD offers, as part of its dance seminars, voluntary participation of young dancers in a "mindful social media fast" in which they delete all social media apps from their cell phones for three days. Although empirical tests of YPAD's seminars are yet to be published, preliminary results of the mindful social media fasts are promising, with pre–post improvements in self-esteem, self-compassion, and – most relevant to body image – body surveillance and body shame (Roberts & Scott, 2016).

Despite dance's largely negative reputation with respect to body image, the relationship between dance and body image is complex, and illustrates that, as Tylka (see Chapter 1) and others have argued, positive and negative body image may not be simple polar opposites and thus dance-based body image interventions ought to be mindful of this complexity. Langdon (2012) argues that dance has a positive impact on body image for many, which can be accomplished any number of ways, as articulated previously (dance as exercise, dance as therapy), via the enhancement of physical self-competence. However, research shows that certain forms of dance are more conducive to this positive sense of physical self-competence, and that greater experience with nearly any dance form is unfortunately associated with increasing body image dissatisfaction. Therefore, as girls continue in dance over time, they may be at risk of body dissatisfaction.

Swami and Harris (2012) compared young adult (M age = 25) female dancers of varying dance type (ballet versus contemporary) and experience (beginner versus advanced) and found that these variables play a significant role in the relationship between dance and positive versus negative body image. Overall, contemporary dancers reported significantly higher body awareness than ballet dancers, regardless of experience level. Advanced ballet dancers had significantly lower body appreciation than beginning ballet dancers. In contrast, advanced contemporary dancers had significantly higher body appreciation than did beginners, suggesting that experience with ballet leads to decrements in body image, whereas experience with contemporary dance improves body image. Swami and Tovee (2009) showed similar positive body image effects in street dancers. These authors suggest that street and contemporary dance may provide dancers with greater opportunities to appreciate their bodies as functional, which in turn may lead to more positive, accepting, and respectful feelings toward their bodies. On the other hand, compared to beginners, advanced dancers of all types reported higher levels of actual–ideal body discrepancy, reflecting a desire to be thinner. Thus, Swami and Harris (2012) warn that dance studios and body image practitioners should be mindful of both the positive and negative impacts that dance participation (depending on type and level) can have on participants' body image.

In sum, dance classes provide important sites for intervening to create positive body image outcomes for youth. Few systematic programs exist that engage dance and dance education as a way to enhance positive body image and positive embodiment for youth. However, the work reviewed in this section suggests that dance studios are in a precarious position, given the surge in popularity of dance and the complex relationship between body image and dance as an art form. With the potential for sexualization in competitive dance and high-profile dance studios with a social media presence, or the emphasis on thinness particularly in ballet, some studios may negatively impact young dancers' body image. If, on the other hand, studios can emphasize physical competence over appearance, then they may provide a truly outstanding platform for positive, appreciative, and respectful embodiment. This may require parents and educators to agitate for change on behalf of young dancers. More empirical work is clearly needed to clarify the dance-specific approaches and outcomes that foster positive body image in youth as a foundation to justify such change.

Conclusion and Recommendations for Practice

As described in this chapter, existing body image programs are largely not informed by theoretical and empirical work on positive body image and positive embodiment. Instead, the focus of this work has been on preventing and/or alleviating body *dis*satisfaction. Reducing body dissatisfaction is clearly an important goal. However, cultivating positive body image is similarly important. Thus, body image researchers should consider incorporating curricula intended to foster positive body image into prevention programs, and should measure change in components of positive image specifically in evaluation work.

Above we provided suggestions and considerations for programmatic approaches to fostering positive body image in specific youth settings, including school, sport, and dance. Here we make a few more general recommendations that apply across contexts. First, we encourage researchers to integrate the theoretical work on positive body image and positive embodiment into the design of body image programs. As noted above, several existing classroom-based programs include a focus on body acceptance skills and include content that may tap other components of positive body image (as outlined by Wood-Barcalow et al., 2010), including appreciation for one's body and its function and feeling comfortable, confident, and happy with one's body. None of the interventions we reviewed, however, seem to address other components of positive body image, including focusing on the strong points of one's body rather than its perceived flaws and taking in positive information about one's body while rejecting negative information. Similarly, despite Piran and colleagues' extensive work on positive embodiment (see Piran, 2016 for a review), most components of that construct have not been integrated into body image programs aimed at youth – the exception is the component of experiences of functionality and agency related to the body. Moving forward, we believe greater consideration of this conceptual work in program design may increase the likelihood of youth developing more positive and enduring attitudes toward their bodies as an outcome of participation in a body image program. In addition, to date, research on the related constructs of positive body image and positive embodiment has primarily unfolded on different trajectories (for an exception see Mahlo & Tiggemann, 2016). Ultimately, it may be useful to integrate these constructs depending on the results of empirical studies. Body image prevention programs aimed at youth would likely benefit from drawing on these, and related, conceptual foundations.

Second, to date, nearly all body image intervention programs have been prevention-focused. That is, the objective is to reduce existing body dissatisfaction or prevent body dissatisfaction in at-risk populations. As we have discussed, research on emotion regulation suggests that attempts at reducing or preventing negative body image likely involve repressive coping strategies that run the risk of engendering short-lived change at best, or even backfiring at worst. Trying *not* to think about aspects or features of the body with which one is dissatisfied (e.g., muscularity in a female athlete or dancer who is worried about "being too big") may backfire via the paradoxical effects of thought suppression. Chronic preoccupation with suppressed thoughts can cause "rebound," yielding more unwanted negative thoughts, emotions and even behaviors. Instead, engaging in mindful acceptance of even negative thoughts (e.g., "there I go, thinking negatively about being too big") or refocusing via self-statements or journaling on appreciation of the positive features of the body (e.g., "muscularity enhances my ability to perform my sport which makes me feel competent and proud") is likely to yield a more sustainable positive body image. Mindful acceptance and refocusing on the positive both map clearly onto Wood-Barcalow et al.'s (2010) positive body image features of body acceptance and focusing on the strong points of one's body rather than its perceived flaws. Developing and working with specific positive self-statements aligns with Piran and Teall's (2012) positive self-talk construct of positive embodiment. We urge body image intervention program researchers to compare, ideally within subjects in a diary-style format, more repressive coping-style framings focused on *not* thinking or feeling negatively about one's body, and more positive, mindful approaches. We imagine this would not only provide empirical evidence for the greater long-term effectiveness of the positive, mindful approach to engender sustainable positive body image, but also would enable individual youth themselves to compare these differing approaches in their own self-talk around their bodies.

Third, Seligman (2011), credited as the founder of positive psychology, has argued that positive human flourishing is not just about the alleviation of negative thoughts and emotions. Indeed, reducing suffering does not necessarily lead to true well-being; the cultivation of distinctly positive attitudes such as contentment, gratitude, and compassion engenders well-being via their own mechanisms. Similarly, positive body image theorists, such as those in this volume, argue that truly positive body image is not simply the opposite end of a continuum of body image and is indeed more sustainable as a source of true well-being. Body image intervention programs that take the approach *not* of reducing such negative body image-related feeling states as shame or dissatisfaction, but instead of cultivating more positive emotions such as pride and appreciation, are therefore likely to yield more sustainable well-being in youth via harnessing the un-doing and upward spiral effects shown in research on positive emotions (Fredrickson et al., 2000; Fredrickson & Joiner, 2002). Therefore, we urge body image intervention researchers to include both independent and dependent outcome variables that are informed by positive body image theoretical and empirical work. Having youth engage their pride, gratitude, appreciation, and compassion for their bodies' functionality and competence may serve to un-do myriad negative emotions such as body shame, disgust, disappointment, or anger engendered by body dissatisfaction. Also, cultivating these positive feeling states and attitudes toward the body may lead to upward spirals of well-being in other areas, such as self-esteem and self-compassion.

In closing, we believe that, going forward, a greater focus on "the positive" is essential in body image programs aimed at young people. If young people hold more positive attitudes toward their bodies, they may be better positioned to appreciate, respect, and enjoy their bodies. Therefore, body image researchers and professionals must incorporate a greater emphasis on cultivating positive body image in the various contexts that young people inhabit.

References

Abbott, B. D., & Barber, B. L. (2011). Differences in functional and aesthetic body image between sedentary girls and girls involved in sports and physical activity: Does sport type make a difference? *Psychology of Sport & Exercise, 12,* 333–342.

American Psychological Association (APA). (2007). *Report of the APA Task Force on the sexualization of girls.* Washington, DC: American Psychological Association. Retrieved from www.apa.org/pi/wpo/sexualization_report_summary.pdf.

Arcelus, J., Witcomb, G. L., & Mitchell, A. (2014). Prevalence of eating disorders amongst dancers: A systemic review and meta analysis. *European Eating Disorders Review*, *22*, 92–101. doi:10.1002/erv.2271

Avalos, L., Tylka, T. L., & Wood-Barcalow, N. (2005). The Body Appreciation Scale: Development and psychometric evaluation. *Body Image*, *2*, 285–297. doi:10.1016/j.bodyim.2005.06.002

Barnes, R. D., & Tantleff-Dunn, S. (2010). Food for thought: Examining the relationship between food thought suppression and weight-related outcomes. *Eating Behaviors*, *11*, 175–179. doi:10.1016/j.eatbeh.2010.03.001

Ben-Tovim, D. I., & Walker, M.K. (1991). The development of the Ben-Tovim and Walker Body Attitudes Questionnaire (BAQ), a new measure of women's attitudes towards their own bodies. *Psychological Medicine*, *21*, 775–784. doi:10.1017/S0033291700022406

Berry, K.-A., Kowalski, K. C., Ferguson, L. J., & McHugh, T.-L. F. (2010). An empirical phenomenology of young adult women exercisers' body self-compassion. *Qualitative Research in Sport and Exercise*, *2*, 293–312. doi:10.1080/19398441.2010.517035

Brown, J. B., Winzelberg, A. J., Abascal, L. B., & Taylor, C. B. (2004). An evaluation of an Internet-delivered eating disorder prevention program for adolescents and their parents. *Journal of Adolescent Health*, *35*, 290–296. doi:10.1016/j.jadohealth.2003.10.010

Buchholz, A., Mack, H., McVey, G., Feder, S., & Barrowman, N. (2008). Bodysense: An evaluation of a positive body image intervention on sport climate for female athletes. *Eating Disorders: The Journal of Treatment & Prevention*, *16*, 308–321. doi:10.1080/10640260802115910

Burgess, G., Grogan, S., & Burwitz, L. (2006). Effects of a 6-week aerobic dance intervention on body image and physical self-perceptions in adolescent girls. *Body Image*, *3*, 57–66. doi:10.1016/j.bodyim.2005.10.005

Cruz, R. F. (2016). Dance/movement therapy and developments in empirical research: The first 50 years. *American Journal of Dance Therapy*, *38*, 297–302. doi:10.1007/s10465-016-9224-2

Daniels, E. A. (2009). Sex objects, athletes, and sexy athletes: How media representations of women athletes can impact adolescent girls and young women. *Journal of Adolescent Research*, *24*, 399–422. doi:10.1177/0743558409336748

(2012). Sexy versus strong: What girls and women think of female athletes. *Journal of Applied Developmental Psychology*, *33*, 79–90. doi:10.1016/j.appdev.2011.12.002

Daniels, E. A., & Wartena, H. (2011). Athlete or sex symbol: What boys and men think of media representations of female athletes. *Sex Roles*, *65*, 566–579. doi:10.1007/s11199-011-9959-7

Desilver, D. (2014, September 2). School days: How the U.S. compares with other countries. Retrieved from www.pewresearch.org/fact-tank/2014/09/02/school-days-how-the-u-s-compares-with-other-countries/.

Diedrichs, P. C., & Halliwell, E. (2012). School-based interventions to promote positive body image and the acceptance of diversity in appearance. In N. Rumsey, D. Harcourt, N. Rumsey, & D. Harcourt (Eds.), *The Oxford handbook of the psychology of appearance* (pp. 531–550). New York: Oxford University Press. doi:10.1093/oxfordhb/9780199580521.013.0038

Erfer, T., & Ziv, A. (2006). Moving toward cohesion: Group dance/movement therapy with children in psychiatry. *The Arts in Psychotherapy, 33* (3), 238–246. doi:10.1016/j.aip.2006.01.001

Fairburn, C., & Cooper, Z. (1993). The eating disorder examination. In C. Fairburn & G. T. Wilson (Eds.), *Binge eating: Nature, assessment and treatment* (12th ed., pp. 317–356). New York: Guilford Press.

Fingeret, M. C., Warren, C. S., Cepeda-Benito, A., & Gleaves, D. H. (2006). Eating disorder prevention research: A meta-analysis. *Eating Disorders: The Journal of Treatment & Prevention, 14,* 191–213. doi:10.1080/10640260600638899

Forman, E. M., Hoffman, K. L., McGrath, K. B., Herbert, J. D., Brandsma, L. L., & Lowe, M. R. (2007). A comparison of acceptance- and control-based strategies for coping with food cravings: An analog study. *Behaviour Research and Therapy, 45,* 2372–2386. doi:10.1016/j.brat.2007.04.004

Fredrickson, B. L., & Joiner, T. (2002). Positive emotions trigger upward spirals toward emotional well-being. *Psychological Science, 13,* 172–175. doi:10.1111/1467-9280.00431

Fredrickson, B. L., Mancuso, R. A., Branigan, C., & Tugade, M. M. (2000). The undoing effect of positive emotions. *Motivation and Emotion, 24,* 237–258. doi:10.1023/A:1010796329158

Garland, E. L., Fredrickson, B., Kring, A. M., Johnson, D. P., Meyer, P. S., & Penn, D. L. (2010). Upward spirals of positive emotions counter downward spirals of negativity: Insights from the broaden-and-build theory and affective neuroscience on the treatment of emotional dysfunctions and deficits in psychopathology. *Clinical Psychology Review, 30,* 849–864. doi:10.1016/j.cpr.2010.03.002

Garner, D. M., Olmstead, M. P., & Polivy, J. (1983). The eating disorder inventory: A measure of cognitive-behavioural dimensions of anorexia nervosa and bulimia. In P. L. Darby, P. E. Garfinkel, D. M. Garner, & D. V. Coscina (Eds.), *Anorexia Nervosa: Recent developments in research* (pp. 173–184). New York: LEA.

Grieser, M., Vu, M. B., Bedimo-Rung, A. L., Neumark-Sztainer, D., Moody, J., Young, D. R., & Moe, S. G. (2006). Physical activity attitudes, preferences, and practices in African American, Hispanic, and Caucasian girls. *Health Education and Behavior, 33,* 40–51. doi:10.1177/1090198105282416

Hagensen, K. P. (2015). Using a dance/movement therapy-based wellness curriculum: An adolescent case study. *American Journal of Dance Therapy, 37*(2), 150–175. doi:10.1007/s10465-015-9199-4

Halliwell, E., Jarman, H., McNamara, A., Risdon, H., & Jankowski, G. (2015). Dissemination of evidence-based body image interventions: A pilot study into the effectiveness of using undergraduate students as interventionists in secondary schools. *Body Image, 14,* 1–4. doi:10.1016/j.bodyim.2015.02.002

Halliwell, E., Jarman, H., Tylka, T. L., & Slater, A. (2017). Adapting the Body Appreciation Scale-2 for children: A psychometric analysis of the BAS-2C. *Body Image, 21,* 97–102. doi:10.1016/j.bodyim.2017.03.005

Holt, K. E., & Ricciardelli, L. A. (2008). Weight concerns among elementary school children: A review of prevention programs. *Body Image*, *5*, 233–243. doi:10.1016/j.bodyim.2008.02.002

Hornyak, L. M., & Baker, E. K. (1989). *Experiential therapies for eating disorders*. New York: Guilford Press.

Iannantuono, A. C., & Tylka, T. L. (2012). Interpersonal and intrapersonal links to body appreciation in college women: An exploratory model. *Body Image*, *9*, 227–235. doi:10.1016/j.bodyim.2012.01.004

Koch, S. C., Mehl, L., Sobanski, E., Sieber, M., & Fuchs, T. (2015). Fixing the mirrors: A feasibility study of the effects of dance movement therapy on young adults with autism spectrum disorder. *Autism*, *19*, 338–350. doi:10.1177/1362361314522353

Krane, V., Choi, P. V. L., Baird, S. M., Aimar, C. M., & Kauer, K. J. (2004). Living the paradox: Female athletes negotiate femininity and masculinity. *Sex Roles*, *50*, 315–329. doi: 10.1023/B:SERS.0000018888.48437.4f

Krane, V., Waldron, J., Michalenok, J., & Stiles-Shipley, J. (2001). Body image and eating and exercise behaviors: A feminist cultural studies perspective. *Women in Sport and Physical Activity Journal*, *10*, 17–54. https://doi.org/10.1123/wspaj.10.1.17

Langdon, S. W. (2012). Body image in dance and aesthetic sports. In T. F. Cash (Ed.), *Encyclopedia of body image and human appearance* (pp. 226–232). San Diego: Elsevier Academic Press. doi:10.1016/B978-0-12-384925-0.00034-1

Levine, M., & Smolak, L. (2005). *The prevention of eating problems and eating disorders: Theory, research and practice*. Mahwah: Lawrence Erlbaum Associates.

Linder, J. R., & Daniels, E. A. (2017). The effects of viewing sexualized images of athletes on self-objectification in men and women. *Sex Roles*. Advance online publication. doi:10.1007/s11199-017-0774-7

Mahlo, L., & Tiggemann, M. (2016). Yoga and positive body image: A test of the Embodiment Model. *Body Image*, *18*, 135–142. doi:10.1016/j.bodyim.2016.06.008

Mahoney, J. L., Harris, Angel L., & Eccles, J. S. (2006). Organized activity participation, positive youth development, and the over-scheduling hypothesis. *Social Policy Report: Giving Child and Youth Development Knowledge Away*, *20*, 3–30.

McVey, G., Tweed, S., & Blackmore, E. (2007). Healthy Schools – Healthy Kids: A controlled evaluation of a comprehensive universal eating disorder prevention program. *Body Image*, *4*, 115–136. doi:10.1016/j.bodyim.2007.01.004

Menzel, J. E., & Levine, M. P. (2011). Embodying experiences and the promotion of positive body image: The example of competitive athletics. In R. M. Calogero, S. Tantleff-Dunn, J. K. Thompson, R. M. Calogero, S. Tantleff-Dunn, & J. K. Thompson (Eds.), *Self-objectification in women: Causes, consequences, and counteractions* (pp. 163–186). Washington, DC: American Psychological Association. doi:10.1037/12304-008

National Federation of State High School Associations [NFSHSA] (2016). 2015–16 high school athletics participation survey. Retrieved from www.nfhs.org/ParticipationStatistics/ParticipationStatistics/.

Neff, K. D. (2003). Self-compassion: An alternative conceptualization of a healthy attitude toward oneself. *Self and Identity, 2*, 85–101. doi:10.1080/15298860309032

Neumark-Sztainer, D., Levine, M. P., Paxton, S. J., Smolak, L., Piran, N., & Wertheim, E. H. (2006). Prevention of body dissatisfaction and disordered eating: What's next? *Eating Disorders: The Journal of Treatment & Prevention, 14*, 265–285. doi:10.1080/10640260600796184

Neumark-Sztainer, D., Paxton, S. J., Hannan, P. J., Haines, J., & Story, M. (2006). Does body satisfaction matter? Five-year longitudinal associations between body satisfaction and health behaviors in adolescent females and males. *Journal of Adolescent Health, 39*, 244–251. doi:10.1016/j.jadohealth.2005.12.001

O'Dea, J., & Maloney, D. (2000). Preventing eating and body image problems in children and adolescents using the Health Promoting Schools Framework. *Journal of School Health, 70*, 18–21. doi:10.1111/j.1746-1561.2000.tb06441.x

O'Neill, J. R., Pate, R. R., & Liese, A. D. (2011). Descriptive epidemiology of dance participation in adolescents. *Research Quarterly for Exercise and Sport, 82*, 373–380.

Petrie, T. A., & Greenleaf, C. (2012). Body image and sports/athletics. In T. F. Cash (Ed.), *Encyclopedia of body image and human appearance* (pp. 160–165). San Diego: Elsevier Academic Press. doi:10.1016/B978-0-12-384925-0.00018-3

Piran, N. (2015). New possibilities in the prevention of eating disorders: The introduction of positive body image measures. *Sex Roles, 14*, 146–157.
  (2016). Embodiment and well-being: The embodied journeys of girls and women. In T.-A. Roberts, N. Curtin, L. E. Duncan, & L. M. Cortina (Eds.), *Feminist perspectives on building a better psychological science of gender* (pp. 43–60). New York: Springer.

Piran, N., & Teall, T. L. (2012). The developmental theory of embodiment. In G. L. McVey, M. P. Levine, N. Piran, & H. B. Ferguson (Eds.), *Preventing eating-related and weight-related disorders: Collaborative research, advocacy, and policy change* (pp. 169–198). Waterloo: Wilfrid Laurier University Press.

National Center on Sexual Exploitation (2016). *Pornification of an art: The sexualization of dance*. Retrieved from http://endsexualexploitation.org/articles/pornification-art-sexualization-dance.

Radell, S. A., Adame, D. D., Cole, S. P., & Blumenkehl, N. J. (2011). The impact of mirrors on body image and performance in high and low performing female students. *Journal of Dance Medicine and Science, 15*, 108–115.

Rauscher, L., Kauer, K., & Wilson, B. D. M. (2013). The healthy body paradox: Organizational and interactional influences on preadolescent girls' body image in Los Angeles. *Gender & Society, 27*, 208–230. doi:10.1177/0891243212472054

Richardson, S. M., Paxton, S. J., & Thomson, J. S. (2009). Is *BodyThink* an efficacious body image and self-esteem program? A controlled evaluation with adolescents. *Body Image, 6*, 75–82. doi:10.1016/j.bodyim.2008.11.001

Roberts, T.-A. & Scott, L. (2016, October). The impact of a social media fast on pre-teen and teen girls' self-objectification, self-esteem and self-compassion. Presented at the Gender Development Research Conference, San Francisco, CA.

Rudd, N. A., & Carter, J. (2006). Building positive body image among college athletes: A socially responsible approach. *Clothing & Textiles Research Journal, 24,* 363–380. doi:10.1177/0887302X06293073

Russell, K. M. (2004). On versus off the pitch: The transiency of body satisfaction among female rugby players, cricketers, and netballers. *Sex Roles, 51,* 561–574. doi:10.1007/s11199-004-5466-4

Schooler, D. (2013). Early adolescent body image predicts subsequent condom use behavior among girls. *Sexuality Research & Social Policy: A Journal of the NSRC, 10*(1), 52–61. doi:10.1007/s13178-012-0099-9

Seligman, M. P. (2011). *Flourish: A visionary new understanding of happiness and well-being.* New York: Free Press.

Smolak, L., Murnen, S. K., & Ruble, A. E. (2000). Female athletes and eating problems: A meta-analysis. *International Journal of Eating Disorders, 27,* 371–380. doi:10.1002/(SICI)1098-108X(200005)27:4<371::AID-EAT1>3.0.CO;2-Y

Stanford, J. N., & McCabe, M. P. (2005). Evaluation of a body image prevention programme for adolescent boys. *European Eating Disorders Review, 13,* 360–370. doi:10.1002/erv.654

Steiner-Adair, C., Sjostrom, L., Franko, D. L., Pai, S., Tucker, R., Becker, A. E., & Herzog, D. B. (2002). Primary prevention of risk factors for eating disorders in adolescent girls: Learning from practice. *International Journal of Eating Disorders, 32,* 401–411. doi:10.1002/eat.10089

Stewart, D. A., Carter, J. C., Drinkwater, J., Hainsworth, J., & Fairburn, C. G. (2001). Modification of eating attitudes and behavior in adolescent girls: A controlled study. *International Journal of Eating Disorders, 29,* 107–118. doi:10.1002/1098-108X(200103)29:2<107::AID-EAT1000>3.0.CO;2-1

Stice, E., Hayward, C., Cameron, R. P., Killen, J. D., & Taylor, C. B. (2000). Body-image and eating disturbances predict onset of depression among female adolescents: A longitudinal study. *Journal of Abnormal Psychology, 109,* 438–444. doi:10.1037/0021-843X.109.3.438

Stice, E., Shaw, H., & Marti, C. N. (2007). A meta-analytic review of eating disorder prevention programs: Encouraging findings. *Annual Review of Clinical Psychology, 3,* 207–231. doi:10.1146/annurev.clinpsy.3.022806.091447

Swami, V., & Harris, A.S. (2012). Dancing toward positive body image? Examining body-related constructs with ballet and contemporary dancers at different levels. *American Journal of Dance Therapy, 34,* 39–52. doi:10.1007/s10465-012-9129-7

Swami, V., & Tovée, M. J. (2009). A comparison of body dissatisfaction, body appreciation, and media influences between street-dancers and non-dancers. *Body Image, 6,* 304–307. doi:10.1016/j.bodyim.2009.07.006

Tylka, T. L., Calogero, R. M., & Daníelsdóttir, S. (2015). Is intuitive eating the same as flexible dietary control? Their links to each other and well-being could provide an answer. *Appetite, 95,* 166–175. doi:10.1016/j. appet.2015.07.004

Tylka, T. L., & Wood-Barcalow, N. L. (2015a). What is and what is not positive body image? Conceptual foundations and construct definition. *Body Image, 14,* 118–129. doi:10.1016/j.bodyim.2015.04.001

(2015b). The Body Appreciation Scale-2: Item refinement and psychometric evaluation. *Body Image, 12,* 53–67. doi:10.1016/j.bodyim.2014.09.006

Varnes, J. R., Stellefson, M. L., Janelle, C. M., Dorman, S. M., Dodd, V., & Miller, M. D. (2013). A systematic review of studies comparing body image concerns among female college athletes and non-athletes, 1997–2012. *Body Image, 10,* 421–432. doi:10.1016/j.bodyim.2013.06.001

Waldron, J. J. (2007). Influence of involvement in the Girls on Track Program on early adolescent girls' self-perceptions. *Research Quarterly for Exercise and Sport, 78,* 520–30. doi:/abs/10.1080/02701367.2007.10599451

Weiss, K., & Wertheim, E. H. (2005). An evaluation of a prevention program for disordered eating in adolescent girls: Examining responses of high- and low-risk girls. *Eating Disorders: The Journal of Treatment & Prevention, 13,* 143–156. doi:10.1080/10640260590918946

Weiss, M. R., Stuntz, C. P., Bhalla, J. A., Bolter, N. D., & Price, M. S. (2013). "More than a game": Impact of The First Tee life skills programme on positive youth development: Project introduction and Year 1 findings. *Qualitative Research in Sport, Exercise and Health, 5,* 214–244. doi:10.1080/2159676X.2012.712997

Whitehead, J. R. (1995). A study of children's physical self-perceptions using an adapted Physical Self-Perception Profile questionnaire. *Pediatric Exercise Science, 7,* 132–151. doi:10.1123/pes.7.2.132

Wood-Barcalow, N. L., Tylka, T. L., & Augustus-Horvath, C. L. (2010). "But I like my body": Positive body image characteristics and a holistic model for young-adult women. *Body Image, 7,* 106–116. doi:10.1016/j. bodyim.2010.01.001

Yager, Z., Diedrichs, P. C., Ricciardelli, L. A., & Halliwell, E. (2013). What works in secondary schools? A systematic review of classroom-based body image programs. *Body Image, 10,* 271–281. doi:10.1016/j. bodyim.2013.04.001

Youth Protection Advocates in Dance (2017). Retrieved from www .ypad4change.org

10 Clinical Applications of Positive Body Image

Nichole L. Wood-Barcalow and Casey L. Augustus-Horvath

Positive body image can be realistic and attainable at any weight. Individuals who struggle with body image disturbance may find this statement difficult to comprehend, let alone incorporate into their belief system. Yet, we have witnessed this transformation occur within our own clients. Clinicians working with this concern might struggle with identifying and implementing effective clinical interventions. In this chapter, we review themes of positive body image research and offer techniques that we, as psychologists, have employed in our own clinical practice, including how to prepare and guide clients through this important therapeutic work.[1] We acknowledge that some information offered here may not be reflected in research to date, but rather is a synthesis of anecdotal information based on clinical experience. The chapter concludes with thoughts about directions which positive body image clinical work might take in the future.[2]

Perspectives from Clinical Practice

We begin by offering basic information about body image, across the spectrum of negative and positive, to elucidate our conceptual background. First, negative body image is pain that is constructed and located within the brain (Doidge, 2007; Ramachadran & Blakeslee, 1998). Body image is a "subjective experience" (Osumi, Imai, Ueta, Nakano, Nobusako, & Morioka, 2014) that emerges and is maintained over time as viewed through different theoretical lenses (Cash & Smolak, 2011;

---

[1] The recommendations are appropriate for those clients who are capable of engaging in self-reflection. Please note that recommendations may need to be adapted for adolescents.

[2] There are some important considerations regarding the application of positive body image that are beyond the scope of this particular chapter and are addressed in earlier chapters of this book: Individuals with varying identities across age and the lifespan (gender, cultural, nationality, etc.) can read Ricciardelli's, Swami's, and Daniels and Roberts' chapters (2, 3, and 9 respectively).

McKinley, 2011; Suisman & Klump, 2011; Swami, 2011). Body image can vary in intensity of both evaluation and investment (Cash, 2008), and be related to a variety of concerns such as activating life events, genetic factors, developmental and sociocultural influences, and identification experiences (e.g., gender, sexuality, race, ethnicity). Body image is a real phenomenon that manifests in the brain and is then experienced via an individual's thoughts, emotions, and behaviors.

Second, body image disturbance can occur: (1) within the general population, as evidenced by the literature addressing normative discontent (Rodin, Silberstein, & Striegel-Moore, 1984; Tantleff-Dunn, Barnes, & Larose, 2011); (2) in the context of a mental health disorder as a symptom or sequelae of that particular disorder (e.g., eating disorder, body dysmorphic disorder, gender dysphoria, trauma and stressor-related disorders, etc.); (3) in the context of a medical disorder (chronic regional pain syndrome; Lewis, Kersten, McCabe, McPherson, & Blake, 2007); (4) as a response to medical interventions (e.g., mastectomy), and/or (5) as an outcome of disfiguring conditions (Harcourt & Rumsey, 2011). As a result, it is important for the clinician to recognize the role and function of negative body image within a larger context to determine whether the issue warrants specific focus itself, or is perhaps a common experience related to other more prominent issues that, once addressed and/or resolved, will then also likely impact the client's body image.

Third, the neuroplasticity of the brain allows for change due to neurogenesis, as well as the possibility to "rewire" long-held connections (Doidge, 2007). As the brain is able to reorganize and relocalize in functioning when an internal and/or external injury occurs (Doidge, 2007), it is possible for brain circuits and pathways to rewire from negative to positive. Practice makes permanence in numerous areas of life, including one's experience of body image.

Fourth, based on our clinical experience, we believe the following to be ineffective, harmful, antithetical, and even destructive when assisting the client's transition from negative to positive body image:

- to ignore, minimize, or devalue body image disturbance, which may be interpreted by the client as though she is at fault or defective;[3]
- to try to convince someone via intellectual dialogue alone to accept her body;

---

[3] We use the pronouns "she" and "her" throughout this chapter as a way to ensure consistency of language. We acknowledge that body image issues exist across gender identities and, as a result, should be assessed and treated regardless of an individual's gender identity status.

- to assume that the client "is making (it) up" or exaggerating issues in order to receive attention, sympathy, or accommodation;
- to believe that inducing guilt or shame within the individual with negative body image (e.g., "you should be happy with the way you look") serves as positive motivation for change.

Preparing for Positive Body Image Work

When preparing for intensive body image work, both the clinician and client need to enter into a mutual agreement that the focus of psychotherapy is to promote positive body image without the additional subversive belief that the *actual body itself* needs to change. Many clients, and some clinicians, believe that positive body image naturally emerges once a defective or disliked aspect of the body is altered, removed, or eliminated. Although this can be an outcome in the aforementioned circumstances, our experience has more often been that clients' body image will shift toward acceptance for an intermediary time and then refocus to baseline levels if additional in-depth body image work is not conducted. An example is the belief that weight loss will spontaneously and automatically correspond with the emergence of acceptance and self-love. There are individuals who experience an increase in positive body image with weight loss, especially when the weight loss increases quality of life and functioning. However, there are many alternate instances whereby individuals lose weight and struggle with "still seeing the fat," resulting in disenfranchisement and frustration. As a point of note, weight loss should not be guaranteed, be expected, or serve as the point of concentrated focus in intensive body image work. Once a commitment to work on this issue is solidified in the therapeutic alliance, there are active components that are required of both the clinician and the client.

Clinician's role. First and foremost, the clinician must entertain the belief that the attainment of positive body image is feasible and attainable at any developmental stage in life for individuals of any race/ethnicity, nationality, socioeconomic class, sexual orientation, gender identity, ability status, and level of mental and/or medical health functioning. The ultimate goal of positive body image is focused on the *process* of transforming from negative to positive body image, not on the outcome alone. Additionally, even after attaining an overall positive body image, the focus is then on maintaining it despite potential external or internal threats.

It is imperative that the clinician uses a conceptual foundation regarding body image that is communicated to the client. Examples include, but are not limited to, evolutionary perspectives (Swami, 2011), sociocultural factors (Tiggemann, 2011), genetic and neuroscientific components (Suisman & Klump, 2011), feminist ideology (McKinley, 2011), and cognitive behavioral perspectives (Fairburn, 2008). It is important to note that the theoretical perspectives are not mutually exclusive; tenets of conceptual foundations can be interwoven and complementary. For example, an older adult female who is dissatisfied with her changed shape upon experiencing menopause (e.g., increased fat storage in the abdomen) can learn about how testosterone levels change in females during this life transition (genetic), how the Westernized feminine beauty ideal to have a flat stomach is discrepant from the actual physical self (sociocultural), and how the objectification of women results in focusing on a woman's appearance versus her assets (feminist), and discuss how strategies such as positive rational acceptance can impact the client's investment in and evaluation of her body (cognitive behavioral).[4]

It is the clinician's role to set established parameters before proceeding with body image work, including amelioration of higher order issues such as maladaptive behaviors: restriction, binge eating, ridding the body of calories via unhealthy measures, body checking or avoidance, excessive/obligatory exercise, nonsuicidal self-injury etc. We believe that addressing such maladaptive behaviors within therapy is a priority before proceeding with in-depth positive body image work. With the recognition that it can be challenging to eradicate destructive behaviors in an absolute manner, the clinician can conceptualize what the threshold is for different clients based upon a confluence of factors. Thus, the clinician upholds the standard that maladaptive behaviors are to be contained or eliminated during positive body image work. We have found that this limit serves as an incentive and can be motivating for those clients wanting to explore positive body image within therapy. If maladaptive behaviors arise or intensify, the clinician tends to those more immediate issues, creates a plan, and informs the client that positive body image work will be resumed once safety (e.g., medical, psychological, nutritional) is ensured. Additionally, for those clients who are below an appropriate weight range, weight restoration needs to occur, as low weight can culminate in cognitive and psychological issues that could interfere with the ability to consider and integrate the principles associated with body image work (Fairburn, 2008).

The clinician plays an invaluable role, educating the client about what positive body image entails. We have experienced numerous clients who want a positive body image but do not have a sense of what it is, what it

---

[4] For additional examples of body image theories and conceptualizations refer to the aforementioned authors' book chapters in *Body Image: A Handbook of Science, Practice and Prevention* (Cash & Smolak, eds., 2011).

looks like for them, how it is attained, and how it is maintained. The clinician therefore assumes a teaching role in providing information synthesized from both research and clinical realms about positive body image. Specifically, positive body image is not just the absence of negative features such as body dissatisfaction; it also includes its own unique variables, such as gratitude toward the functioning of the body, and it can be both constant and fluid depending on various factors (Avalos, Tylka, & Wood-Barcalow, 2005; Frisén & Holmqvist, 2010; Holmqvist & Frisén, 2012; Tylka, 2011; Tylka & Wood-Barcalow, 2015; Wood-Barcalow, Tylka, & Augustus-Horvath, 2010).

To discern the starting point associated with body image work, the clinician can integrate standardized assessments.[5] General body image assessments can include, but are not limited to, the Figure Rating Scale (Thompson & Altabe, 1991), Body Esteem Scale (Franzoi & Shields, 1984), Body Shape Questionnaire (Cooper, Taylor, Cooper, & Fairbum, 1987), Physical Appearance State and Trait Anxiety Scale (Reed, Thompson, Brannick, & Sacco, 1991), Sociocultural Attitudes towards Appearance Questionnaire-3 (Thompson, van den Berg, Roehrig, Guarda, & Heinberg, 2004), and Body Image Avoidance Questionnaire (Rosen, Srebnik, Saltzberg, & Wendt, 1991). Clinicians can utilize the assessments included in Cash's *Body Image Workbook* (2008) as treatment outcome measures. Additionally, when working with individuals who identify as male, it is important to include specific measures that are created for and normed for boys and men, such as the Drive for Muscularity Scale (McCreary, Sasse, Saucier, & Dorsch, 2004), Body Parts Satisfaction Scale for Men (McFarland & Petrie, 2012), and Male Body Attitudes Scale (Tylka, Bergeron, & Schwartz, 2005). Some of the aforementioned instruments, and others, are reviewed in Menzel, Krawczyk, and Thompson (2011).

Additionally, the clinician should include instruments focused specifically on body acceptance. Examples include the subscale from the Multidimensional Body Self-Relations Questionnaire (Brown, Cash, & Mikulka, 1990), the Embodied Image Scale (Abbott & Barber, 2010), the Broad Conceptualization of Beauty Scale for Women (Tylka & Iannantuono, 2016), and the Body Appreciation Scale-2 (Tylka & Wood-Barcalow, 2015). Although the clinician might question the inclusion of assessments that focus on positive aspects of body image at the beginning of treatment, it is possible that the client already endorses positive components at that time, which can be highlighted and

---

[5] Review *Cognitive-Behavioral Approaches to Body Image Change* (Jarry & Cash, 2011) or *The Body Image Workbook* (Cash, 2008) for step-by-step instructions on body image change.

enhanced during the course of treatment. By doing so, the clinician challenges the notion that negative and positive body image are opposite ends of one spectrum while also acknowledging the positive elements already inherent within the client. This strengths-based approach serves as motivation for additional change.

Finally, it is imperative that the clinician assisting with body image work has done (or is doing) their own personal work (if necessary) related to body acceptance. This allows the clinician to have an authentic and congruent relationship with her own body that is reflected in her own comfort and confidence in working with clients struggling with body image concerns. Similar to Levine and Chapman's (2011) encouragement to clinicians to be "a model of critical consciousness and active resistance for their patients and their families" (p.108) in relation to social media, we encourage clinicians to model and emulate positive body image as a source of inspiration for clients.

Client's role. Using the Stages of Change Model as a foundation, the client ideally should be in at least a preparation stage as it relates to maladaptive behaviors (if present), and at least the contemplation stage related to body image work specifically (Prochaska, DeClimente, & Norcross, 1992).[6] It is helpful for the client to create an "I commit to" list at the beginning of the body image work to serve as a reminder of why doing the work is important when she experiences psychological discomfort later in the treatment process. If a client is either unwilling and/or unable to participate in body image work for whatever reason (e.g., cognitive challenges, maturity issues for children/young adolescents, lack of investment, being pressured to do so by others, etc.), it is important to communicate what can and cannot be done until both investment and engagement are endorsed by the client. We offer two examples to illustrate this point. One example is when a client touts that she wants body acceptance, but she is unable or unwilling to engage in the self-reflection required and neglects to make the recommended behavioral changes offered by the clinician (e.g., cease dieting). Another example relates to clients who are minors, whereby parents set a treatment goal for the child to "like her body" or for the child "to see herself like I do" without considering whether that goal is actually shared by the minor. If it is not a goal for the minor, then it is important for the clinician, parent, and minor to discuss how that goal will only be of focus when there is specific and intentional buy-in from the minor.

---

[6] Stages of Change is a transtheoretical model of stages related to intentional behavior change: precontemplation, contemplation, preparation, action, maintenance and relapse. Read Prochaska, Diclemente, and Norcross (1992) for more information.

Having secured the client's commitment to engage in the clinical work, the next step is to prepare her for the behavioral changes which need to be maintained while working on body image issues within therapy: healthful nutritional intake; appropriate physical movement that is not excessive, compulsive, or driven; moderate weighing practices; and if necessary, cessation of specific eating disorder behaviors (e.g., dietary restriction, purging of all forms, binge eating) and amelioration of self-injurious behaviors. By encouraging moderate weighing, we distinguish between excessive and avoidant practices, as both can be impediments to authentic positive body image. Excessive weighing (e.g., several times a day) can serve as a way to punish oneself psychologically, inadvertently reinforce that a specific weight is necessary for body image acceptance, and generate as well as perpetuate rule-governed behaviors (e.g., reducing caloric intake, driven exercise) that reinforce negative cognitions and uncomfortable emotions. Alternatively, complete avoidance of weighing can also impede the attainment of a positive body image due to the potential aversive emotions and cognitions attached to weight(s) that cannot be directly addressed or challenged due to avoidance. The clinician should provide education about the potential concerns associated with excessive or avoidant weighing practices and encourage the client to surrender destructive practices for an indeterminate period of time that is based on the client's specific needs. If the client is unable to commit to examining and possibly changing her weighing practices, the clinician can offer some of the following options: (1) implement in-session weighing as a way to monitor and track the trajectory with the client's commitment to refrain from weighing outside of therapy, along with time in session devoted to discussion of any thoughts/feelings that arise from in-session weighing; (2) incorporate experiments whereby the client either decreases or increases weighing (contingent upon excessive versus avoidant practices) for a specific period of time while tracking emotions and cognitions to determine the many purposes of weighing (both constructive and destructive); (3) identify a goal with a specific timeline whereby the client transitions to moderate weighing practices (e.g.,. once a week); and (4) engage in exposure to current weight and imagined weights coupled with self-compassion and affirmative statements, while deconstructing how the strong responses to various weights are constructed and reinforced both externally and externally. The ultimate challenge is for the client to consider how weight has served as a metric of self-acceptance that, once eliminated from the equation of typical functioning, requires her to gauge emotions, cognitions, and behaviors through an alternate lens.

The clinician and client are encouraged to identify how the use of individualized "rules" and expectations about the body (both actual and ideal) are created, maintained, and reinforced over time. Examples of "rules" that our clients have shared include: "Only women who look like (insert client's beauty ideal) can wear (insert clothing item)," "I will only accept myself once I have (lost weight/toned up)," "I need to look a certain way to be attractive," and "I can't do (insert activity) while I look like this." By understanding the client's rules, the clinician can assist the client to challenge the cognitions and to engage in behaviors that counter them, as a way to conquer them.

Having identified the rules either in session or as a homework assignment, clients can then examine whether their specific "rules" or expectations get them closer to or farther away from body image acceptance. The clinician plays a pivotal role in this discussion by challenging the client in a meaningful and authentic manner that is not judgmental, but rather curious and consistent with the Socratic dialogue technique in cognitive behavioral therapy (Beck, 1979). It is imperative that the clinician is aware of her own potential biases and those of the larger cultural context to ensure that stereotypes are not reinforced inadvertently with the client. For example, a female client who wants to attain the thick ideal (flat stomach, curvy hips/buttocks) might believe in and follow a rule about completing a certain number of sit-ups a day as an attempt to attain this ideal and positive body image. Rather than the clinician supporting the belief and behavior as effective, it is their mission to challenge whether a flat stomach is necessary for positive body image (question the entrenched belief) and how current behaviors may be leading the client further from self-acceptance (challenge to redirect toward the actual goal of self-acceptance as she exists currently). Another example might be when the clinician has internalized weight bias that is pervasive within the larger culture, resulting in the clinician agreeing with the client about acceptance being predicated on attainment of certain beauty ideals. The clinician may refer to Koenig and O'Mahoney (2017) for further discussions and ideas related to recognizing and attending to weight stigma.

A next important step is for the client to explicate what positive body image personally means to her. Although seemingly an easy task, many clients in our work have experienced difficulty in describing *what they want* versus the often automatic response of identifying *what they don't want*. The clinician's expertise in this matter is paramount in helping the client to identify and understand the nuances in what positive body image would look like from the following perspectives: emotional, cognitive, interpersonal, behavioral, social, and spiritual (if appropriate).

Short-term, intermediate, and long-term goals can be created from this imagined future, including practical applications. An example is a client wanting to wear a bathing suit at the pool as a long-term goal that would be one indicator of positive body image for her. The clinician can help the client identify short-term and intermediate challenges that get her nearer to the long-term goal: try on a bathing suit at the store, purchase a bathing suit, try the bathing suit on at home, wear the bathing suit to a pool with other attire over it, sit at pool with bathing suit on, put feet in pool while wearing suit, get into the pool while wearing suit.

Next, the clinician assists the client with creating a body image timeline that includes seminal life events pertaining to the body that are viewed as positive, negative, or neutral by the client. Instruction on how to create the timeline is ambiguous purposely to allow the client to engender her own creative outlet. Some of the timelines created by our clients include pen and paper descriptions, photographs to catalogue different life experiences, collages of images from magazines, artwork, and more. The timeline is explored during a therapy session so that the client and clinician have a coconstructed understanding of the contributing and maintaining factors associated with that particular client's body image experiences. Discussion of the timeline allows for identification of challenges and barriers to achieving a positive body image both intrapersonally (e.g., entrenched views about the ideal body) and interpersonally (e.g., critical family members who make frequent comments about the current state of the client's body). The timeline is referenced throughout the therapeutic process and, as a result, should be readily accessible at any point.

Positive Body Image Themes and Interventions

Now that we have defined the various roles and tasks for both the clinician and the client, we offer psychotherapeutic interventions for positive body image work, organized by themes identified in various studies that specifically addressed positive body image: (1) body appreciation and acceptance; (2) a broad conceptualization of beauty; (3) unconditional acceptance from others; (4) faith, (5) taking care of the body; and (6) filtering information (Andrew, Tiggemann, & Clark, 2014, 2016b; Avalos, Tylka, & Wood-Barcalow, 2005; Frisén & Holmqvist, 2010; Gillen, 2015; Holmqvist & Frisén, 2012; Wood-Barcalow et al., 2010). We recognize that these themes might be specific to the samples included in the original studies, and as a result may not be inclusive for all genders of different cultures, ages, race/ethnicities, sexual identification, and more. Therefore, the clinician is encouraged to use their respective expertise and acumen in assessing and tailoring different approaches based on the individual needs of the client.

Appreciation and acceptance. A theme that has emerged in positive body image research is that of satisfaction, appreciation, and acceptance of one's body (Avalos et al., 2005; Frisén & Holmqvist, 2010; Holmqvist & Frisén, 2012; Wood-Barcalow et al., 2010). Adolescent participants in a Swedish study about positive body image described themselves in terms such as "average looking" or "good looking" (Frisén & Holmqvist, 2010). Adult female participants described acceptance as love directed toward the self (Wood-Barcalow et al., 2010). It is important to note that body appreciation and acceptance does not translate into perfectionism, egotism, and the *actual* body corresponding with an *ideal* body. In fact, acknowledging perceived imperfections and undesirable traits is an important part of the process, without imbuing conditional standards or expectations for appreciation.

Next, we offer some specific ideas on how to acknowledge and promote both appreciation and acceptance of the body within the therapeutic experience via identifying areas of gratitude, participating in mirror exposure work, and incorporating self-compassion.

Gratitude. Research examining gratitude in relation to medical and mental health has received attention in recent years (Mills et al., 2015; Wood, Froh, & Geraghty, 2010; see also Dunaev and Markey, Chapter 8 in this book). In our work, we encourage clients to acknowledge gratitude related to the function, health, and features of their bodies. The clinician can encourage the client to list and record all the benefits that her overall body and various body parts provide in relation to daily living (e.g., my arms help me to lift weights, to wash myself, to hold my children). With direction and encouragement, the client can learn how to express gratitude for the healthy functioning of the body in its current state (e.g., I'm thankful that my heart beats about 115,000 times a day without any problems).

We have observed that this task may prove challenging for those clients with extreme body dissatisfaction, as they often perceive and relate to their overall body and its various parts in a derogatory manner. Being asked to identify gratitude for the body may be disconcerting and sometimes embarrassing. The clinician's nonjudgmental, steady, and determined response helps to assist the client in this task.

Mirror exposure work.[7] Many individuals with negative body image tend to exhibit perfectionism, rigidity of thoughts, and an altered

---

[7] Mirror exposure work is a form of exposure therapy in which clients stand in front of a mirror in session and as homework with the goal of decreasing the negative thoughts and feelings associated with the body.

perception of their bodies that can be transformed into appreciation and acceptance via mirror exposure (Cash, 2008; Delinsky & Wilson, 2006; Hildebrandt, Loeb, Troupe, & Delinsky, 2012; Jansen, Bollen, Tuschen-Caffier, Roefs, & Braet, 2008; Luethcke, McDaniel, & Becker, 2011). Although an overview of the mirror exposure literature and description of how to employ the method extend beyond the scope of this chapter, we offer a few considerations that we have found beneficial when implementing this method with our clients. It is essential for the clinician to discuss the rationale of the approach in advance of implementing it, as well as to acknowledge the potential discomfort that may arise from this work and how to manage it without resorting to maladaptive behaviors. During mirror exposure work, we have found the following interventions beneficial across a range of clients: describe body parts using only neutral and objective terms; identify the purpose and function of body parts; and incorporate the phrases "I appreciate" or "I accept" for each body part. We encourage repetition of the approach both during therapy sessions and in homework assignments. The clinician can highlight positive changes that emerge across therapy sessions as a way to provide positive reinforcement for the work in getting closer to positive body image. We have been amazed to witness the positive transformation in our clients in not only eradicating negative thoughts and emotions regarding the body, but also impacting the perceptual component, whereby they are able to view themselves in an accepting manner.

Self-compassion. The burgeoning area of self-compassion intertwines with positive body image work and, more specifically, appreciation and acceptance. Self-compassion addresses three primary components: *self-kindness* versus self-judgment, *common humanity* versus isolation, and *mindfulness* versus over-identification (Neff, 2003). It is related to body appreciation in female undergraduate students (Tylka & Homan, 2015) and young adult women (Andrew, Tiggemann, & Clark, 2016b), and corresponds with lower levels of body preoccupation and weight concerns (Wasylkiw, MacKinnon, & MacLellan, 2012). An overview of the self-compassion literature can be found in Cook-Cottone's chapter in this edited volume as well as in Braun, Park, and Gorin (2016). We next offer considerations of how this construct can be promoted in the therapeutic process through the incorporation of the Self-Compassion Scale Short Form (Raes, Pommier, Neff, & Van Gucht, 2011) to determine baseline levels at the beginning of body image work and to guide interventions henceforth.

If a client scores low on self-kindness and high on self-judgment on the Self-Compassion Scale Short Form (Raes et al., 2011), the clinician can assist the client in understanding how different types of negative self-talk (critic, worrier, perfectionist, victim) contribute to judgments about the body (Bourne, 2015). When a type of negative thinking emerges in a therapy session, the clinician can identify and externalize it as a form of negative self-talk, and encourage the client to reframe it using statements focused on self-kindness. For example, a client who endorses self-talk associated with the perfectionist or critic – "I need to get ripped (more defined muscles)" – can be encouraged to identify and repeat alternate thoughts that imbue self-kindness, such as "I may never be as defined as a body builder but I can appreciate the hard work that I've done to try to be healthy." Homework assignments can include completing a thought record about body-related themes and identifying the types of cognitive distortions and negative self-talk contained therein. Doing so shifts the focus from criticism of individual body parts to understanding how overall self-talk contributes to negative body image, and likely impacts other areas of life as well. It is helpful to address how individual and sociocultural rules and expectations about the body correlate with self-judgment. Additionally, the clinician can highlight examples of rules (as noted earlier in this chapter) in the therapeutic moment and challenge the client to consider how self-kindness might unfold when those rules are refuted, dismissed, or challenged on a consistent basis.

Another construct of the Self-Compassion Scale Short Form is *mindfulness* ("holding one's experience in balanced perspective rather than exaggerating the dramatic storyline of suffering" Raes et al., 2011, p. 250) versus *overidentification* with thoughts and emotions (Neff, 2003; Raes et al., 2011). If a client scores *low on mindfulness* and *high on over-identification*, then the clinician can assist the client to assess how an overidentification with or overemphasis on perceived body flaws corresponds with emotional suffering, including the intensity and frequency of it across various areas of life. The clinician can encourage the client to shift toward mindfulness by identifying and considering how her own physical attributes and personality characteristics (including perceived flaws) contribute to her unique being. Helping the client shift from a negative, flaw-based perspective to one of openness with one's features and acknowledgment of the body's current health and functioning assists the client in moving more toward acceptance and appreciation. During session, the clinician can facilitate guided meditations such as the ones identified in Albertson, Neff, and Dill-Shackelford's (2015) study (i.e., Compassionate Body Scan, Affectionate Breathing, Loving-Kindness that incorporates self-compassion).[8] In this study, participants

---

[8] Podcasts can be accessed at www.selfcompassion.org.

received three weeks of self-compassion training that included listening to twenty-minute podcasts daily. A three-month follow-up indicated that compared to those in the randomized waitlist control group, participants in the self-compassion intervention group reported significantly higher gains in body appreciation and self-compassion, and greater reductions in body shame, body dissatisfaction, and contingent self-worth based on appearance (Albertson et al., 2015).

Another component of self-compassion is that of *common humanity* (recognizing that the human experience is shared with others) versus isolation (experience of feeling alone and detached from others; Neff, 2003). If a client scores low on common humanity and high on isolation on the Self-Compassion Scale Short Form, then the clinician can highlight how negative body image is a pervasive issue that exists within many cultures, commonly referred to as "normative discontent" (Tantleff-Dunn et al., 2011). The client's experience of negative body image can be validated by the clinician while simultaneously addressing how pervasive sociocultural beauty ideals promote body dissatisfaction by creating a discrepancy between the actual and ideal selves. To increase the common humanity perspective, the client can be prompted to consider the positive attributes within her respective culture(s) and identities while simultaneously celebrating beauty more broadly (Tylka & Iannantuono, 2016). As an example, some of the female participants in our 2010 study reported that they rejected and refuted dominant sociocultural beauty ideals that were inconsistent with what was desirable and honored within their respective racial/ethnic identities, as a way to increase body acceptance (Wood-Barcalow et al., 2010). To reduce isolation, it can be healing for the client to learn about the experiences of others who have suffered with negative body image and have been able to transform this into a positive body image. Examples can be found on the National Eating Disorders Awareness website under *Stories of Hope* (www.nationaleatingdisorders.org/stories-of-hope-list).

Broadly conceptualizing beauty. Another theme that has emerged as a component of positive body image is the perspective of beauty as a broad construct that extends beyond the sometimes narrow and limited definitions imbued within sociocultural lenses. Rather than accept and internalize certain appearance ideals, persons with positive body image report wanting to look like themselves rather than conform to "unrealistic ideals," and understanding that beauty is both an inclusive and subjective experience (Frisén & Holmqvist, 2010; Wood-Barcalow et al., 2010; Holmqvist & Frisén, 2012). The adult women in our above-mentioned study

(Wood-Barcalow et al., 2010) reported the importance of acknowledging the significance of heritage and ethnicity as it relates to positive body image.

The clinician serves an important role in educating the client about how beauty ideals shift over time and within cultures based on a confluence of issues such as values, mores, political influences, access to resources, and more. Furthermore, it can be highlighted that different cultures around the world have their own beauty standards. The clinician can encourage the client to identify how beauty ideals are promoted within her respective cultures and identities, as well as to challenge the notion that the oft-touted ideals are the *only* definition of beauty. With encouragement, the client can identify famous individuals who demonstrate beauty without meeting stereotypical standards. A next step is for the client to identify people in her own life (family, friends, acquaintances, community members, and more) whom she deems beautiful. Additionally, we have found it beneficial to encourage clients to identify how beauty is demonstrated within their specific heritage and family system. For example, a client who is displeased with the color of her skin can focus on how her unique coloring is related to her family of origin and ancestors. With guidance, the clinician helps the client to achieve the realization that if this contributes to beauty for others, then the same principle holds true for her as well.

The clinician can encourage a client who identifies as female to complete the Broad Conceptualization of Beauty Scale (BCBS), which assesses the extent to which women define female beauty regarding external or internal characteristics (Tylka & Iannantuono, 2016).[9] The client can ponder her responses to items such as "I think that a wide variety of body shapes are beautiful for women" and "I think that women of all body sizes can be beautiful" and what experiences in her own life have contributed to these specific beliefs, as well as how they relate to her personal experience.

Unconditional acceptance from others. Unconditional acceptance from others is another resounding theme that has emerged in positive body image research. For example, Swedish adolescents shared a perspective that the "body itself (is viewed) as peripheral," in which they assumed that others liked their appearance and dismissed negative feedback about their bodies when it occurred (Frisén & Holmqvist, 2010, p. 208). College-aged women noted that explicit and implicit messages from others about their body acceptance shaped the process of having a

---

[9] Tylka and Iannantuono (2016) found that higher scores on the BCBS corresponded with higher body appreciation and self-compassion while simultaneously being inversely correlated with antifat attitudes and thin-ideal internalization.

positive body image (Wood-Barcalow et al., 2010). It is possible that the family dynamics, upbringing, and socialization processes of people with positive body image differ from those of people with negative body image, though this particular line of inquiry has yet to be investigated thoroughly. Although more can be learned about elements directly related to the creation of positive body image (Andrew et al., 2016), and specifically ways in which unconditional acceptance from others is cultivated and related to positive body image, our efforts with clients focus on what clients can do moving forward within the interpersonal context. We acknowledge that it is impossible to completely alter or control the interpersonal environment in which one exists; however, there is benefit in acknowledging and focusing on the element of unconditional acceptance that already exists from others.

Upon instructing the client to review seminal events associated with her body image development as part of the timeline intervention, the clinician can encourage the client to identify those individuals in her life who have been key advocates of body acceptance. As part of a therapy session or a homework assignment, the client reflects on what positive messages she received, in both general and specific ways, about her body. This process is especially illuminating for clients to discern the overall influence of these positive messages and how it is likely that they have not been internalized over time, versus the assimilation of negative information. With the clinician's assistance, the client records these examples in a readily accessible format (e.g., journal, blog, audio file) that can be reviewed at times when body dissatisfaction is overwhelming and interfering with functioning. We have received feedback from clients stating that this is helpful to shift the perspective from negative to positive, with the ultimate goal of rewiring the brain through repetition.

An interesting finding from our 2010 study with adult women was the notion of positive body image having a "ripple effect," through which it can be transferred or passed on to others via formal or informal mentoring efforts (Wood-Barcalow et al., 2010). Some clients have recognized that being around others who embrace positive body image impacts their own body image in both the short-term and long-term. The client can interview these influential people and ask about their own experiences with body image as a way to gain personal knowledge and insight. Additionally, the client can increase time spent with these individuals versus those who engage in negative body communication and focus on appearance-based issues. Furthermore, the clinician can assist the client in finding ways to educate others about the importance of healthy body image by discussing these topics via informal and formal venues such as teaching a class, posting info on social media forums, and more.

Some clients can benefit from having family and friends join a session of therapy to discuss how they can be supportive in promoting healthy body image. The clinician can educate family and friends regarding certain statements and behaviors that can impact the client's progress. Examples include refraining from negative body talk, using affirmative statements when discussing appearance, focusing on talents and strengths outside of appearance, and encouraging constructive behaviors such as healthful nourishment and physical activity.

Faith. Many of the clients we have worked with over the years cite their faith, spirituality, and/or religion as a component contributing to positive body image.[10] Research to have emerged in recent years supports this connection to the clinical realm; we provide a brief overview of those findings here. In our 2010 study, twelve of the fifteen female respondents believed that their positive body image was influenced by a higher power who created them to be special and unique, along with providing unconditional acceptance (Wood-Barcalow et al., 2010). Jacobs-Pilipski and colleagues reported that a portion of female participants in their qualitative study reported using "faith beliefs" to alleviate negative feelings directed toward their bodies (Jacobs-Pilipski, Winzelberg, Wilfley, Bryson, & Taylor, 2005). In another study, a small proportion of females noted that focusing on faith was an effective way to respond to "bad body image days" (Smith-Jackson, Reel, & Thackeray, 2011). Additionally, research participants who utilized spiritual body affirmations when viewing photographs of models reported higher levels of body image satisfaction than the control group (Boyatzis, Kline, & Backof, 2007).[11]

For those clients who identify with a particular faith, we offer the following interventions for consideration in therapy sessions. The clinician can encourage the client to identify specific spiritual texts or tenets that address body acceptance, to use as a meditation or focus when experiencing negative body image. The client can be reminded of her unique relationship with a higher power that includes unconditional acceptance, as well as to practice spiritual body affirmations such as "my body is whole and perfect because it is created in the image of God" (Boyatzis et al., 2007). The client can be encouraged to discuss the concepts that "God accepts them as they are" (p. 329; Homan, 2012) and that "God's approval does not depend on weight or shape" (Homan, 2012;

---

[10] While a full discussion of the nuances of terms such as religion and spirituality, and the potential overlap and distinction between the terms is beyond the scope of this section, interested readers are referred to works such as that of Paloutzian and Park (2013). We use the term faith henceforth.

[11] It should be noted that the majority of research on positive body image and spirituality/religion includes samples who identify Christianity as their faith.

Scott Richards, Berrett, Hardman, & Eggett, 2006). Furthermore, the client can be reminded that spiritual texts do not include appearance-specific standards associated with beauty that are promoted in today's society.

In addition to using prayer, gratitude journals, and mindfulness practices, the clinician can assist the client to conceptualize self-care as a form of body sanctification – the belief that the body has divine significance (Jacobson, Hall, & Anderson, 2013). The clinician can reinforce that eating in a way that properly nourishes the body, resting when necessary, and engaging in movement are some concrete ways to demonstrate respect for the body and soul.

If faith issues transcend the scope of the clinician's training or comfort levels, she can advocate for the client to connect with a faith-based leader for one-on-one consultation on the intersection between faith and body acceptance. Additionally, the client's faith-based community can serve a vital role in providing support, education, and mentoring during the transition from a negative body image to a positive one. Examples of this might include the client's participation in study groups or support groups (e.g., Celebrate Recovery, 12-step programs).

Taking care of the body. Another consistent theme of positive body image research is the importance of taking care of the body by getting appropriate sleep and rest, eating in a healthful manner, moving the body for joy and pleasure, pampering, and adhering to medical and preventa-tive care procedures (Andrew et al., 2014; Frisén & Holmqvist, 2010; Holmqvist & Frisen, 2012; Wood-Barcalow et al., 2010). These com-ponents are elucidated below.

Sleep. The clinician can emphasize the importance of tending to and improving both the quantity and quality of sleep as a means of caring for the body. Some of the women in our 2010 study emphasized that getting an appropriate amount of sleep and rest was integral for their overall medical and mental wellbeing, including positive body image (Wood-Barcalow et al., 2010). Research has demonstrated that those with better sleep patterns report significantly lower levels of anxiety and depression as compared to people with insomnia (Taylor, Lichstein, Durrence, Reidel, & Bush, 2005). More information is needed regarding the inter-action of sleep and positive body image.

Eating. Numerous studies have linked positive body image with healthful and intuitive eating, as well as fewer unhealthy dieting behaviors (Augustus-Horvath & Tylka, 2011; Avalos & Tylka, 2006; Gillen, 2015). Avalos and Tylka (2006) demonstrated that appreciation of the body actually predicted intuitive eating and corresponded with awareness of body signals. The client can be encouraged to eat in a mindful, balanced manner that eschews fad diets, caloric restriction, and/or the elimination of macronutrients. Clients can work with registered dietitians who are trained specifically in treating individuals with body image concerns in order to ensure that nutritional goals focus on increasing function and acceptance, versus targeting weight loss or changing the body.

Body functionality and movement. The clinician can assist the client in becoming aware of her body functionality as well as what her body is capable of doing (e.g., movement, sensing), as a way to shift from an appearance focus (Abbott & Barber, 2010; Alleva, Martijn, Van Breukelen, Jansen, & Karos, 2015; Alleva, Veldhuis, & Martijn, 2016). In the *Expand Your Horizon* program, Alleva and colleagues demonstrated that body appreciation can increase in women following structured writing assignments that focus on body senses, physical capacities, health, creative endeavors, self-care, and communication (Alleva et al., 2015). The clinician can replicate this intervention within the therapeutic process by asking the client to do similar writing assignments as homework; the assignments can then can be discussed during therapy sessions.

The clinician can encourage movement/exercise as a form of self-care to increase body image.[12] The clinician can help the client to explore the relationship she has with movement and exercise (currently and in the past), including the use of specific assessments to differentiate between pleasurable movement and obligatory exercise.[13] Activities that are uncomfortable, promote physical pain, focus solely on caloric elimination, or target changes to the body due to dissatisfaction should be eliminated in favor of movement that is fulfilling, enjoyable, and satisfying (Martin Ginis & Bassett, 2011). The clinician can educate the client about the numerous purposes of physical activity that extend beyond weight control and include health, fitness, stress management, socialization, and mental challenges (Tylka & Homan, 2015), and help shift the client from a calorie-burning mindset to one of improving mental health and body acceptance. Furthermore, the client can learn how focusing on functional motives for physical activity (e.g., increased cardiovascular health and flexibility, more balance) has been linked to body appreciation for both men and women (Tylka & Homan, 2015).

Examining the role of movement during childhood, adolescence, and adulthood can reveal opportunities for current enjoyment such as biking,

---

[12] Reviews of the interactions between exercise and body image can be found in Campbell and Hausenblas (2009) and Martin Ginis and Bassett (2011).
[13] Exercise Dependence Scale-21 (Symons Downs, Hausenblas, & Nigg, 2004); Compulsive Exercise Test (Taranis, Touyz, & Meyer, 2011).

swimming, and team sports. For example, an adult man who has run regularly for years but now finds it laborious might recall the joy he experienced from swimming during adolescence, and make a transition from running to swimming. It is important to note that sometimes the client will need assistance in identifying alternate physical activities that are not grounded in pathological and unhealthy thought processes that correspond with body image disturbance. The clinician can collaborate with local trainers who share a similar philosophical perspective of promoting health and wellness associated with positive body image as possible referral options.

Pampering and preventative care. In our 2010 study, women identified pampering as a component of positive body image, offering examples such as getting a manicure or pedicure and engaging in grooming activities that are considered pleasurable (Wood-Barcalow et al., 2010). In our experience, some clients are reticent to pamper themselves as they feel unworthy to do so, based on a lack of current body acceptance. It can be beneficial to share with the client that engaging in these behaviors is a step toward positive body image as they require the client to challenge thoughts of unworthiness, rather than postpone pleasure and enjoyment. Additionally, the clinician can assist the client with understanding the importance of regular preventative measures associated with medical health and functioning. Two independent studies (one with Australian females and one with American men and women) demonstrated that individuals with positive body image intentionally protected their skin from UV exposure and damage (Andrew et al., 2014; Gillen, 2015), got screened for skin cancer, and sought medical attention when appropriate (Andrew et al., 2016).

Filtering information. Positive body image research suggests the importance of filtering information to accept that which is positive and dismiss or refute that which is negative. We have described this process as a filter in which information that is commensurate with positive body image is preserved and information incongruent with it is rejected (Wood-Barcalow et al., 2010). As an example, adolescents with positive body image described how negative comments about their own bodies were not given importance (Frisén & Holmqvist, 2010).

In clinical practice, we have found it useful to educate clients about the filtering process, empowering them to choose what information they retain and what they reject. Although it can be challenging to first identify and then refute negative information about the body, it is imperative to do so as a way to promote more healthy conceptualizations of the body. The client can learn how to identify both internal and external messages to which she is subjected that are focused specifically on body-related topics (e.g., appearance, weight, shape, height, muscularity, fat to muscle ratio) and to evaluate whether the messages are neutral, negative, or positive. Interestingly, we have found that it can be challenging for clients to discern the valence of the messages, especially when they are couched as positive or neutral but include insidious underlying beauty ideals.

Knowing that body comparison with others is a prominent process that exists for many clients, the clinician can educate about social comparison theory (Festinger, 1954) and how it relates to body image. In social comparison theory, individuals compare to others in an upward direction (e.g., idealizing the other individual, belief that the other individual is "better off") or a downward direction (e.g., belief that the other individual is "worse off"), which can impact a person's emotions and self-concept (Festinger, 1954; Fitzsimmons-Craft, 2011). To integrate this theory into body image work, the clinician and client can investigate the motives underlying the comparison(s), such as *self-improvement* (comparing to others who are perceived as better to serve as motivation for change), *self-enhancement* (comparing to those who are perceived as less fortunate as a way to feel better), and *self-evaluation* (comparing to others who are similar; Hegelson & Mickelson, 1995; Knobloch-Westerwick & Romero, 2011). The clinician can encourage the client to be aware of when comparisons occur and the impact of them, including her mood before, during, and after the comparison process. Examples might include the client following blogs about those who have positive body image, resulting in inspiration (self-improvement); imagining the potential hardships of others to put her own pain into context (self-enhancement); or making comparisons with the social media sites of similar peers (self-evaluation). It is helpful to note that comparisons, regardless of the type, can result in various outcomes, from positive to negative, depending on the client's unique experiences and filtering processes (e.g., self-improvement comparisons can be inspiring for one client and cause despair for another). Furthermore, there is research which suggests that self-evaluation creates an opportunity for negative information to be absorbed or highlighted (Holland & Tiggemann, 2016). Upon learning how the different types of comparison impact the client's own body image, the clinician and client can create specialized interventions in which the client filters incoming and outgoing information as a way to move toward or maintain positive body image. Here are examples of interventions that we use with our clients: to refrain from accessing social media when focused on what is unacceptable or not good enough regarding the body (self-improvement), to focus on the benefits and proper functioning of the body currently (self-enhancement), and to remember times in the past that corresponded with positive body image (self-evaluation).

Upon gaining greater knowledge of the role of social comparison, the client can then assess and analyze the interpersonal environment in which she exists. In essence, she can intentionally focus on how to create an intrapersonal and interpersonal "safe environment," free from negative body image information. The client defines what this means, which could include such elements as not having shape- or weight-based dialogue with friends and family, refraining from media images that focus on appearance and promote stereotypical beauty standards (e.g., reality TV shows, certain magazines; Levine & Chapman, 2011), talking about current issues happening in the world versus disparaging body talk, redirecting conversations that focus on appearance to other topics, highlighting the strengths of herself and others, and educating others about the importance of limiting judgment and increasing acceptance. The client can create a "positive body image box," in which she includes specific items that conjure positive recollections associated with body acceptance (e.g., a letter from a friend, a photograph of a time when body acceptance occurred, an "I commit to" list, etc.), reasons for recovery, and cues to use coping skills and social support networks as effectively as possible.[14]

Conclusions and Future Directions

This chapter has reviewed relevant research on positive body image and offered specific interventions that can be integrated into therapeutic care. Although a great deal of positive body image literature has emerged in the past decade, there are still gaps in terms of how research informs the practice of clinicians. We offered a sampling of our own clinical techniques that we have found valuable to our clients working toward positive body image. We acknowledge that our training experiences, identities (gender, cultural, national, sexual, etc.), location of practice, and access to clients of certain socioeconomic backgrounds likely shape our interventions and can limit the generalizability of these interventions. In the future, we hope that additional assessments, training manuals, and workbooks on positive body image will be inclusive of people of various cultural and minority social identities. We look forward to future positive body image research and clinical advancements that will benefit both clinicians and clients alike.

---

[14] Similar to that of the "Virtual Hope Box" (Bush et al., 2015) or "Hope Kit" or "Hope Box" (e.g., Wenzel, Brown, & Beck, 2009).

References

Abbott, B. D., & Barber, B. L. (2010). Embodied image: Gender differences in functional and aesthetic body image among Australian adolescents. *Body Image, 7*, 22–31. https://doi.org/10.1016/j.bodyim.2009.10.004

Albertson, E. R., Neff, K. D., & Dill-Shackleford, K. E. (2015). Self-compassion and body dissatisfaction in women: A randomized controlled trial of a brief meditation intervention. *Mindfulness, 6*, 444–454.

Alleva, J. M., Veldhuis, J., & Martijn, C. (2016). A pilot study investigating whether focusing on body functionality can protect women from the potential negative effects of viewing thin-ideal media images. *Body Image, 17*, 10–13. https://doi.org/10.1016/j.bodyim.2016.01.007

Alleva, J. M., Martijn, C., Van Breukelen, G. J., Jansen, A., & Karos, K. (2015). Expand Your Horizon: A programme that improves body image and reduces self-objectification by training women to focus on body functionality. *Body Image, 15*, 81–89.

Andrew, R., Tiggemann, M., & Clark, L. (2014). Positive body image and young women's health: Implications for sun protection, cancer screening, weight loss and alcohol consumption behaviours. *Journal of Health Psychology, 21*, 28–39. https://doi.org/10.1177/1359105314520814

(2016a). Predictors and health-related outcomes of positive body image in adolescent girls: A prospective study. *Developmental Psychology, 52*, 463–474.

(2016b). Predicting body appreciation in young women: An integrated model of positive body image. *Body Image, 18*, 34–42. https://doi.org/10.1016/j.bodyim.2016.04.003

Augustus-Horvath, C. L., & Tylka, T. L. (2011). The acceptance model of intuitive eating: A comparison of women in emerging adulthood, early adulthood, and middle adulthood. *Journal of Counseling Psychology, 58*, 110–125. https://doi.org/10.1037/a0022129

Avalos, L. C., & Tylka, T. L. (2006). Exploring a model of intuitive eating with college women. *Journal of Counseling Psychology, 53*, 486–497. https://doi.org/10.1037/0022-0167.53.4.486

Avalos, L., Tylka, T. L., & Wood-Barcalow, N. (2005). The Body Appreciation Scale: Development and psychometric evaluation. *Body Image, 2*, 285–297. https://doi.org/10.1016/j.bodyim.2005.06.002

Beck, A. T. (1979). *Cognitive therapy of depression*. New York: Guilford Press.

Bourne, E. (2015). *The anxiety and phobia workbook*. New Harbinger Publications.

Boyatzis, C. J., Kline, S., & Backof, S. (2007). Experimental evidence that theistic-religious body affirmations improve women's body image. *Journal for the Scientific Study of Religion, 46*, 553–564.

Braun, T. D., Park, C. L., & Gorin, A. (2016). Self-compassion, body image and disordered eating: A review of the literature. *Body Image, 17*, 117–131. https://doi.org/http://dx.doi.org/10.1016/j.bodyim.2016.03.003

Brown, T. A., Cash, T. F., & Mikulka, P. J. (1990). Attitudinal body-image assessment: Factor analysis of the Body–Self Relations Questionnaire. *Journal of Personality Assessment, 55*, 135–144.

Bush, N. E., Dobscha, S. K., Crumpton, R., Denneson, L. M., Hoffman, J. E., Crain, A., Cromer, R., Kinn, J. T. (2015). A virtual hope box smartphone app as an accessory to therapy: Proof-of-concept in a clinical sample of veterans. *Suicide and Life-Threatening Behavior*, *45*, 1–9.

Campbell, A., & Hausenblas, H. A. (2009). Effects of exercise interventions on body image: A meta-analysis. *Journal of Health Psychology*, *14*(6), 780–93.

Cash, T. F. (2008). *The body image workbook: An eight-step program for learning to like your looks*. Oakland, CA: New Harbinger Publications.

Cash, T. F., & Smolak, L. (2011). Understanding body images: Historical and contemporary perspectives. In T. F. Cash & L. Smolak (Eds.), *Body image: A handbook of science, practice, and prevention*, 2nd ed. (pp. 3–11). New York: Guilford Press.

Cooper, P. J., Taylor, M. J., Cooper, Z., & Fairbum, C. G. (1987). The development and validation of the Body Shape Questionnaire. *International Journal of Eating Disorders*, *6*, 485–494.

Delinsky, S. S., & Wilson, G. T. (2006). Mirror exposure for the treatment of body image disturbance. *International Journal of Eating Disorders*, *39*, 108–116.

Doidge, N. (2007). *The brain that changes itself: Stories of personal triumph from the frontiers of brain science*. New York: Penguin Books.

Fairburn, C. G. (2008). *Cognitive behavior therapy and eating disorders*. New York: Guilford Press.

Festinger, L. (1954). A theory of social comparison processes. *Human Relations*, *7*, 117–140.

Fitzsimmons-Craft, E. E. (2011). Social psychological theories of disordered eating in college women: Review and integration. *Clinical Psychology Review*, *31*, 1224–1237. https://doi.org/10.1016/j.cpr.2011.07.011

Franzoi, S. L., & Shields, S. A. (1984). The Body Esteem Scale: Multidimensional structure and sex differences in a college population. *Journal of Personality Assessment*, *48*, 173–178.

Frisén, A., & Holmqvist, K. (2010). What characterizes early adolescents with a positive body image? A qualitative investigation of Swedish girls and boys. *Body Image*, *7*, 205–212. https://doi.org/10.1016/j.bodyim.2010.04.001

Gillen, M. M. (2015). Associations between positive body image and indicators of men's and women's mental and physical health. *Body Image*, *13*, 67–74.

Harcourt, D. & Rumsey, N. (2011). Body image and biomedical interventions for disfiguring conditions. In T. F. Cash and L. Smolak (Eds.), *Body image: A handbook of science, practice, and prevention*, 2nd ed. (pp. 404–412). New York: Guilford Press.

Helgeson, V. S., & Mickelson, K. D. (1995). Motives for social comparison. *Personality and Social Psychology Bulletin*, *21*, 1200–1209.

Hildebrandt, T., Loeb, K., Troupe, S., & Delinsky, S. (2012). Adjunctive mirror exposure for eating disorders: A randomized controlled pilot study. *Behaviour Research and Therapy*, *50*, 797–804. https://doi.org/10.1016/j.brat.2012.09.004

Holland, G., & Tiggemann, M. (2016). A systematic review of the impact of the use of social networking sites on body image and disordered eating outcomes. *Body Image, 17,* 100–110. https://doi.org/10.1016/j.bodyim.2016.02.008

Holmqvist, K., & Frisen, A. (2012). "I bet they aren't that perfect in reality": Appearance ideals viewed from the perspective of adolescents with a positive body image. *Body Image, 9,* 388–395.

Homan, K. J. (2012). Attachment to God mitigates negative effect of media exposure on women's body image. *Psychology of Religion and Spirituality, 4,* 324–331. https://doi.org/10.1037/a0029230

Jacobson, H. L., Hall, M. E. L., & Anderson, T. L. (2013). Theology and the body: Sanctification and bodily experiences. *Psychology of Religion and Spirituality, 5,* 41–50. https://doi.org/10.1037/a0028042

Jacobs-Pilipski, M. J., Winzelberg, A., Wilfley, D. E., Bryson, S. W., & Taylor, C. B. (2005). Spirituality among young women at risk for eating disorders. *Eating Behaviors, 6,* 293–300. https://doi.org/10.1016/j.eatbeh.2005.03.003

Jansen, A., Bollen, D., Tuschen-Caffier, B., Roefs, A., Tanghe, A., & Braet, C. (2008). Mirror exposure reduces body dissatisfaction and anxiety in obese adolescents: A pilot study. *Appetite, 51,* 214–217.

Jarry, J.L., & Cash, T.F. (2011). Cognitive-behavioral approaches to body image change. In T. F. Cash and L. Smolak (Eds.), *Body image: A handbook of science, practice, and prevention,* 2nd ed. (pp. 415–423). New York: Guilford Press.

Knobloch-Westerwick, S., & Romero, J. P. (2011). Body ideals in the media: Perceived attainability and social comparison choices. *Media Psychology, 14,* 27–48.

Koenig, K. R. & O'Mahoney, P. (2017). *Helping patients outsmart overeating: Psychological strategies for doctors and health care providers.* Lanham: Rowman & Littlefield Publishers.

Levine, M.P., & Chapman, K. (2011). Media influences on body image. In T. F. Cash and L. Smolak (Eds.), *Body image: A handbook of science, practice, and prevention,* 2nd ed. (pp. 101–107). New York: Guilford Press.

Lewis, J. S., Kersten, P., McCabe, C. S., McPherson, K. M., & Blake, D. R. (2007). Body perception disturbance: A contribution to pain in complex regional pain syndrome (CRPS). *Pain, 133,* 111–119. https://doi.org/10.1016/j.pain.2007.03.013

Luethcke, C. A., McDaniel, L., & Becker, C. B. (2011). A comparison of mindfulness, nonjudgmental, and cognitive dissonance-based approaches to mirror exposure. *Body Image, 8,* 251–258. https://doi.org/10.1016/j.bodyim.2011.03.006

Martin Ginis, K. A., & Bassett, R. L. (2011). Exercise and changes in body image. In T. F. Cash and L. Smolak (Eds.), *Body image: A handbook of science, practice, and prevention,* 2nd ed. (pp. 378–386). New York: Guilford Press.

McCreary, D. R., Sasse, D. K., Saucier, D. M., & Dorsch, K. D. (2004). Measuring the drive for muscularity: Factorial validity of the Drive for Muscularity Scale in men and women. *Psychology of Men & Masculinity, 5,* 49–58. doi:10.1037/1524-9220.5.1.49

McFarland, M. B., & Petrie, T. A. (2012). Male body satisfaction: Factorial and construct validity of the Body Parts Satisfaction Scale for men. *Journal of Counseling Psychology, 59,* 329–337. https://doi.org/10.1037/a0026777

McKinley, N. (2011). Feminist perspectives on body image. In T. F. Cash and L. Smolak (Eds.), *Body image: A handbook of science, practice, and prevention*, 2nd ed. (pp. 48–55). New York: Guilford Press.

Menzel, J. E., Krawczyk, R., & Thompson, J. K. (2011). Attitudinal assessment of body image for adolescents and adults. In T. F. Cash and L. Smolak (Eds.), *Body image: A handbook of science, practice, and prevention* (2nd ed., pp. 154–169). New York, NY: Guilford Press.

Mills, P. J., Redwine, L., Wilson, K., Pung, M. A., Chinh, K., Greenberg, B. H., . . . Chopra, D. (2015). The role of gratitude in spiritual well-being in asymptomatic heart failure patients. *Spirituality in Clinical Practice*, 2, 5–17. https://doi.org/10.1037/scp0000050

Neff, K. D. (2003). The development and validation of a scale to measure self-compassion. *Self and Identity*, 2, 223–250.

Osumi, M., Imai, R., Ueta, K., Nakano, H., Nobusako, S., & Morioka, S. (2014). Factors associated with the modulation of pain by visual distortion of body size. *Frontiers in Human Neuroscience*, 8, 137. http://doi.org/10.3389/fnhum.2014.00137

Paloutzian, R. F., & Park, C. L. (2013). *Handbook of the psychology of religion and spirituality* (2nd ed.). New York: Guilford Press.

Prochaska, J. O., Diclemente, C. C., & Norcross, J. C. (1992). In search of how people change: Applications to addictive behaviors. *American Psychologist*, 47(9), 1102.

Raes, F., Pommier, E., Neff, K. D., & Van Gucht, D. (2011). Construction and factorial validation of a short form of the self-compassion scale. *Clinical Psychology & Psychotherapy*, 18, 250–255.

Ramachandran, V. S., & Blakeslee, S. (1998). *Phantoms in the brain: Probing the mysteries of the human mind*. New York: Morrow & Co.

Reed, D. L., Thompson, J. K., Brannick, M. T., & Sacco, W. P. (1991). Development and validation of the physical appearance state and trait anxiety scale (PASTAS). *Journal of Anxiety Disorders*, 5, 323–332.

Rodin, J., Silberstein, L., & Striegel-Moore, R. (1984). Women and weight: A normative discontent. In *Nebraska symposium on motivation* (Vol. 32, pp. 267–307). University of Nebraska Press.

Rosen, J. C., Srebnik, D., Saltzberg, E., & Wendt, S. (1991). Development of a body image avoidance questionnaire. *Psychological Assessment: A Journal of Consulting and Clinical Psychology*, 3, 32.

Scott Richards, P., Berrett, M. E., Hardman, R. K., & Eggett, D. L. (2006). Comparative efficacy of spirituality, cognitive, and emotional support groups for treating eating disorder inpatients. *Eating Disorders*, 14, 401–415. https://doi.org/10.1080/10640260600952548

Smith-Jackson, T., Reel, J. J., & Thackeray, R. (2011). Coping with "bad body image days": Strategies from first-year young adult college women. *Body Image*, 8, 335–342. https://doi.org/10.1016/j.bodyim.2011.05.002

Suisman, J., & Klump, K., Cash, T. F. (2011). Genetic and neuroscientific perspectives on body image. In T. F. Cash and L. Smolak (Eds.), *Body image: A handbook of science, practice, and prevention*, 2nd ed. (pp. 29–38). New York: Guilford Press.

Swami, V. (2011). Evolutionary perspectives on human appearance and body image. In T. F. Cash and L. Smolak (Eds.), *Body image: A handbook of science, practice, and prevention*, 2nd ed. (pp. 20–28). New York: Guilford Press.

Symons Downs, D., Hausenblas, H. A., & Nigg, C. R. (2004). Factorial validity and psychometric examination of the Exercise Dependence Scale-Revised. *Measurement in Physical Education and Exercise Science, 8*, 183–201.

Tantleff-Dunn, S., Barnes, R. D., & Larose, J. G. (2011). It's not just a "woman thing": The current state of normative discontent. *Eating Disorders, 19* 392–402. https://doi.org/10.1080/10640266.2011.609088

Taranis, L., Touyz, S., & Meyer, C. (2011). Disordered eating and exercise: Development and preliminary validation of the compulsive exercise test (CET). *European Eating Disorders Review, 19*, 256–268. https://doi.org/ 10.1002/erv.1108

Taylor, D. J., Lichstein, K. L., Durrence, H. H., Reidel, B. W., & Bush, A. J. (2005). Epidemiology of insomnia, depression, and anxiety. *Sleep, 28*, 1457–1464.

Thompson, J. K., & Altabe, M. N. (1991). Psychometric qualities of the figure rating scale. *International Journal of Eating Disorders, 10*, 615–619.

Thompson, J. K., van den Berg, P., Roehrig, M., Guarda, A. S., & Heinberg, L. J. (2004). The sociocultural attitudes towards appearance scale-3 (SATAQ-3): Development and validation. *International Journal of Eating Disorders, 35*, 293–304.

Tiggemann, M. (2011). Sociocultural perspectives on human appearance and body image. In T. F. Cash and L. Smolak (Eds.), *Body image: A handbook of science, practice, and prevention*, 2nd ed. (pp. 12–19). New York: Guilford Press.

Tylka, T. L. (2011). Positive psychology perspectives on body image. In T. F. Cash and L. Smolak (Eds.), *Body image: A handbook of science, practice, and prevention*, 2nd ed. (pp. 56–64). New York: Guilford Press.

Tylka, T. L., Bergeron, D., & Schwartz, J. P. (2005). Development and psychometric evaluation of the Male Body Attitudes Scale (MBAS). *Body Image, 2*, 161–175.

Tylka, T. L., & Homan, K. J. (2015). Exercise motives and positive body image in physically active college women and men: Exploring an expanded acceptance model of intuitive eating. *Body Image, 15*, 90–97.

Tylka, T. L., & Iannantuono, A. C. (2016). Perceiving beauty in all women: Psychometric evaluation of the Broad Conceptualization of Beauty Scale. *Body Image, 17*, 67–81. https://doi.org/10.1016/j.bodyim.2016.02.005

Tylka, T. L., & Wood-Barcalow, N. L. (2015a). A positive complement. *Body Image, 14*, 115–117.

(2015b). The Body Appreciation Scale-2: Item refinement and psychometric evaluation. *Body Image, 12*, 53–67. https://doi.org/10.1016/j.bodyim .2014.09.006

Wasylkiw, L., MacKinnon, A. L., & MacLellan, A. M. (2012). Exploring the link between self-compassion and body image in university women. *Body Image, 9*, 236–245. https://doi.org/10.1016/j.bodyim.2012.01.007

Wenzel, A., Brown, G. K., & Beck, A. T. (2009). *Cognitive therapy for suicidal patients: Scientific and clinical applications.* Washington, DC: American Psychological Association.

Wood, A. M., Froh, J. J., & Geraghty, A. W. A. (2010). Gratitude and well-being: A review and theoretical integration. *Clinical Psychology Review, 30,* 890–905. https://doi.org/10.1016/j.cpr.2010.03.005

Wood-Barcalow, N. L., Tylka, T. L., & Augustus-Horvath, C. L. (2010). "But I like my body": Positive body image characteristics and a holistic model for young-adult women. *Body Image, 7,* 106–116. https://doi.org/10.1016/j.bodyim.2010.01.001

Index

CPSIA information can be obtained
at www.ICGtesting.com
Printed in the USA
LVHW051506240621
691067LV00008B/720

9 781108 410427